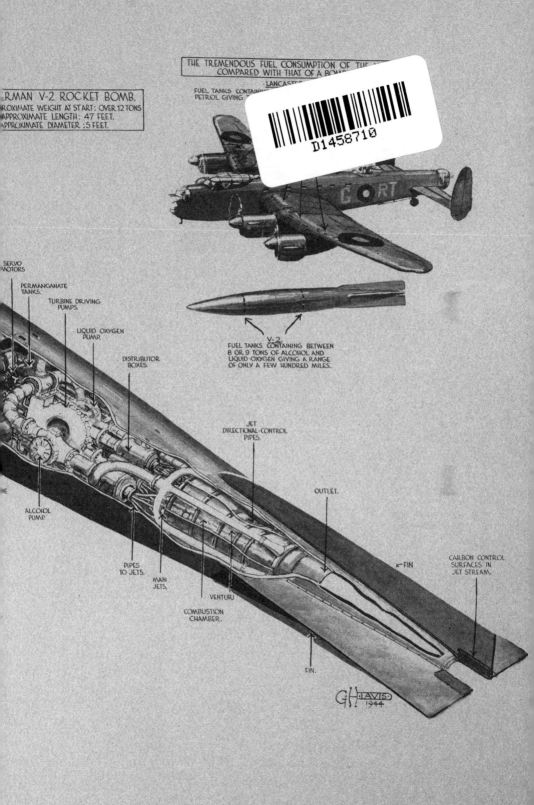

GERMAN V-2 ROCKET BOMB.
APPROXIMATE WEIGHT AT START: OVER 12 TONS
APPROXIMATE LENGTH: 47 FEET.
APPROXIMATE DIAMETER :5 FEET.

THE TREMENDOUS FUEL CONSUMPTION OF THE
COMPARED WITH THAT OF A BOMB
LANCASTER
FUEL TANKS CONTAINING
PETROL GIVING

V-2
FUEL TANKS CONTAINING BETWEEN
8 OR 9 TONS OF ALCOHOL AND
LIQUID OXYGEN GIVING A RANGE
OF ONLY A FEW HUNDRED MILES.

SERVO
MOTORS

PERMANGANATE
TANKS.

TURBINE DRIVING
PUMPS.

LIQUID OXYGEN
PUMP.

DISTRIBUTOR
BOXES.

ALCOHOL
PUMP.

JET
DIRECTIONAL-CONTROL
PIPES.

OUTLET.

FIN

CARBON CONTROL
SURFACES IN
JET STREAM.

PIPES
TO JETS.

MAIN
JETS.

VENTURI

COMBUSTION
CHAMBER.

FIN.

G H DAVIS
1944

Private Battles

How The War Almost Defeated Us

For Rena

Private Battles

How The War Almost Defeated Us

SIMON GARFIELD

EBURY
PRESS

First published in Great Britain in 2006

10 9 8 7 6 5 4 3 2 1

Ebury Press, an imprint of Ebury Publishing.
Random House, 20 Vauxhall Bridge Road,
London SW1V 2SA

Random House Australia (Pty) Limited
20 Alfred Street, Milsons Point, Sydney,
New South Wales 2061, Australia

Random House New Zealand Limited
18 Poland Road, Glenfield, Auckland 10, New

Random House (Pty) Limited
Isle of Houghton,
Corner Boundary Road & Carse O'Gowrie,
Houghton, 2198, South Africa

Random House Publishers India Private Limited
301 World Trade Tower, Hotel Intercontinental Grand Complex,
Barakhamba Lane, New Delhi 110 001, India

The Random House Group Limited Reg. No. 954009

www.randomhouse.co.uk

A CIP catalogue record for this book is available from the British Library.

Cover design by Two Associates
Text design and typesetting by Textype, Cambridge

ISBN 9780091910761 (From January 2007)
ISBN 0091910765

Papers used by Ebury Press are natural, recyclable products made from
wood grown in sustainable forests.

Printed and bound in Great Britain by Clays Ltd, St Ives Plc

Copies are available at special rates for bulk order. Contact the sales
development team on 020 7840 8487 or visit *www.booksforpromotions.co.uk*
for more information.

Introduction

This book concerns the lives of four ordinary people in extraordinary circumstances, and they are not famous people, and they are not professional writers. They write of their experiences in an honest, moving, humorous and brave way at a time when their lives and those of their friends were in danger, and they illuminate what it was like to live through the Second World War in a way that most books cannot – with immediacy and intimacy, and with great regard for commonplace detail. More than 60 years on, the reader stands in the diarists' butcher's queue, or sits by their side at work, and they whisper in our ear as if we had known them all our lives.

This book is also the last to be published in a trilogy but not the last in the sequence. The first of the three, *Our Hidden Lives*, concerns the three years of austerity following the war. The second, *We Are At War*, covers the start of the conflict until the middle of the Blitz in October 1940. *Private Battles* takes up the story from November 1940 to May 1945. Needless to say, this was not an entirely planned order of events.

A few years ago I was asked by my editor whether I thought there might be a book in the Mass-Observation archives at the University of Sussex. I had only heard vaguely of Mass-Observation. I knew it had been started in the late 1930s by three men – Tom Harrisson, Humphrey Jennings and Charles Madge – who were interested in what ordinary people thought about their lives and the world around them. They began by observing them close at hand in their factories and pubs, and they asked them to write about certain issues – their political views, the prospect of war, how they spent their Saturdays. When war looked inevitable, the Mass-Observers were also asked to keep personal journals about their daily activities and send them to an office in London each month. Several hundred people of all ages and backgrounds wrote from all over Britain, and they wondered what possible purpose their daily rituals and regular engagements would serve.

1

Initially, their opinions were used to gauge morale; the government ministers took a keen interest in Mass-Observation, for they recognised it as a true and spontaneous expression of the mood of the country. Subsequently, historians have consulted the diaries for all manner of reasons, the task made easier when the material was deposited by Tom Harrisson at the University of Sussex in the late 1960s.

When I first encountered the diaries, I was struck by their great richness and variety, and by the daunting amount of pages to examine. Some correspondents had sent only the most perfunctory accounts ('woke up . . . went to work . . . came home'), but some wrote several pages a day about every aspect of their lives, devoting many hours each week to write up notes they had often taken surreptitiously. I was surprised that more historians had not utilised the diaries in a comprehensive way, using larger, more revealing passages rather than little snippets. I decided to try to tell the story of the war and its aftermath in two ways: in the usual chronological format dominated by the big turning points, and also in a manner that juxtaposed several lives to provide a level of personal detail not generally considered relevant (but in truth highly instructive).

I began with the post-war period, partly because there were fewer diarists to read and select from, and partly because it was a period that had been relatively under-examined. The result was *Our Hidden Lives*, an account from VE Day to the birth of the NHS as witnessed by five writers. The book struck a chord, sold well, and was made into a BBC film. I loved working on it, and was keen to edit some more. The immediate thought was to resume the stories of the diarists for another few years, but their output dwindled and became less involving. So I looked at the diaries that had been written during the war, initially fearful that they wouldn't yield enough fresh material to stand up well against the many other war books published every month.

But I was wrong. The diarists' lives were unique, and *We Are At War* revealed fascinating and unanticipated insights. This third book completes the story. There are only four writers this time, for the period covered is longer, but I hope their observations are no less engaging and rewarding.

The grand theme is a simple one: just getting through it all. An early title for this book was *Keeping It Together*, a phrase the diarists would never have used but would easily have understood. How to get enough nutrition. How to pay the fines imposed for not blacking out at night. How to feel that you were doing something valuable for your country. How to criticise the government and those in authority

2

without appearing unpatriotic, ungrateful or Communist. How to scheme, particularly where food was concerned. How to plan for a post-war world, as hard sometimes as that was to envisage. How to avoid being ill all the time (poor nutrition again, working longer days, standing around for hours in food and transport queues). How to accept the devastating RAF bombing raids while retaining a sensitive and pacifist outlook. And then there was the question of how not to be killed.

Taken as a whole, two other patterns emerge, both forcible rejoinders to the notion that we were all pulling together during these years. The diarists writing here – by no means a representative sample of the country's mood, but nonetheless a valuable snapshot of it – describe a wartime Britain we may be a little unfamiliar with. Displays of genuine camaraderie and the Blitz/Dunkirk spirit of legend are matched by acts of selfishness and expressions of spite. Usually these are the result of the daily grind: beating someone else to the rationed fruit or shoes, feeling resentful about the lack of support when fire-watching. But there is a deeper malaise too, a belief that the war is not being prosecuted well and that those in power do not understand the prolonged suffering of the less privileged. Churchill is by turns revered, mocked and scolded, his ministers treated with equal parts respect and disdain.

Two of the diarists may be familiar. Maggie Joy Blunt, who has appeared in both previous volumes, is a frustrated freelance writer in her early thirties, living in Burnham Beeches near Slough. She begins work as a publicity and marketing officer for an alloys firm involved in aircraft manufacture, but her heart is elsewhere: with her many friends in London, with her male friend S fighting in Europe, with her literature and love of politics, with her cats. She does not contribute as frequently as the other diarists, but she writes with heartfelt passion and a memorably lyrical turn of phrase.

Readers of *We Are At War* will remember Pam Ashford, the secretary at a coal shipping firm in Glasgow. She is 38 when we meet her again, still living with her mother and in daily pursuit of both office gossip and affordable food. She changes jobs twice in the course of these diaries, and we follow her emotional turmoil as she leaves and meets new colleagues. She brings a fascinating insight to the American presence in Glasgow, and she is enthralled and horrified by their modern manners and morals.

And then there are two new writers, both men. Edward Stebbing is a soldier in his early twenties. He was born in Essex, and enjoyed a conventional grammar school and Church of England upbringing. His experiences as a private in Aldershot, London, Yorkshire and

Scotland he finds disorientating, but he reports faithfully the views of his fellow recruits. He is delighted to be discharged in 1941: 'My service in the Army has seemed to me a sheer waste of time. Now, paradoxically, I am going to see what the war is like.' He finds a job in the clinical pathology department at Clare Hall Hospital in Potters Bar, and writes with great frankness of his thoughts and those of his workmates and landlady as the war progresses; as he concludes, 'what is difficult for historians to convey . . . is that such a multitude of different events [are] happening simultaneously'.

The fourth diarist is Ernest van Someren, 36 at the outbreak of war, a research chemist in Hertfordshire, a husband and father, a keeper of hens and keen Quaker, a determined individualist. He worked for Murex Welding Processes Ltd in Waltham Cross, where he employed his skills in chemical analysis by emission spectroscopy and became involved in aspects of manufacturing steel products by welding. In the diaries he is often vague about precisely what it is he does, quite possibly because one of his projects produced the huge steel spools required to wind pipe for the cross-channel fuel supply for invading forces after D-Day. This was called PLUTO, Pipe Line Under The Ocean. His job was almost certainly protected from conscription, which suited his position as a Conscientious Objector. In the days before iPods and mobile phones, people practise their recorders on the train home. Well, not everyone; but Ernest van Someren does, and he does other unorthodox things too. He shuts his son Laurie in the greenhouse to calm him down, and he reports on the amount of blood spilled at a children's birthday party.

As ever, the glory is in the minutiae. We learn about the exact nature of a shop window's contents and the meals they inspire; we read the precise words spoken in favour and disgruntlement at a particular turning in a far-flung battle. We envisage a scene of such vividness at a job interview or gathering of friends that we have no trouble rooting for the participants. There is no hindsight in these diaries, no ability for the writers to edit with the benefits of a retrospective and more refined judgement. There are two teasing coincidences, when the diarists overlap and meet, at least in text. In September 1944, Pam Ashford discusses a comment from Judge van Someren, although whether he was a relation of Ernest van Someren is unclear. And shortly afterwards Ernest visits Burnham Beeches, the home of Maggie Joy Blunt. Our four writers express not only fortitude but also courage that their words would not be misused. Their agreement with the founders of Mass-Observation and its trustees specified that their work would be used as they saw fit and fair, and their identity would be protected. As with the first two books, this arrangement has been upheld (with the exception of Edward Stebbing and Ernest van Someren, whose sons kindly agreed to the use of their real names). All the other names, places and events are unchanged, although the total length of the diaries has been greatly reduced. Unedited, the full text would run to about 800,000 words, or more than four times the present length. No words have been added, although very occasionally the sequence of a particular entry has been rearranged to improve clarity. There are several gaps in the writers' journals, caused by illness, time spent revising for exams, pressures of work. Sometimes, I think, entries have just got lost in the post or were mislaid in the years before Tom Harrisson transferred them from London to Sussex.

But much of an important and engrossing nature survives, and this is what may be learnt from this volume alone: why there was an increased demand for pianos; how best to feed canaries at a time of seed shortage; what happened when you agreed to 'See the Lovely Lovelies'; how unpopular was Neville Chamberlain even as he fell ill; how Sugarettes proved a poor substitute for real sugar; what happened when official summertime lasted until November; how not to secure an additional personal supply of eggs; and how much Iceland craved British cosmetics and underwear.

We may also read how successful was Woolworth's restaurant, and the fact that the cooking was done by electricity; precisely why the Italians had given up fish and chips; how difficult it was to buy a comb; how many days it usually took for the government to admit that German claims about damage inflicted on the Allies was in fact true; how wartime wedding cakes were really a sham and excessive marzipan was illegal; how best to pilfer goods from wooden crates at the docks; how the latest offerings of 'fish flesh' were probably whale; and how one diarist was personally affected by a particularly terrible event after working at Gracie Fields' house.

And then we may discover just why 'The Star Spangled Banner' became the American national anthem; how small boys were employed in the war against VD; how Sir William Beveridge was considered conceited and his Report mistrusted; how there was strong belief that Germans should face post-war firing squads rather than the courtroom; how short films about welding and forgings proved to be both rewarding and popular; how tomatoes can have therapeutic uses in the treatment of anxiety; and how the ending of the conflict was expected almost a year before it came.

As one protagonist may have put it, this is not the whole story, it is not even half the story, but it is perhaps one of the best ways of telling a part of the story. Everyone has their own individual experiences of the war, but human hopes, anxieties and pleasures don't vary that much from person to person, and don't change very much over time. If you lived through it, you will recognise these emotions. And if you were born later, these diarists have done all they can to explain what it was really like.

Chapter One

ANY CRUM IN THE KINGDOM

As much emphasis on the tease as on the strip: soldiers contemplate a night at the Prince of Wales Theatre, London.

31 October 1940–2 January 1941

31 October 1940 This month in Britain, 6350 civilians were killed by enemy action.

5 November President Roosevelt wins a third term by a landslide.

8 November RAF bombs Munich, delaying Hitler's annual speech.

9 November Neville Chamberlain dies of cancer at the age of 71.

11 November The British attack Italian fleet at Taranto in southern Italy.

14 November 568 people die and 863 are injured in a raid on Coventry.

15 November The ghetto in Warsaw, with 400,000 Jews, is sealed off from the rest of the city and is starved of food.

20 November Severe Luftwaffe raids on Birmingham, followed by Liverpool, Bristol and Southampton.

21 November The Italians surrender in Greece.

26 November The ban on banana imports is announced, but sugar and tea rations are increased for Christmas.

8 December The House of Commons and Tower of London bombed.

14 December Churchill watches Charlie Chaplin's *The Great Dictator*.

17 December General Wavell leads a series of British advances in North Africa.

23 December Anthony Eden becomes Foreign Secretary as Viscount Halifax becomes Ambassador to Washington.

27 December The Luftwaffe launches prolonged attack on London, culminating in the second 'Great Fire' two days later.

1 January 1941 The BBC *Brains Trust* takes to the air.

THURSDAY, 31 OCTOBER 1940

Maggie Joy Blunt
Metal factory worker living in Burnham Beeches, near Slough, age 31
The winter is here. It seems to have come so quickly. Yesterday I found the dahlia leaves blackened by frost and I lifted and stored the tubers and cut the remaining flowers. They are in a vase now in front of me: their delicately crinkled petals spread in perfect circles of pale colour. I didn't realise dahlias were so lovely. What shall I be doing and feeling, and what shall I have done and felt, by the time those tubers bloom again . . .

SATURDAY, 2 NOVEMBER

Ernest van Someren
Research chemist in Broxbourne, Hertfordshire, age 37
Jean R. came to see us. We sat and talked most of the afternoon and evening, largely about incidents in London. She has just moved from an old house very near a railway to a steel and concrete block of flats. She told us about a woman having a bath in Kentish Town whose house was damaged by a very close hit, so that her bath slid down into the street without spilling the water or hurting her in any way. It was dark too.

MONDAY, 4 NOVEMBER

Pam Ashford
Secretary in coal shipping firm, Glasgow, age 38
At 2.45am the alert woke me up, but I went to sleep again, and did not hear the all clear; this is said to have gone at 3.50. I have been surprised by the changed attitude so many people are showing – they stayed in bed. Familiarity must be one factor, and I should think the cold nights another.

My friend Miss Whittan was 'phoning London friends this morning and they reported that last night – the first for 56 nights without an alert – was so quiet as to be 'eerie'. There they were in their shelters expecting something to happen and nothing did. The ears get used to the noise and then quiet keeps one awake.

Miss McKirdy has heard of a house that was bombed in London, and immediately the salvagers began to go all over the debris looking for a pair of pink corsets. The owner had £2000 sewn in and had not happened to be wearing the garment at the time the bomb fell.

Ernest van Someren

Up early for Jean to get a coach back to work. A good post, letters from my brother and bro-in-law in RAF and a note from my mother with some ham from my sister in USA. Tony, my brother, has been moved from Scotland to Lancashire to a RAF training camp where he is allowed to do some consultant work as a psychiatrist, which he had hoped to do.

During the day a parcel arrived from [my sister] Tessa with assorted sweets and two pairs of nylon stockings. After we had sampled the sweets we found a letter saying that they were for Esmee and her two boys. We sent on the rest of the sweets the next day.

In the evening wrote diary and letters. It was fairly noisy.

Maggie Joy Blunt

Heart of my heart! It seems six or seven bombs have just fallen outside my back door. I heard a plane and then zzzoom! zzzoom! *zzzoom*! – one after the other. I felt the ground shaking and dived for the table. We have had bombs at H Corner which destroyed two council houses and the landmine in the Beeches but nothing as near as this. What damage now is done? I heard the soldiers stationed in the woods shouting 'Lights! These people aren't blacked out at all!' But it's not easy to keep a slither of light from showing now and then. The times I have pulled and tacked and padded my black-out.

The silence now . . . and the darkness! Outside never was such a dark night and that one plane swooping from the clouds, dropping its bombs without warning . . . I have heard no siren . . . In this quiet, withdrawn spot it is the unexpectedness of such an event that is so terrifying. I would rather be in a town and hear the barrage guns.

TUESDAY, 5 NOVEMBER

Pam Ashford

I am told there has been an increased demand for pianos – people are having musical evenings at home and canteens want pianos. And of course there are munition workers with big packets of money that they want to spend, despite the appeals of the War Savings Committee.

WEDNESDAY, 6 NOVEMBER

Pam Ashford

Nowadays I look at [my brother] Charlie's *Herald* before leaving for work and today there was a post in a shipping company advertised. It might be an opportunity and I have replied. Nevertheless Mr Mitchell has always been so good to me that I would be dreadfully unhappy leaving him. Today I have been reduced to copying a directory so as to look busy!

Mother went to a whist drive at Marie's church this afternoon, and found herself with quite a different class of women from her English Society and its friends. Partick is, of course, a shipbuilding area and the members of the church seemed to be in that swim. These women were all saying what terribly long hours their husbands worked, how worn out they are, and how much they fear for their health. One man got home at midnight last night and had to get up at 4am.

There's something terribly wrong with the way the activities of the nation are organised. Shipyard workers pressed like that, and people in commerce longing to do something and not being able to find anything to do.

THURSDAY, 7 NOVEMBER

Ernest van Someren
In the evening took Laurie [two-year-old son] out to see a neighbour, as he had not been out all day. He surprised me by identifying a car in the dark as Mr Randall's, by the sound of its engines (it's a 1926 Clyno). We were caught at neighbours by a warning, started home but turned back when there was gunfire near us. L was slightly but definitely scared, I carried him a little way back and he said, 'Panda doesn't mind the bangs,' about the pet he was carrying.

Pam Ashford
Mr Hutchison has lent Mr Mitchell a book called *The Martyrdom of Poland*, presented to him by the Pole who is billeted at his home in Biggar. Mr Mitchell declines to let me look at it on the grounds that it would shock me, and keeps on reading out atrocities to show me that this is the case.

People are contrasting the winter that they anticipate and the winter of last year. Last winter was one of the healthiest on record, thanks to people getting extra rest in the evenings. This winter we anticipate the ailments associated with damp and frost. I have not, and I should not be surprised when figures come to be told if we don't find out that the air-raid casualties fall short in number of the number that get 'flu, measles, diphtheria – and possibly worse illnesses.

There is a story going about that Lord Haw Haw has said that tonight Glasgow is to be razed to the ground.

There seems a general opinion that old people don't take the air raids so seriously as younger ones. They may even think that sudden death is better than years of senility.

Ten days ago the BBC said that carrier pigeons were to be rationed and it made me a little anxious about canaries. When the war broke out the Ministry of Food announced that the Government would let neither man nor beast go hungry, but all the same we have kept half a stone of seed always on the premises. I enquired from my dealer today of mixed canary seed, but loose there is none, and he does not know when there will be any. All he knows is that the Government have clapped 50% on the price, i.e. from 6d a pound to 9d. Of course, I would never think of my bird in terms of money like that, but I bought a packet of bird seed and it looks the same as what Dick has always had. What does make me savage is that ever since his quarrels with Mr Ross's bird in June he has refused to sing a note. At first he had the excuse of moulting, but now it is either sulks or laziness.

FRIDAY, 8 NOVEMBER

Edward Stebbing
New recruit stationed in England, age 21
Roosevelt's re-election seems to have been taken for granted and as nothing much happens in Greece there is not much comment about that either.

The popularity of strip tease . . . Tonight the theatre was more crowded than before, people standing at the back and at the sides all through. The show was entirely altered, and if anything better than before, but more daring and sexier too. Posters invited one to 'See the lovely lovelies'. The strip tease act appealed to me because there was as much emphasis on the tease as on the strip. The artist digs at the audience were amusing because true.

Ernest van Someren
I went to town instead of to the works, and I left at about four and did some shopping. With great difficulty bought a beret for L, had no idea small boys' hats were so rare until I had to hunt for one. Then I went to a music shop and bought a recorder in a synthetic plastic for 5/- (intending to sell it to a friend) and some music on approval. I was rather depressed by the mess around Oxford Street. Went home on the 5.10 train which was very full. I sat on a ledge in the guards van

and played the recorder most of the way, after asking the guard if there was any regulation against it.

Pam Ashford
Miss Smith was saying that Reginald Foort is in jail for communicating with the enemy – he selected his tunes on the organ in such combinations as to convey messages. I said 'That yarn has been fastened to nearly every regular broadcaster by now!' My scepticism was brushed aside, and people are going to watch the BBC programmes closely to find out if he appears again. Then it is said that in Parliament questions were asked about the German wife of a BBC announcer. I myself had sometimes wondered why he does not read the news nowadays, but I never hit on that notion.

Mr Mitchell is feeling ill today and says he has 'war nerves in the stomach'. Miss Bousie says, 'So have I; so has everyone; this continuous strain is more than human nature can stand.' My observations would not bear out that 'everyone' has 'war nerves in the stomach', though naturally I can only speak definitely of myself, and my experience is that the stimulating atmosphere of war has benefited my health, with one or two breaks – such as the Collapse of France – when the strain has made me sick.

Laughing I said, 'This is Friday – the Germans' favourite night,' but it transpires that Mr Ferguson on leaving had said just the same and thrown half the women in the office into the depths of despair. Miss Bousie: 'That terrible sound!' There seem to be lots of people who find the siren an unpleasant sound. Perhaps if we lived beside a siren – as Mrs Wallace does – we should think so, but at a distance I can't see anything unpleasant about it. I am sure that these people project their own feelings on to this quite inanimate object.

I was terribly shocked at 6 to hear that Mr Neville Chamberlain is dangerously ill. There are few things that anger me so much as the way he is sneered at in so many quarters. While there's breath in my body I'll stand up for him.

SATURDAY, 9 NOVEMBER

Ernest van Someren
It was rather a noisy evening. We live on one of the naturally defined routes into London (the Lee Valley) and often hear planes flying over even when there is no gunfire or bombing until they get nearer to town.

Edward Stebbing

Soldier comment on Chamberlain's illness: 'That's it, you old b******, die.' Another soldier: 'Why, is he ill?' Reply: 'I hope so.'

SUNDAY, 10 NOVEMBER

Pam Ashford

I learnt of Mr Chamberlain's death with deep sorrow, mingled with indignation at the abuse that has been thrown at him during the past two years. Mother, Charlie and I have not as much in common as you may find in some households, but in this sorrow we are at one. Mother has been saying, 'There is not a soul in the nation will not grieve. There won't be so many grieve at my passing.' I can't set down how deep is my respect for the late Prime Minister.

The bus seasons are up to 3/6 now, and one is limited to four journeys a day.

MONDAY, 11 NOVEMBER

Edward Stebbing

Had a letter from home. My sister says 'Aren't you glad Roosevelt got in? We all are, for we do know how he feels about things and I'm sure he will help us all he can.'

Observed the two minutes' silence, but only thought how futile the last war was and how futile this one is. Reluctantly bought a poppy.

Of four papers read today, only the *News Chronicle* seemed to be sincere in its comments on Chamberlain. The *Daily Mail* and *Daily Sketch* seemed to be making desperate efforts to whitewash him.

Pam Ashford

Mother says that the grocer boy, aged about 15, asked the time when he came to the door at 10.55 so as to observe the silence. Surprised, I said, 'There is no silence this year.' Mother herself was moved and on her own observed the two minutes, during which she was thinking of a picture in one of the newspapers two or three years ago. I remember it too for its extreme beauty and pathos – a farm labourer, alone, with bowed head, in a field. I myself feel that in these days we have increased reasons for remembering those who fell in the Great War.

Mr Chamberlain's death has touched many people. Miss Carswell said that on the bus yesterday two girls sat saying they were glad he was dead and abused him and Mrs Chamberlain terribly. Mr Mitchell has been saying, 'He was too much of a British gentleman to fight gangsters,' and Miss Bousie is praising his home life and good character.

Ernest van Someren
At work had a warning a bit before 11, went to the shelters, came out before 11 and forgot the two minutes' silence for the first time in many years.

At home I had supper early and typed an article afterwards (technical, commissioned and overdue) and after the news [my wife] Kay copied out and made a fair copy for me to send off, from which I hope to earn 3 guineas for Christmas presents. We have decided to give only to relations and children and the household – not to friends at a distance this year.

TUESDAY, 12 NOVEMBER

Maggie Joy Blunt
The bombs fell in the gardens of houses about a quarter of a mile from the cottage. Glass broken but no one hurt.

Spent the weekend with Stella and Paul in their new house in South Mimms. A romantically charming place – parts of it very old – but awkward, cold and uncomfortable. SS is sharing with them – she is as pro-Fascist, cynical, unstable, depressing as ever. Yet not without charm and a good deal of intelligence. She and P and S seem inevitably of the stuff of which Fascists are made. The way they talk makes me feel sick. They delight in counting up the bomb craters in London, and nosing out new damage. They ignore the miles and miles of untouched streets, the buildings that have escaped destruction . . . I still feel that they would rejoice to . . . see German military might supreme and the Fascist idea of socialism established in Britain. But I may be being unfair to Paul. Should like to have a discussion with him on his own . . .

Pam Ashford
On the way into town this afternoon a passenger beside me asked how to get to St Enoch Square, and as that necessitates alighting at the same stop as I use, I promised to put him right. He is attached to a ship (not the Navy), and was in London (apparently between two voyages) last week. He said that at 3pm the children began to queue up to take their places in the shelters. 'It was pitiable. There is no part of London that has not had some damage by now. There is broken glass everywhere.' He stayed beside St Clement Dane's Church and used the crypt as his particular cover. He was crossing the road to enter it when the bomb fell on the church and damaged it severely. He evidently appreciated its beauty and felt the loss. He went to see a Dutch church in Leadenhall Street and found there was nothing left

of it at all. I said, 'Well you will be able to get some sleep now you are in Glasgow.'

WEDNESDAY, 13 NOVEMBER

Pam Ashford
Those people who take tea umpteen times a day and always with heaped spoonfuls of sugar are taking the rationing system badly. Agnes says that there is no sugar left from this week's ration, and she will have to buy a sugar substitute at a health food shop (pills called Sugarettes). She ended her dismal story with, 'I never thought I could come to this. I always thought we should get at least enough sugar.'

Agnes came back from lunch with the Sugarettes, still declaring that she never thought she would fall so low as to eat chemicals.

One thing we do use at home is biscuits. Perhaps it is because there is no economic basis to our housekeeping, and everything is on labour-saving lines. We have only one course at lunch, with coffee and fancy biscuits to follow. Supper: biscuits and cheese; Charlie breakfasts off Butterette biscuits; my Saturday lunch consists of Healthy Life biscuits nibbled in the darkness of the cinema. A year ago I laid in large stocks which I let go down as the shops always seem to have plenty, but it has been a deceptive plenty. I went to Cranston's this morning (a shop that normally carries a very large assortment) and there were only plain biscuits on the premises. After work I got some chocolate biscuits from Cooper's.

There was a time when everyone who could listened in at 1. Mother and I still do, but our continuance would seem rather the exception than the rule. Today we happened to have the set still on at 1.10 when the news of the naval victory came through. How thrilled we were. Returning to work I saw crowds reading chalked notices on Sauchiehall Street and ran up the three flights of stairs to the office to tell the news. Believe it or not, such is the boredom in certain quarters that I raised not one flicker of interest in the three who were in, viz. Miss Crawford, Margaret and Lottie. As Margaret put it, 'You say often that this or that was given out in the one o'clock news, but how could one day be more important than another?' Mr Ferguson came in then. He knew the news and was jubilant. Mr Mitchell was the last to hear, and his enthusiasm was intense and infectious. (He was in the Navy last time.) He went all over the place telling everyone a second time of how 'Half the Italian fleet was out of commission'.

THURSDAY, 14 NOVEMBER

Edward Stebbing

I have heard a good many members of this unit say that they wished the war would end whether we win or lose, or that they would be glad to get out of the army (myself included). If there were only one or two of this opinion, I should not take much notice, but almost every day I hear some variations of the same idea, the common reason being that most of us are fed up with the whole business.

The Government is criticised for its lack of aggressiveness and the attack on Taranto came as a welcome bit of excitement: concentrate on Italy – in Greece, in Egypt, in the Mediterranean, with air attack – seems to be a widely held view.

FRIDAY, 15 NOVEMBER

Pam Ashford

Today is foggy. Miss Bousie fears to have the lights on in a fog during the day lest the light gives us away to enemy aircraft overhead. As if it would! She also thinks fog will help the enemy get away after dropping their bombs on us. This began talk on flying with instruments, and several people put it down as 'eye-wash' that the Germans are not so well equipped or so skilful as we. There was an idea that Birmingham and Coventry had it badly last night. Miss Bousie: 'They said serious damage.' Miss Smith: 'And heavy casualties.' I listened to the eight o'clock news at a distance and with half an ear, and I did hear something about serious damage but failed to take the item in. It must have been a more conspicuous item at one o'clock for when I got in at 1.15 – late – Mother was seriously alarmed about a report of 1000 killed.

There is no doubt that stocks in grocers' shops are not as large as they were, and Charlie who has always scoffed at Mother's hoard (to which I have contributed generously) has now advised me to build up a reserve again. I know that mother and I saved pounds on our 1939 purchases, but things are dearer now. To build up a reserve is less easy. In fact I often wonder about the ethics of it. If it were that I did the housekeeping I should run more risks, for I have the strength (if need be) to stand in queues and to devise new dishes from available supplies. But with Mother at 73 as the housekeeper, we should be in a pickle if we were thrown back to the situation that prevailed in 1918.

I am surprised that today's entry has been so long, for since 12.30 my mind has been pinned on another matter. A fatal accident happened beside Campbell's in Union Street while my bus was beside Peacock's. A lady was killed by a tram which had to be raised. I have said to myself, 'If you feel a street accident so deeply, what would you be like in a Blitzkrieg? Perhaps you are wrong in thinking you are not afraid of air raids.' Again (after finding the fatality not in the evening papers), 'The nation attaches horror to Coventry, but not to a street accident. I am the other way round. It all depends on how far off you are.'

SATURDAY, 16 NOVEMBER

Maggie Joy Blunt
News Chronicle: 'Heavy bombs were dropped last night during one of the biggest recent attacks on the capital. An ARP [Air Raid Precautions] warden said, "For numbers (of planes) it is the worst night of my experience."'

Jules and I were hanging out of the window of SM's top floor flat in Marylebone High Street from 1 to 3 o'clock in the morning. Plane followed plane over our heads and we got to know almost to the second when they would release their bombs. '*He's* due to lay!' Jules would say. And down they would screech – to the right, to the left and far ahead of us. The awful noise of rent air; the scream of metal as it hit the waiting city; the explosion blast and shiver of the wounded earth . . . rooftops pallid in the light of a full moon, echoes of gunfire rolling along the still streets, shrapnel sweeping past our window like hailstones, and in the distance a carillon of fireballs and the horizon above the chimney pots coloured like the afterglow of sunset . . . We didn't know whether the next bomb would be ours or not but it didn't seem to matter. I felt no fear. It was terrible and splendid.

I said, 'Isn't it rather rash to be standing at a window like this?' Jules replied, 'A man was saved standing at his window – the house was cut away behind him . . .' It never was any use trying to influence Jules. SM had gone to bed quite early but Jules had a feeling that it was going to be a spectacular evening and would not let me join her. I didn't want to die, naturally – what would happen to my cottage and the cats? – but I didn't think I would. And if I did – '*tant pis*'. No one is indispensable.

Home again now after an exhausting journey full of delays owing to damage at Southall. It was strange to see early this morning in London people quietly getting on with their work, sweeping up glass, walking along the streets. Logically, somehow, everyone should have been prostrate with reaction, confused, paralysed . . . But no. Shop doors were open, women went about their marketing as usual, men were climbing onto buses in the normal way. There was a sad, grey atmosphere over the town but nothing on the surface betrayed the horror so recently suffered. It is night again now. Planes are once more overhead, the guns in action.

Last Monday afternoon as I was coming back from Slough a plane swooped from low clouds just over the bus I was in and machine gunned the road. People looked bewildered, terror-stricken and ran for shelter. The conductors on our bus – it was stationary and people were descending – cried, 'Get down on the floor, away from the glass.' I ducked but there wasn't much room. It was all over in a few seconds. I don't think anyone was hurt. The nights are very long. I think I shall grow tired of such excitement.

This afternoon in a railway carriage crowded with Tommies and workers returning home – a wizened man, like a peevish dwarf, who had been complaining at the delay and muddle at Paddington, began to attack the Government. There was general grudging admission of mistakes made until a cheerful little Welsh soldier said, 'But it's the people's fault. Our Governments *have* been rotten but we've put 'em there.'

Ernest van Someren

I went to Waterloo and got an electric train to Reading. The damage to houses near the line of S.R. in London was very serious in the first few miles. I travelled alone in a first class car and read a history of the Quakers, or alternately practised the recorder a bit, which I can do while looking out of the window.

Got to Reading at 12.30 instead of 11 and took a bus to the University for a meeting of a new body, the British Rheologists Club. After lunch we went in various cars (about 20 of us) to a show of rheological apparatus, where I found something very interesting to me in connection with my work. I also listened to short talks on how to test for pregnancy in cows, and how we judge firmness by touch.

Pam Ashford

The tea store that individuals gathered in the early days of the war must be going down – at any rate two people have referred to cocoa today. Miss Smith said, 'The man on the BBC said "Why not try cocoa? This is how it is made, you put cocoa and sugar at the bottom of a cup, make a paste with milk and pour the water on!" So I tried it and quite liked it.' The others showed intense interest in this novel method, while I was flabbergasted that it should be regarded as an innovation. It transpires that in these parts people boil cocoa in a saucepan. I have lived in Scotland 23 years and never knew that before.

Edward Stebbing

Overheard at breakfast: 'I hear Churchill is talking about a campaign in 1944.' 'Of course I think most of that's propaganda.' I had been thinking the same thing myself for some time – and very clever propaganda, too. Notice that nothing is said in the papers about the damage which must have been done to factories and other military objectives in Coventry.

MONDAY, 18 NOVEMBER

Pam Ashford

The Soroptomists again. Miss Forster has a London friend who in the black-out drove her car into a bomb crater. Unable to extricate it in the darkness she left it. She returned next morning only to find that another bomb had fallen, and her car was blown away this time.

TUESDAY, 19 NOVEMBER

Ernest van Someren

A fairly quiet night, we stayed in bed till nearly nine. A fine morning, I did the chickens and then some jobs in my greenhouse. I also cut a chopping block from a large log and K chopped some twigs for kindling. Ron played with L in the morning, then got a fit of crying and refused to help tidy the playroom. I was annoyed with him and after everyone else had tried to persuade him I carried him out and locked him in the greenhouse, where he yowled all the time we had lunch. When we asked him to come in he just sulked. He's a spoilt and loathsome brat.

WEDNESDAY, 20 NOVEMBER

Pam Ashford

On Saturday morning the staff [at the office, the Forth & Clyde Shipping Company] suffered its most profound shock in my experience there, and for five days practically nothing else has been talked about. Mr Ferguson (Managing Director) had put up on the wall a notice that as from 19th inst. we should only have three-quarters of an hour for lunch. At one that day after he had gone Miss Smith said we should not start till the 19th inst., and that would give us Monday to arrange our times. I was thankful for that respite as that assured another Soroptomist Lunch, but Miss Carswell not having heard of it turned up on Monday with her packet of sandwiches, a day too soon! When 9 people are in the welter of emotion simultaneously, you don't half get feeling running high. However, this afternoon Mr Ferguson has changed his mind, and tomorrow, Thursday, we are back to the old arrangement of 1½ hours. Probably by then the storm of indignation will have subsided and we shall look on the humorous side. There has been humour in the way we have inspected each other's lunches to find out what variation can be rung on bread and hot water (particularly when we have been forbidden to use the hot water for any hot drinks that smell – Oxo etc.)

The extension of summertime is upsetting our preconceived ideas of November. Daylight at 5.30 does not seem right. What seems even further from what is right is the darkness in the morning. When I clear out at 8.15 there is enough light to see the way, but no more.

How prices are rising in all directions! When the purchase tax begins to show its effect, things are going to be very hard. Scarcity is showing itself too. I have been reading about a milk shortage and now it has touched Hyndland – last Saturday and again today there has been none. Do the Government intend the civilian population to live on potatoes and bread? I have been looking for the 1s 3d chilled cod ever since the Government fixed the price, but like the onions, it has not arrived in Glasgow yet.

THURSDAY, 21 NOVEMBER

Ernest van Someren
Stayed in bed for my cold, as I had a thick head in the morning. I read the history of the Quakers, and then Eric Linklater's *Impregnable Women*. L came up and tried to keep me company, offering me a jigsaw puzzle, later he went to fetch my recorder for me and I practised a bit. He got hold of a curtain rod and torch and went through the motions of playing a cello.

Today we heard that Hertfordshire has received 4000 bombs, which only caused 20 fatal casualties. I don't know if this includes incendiaries.

Edward Stebbing
Opinion of a soldier (age about 25) is that this country still lacks imaginative leadership. Although the help given to Greece was an improvement on Norway, the Government should have had plans ready supposing Greece was to be invaded, whereas it seemed that they did not start making plans until after the invasion.

Sir Neville Henderson's astonishing statement that before September 1938 we had no Spitfires and few AA guns is considered by two of my friends to be a lie.

22

Pam Ashford

With fish so scarce, I have had the experience of taking it on Monday, Tuesday and Wednesday. The Soroptomists had cod; on Tuesday I had a kipper (a present from a friend), and on Wednesday Mother fed me up at teatime on a crum. She says they had parcelled it up before saying the price, which was 10d. I appreciate her generosity, but don't think any crum in the Kingdom is worth that much. Marie Wilson has been saying she paid 1/1 for a small piece of sole, at 3/6 lb. And we live on an island. Before the war you used to hear that the waters around our shores were fished to such an extent that the fish population was declining. They are having their day now. Marie said she used to buy eggs at a small dairy. When she was in yesterday she said to the owner, 'Why can I never get any eggs?' He said, 'It is your own fault.' She said, 'How?' He said, 'You always ask me when I have a shopful of customers.' She said, 'There is no one else in the shop now.' He said, 'Go and look out of the door and see if there is anyone in the street.' She did this and reported that the coast was clear. He promptly produced three eggs.

Miss Bousie thought it was only polite to thank Mr Ferguson for reverting to the old hours (no one else had any such idea), and he thereupon turned on her saying that 'she was the cause of the trouble. She had gone round to each individual stirring up discontent. We were all pleased with the new arrangement till her evil influence turned us against it. If any of us were bombed now on the way home our deaths would be at her door.'

FRIDAY, 22 NOVEMBER

Edward Stebbing

Best news I have heard today is that I am going on leave next week. After six months of army life without a break, the thought of going home and not having to do anything I don't want to is a tremendous relief. For the last few months my idea has been whenever possible to escape from it all. I have spent more money at the cinema, theatre and dances than I have ever spent in an equal period in civilian life. This escape is, of course, only temporary and I should not wish it to be permanent.

I still read as much as I can, am now reading Sir Richard Acland's *Unser Kampf* and so far am almost completely in agreement with him. Still spend about the same amount on tobacco, allowing for the rise in prices. Yet I also manage to save more and I have food and clothes provided, do less travelling, have things sent to me which I might have bought myself in civilian life, entertainment is fairly cheap and I do not indulge in so many little luxuries. Now that I shall get 1/- a day extra, having qualified as a laboratory assistant, I shall probably save still more.

Pam Ashford
The onions scarcity is upsetting householders seriously – there is no sight of the 4½d Government onions. The milk famine is much worse. They give it away free to children (which is right), and the civilian population (the rest of it) never know whether they are going to have any or not.

SATURDAY, 23 NOVEMBER

Ernest van Someren
Was busy after lunch building a pen for two hens in one end of the greenhouse, so that we can fatten them separately for Christmas.

We had a lazy evening reading, and answered an advert in the *New Statesman* for someone who might possibly come and live here, a woman with a child.

TUESDAY, 26 NOVEMBER

Maggie Joy Blunt
And now the problem of M. Should she come and live with me until after Xmas until the confinement? I am willing to have her, but I wonder if it is wise, the best plan. She should get right away from bombs.

June's CO friend, who objects to fighting in this war although he went to Spain because he believed in the cause of the Spanish people, thinks we shall have Fascism here whether we win or lose, financial interests have such a hold upon our country and its institutions. He is prepared to go to prison for his convictions.

WEDNESDAY, 27 NOVEMBER

Edward Stebbing
Randolph Churchill's maiden speech in the House of Commons attracted my attention today. In my opinion it was a stupid speech and the papers made an unnecessary fuss over it. What does he, as an officer, know about what the men talk about in the barrack rooms? It is true that the main aim of many of them is simply to defeat Hitler but there are just as many who think that this war will only be worth fighting if there is a new order of things to follow. Merely to fight to

salvage all that was good in the old world, which wasn't much, is a restricted outlook, showing poor imagination of what is necessary to make the world a better place. I have detected signs of suspicion that we may not be fighting for all that we are supposed to be, of fears that the peace may be much more difficult to win than the war, of hopes that we may never go back to the pre-war state of affairs.

Arrived home [a small village near Chelmsford in Essex] on leave in the afternoon. Found it more or less unaltered, except that the black-out has been improved and my father and sister now sleep downstairs. My sister says she has not been to a cinema or other entertainment all the time I have been away. My father is late home from work and by the time he has had his evening meal and everything has been cleared away there is not time to do anything much. Saturday night's radio programme seems to be the main entertainment of the week.

Pam Ashford
It has just been announced that the importation of bananas is to stop owing to the amount of space they occupy on ships. Mother is filled with pity for the monkeys at the zoos, but I feel that the curators will cope with that.

THURSDAY, 28 NOVEMBER

Ernest van Someren
Frosty, but I cycled. Busy with photographic work. Left a little early to go to Enfield shopping, bought a suitcase and umbrella set to give to our assistant, and a pair of bedroom slippers for my wife to give me at Christmas.

FRIDAY, 29 NOVEMBER

Pam Ashford
A man in Bristol phoned wanting cargoes for Plymouth, Falmouth, Bristol, Fremington, Hayle and Penzance. The possibilities of business are slight, partly because boats are scarce, and partly because these South of England people have a bias in favour of bright shining coals and fight shy of dull coals, never having learnt that brightness and dullness have nothing to do with burning characteristics. Our Newcastle-on-Tyne friends have found someone in Portugal interested in British coal. The sudden transition from the extreme of quietness to – not the extreme of busyness – but to a busier state, makes one feel one had turned a somersault.

Most of those in the office have shown no interest whatsoever in the Italian defeat by our Navy. I expressed my pleasure to Miss Bousie who revealed herself (unexpectedly in view of her pacifist tendencies) as full of hatred for the Italians. The seizures of Abyssinia and Albania and the stab in the back of France she clearly regards as far worse crimes than any of Hitler's.

And here is an even more unlikely story – coming from that perennial home of rumour, the Royal Exchange. Mr Mitchell was told that we have some 'suicide' troops who take on particularly hazardous jobs. Recently they were landed at Dunkirk with some tanks and captured 150 highly placed Germans. The tanks may or may not have been lost, but the gain in depriving the enemy of these leaders is immense. On another occasion 2000 landed at Guernsey and killed every German on the Island. The office accepted the former story, but hesitated about the latter.

SATURDAY, 30 NOVEMBER

Pam Ashford
The BBC reported that the most intense air activity was over London last night. Miss Bousie: 'How can the Londoners stand it?' Miss Carswell: 'See how you feel if you lose a night's sleep, an absolute wreck, and with them it goes on night after night.' Miss Bousie: 'They say you can get used to it, but I don't believe it.'

I am reading a book on reincarnation (to which I am not a convert, though the book is full of thoughts that are good and true), and having mentioned the book casually I was startled to find that practically everyone believes that they are going to have another turn on earth and are looking forward to being reborn in a better era. Miss Smith hopes she will be a cannibal next time. The whole conversation surprised me, for I am overjoyed to think that my lot has fallen to the twentieth century. In this clash between Christian Ethics and the New Paganism, the angels can only stand and watch, but we can act.

However, food crops up in conversation far oftener than angels.

SUNDAY, 1 DECEMBER

Edward Stebbing
Just before eleven o'clock tonight we heard a whistling noise. I did not realise what it was, but my father said 'look out!' and dived under the table. I followed suit, just as a bomb exploded not far away. My sister came running downstairs and got under the table too, where we stopped for a little while.

26

MONDAY, 2 DECEMBER

Pam Ashford

The speaker at the Soroptomist Club should have been Dr Honeyman but he sent his assistant as substitute, viz. Mr Fleming, who spoke on 'The Art Galleries in Wartime'. He said he chose this title because at a recent meeting at Knightswood a member of the audience asked, 'What was the good of having an art gallery in wartime? Why not spend the money on munitions?' Mr Fleming set out to show us that the atmosphere in an art gallery was one of the few in which you could escape from the war. At a cinema you could not. It strengthened you to face things.

There is no time of the day when men in the forces are not to be found wandering around the galleries – mostly they come in because there is nowhere else to go. The most intelligent groups of all are the Poles, practically all of whom are cultured. A party of 600 turned up one morning.

TUESDAY, 3 DECEMBER

Edward Stebbing

My leave goes much too quickly. Tomorrow I shall have to go back. I wish that I had never got to return.

Everyone says it won't be much of a Christmas this year, that nobody will keep it as usual. My father says he is going to have a chicken for Christmas dinner.

A walk round the village shows it to be more or less unaltered. Noticed surface shelters in the school playgrounds, a huge heap of scrap metal on a piece of waste ground. The bomb the other night caused considerable damage, but no deaths.

We were talking about the war and my sister asked, 'Can we stick all this bombing?' and with reference to the shipping losses, 'Can we hold out?' This is the first time I have heard doubt expressed, about our ability to win. Nobody, of course, could give definite answers to the questions, except that if we can destroy the Italian fleet we can spare more ships to attack the U-boats.

WEDNESDAY, 4 DECEMBER

Ernest van Someren

Took the morning off to go to town to visit a library, and Kay came too to do some shopping. We left L with the money to pay the gardener, and instructions about the laundry, so as to make him feel he was indispensable at home.

We went first to the E.M.G. gramophone shop, a most fascinating place where they found us just what we wanted in gramophone records, and sold us three. I had some cash in hand from my birthday which I was told to spend on records or books. We bought a Dolmetsch record of a Handel sonata for recorder, viol di gamba and harpsichord; a piano record of 'The Lambeth Walk' played in the style of Verdi, Chopin, Beethoven etc. and a Poulenc record to complete a trio of which I have the other record. The second purchase was made especially with a view to the listening group, when the question of style arises.

Then we bought a slab of chocolate at de Brys, and went to the Dryad shop for some cane and a book for a child's present. We had a long session in Gamages toy dept trying to find a toy car for L to sit in and drive, with pedals, but they all had too wide a turning circle to manage the corners on the paths in our garden. We separated. Kay bought a smock and I bought a pair of flannel trousers, some coffee, and made a visit to a library where I rapidly abstracted two long German articles, the last two references for my booklet of Spectrochemical Abstracts.

Pam Ashford

The Billeting Officer called on Mother this morning to know what accommodation we had. Mother had heard that he was in Hyndland from Mrs Heddon and pointed out to him that our house was full of private papers of the Ministry of Aircraft Production [brother Charlie's work]. She thinks she warded him off. Mother keeps saying that at 73 she cannot take on any more work. I say, wait and see, but in any case I don't think that giving up a room is much of a sacrifice to a family that has given up no-one to the Forces, and happens – till now – to have kept its income intact. And has not been bombed either.

THURSDAY, 5 DECEMBER

Pam Ashford

People keep on saying how many English people there are in Glasgow now, and for the most part they are spoken of in disparaging terms. In one case an English woman has gone out to work and left her child on her landlady's hands all day. Someone else ruined a carpet (how?) the first night.

SATURDAY, 7 DECEMBER

Pam Ashford
A lady was saying how miserable the soldiers look going about the town – in the last war there was glamour, with bands to see them off at the station etc. There are, of course, exceptions – even in pre-black-out days Glasgow itself was enough to give any stranger the blues! But the fact remains that this war has not evoked a 'martial' frame of mind. Mr Churchill said of the Londoners 'grin and bear it' attitude; but here in this 'safe' area it is mostly boredom.

Mother found a paragraph in the evening paper giving alternatives to seed for canaries. We know from past tests that Dick will not eat many things that other bird owners give as titbits (sugar, egg, apple, watercress – he only eats lettuce occasionally). The paper said 'carrot', and we gave him a piece, which he evidently delighted in. Thank goodness! Mother has always said that she would have him put away rather than see him hungry.

Ernest van Someren
After L's rest we went to Hertford and did some shopping – tried to buy him a small car, and to get some presents. I bought a recorder for a colleague. We stopped on the way home and bought a car at a shop in Hoddesdon, to be delivered next week.

SUNDAY, 8 DECEMBER

Edward Stebbing
In an overheard conversation amongst four or five men of this unit the following conclusions were more or less unanimously reached: that Chamberlain would have surrendered after the first big raid on London; that Churchill has saved this country from defeat; that Russia would be the only one to benefit from this war; that Hitler was mad, but a genius, and the chief victories of this war had been Hitler's diplomatic victories; that all Germans should be exterminated (shoot them, sterilise them etc., and also make them work for us as slaves).

MONDAY, 9 DECEMBER

Maggie Joy Blunt
A pretty, fading widow serves at the canteen on Monday mornings. She is slender, frail looking, her pale hair fluffs out in little curls from under a nigger brown bandeau. She was full of the news of last

night's bad raid on London. 'Another Coventry, the paper says. The screams of children under the debris . . . terrible! Hitler is a wicked man. There never has been a wickeder. I would like to hang, draw and quarter him. Really, if only I could get my hands on some of these Germans that come murdering our women and children! We *must* go on with this war. Did you see that six men in parliament had the nerve to propose making peace terms?'

Then Mrs D began. 'I never did like Germans. My husband and I have nearly come to blows on this subject more than once. I won't have Germans in my house. I had an Austrian maid when the war began, but I packed her off. They ought none of them be allowed to stay in this country. They must in their secret hearts be in sympathy with their own people. I was brought up to believe that my country came FIRST. My father was very strong on this point. He would say, "Even if you found your nearest and dearest are traitors, if you found *me* betraying my country, you should give us up to the authorities." Country before everything.'

Edward Stebbing
Slogan seen in restaurant, burnt on a piece of wood: 'Act victory, think victory, talk victory. Otherwise – well shut up.'

Pam Ashford
The wretch has now turned up his nose at carrots.

TUESDAY, 10 DECEMBER

Pam Ashford
The consignment for Iceland is being boarded today. There are 17 packages including hundreds of items – underwear, stockings and socks, frocks, blouses, toys, perfumery, cosmetics, handkerchiefs, scarves etc. Mr Mitchell and Mr Hutchison don't seem to be conscious of any reason why they should not conduct such transactions, and I myself think of it as just business. Some of the ladies are annoyed. One considers that there is no other coal exporter in Glasgow who would have agreed to act as agent for general merchandise. I am glad to see the profit (£120) coming in and as for Mr Mitchell, the beneficial effect on his nerves is noticeable.

Mother went to a whist drive and someone brought an attaché case of felt nosegays. A refugee in her tenement makes them, but as she is not allowed to make money herself she gives them to this lady to sell, and the lady hands her the money. I certainly think that the lady would do better business if she kept her mouth shut.

As for Dick, Mother gave him a sandwich (1 inch cube) of bread, sugar and butter, and he would have none of it.

THURSDAY, 12 DECEMBER

Pam Ashford

There is one enjoyable wireless feature, *David Copperfield*, serialised on Monday nights. Last time Mr Micawber wrote David a tragic letter representing himself on the point of suicide; David ran to the address, but on the way saw a coach with Mr Micawber sitting in the front, the picture of health and happiness. The wireless stopped there, and I could not but exclaim, 'I have been through that situation many times. Nothing could be more like Mr Mitchell.' How that is being exemplified now. Only on the 2nd inst. he was in the hands of the doctor, and came back on the 3rd in deep gloom. On the 5th the Icelandic order came and the effect has pitch-forked him to the opposite extreme. He is full of schemes for developing this Icelandic connection, and already our fortunes are as good as made.

There is a story going around the Exchange that a wounded German lay in hospital beside a Glasgow man. The German said, 'The people of Glasgow are safe. We cannot reach Glasgow. From one large-scale attack planned on Glasgow only three planes returned. The magnetic disturbances that the hills produce are too much for our compasses.' No doubt enemy airmen dislike the thought of flying over the Southern Uplands in the dark – and the Highlands too, probably, but would you believe that anyone would accept the story with confidence! Yet it was so – satisfaction was expressed all round.

Ernest van Someren

After breakfast L had a sweet, and although there were only four left he gave me two in a paper bag to take to work for my elevenses – most impressive generosity. I came home in good time and brought him some different sweets from the works canteen. His car had arrived and he is very pleased, though steering is still a mystery to him.

Edward Stebbing

Received a letter from my sister, saying she was going to be married. 'We had been thinking about it since last summer when we postponed the plans we had made between us because of the war, but as it seems the war is going on years we are not going to wait.'

Marriages seem to be on the increase now. Several of my friends and acquaintances have been married recently, as well as my brother.

Another couple are going to be married as soon as they can find a house, which is a big problem for newly-weds nowadays.

FRIDAY, 13 DECEMBER

Pam Ashford
Mr Mitchell's mind is full of the exportation of general merchandise to Iceland, and he has been searching out all sorts of people who might have things to sell. A Paisley firm has offered him tartan scarves for Iceland, and he hopes to set a new fashion going there.

SATURDAY, 14 DECEMBER

Pam Ashford
The defeat of the Italians is bucking everyone up immensely. It is more like what we have understood war to mean. After work I went to see Maurice Chevalier in *Pièges* and found it fine. I was only 20 minutes late for the Music Lecture – my best time so far. They finished *Madame Butterfly*; a student sang some Verdi; as it was our 'breaking up day' there were some negro spirituals sung by Paul Robeson, followed by a thing called *Peter and the Wolf* (Russian) that was absolutely great!

MONDAY, 16 DECEMBER

Ernest van Someren
After tea at home I fixed up an old dry-shaver and some string and wire in the kitchen to try to demonstrate vibrations for a talk on sound. L was much intrigued, and I wasted a bit of time trying to get the thing to work without proper apparatus. This morning we posted the last of our Christmas cards, of which we did 60 this year.

Pam Ashford
At Cooper's I located Kraft cheese, but they would not sell it by virtue of a notice on the wall limiting sales of Kraft to people who are registered for butter. The assistant said no cheese is being made in this country and it now comes from Canada alone. They let me have a box of Chedlet, and while purchasing it I made a mental note that it must be ancient. Then in the health food department I got the last box of Ryevita.

Reaching the office I heard much about a sweet scarcity. I knew this had begun, for Charlie who buys mother a box of Black Magic each Saturday had to take caramels last time.

WEDNESDAY, 18 DECEMBER

Pam Ashford
Mr Mitchell's scheme for sending general merchandise to Iceland is developing. McDonald's the biscuit makers have given him two big cases filled with eight varieties of their biscuits, one case for Iceland and one for us to keep 'for reference' (i.e. a biscuit for the ladies' tea, a box for Miss Crawford, a box for me, and five for the Mitchell household). McDonald's say they cannot get treacle for ginger nuts for home consumption but they can for biscuits for export.

Edward Stebbing
All the wards now are showing Christmas decorations of some sort, but in spite of this the Christmas atmosphere seems to me to be entirely absent. It is difficult to explain this feeling of it not being Christmas time, but the feeling is definite. Christmas is perhaps the time of year I like best, it always seems different, but this year there is no difference, it is the same as any other time.

THURSDAY, 19 DECEMBER

Pam Ashford
This coming Christmas seems to be interesting my associates only mildly – I say my associates, but the remark applies to myself too. Half the Christmas pleasure lay in buying the presents, which involved shop window gazing after work throughout most of December – would this friend like that? But you cannot window gaze in the black-out.

Miss Bousie's Birmingham brother has written to say things are terrible there. His house is intact, but the house on either side has been knocked down, and the opposite house was burnt. Last week they were in the shelter at night for 13 hours.

Auntie Nellie's (Portsmouth) letter is to hand and she speaks of the terrifying experiences they have gone through. All our relatives in Portsmouth, Southampton and the South of England are unharmed, though some have lost their windows.

Ernest van Someren
After tea played with Laurie, dividing the room in two with a barrier and throwing a very soft ball about. His first idea of the conventions which define a game are developing, about such details as always using the chairs in the same way on the floor, and that we should keep on opposite sides of the barrier.

FRIDAY, 20 DECEMBER

Edward Stebbing
Sent off my Christmas cards, which will be almost my only Christmas shopping this year. I wish that I was spending Christmas at home.

Pam Ashford
The exchange of Christmas presents has started. Mr Mitchell has given me a book token and I have given him a box of chocolates for the family and a cigar for himself.

Ernest van Someren
Busy at work with a long dull job. People's attitude to the war news soon changes from resignation to ill-controlled optimism, and they are expecting the Western Desert campaign to develop into a sweeping movement across N. Africa.

In the evening loafed, read a little, and listened to the Sibelius symphony although the reception was bad.

SATURDAY, 21 DECEMBER

Pam Ashford
I have always written to 'everyone' at Christmas and this involves about 24 letters. I got Eda's (5 pages of pad paper) and Janet's (6 pages) done after tea. I take great pains over the first half-dozen or so, deliberately treating different subjects in each. That gives me so much material already composed in my head that the remaining 18 letters flow off the pen. But this year I feel that no one must be passed over. I want people going through the Blitzkrieg to know we care, and in so far as possible I want them to write back to say they are still here.

SUNDAY, 22 DECEMBER

Ernest van Someren
We got together the parcels which have arrived and opened them all. Laurie had some painting books and a bed with proper bedclothes for a doll, which Kay made him for his play and to teach him how to make a bed neatly. Kay gave me bedroom slippers and some chocolate. I gave her a silk smock – both self-chosen gifts. My sister sent us a tin of fancy biscuits. The daily help gave L a soft toy horse and some sweets – someone else gave him a mug and plate.

MONDAY, 23 DECEMBER

Ernest van Someren
L shows one or two signs of having started a cold. I went to work by train, later K and Laurie set out to York, where she is to stay for a week with her parents in a house near her sister's home at Wetherby. Christmas cards are coming in well, as usual.

Edward Stebbing
Soldiers remark on Halifax's appointment as US Ambassador: 'I hope he gets torpedoed on the way.'

Pam Ashford
Both the leading Sunday papers, *Times* and *Observer*, had their leaders that Hitler might try to invade us soon. I should not be surprised if that is not what Mr Churchill is going to say in his broadcast. Hitler is just the type that might land on Christmas Day.

Miss Bousie thinks that as canaries are sub-tropical birds they should like sub-tropical fruit and has given hers three sultanas, which it rejected scornfully. Agnes is experimenting with her budgie, who is likewise holding out for seed.

Mr Mitchell returned at 4 with a newspaper revealing recent damage to the House of Commons. This excited comment. Mr Mitchell: 'It does not matter how many buildings we lose, so long as we gain victory.' I: 'It does not matter how many historical buildings we lose, so long as we keep our aircraft factories intact.'

Mr Churchill spoke at 9. I do think this is the greatest speech I've ever heard.

TUESDAY, 24 DECEMBER

Pam Ashford
Mr Churchill's speech formed the chief topic of conversation this morning. Miss Smith praises it. Miss Bousie was shocked and antagonistic. 'What venom! I dislike such speeches. He made me quake.' I: 'You quake. It is to be hoped he made the Italians quake.' She: 'Yes. But what will they not do to us in revenge?'

CHRISTMAS DAY

Edward Stebbing
No presents, no games, no visitors. Actually 'no presents' is not quite true, as there was one present from the sister of the ward which came as a pleasant surprise and two extremely good Christmas dinners, one at midday the other at tea-time, helped to mark the occasion. After dinner someone came round dressed in the red robes and beard of Father Christmas and gave each patient a present off the Christmas tree.

Pam Ashford
Christmas Day! Today has been of the happiest, not because of the 'highlights', but because of the absence of highlights. No newspapers today. No lengthy wireless bulletins, but just the reassurance that there were no enemy aircraft over the country! No getting up and journeying into town before dawn, but waking up at 10 and Mother coming into the room. We hugged, she saying 'Thank God for another Christmas Day!' and I, 'Thank God we have a roof over our heads.' Mother then went down the stair to wish Mrs Stewart a happy Christmas Day and found her cooking for 16 soldiers whom she had invited to breakfast.

As long as we have a peaceful Christmas Day there is hope for this civilisation of ours. Today has been a lovely experience.

Ernest van Someren
Got up at 8.00 after the quiet night which I expected. After breakfast I packed a rucksack and went to town by coach, got to my mother's home at about 11.30 and had a snack. She has in the house her mother aged 84 and an elderly couple of cousins H and D van Someren, who are living there temporarily.

At about 1.30 we had dinner, with a fat capon and some white wine which my mother has hoarded for 10 years – good stuff. Afterwards we sat and talked, listened to the King at 3.00 and made the usual polite remarks about how he hates speaking and how his fluency is slowly improving.

THURSDAY, 26 DECEMBER

Pam Ashford
Miss Bousie was full of praise for Hitler. 'He did not send any planes over. If we would only meet him, he would never send another. Why should people stop fighting for one day, when they could stop fighting for all the days of the years?'

Elsie came from Edinburgh to have lunch with us in Glasgow. She says that £700 of damage was done at the Edinburgh Zoo by the bombs there, and that the Holyrood bomb fell in the adjoining graveyard and some of the old kings of Scotland have been disinterred. For some reason this sounded funny, and we asked if Darnley had been blown up again. She could not give details.

After work I went to Grant's with two book tokens (total 11/-) and bought *The Seven Pillars of Wisdom* by T.E. Lawrence.

FRIDAY, 27 DECEMBER

Ernest van Someren
I got a bus to Westminster, bought a snack and went to the Fabian Society head office and got into a private coach. We set out to the Christmas School at a large school in Surrey. After dinner there was a dance to gramophone records in a fine ballroom. Made friends with a Mrs H, slightly younger than me, who knew some people I knew in Birmingham. She was rather beautiful and her husband, in the army, was absent. We went to bed soon after 11, I slept in a small dormitory with 4 other men.

SUNDAY, 29 DECEMBER

Ernest van Someren
In the afternoon more people arrived, the lecture was by Francis Williams on the prospects of a Revolution in Europe and the discussion was very lively. Then some more ping-pong before dinner. A collection was taken among the members to buy some drinks, we all had sherry and biscuits before dinner.

The party began with games and a sing-song and political charades. I led some rounds with my recorder, including 'London's Burning'. Drinks were served, we played balloon games, finishing with the Internationale.

Pam Ashford
Alice came to tea. She was at Montrose for 5 weeks in the summer and twice they were bombed by day. A woman was killed through a piece of shrapnel severing the jugular vein and the entire population went to the funeral.

MONDAY, 30 DECEMBER

Pam Ashford
From the 8am bulletin it was obvious that last night's raid on London was very bad, and each subsequent bulletin has brought further confirmation. Agnes had a letter from a friend in Sheffield saying things were terrible there and that her mind will never recover from the shock. Wherever you go you see severed legs and arms lying about.

'We must do the same to the Germans, destroy their homes too,' said Mr Mitchell. I said, 'Let us keep our hands clean of that evil. In any case bombing their munition works is more effective.' Mr Mitchell thinks we are only playing for time. In the Spring thousands of American planes will be here and then we shall do to the German civilians what the Germans have done to ours. Distinctions between 'Nazis' and 'the other Germans' are all swept away now, in a raging hatred for every man jack of them.

Edward Stebbing
Managed to get home for a few hours before being moved to another unit on Jan 2nd. Going home and coming back I saw the shelters in the tubes for the first time, and noticed how they seemed to accept all this business of carrying bundles of bedding, food, etc. down to the tubes and spending the night. This is a normal part of their existence, without fuss, without excitement. All this was strange to me and rather wonderful. At home the most interesting observation was that there is a pretty general opinion that the war will end next year, or that the worst part of it will be over.

The next instalment, beginning a new year, will be written from Sheffield, among different surroundings, different people in different conditions of life

No. 7379659
Pte E A Stebbing
E Barrack Avon
No 2 boy, R.R.M.C
Connaught Hospital
Aldershot
Hants

TUESDAY, 31 DECEMBER

Pam Ashford

I am thrilled when I think that after war this generation will have the opportunity that Wren's generation had and let slip, the opportunity to rebuild London. Mr Mitchell regards London as an 'octopus . . . the bane of Great Britain'. I said, 'The concentration of industry on London has had a reverse. After the war the Clydeside will have its day.' Mr Mitchell, 'And so it should have with iron and steel here.'

Miss Bousie is thankful the Guildhall is gone. It means an end of the Lord Mayor's Banquets, flunkeys in white wigs, and 'Pray silence for My Lord So-and-So' and all that sort of nonsense.

Home in time to hear a very serious talk on fire fighting by Mr Morrison.

THURSDAY, 2 JANUARY 1941

Pam Ashford

Mother and I went to see *Theodora Goes Wild* at the La Scala at 11.15. We got home at 2 and had just crossed the threshold when the siren went. Glasgow's only previous experience of a daylight warning was on 23rd July. The trams and buses continued, and people walked about the streets as normal.

Letters replying to our Christmas greetings are coming in now. News from Exeter (get many alerts but not raids), Southampton (like hell let loose), I of W (terrible), Plymouth (some raids but quite bearable). What a New Year to enter!

Chapter Two

THESE ARE THE SHADOWS

Londoners are used to these shocks by now: another victim of a V-1 rocket receives attention.

4 January–25 February 1941

4 January German-born Marlene Dietrich becomes an American citizen.

9 January The Lancaster bomber makes its maiden flight.

10 January All Jews are required to register in the Netherlands; Stuka dive-bombers attack HMS *Illustrious*.

11 January Portsmouth devastated as the Luftwaffe drops 50,000 incendiaries.

13 January James Joyce dies in Zurich.

22 January Australian and British forces capture Tobruk from the Italians.

28 January Home Secretary Herbert Morrison closes the Communist *Daily Worker*.

4 February The British Chancellor Sir Kingsley Wood announces that the cost of the war is currently £11 million a day.

9 February Churchill ends five months of radio silence, entreating, 'Give us the tools and we will finish the job.'

22 February An estimated 400 Jews a week die of starvation in the Warsaw ghetto, while Jewish protests in Amsterdam lead to shootings and deportations to Buchenwald.

SATURDAY, 4 JANUARY 1941

Ernest van Someren
The Christmas mail from the USA was lost, so we have nothing from my sister there. One of my cousins who was a prisoner in Germany from 1915 to 1918 subsequently went to live in Holland, and has been taken by the Germans again, this time as an internee – there was no news except that he is alive.

Pam Ashford
The Manchester premises of one of our customers has been burnt down. The books in the safe were roasted. The rubber and metal in the covers melted and encased the books. It will take a hatchet to open them.

Mrs Stewart visited Mother to say that Waddell's sausage factory was machine-gunned. Mr Stewart (butcher) says, 'Now they have gone for Waddell's sausages, I suppose they will be after mine next.' Local opinion is that the Germans mistook the sausage factory for something else.

SUNDAY, 5 JANUARY

Edward Stebbing
Life in Sheffield so far has not been very inspiring. One of my Aldershot comrades is billeted in the next house but one so shall not have to make all new friends. In that house they have water and light and we go there to wash. When we get the water and gas put on and something softer than the floor to sleep on it shouldn't be too bad. We are here to form a unit to go abroad so there is nothing much to do. The main job is to keep warm.

Sheffield has suffered much from the Blitz. Before then, I am told, it was one of the liveliest places you could wish to be in. Most places of entertainment close early (about 6), the shops close early, the cafes close early now. It is hard to find a place where one can get a good meal. Woolworth's, about the only place serving reasonably priced hot meals, is doing a roaring trade. Last night I discovered a dance-hall where they have dances every night. It was crowded out (99% civilians) but I enjoyed myself. Admission is 1/6d so I shan't be able to afford to go there often and buy meals as well. Reading will be my chief pastime, I think.

MONDAY, 6 JANUARY

Ernest van Someren
I woke with facial neuralgia and a cold in my head, so stayed in bed.
Got rid of the face ache with aspirin and coffee.

TUESDAY, 7 JANUARY

Ernest van Someren
Felt better, with mild cold, went to work throughout the day-old
snow. I might as well have stayed in bed again, we had local spotter's
warnings thrice and spent 2 hours in the shelters, coolly disgusted. In
the evening K had a sore throat, we warmed up the bathroom
carefully with an electric fire and had a very hot bath.

Edward Stebbing
Listened to a discussion among some soldiers in a Salvation Army
canteen. These were some of the remarks of the two with the most to
say: 'Italy won't stick it much longer . . . But the war will go on a
long while yet . . . If Germany wins the war, the average German
won't benefit, but the ruling classes will. Come to that, the average
Englishman won't benefit if this country wins. The ruling classes will,
but people like you and me will still have to work hard for our £3 or
£4 a week. Still I shouldn't wonder if the working man doesn't stick
up for himself a bit more after the war, when he sees all the money
that's been spent . . .' Reply: 'Oh I don't know. There'll be greyhound
races, and football matches again to help him forget. It's only while
all those things are closed down that he has to sit at home and either
mope or think about the war. When it's over it'll be back to the good
old days of Greta Garbo and Robert Taylor.'

Pam Ashford
About a year ago this diary contained a record of a nightmare tram
journey home in a Glasgow fog. Today we had a taste of the same
thing, but in the black-out. For the first morning this winter I needed a
torch. My only operating one is a big one at the bedside and I wrapped
much tissue paper around it. It was awful outside. At one point I met
a policeman who said, 'Are you the sun?' I am still undecided as to
whether this was a reference to the brightness of my light, but I said,
'See what layers of tissue paper I have it screened with.'

At last it is stated officially that Broadcasting House has been
struck. So the noise that was unmistakeably a bomb one news-time
has been confirmed.

WEDNESDAY, 8 JANUARY

Pam Ashford

After work I went to the Royal Philosophical Society to hear Mr Robieson, the Editor of the *Glasgow Herald*, speak on the Press in wartime. When I entered (as ever late) he was discussing the paper shortage and its effects, then he dealt with the Press and Censorship Bureau, the way papers were co-operating and would co-operate to keep going, with allusions to the damage to Fleet Street. In his view the vagueness of the Air Ministry's reports on raids on this country was harmful to public morale.

There were questions from the audience. A man could not understand how things could be transmitted to the enemy sufficiently quickly to be of any use. Mr Robieson said, 'Of course the Authorities don't tell us why they are so particular about references to the weather, etc., but we assume that they believe that there are still some secret wireless transmitters.' At a recent conference at the Ministry of Information, the newspapers were told that at 11am a summary of all the leading British papers was in the hands of the German Government Officials.

Ernest van Someren

Hurried home after work to have tea and then go to the dentist, who repaired two teeth I chipped on a nutshell in a cake at Christmas. We have started Laurie on the exercises in Muller's *My System for Children*. He does a few by the fire after his evening bath, likes the idea and keeps looking at the pictures in the book to make sure he is doing the right thing – he hardly likes me to interpret the text unless it confirms the pictures precisely.

We have the performance figures for our poultry for the Oct–Dec quarter: 320 eggs of which we had 137. The cost was about 44 for food, and the market value for the eggs 5 guineas, so they are beginning to repay the capital outlay.

FRIDAY, 10 JANUARY

Pam Ashford

Iceland has ordered a second consignment of underwear. They also want an offer of half a million fish hooks (these are scarce) and 1000 barrels of cement. Entering into these new markets worries Mr Mitchell. I am flabbergasted at the large profits that can be plucked. On coal for abroad 3% is laid down by law, but with non-skid chains the manufacturers have covered us for 33 and a third. On the underwear we get 25%.

46

Everyone has strong views on what to do in an alert. Miss Bousie: 'If I were in a munitions factory I would work during an alert. What good would I do here? I might be killed by a bomb. There is nothing glorious in being killed by a bomb. There is something glorious in being killed in battle, but not by a bomb. The important thing is to keep ourselves sound in body and mind, absolutely fit to rebuild the country when the politicians have finished smashing it up. I blame myself for this war. I did not press hard enough for proportional representation. I did not work hard enough for the League of Nations Union.'

SATURDAY, 11 JANUARY

Pam Ashford
After work I went to the Cosmo to see *The Postman Always Rings Twice*. Sombre.

Edward Stebbing
Visited one of the two pantomimes running in Sheffield. Because of the Blitz they have a morning and afternoon performance daily instead of afternoon and evening.

The theatre was packed out in the afternoon and I had to stand for half the performance. Jokes against the Italians were well received, e.g. 'Did you know the Italians have given up fish and chips?' 'Given up fish and chips? No, why?' 'Because they've run out of Greece.'

As far as I know the two theatres I have mentioned are the only ones open. Another is closed with a notice up – 'Closed until happier times'. Found another dance hall tonight, a fair distance from the city. Run by the soldiers the admission was only 3d and there was a big crowd there and plenty of girls.

SUNDAY, 12 JANUARY

Maggie Joy Blunt
N and I went to London on Friday – she to stay with M at Swiss Cottage and me to stay with Jules and Mavis in their new flat in Gloucester Place. Jules and I worked most of the time on the novel – he as usual tearing my efforts to pieces – except on Saturday afternoon when we went to see Bette Davis and Charles Boyer in *All This and Heaven Too* at the Warner in Leicester Square. The Blitz began in the middle of it. A bomb fell somewhere near and the building rocked. (This bomb was I think the one that wrecked Green Park Tube Station.) No one moved, there was scarcely even a

murmur. When we came out Jules said, 'I am not given to singing the praises of the British nation but when I see the way we can behave when something like that happens I begin to think we are not such a bad race after all. Abroad there would have been pandemonium.' Perhaps Londoners are used to these shocks by now and anyway only the type who can endure them are in town, the rabbits have long since fled to the country. The excitable, panicky foreigner has left too. A visit to London is a tonic.

We walked back from Leicester Square to Gloucester Place. Guns were going but no shrapnel was falling in our direction. Fires lit the dusk to the east and west of us. We could see one raging at the end of Bond Street from where we stood in Oxford Street. This evening the buses were making a detour round Hyde Park Corner and I had to pick up my Green Line in High Street Kensington.

We have had an orgy of reading. John Hampden's *Great English Short Stories*. Maugham's *Altogether* and extracts from his *Gentlemen in the Parlour*. Some Hazlitt essays. John Steinbeck's *Red Pony. Richard II*. Around me now I have Clough Williams Ellis' *Pleasure of Architecture*, J.M. Richards' *Introduction to Modern Architecture*, Ramsay Muir's *Future for Democracy*. Have finished *Idiot's Delight* and Shaw's *Major Barbara* and begun *John Bull's Other Island*. So much and so much and so much more to read. Wintringham's *Armies of Freemen* for instance. One gets mental dyspepsia with it all.

MONDAY, 13 JANUARY

Maggie Joy Blunt

This morning a sharp white frost had feathered the trees but later in the day the sun had in it the first warm promise of spring. I ache for the spring and the longer hours of daylight and the garden in growth again above ground. There are snowdrops out already – one was in bud before Xmas. Oh, for warm days, long days, open windows and light clothes! I think when one has to clear and lay one's own fires one loves the summer more. But the trees in winter are more beautiful rising clear to the sky from a bronze, copper and sepia bed.

I am selling some of my furniture to cousin PJ who married last autumn. His sister and mama propose coming to collect the small pieces from here on Wednesday in their car. The what-nots, the davenport, and one small table. I am planning all manner of exciting rearrangements and may visit some of those fascinating antique shops in Beaconsfield.

Edward Stebbing

Food is chief problem here and I personally spend more on it than anything else. The food we get from the Army is poor and insufficient. Hot meals are hard to find and supply has been upset by air-raids. Woolworth's is the best place to go. Went there today and had two sausages, an egg and chips, bread and butter, tea, and a sweet for only 1/11 – the best meal I have had since I've been here. The cooking is done by electricity.

Pam Ashford

Yesterday both wireless and Sunday papers gave accounts of the destruction of publishing houses at Paternoster Row during the fire of London. Charlie says that all the unsold copies of his books were stored at Stationers Hall, and have gone up in flames. He seems tickled about it. He has three published but only one still producing royalties. Two others are not yet in print, the publishers having bought them in the summer of 1939 and held them over till after the war. The MMS are safe.

Mother warned me that there were no sausages in Hyndland last week. (We associate this with the meat scarcity rather than the machine-gunning of Waddell's sausage factory.) I promised to keep my eyes skinned down town.

For the first time the Soroptomists had a vegetarian dish for the main course, viz macaroni and cheese (with peas and potatoes). I was sitting beside Miss Mary McKirdy, the cookery teacher at the Dough School. I said, 'We live off tins, and dear knows what we shall do if the tins are cut off.' This natural utterance was not perhaps discreet to such a hearer, for Miss McKirdy says she has spent her life getting people away from tin openers, and she has been most upset because last week the Dough School Canteen had to use a tin of tongue.

In the office today Miss Carswell was full of something she read in a Sunday paper, viz that the Germans had announced that when they had conquered this country, British women would be given to Nazis as additional wives, but only blondes of Nordic stock. Other types would be mated with less desirable breeds. I burst out laughing and said, 'Then I'm booked for an Italian. That's great. I always wanted to see Venice.' (My physical appearance is 100% Mediterranean, though why I don't know.)

At lunchtime Miss Bousie called me to her and with a chuckle said, 'What do you think of the stories they get out of the Sunday papers?' I said, 'The stories of atrocities done to the Poles are true. If the Germans conquered this country they would wreak the same vengeance on us.' Miss Bousie was astonished that I should think that. I mentioned it to Mr Mitchell who said, 'They would annihilate us.' What is beyond me is what Poland's position will be when we have won the war. Mr Mitchell's answer to that is that the Poles will murder every German in Poland.

TUESDAY, 14 JANUARY

Pam Ashford
The news that Plymouth suffered a severe raid last night moves me far more than Portsmouth. I lived at Plymouth from 1½ till 14 and love every stone and blade of grass. The houses, roads, that church, that school are all parts of me. Houses that I have lived in in Glasgow don't matter, but the house in Fitzroy Terrace, Plymouth, does. To think of injury possibly done to Stoke Damerell Church or DSS, is like touching the pupil of the eye. And is my father's grave untouched?

WEDNESDAY, 15 JANUARY

Maggie Joy Blunt
Snow has prevented my relations from coming here today. Spring seems a long way off now. It was only a dream in the sun on Monday. But it will come. And with it what more horrors of war?

Cousin J sent me for Xmas a small coloured reproduction of Van Gogh's portrait of an artist – Mediterranean greens and yellows and burnt sienna. A lovely, warm exciting little picture. It was one of the nicest presents I had.

THURSDAY, 16 JANUARY

Ernest van Someren
Laurie's 3rd birthday. To his delight the morning post was all for him, just two birthday cards. Busy at work again. After work brought one of my colleagues home, and L greeted us when we opened the door with 'Hello, Mr Roberts' and at once started to show off his birthday presents of books. We had a large high tea at once, then a little chat before Mr R continued his trip home by train. Laurie was rather conspicuous, but fairly polite and very cordial, and he is not shy with me at all now. Then we listened in a bit, and also did some recorder practice.

FRIDAY, 17 JANUARY

Pam Ashford

So the papers report that Mr Churchill was in Glasgow yesterday. But they don't tell you he is here till he is on the way back.

Squads for fire fighting are news now. Our tenement in 188 Hyndland Road is the most hopeless place imaginable. Two unoccupied houses, two houses each occupied by an old lady living alone, a Jewish family that keep themselves to themselves and are an indeterminable factor, Mr Fuller, living alone, a bag of nerves, and in any case ruled out as a civil servant; that leaves the Stewarts (Mr Stewart 100% disability pension from last war, both arms useless) and ourselves – Charles prohibited from ARP by the Government.

Miss Bousie has been telling me about friends in London. They have just written to say that they have not had their clothes off since August (I felt like saying they must be dirty by now, but refrained from ribaldry), and last week they went to bed for the first time since August. I said, 'But there have been a number of nights when it has been announced that London had a night with no alerts.' Miss Bousie: 'Don't you believe it.' I: 'But Christmas Eve . . .' Miss Bousie: 'Well they never went to bed.'

The meat scarcity! The papers report that sausages are likely to disappear. There goes another unrationed dish. Fish is beyond our purse. Haddock is today at 4/- per lb. Our butcher can no longer get chickens. I said to Mother, 'Then I must eat rabbit.' I so dearly love the bunnies scampering over the fields that the thought of eating one thoroughly upsets me, to which Mother replied, 'But there are no rabbits. They have been exterminated.' Frankly I don't believe this, and have promised to watch the City shops.

SATURDAY, 18 JANUARY

Ernest van Someren

At about four, five children came with two mothers. We took off them enough wet clothes to fill the entire 'airer' in our kitchen. We put two tables together and had tea in our ex-bedroom, usually called the playroom now. They began with jellies and Kay had made a cake and iced it (real icing sugar bought by our daily help) and there were three candles. Laurie ate hard and took little notice of the visitors.

After tea we played in the sitting room, blowing bubbles, knocking balloons about, blind man's buff, and a bit of hide the thimble, the party was a screaming success. It broke up soon after six, and I took one of the girls home while K put L to bed. On the way he announced that he preferred to have tea with Mummy and Daddy and play at hiding an orange afterwards.

SUNDAY, 19 JANUARY

Edward Stebbing

Four of the chaps were talking this morning about the army. Three of them announced their intention of getting out of it as soon as possible when the war is over. The other, not so sure, said, 'Don't be too sure. They won't let you go as soon as the war is over. They've only got to pass another Act of Parliament and they can do what they like.' 'They can't do it, without our consent,' said another, 'because we're fighting for freedom.' Are we? I wondered.

MONDAY, 20 JANUARY

Pam Ashford

'Fire in the galley, fire down below, get a bucket of water lad, there's fire down below.' (Sea shanty).

I cannot but laugh, for a day in which fire fighting has cropped up again and again has actually been brought to a close by – a fire!

Mr Roxburgh said, 'I have been listening to this German broadcaster. There is a certain amount of truth in it. We were going to make this a land fit for heroes after the last war, and we did not. He is a dangerous broadcaster. The Germans understand the psychology of the public better than the BBC.'

Through this Iceland business I did not get away from work till 6.30 when it was dark of course. At Charing Cross the bus had to stop to let a fire engine pass, and away the engine went up Woodlands Road. Even then there seemed a pinkness to the west, and by Park Road there was no doubt about it being a redness. As we passed the end of Sutherland Street, there it was. The upper floors of two large tenements ablaze, great flames, feet long, belching up from an inferno. I got up the bus, you can bet. That one lone engine was there with the fire escape extended to roof level and a fireman trickling a tiny jet of water, which after a little ceased altogether.

What hundreds and hundreds of people turned out. And what comments they made as they saw the fire spread and the brigade doing nothing. 'It is a disgrace to Glasgow.' 'It will be a month before they get that fire out.' 'If that is what they are like with an ordinary fire, what will they be like in a blitz?' 'What a beacon for a Jerry.' Of course, I enjoyed the spectacle immensely, but I felt deep grief too for the people whose homes were totally destroyed. It might have been mine. I dared not stay till the end, for it was 7.30 and I knew Mother would have made up her mind that I had been run over in the black-out.

WEDNESDAY, 22 JANUARY

Ernest van Someren
Got home after dark. There was a parcel of sweets from my sister in USA, mixed candies and chocolate raisins, in good condition. For two weeks I have been unable to buy my favourite chocolate, and have drawn a little on my reserve.

THURSDAY, 23 JANUARY

Pam Ashford
Mr Mitchell is very ill and has been taken to a nursing home for observation. He had been X-rayed and they think he will have to have an operation. Oh! I do hope that Mr Mitchell being away for some weeks does not mean that Iceland falls through our grip.

FRIDAY, 24 JANUARY

Edward Stebbing
Food works out on an average of 9/6 a week, nearly half my wages. Learnt today that I shall not be going abroad after all, not being physically fit for service in tropical climates. This will please my family and they will not worry about me. I'm not sorry either to leave Sheffield as I know it. Tomorrow I go to Leeds.

SATURDAY, 25 JANUARY

Edward Stebbing
Arrived in Leeds late in the afternoon. Not knowing my way about could not go anywhere far from the tram-stop where I could catch a train back to my billet. Went to a wine lodge, where it was warm and bright and there were plenty of people and had a drink. The bar was circular and underground so could be used as air-raid shelter. Stopped down there and just looked at the people.

MONDAY, 27 JANUARY

Edward Stebbing
One of the first things I noticed here was that the Army food is a

great improvement on that at Sheffield. It is adequate and well-prepared. Why can't it be the same everywhere?

Went to the pictures (the cinemas and theatres open in the evening) for the first time in weeks. Missed the last tram back; spent the night at the YMCA which is open all night.

TUESDAY, 28 JANUARY

Ernest van Someren
An annoying day, with two warnings at lunchtime, and another in the afternoon, which wrecked the day's work. Laurie's cold is rather bad, when I got home he was a bit limp and feverish, K had been to see the doctor and for some odd reason didn't mention L. I went out to see someone about a WEA meeting, came home to supper and a quiet evening putting wax on old gramophone records.

We looked through our 1941 accounts recently, and I can produce a statement to compare with the budget of 1939.

	1939	1940
Food	120	121
House, cleaning, labour	68	64 + 5 for garden
Rent and rates	86	88
Insurance personal, income tax	37	37
Gas, electric (coal 1940 inc)	33	35 including a stove
Self, personal, holidays &c	82	74
Wife, ditto ditto	60	40
Laurie	3	13
Medical expenses	(under personal) 6	
Telephone & postage	11	11
Chicken keeping		6 – against which credit about 240 eggs & some hens
Periodicals	3	4
Subscriptions	10	10
	548	546

Total income for 1940 about 570, excluding contribution to works pension fund, deducted at source, of £26.

Problem is, what shall we cut next year to compensate for double

54

the income tax and another baby? We have in the bank about 95 for the latter, which is sure to be expensive.

Edward Stebbing
Went to the pantomime. Arthur Askey in *Jack and Jill*. Very good show, well attended.

FRIDAY, 31 JANUARY

Ernest van Someren
I went out to a meeting of the local Hospitality Committee, which has completed 2 years of work looking after two refugee girls from Germany. One is now 18 and earning money in an office, the other is still at school, will train to be a nurse afterwards. We have collected enough for her maintenance till the summer.

Then home to put L to bed while K got supper. He is a bit bad-tempered while not quite well and we had a row, during which he hit me so hard with his head that I cut my lip off a tooth and it bled, and hurt me so badly that I smacked him hard. This and the bloodshed made some impression.

After supper the WEA class met here, to listen to the BBC talk on the drama and discuss it a bit. Then we had tea, when the BBC orchestra came on we turned off the lights and sat listening to the Schumann piano concerto keenly.

Edward Stebbing
Last three or four letters from my sister have shown that she is very busy preparing for her wedding tomorrow, but it is a big disappointment for both of us that I shall not be able to be there. She says, 'I wish more than anything else that you will be there.' Family events such as this seem more important to me than the progress of the war etc. You cannot live your own life in the Army, you are one of a million machines, your life is planned out in advance and you're forced to live it.

Maggie Joy Blunt
Have had another idea for writing this diary. From notes made daily or weekly I will write it up once a month – a regular monthly report rather than all these casual jottings. Beginning now.

There has been a sinister lull in enemy attacks on this country since Xmas. Except for the fire Blitz on London and short concentrated raids on Cardiff, Portsmouth, Plymouth and Southampton our nights have been so quiet 'you could hear a bomb drop' as David Low told

America. There have been a few daylight alerts but they have not hindered the normal life of the country.

The weather may be one very good reason for this pause – and it can only be a pause. We have had sharp frosts and heavy falls of snow that have thawed in a few days into dreary slush and chill rain. We long for the spring and welcome the first snowdrop but wonder all the while what is brewing, what more horrors are in store for us. War activity has veered to the Mediterranean as we were warned it would. The Greeks continue their advance in Albania. Haile Salassie is leading his patriots in revolt against their conquerors in Abyssinia. Bardia has fallen and we have taken Tobruk. Our successes against the Italians in North Africa should have heartened us, yet somehow they haven't. We have made so many blunders, the Nazis have achieved so many efficient victories that we cannot help feeling a little cynical. Hitler and Mussolini have met and are reported to be 'in full agreement on all questions of mutual interest', but I can only picture now an exchange of macaroni and custard between Charlie Chaplin and Jack Oakie. There is trouble brewing in the Balkans. A new and vast trade pact has been signed between Germany and Russia and it seems that Russia stands to Germany in the same relation as America does to us. We have been promised material help in abundance from America and we shall need it.

It is as though we are beginning to see at last the slow subsidence of our river of wealth. We are not starving, we are not even underfed, but our usually well-stocked food shops have an empty and anxious air. Cheese, eggs, onions, oranges, luxury fruits and vegetables are practically unobtainable. The fruit shops fill their windows with tinned goods and expensive spring flowers. Housewives are having to queue for essential foods. We live on potatoes, carrots, sprouts, Swedes, turnips, artichokes and watercress. We are encouraged to use oatmeal to help out the meat ration which was cut at the beginning of the month and now includes all the offal we could once buy without coupons. Cigarettes and sweets are difficult to get though not impossible if one has time and patience to search the shops. Prices are rising. We hear mutterings about inflation and hope that something will be done to prevent it, though how, when we are spending 12 millions a day on our war effort, is hard to imagine. We are warned by statesmen repeatedly that Hitler intends to invade us if he can when the weather improves. Our men are still called up in large numbers, those under 19 and over 36 and women from 18 to 23 are to register soon. The outlook really seems very grim indeed.

The talk that week in the village was all of the fire Blitz on London. But what we need is a new City – not the present one cleared a little here and there and patched up. A new City built to a modern, controlled plan of the whole capital, incorporating what is worth preserving and dynamiting the blocks of hideous, unhygienic offices and commercial buildings which have destroyed the beauty of London more effectively than any bomb.

An uneventful month for me in my own affairs, but so crowded with voices from beyond the confines of my immediate circle, brought to me by radio, newspapers, journals and books that I find it difficult to sort out and digest the ideas and news and rumours they introduce. Daily I receive the *News Chronicle* and *Daily Telegraph* (the DT's offices had been badly damaged). Once a week comes the local paper, the *New Stateman*, the *Listener*, the *Radio Times*, the *Architects Journal*, and the *Sunday Times*; every month the *East End Star*, *Civil Liberty*, pamphlets and newssheets from the Fabian Society, the *Labour Book Services Bulletin*. I am never without two or three books from the public library, new Penguins and books that have been lent to me or that I am re-reading from my own collection. I wonder that I have time to do anything but read and if I read every journal and book that accumulates during the month carefully from cover to cover I don't think I should. As it is I glance at headlines and skip.

This year's first issue of *Picture Post* I must mention. It is devoted to the problem of planning New Britain, and devoted magnificently. Its articles discuss the present situation, work for everyone in the future, social security for all, agriculture, rebuilding, modern planning of the home, education, health, medical services and the use of leisure. The contributors are well-known experts in their subjects with pronounced progressive views. An inspiring number.

Such evidence of an honest desire for a better world, acknowledgement of past mistakes, lethargy, eagerness for reform and improvement I find again and again in the columns and pages of my periodicals, even sometimes in the *Telegraph* and *Times*. Evidence of a revolution in the spirit and mind of man. Priestley is our spokesman. He has become the representative of British Everyman. I am continually astonished at his popularity. He has even impressed some of my most conservative relatives – though the head of this family still splutters at the mention of his name. He voices the opinions and hope of millions – plainly and with understanding, as one thoughtful man to another.

It will come, our better world, though through how much more pain it is impossible to say. As much, perhaps, as our past sins demand. Reactionary discrepancies are much harsher than they were last May. In consumption, living conditions, education and social security the position of the poorer classes has grown worse in relation to the position of the well-to-do. Our economic machinery is not working at the pace or with the efficiency it should and could. Labour MPs hesitate on certain issues of importance. Powers that were to be confined to the circumstance of invasion have been wielded dictatorially to suppress the *Daily Chronicle* and *The Week*.

I think that an important point is that we are not only fighting the Nazis but also forces which want to obstruct progress in our land, among our own people, which we should have fought with vigour before the war and must continue to fight when this war ends.

SATURDAY, 1 FEBRUARY

Edward Stebbing
Fellows on sick parade this morning were talking about the invasion. General reaction was 'Let Hitler come, and get what's waiting for him.' It is generally thought that any invaders will get a very hot reception.

MONDAY, 3 FEBRUARY

Edward Stebbing
Saw a new (to me) poster today, the first one for a long time which seemed to have significance. It showed a picture of a tank in action and the slogan was 'Land to Attack'. The change-over from 'Land to Defend', coming as it does at a time when Britain is attacking in Africa, represents a difficult change in attitude and skilful variation in propaganda. It opens up a wide field of differences between the Government which was responsible for the 'Land to Defend' poster and the present govt.

Went to a Locarno dance-hall and found it not what I expected. There was no MC, no social dances, nothing to get the dance going in a lively manner. The floor was small and rather rough, the girls on the whole not very attractive, and the dance band consisted entirely of women and although it was probably OK technically it wasn't too good for dancing purposes. As a result I only had three or four dances then left. The only redeeming feature was that admission was only 6d for the forces. I do not know whether it is always like this, but I am prepared to believe that it is an exception to other Locarno halls.

TUESDAY, 4 FEBRUARY

Edward Stebbing
Went to see *The Great Dictator* which is being shown at two cinemas here this week. As comedy it was excellent, but as a take-off on the dictators not up to my expectations. It certainly seized on many superficial features of dictatorship and ridiculed them, but it did not bite deep and show up the evil roots of Fascism except slightly in the speech at the end. This confirms the opinion of a friend of mine, a soldier, who wrote to me about it: 'It was a great deal less funny than his earlier films, while the way he takes off Hitler without in the least seeing (or showing) *why* Fascism exists and *how* to eliminate it in all its forms, is nothing short of tragic in a man of such one-time genius. No wonder British Imperialism has played up his film the utmost, as it makes the sort of image negative, pseudo-anti-Fascist propaganda that suits their book perfectly.'

THURSDAY, 6 FEBRUARY

Ernest van Someren
L is better and got up this afternoon. Before lunch he was alone in his cot in the sitting room and pulled down (accidentally, perhaps by swinging it) a large framed and glazed kakemono on the wall. It damaged a bookcase and my desk and the wainscot, but did not break its glass or frame. He doesn't admit that he did it, but was rather frightened and showed slight signs of remorse.

Pam Ashford
A fortnight ago I had to interrupt the diary. Mr Mitchell's illness involved me in such intense work and long hours that it was impossible to go on. He is back again now, not perfectly well, but soon will be, I hope.

During the diaryless spell I used to think . . . the fact was constantly staring me in the face that the pace of the war was gathering, and sometimes I thought, 'Crikey me! If the invasion starts before I am back on this diary . . .' but it has not.

Last week the tenants in our block were summoned to the ARP HQ to approve the establishment of a MAGNA group (Mutual Aid Good Neighbours Association) and to elect a committee. Nine gentlemen were elected last night. At 10 two of them called to ask what fire fighting equipment we had. They detailed the things each tenant was to provide: 2 buckets of water, 1 bucket of sand, 6 sand pillows, first aid, 12 candles, matches, and the things that should be communal property of the tenement – 2 stirrup pumps, 2 scoops, 2 rakes, 2 inverted dustbin lids, 1 ladder, 1 hatchet.

I mentioned that lately I have been sleeping in my dressing gown. 'If the house falls down when I am asleep, I shan't catch pneumonia while I am lying in the debris waiting to be dug out,' I explained, which seemed to tickle them.

Mrs Stewart's pernicious anaemia is trying her again and she cannot give the big parties for soldiers. Instead she has a youth from the sea with her. This lad was torpedoed in the Atlantic and drifted in a rowing boat for three weeks with only water and biscuits. Brought to Glasgow he went to one of the hostels, which sent him to Mrs Stewart. He has been there three weeks now and next week will join a 23,000 tonner, about which he is thrilled. This holiday is the first time in his life he had stayed in an ordinary house. He has little education and is desperately anxious to learn. He knew nothing about 'manners', 'etiquette', or call it what you will, and Mr S and Mrs Stewart have been grooming him.

As a present to take away to sea they have given him Pear's Encyclopaedia, and his joy is immense. It turns out that his idea is that when the war is over he will go to America, saying, 'You can get on there. Here you have to be educated to get on. In America they want people who are strong and able.' Mrs Stewart had agreed and went on, 'That it true. Here you cannot get on without education and influence.' Doubtfully, I said, 'Yes, but after the war things will be totally different. Class barriers are crashing in all directions.'

Mr Stewart went on to say that the English public schools' day is over.

FRIDAY, 7 FEBRUARY

Pam Ashford
Glasgow is getting conscious of its position. Sand bags are being placed around George Square, bowling greens, grass plots in the middle of streets, etc. I collected a bag at the ARP sand pit tonight. Quite a number of buildings have got boards around their roof edges to help roof spotters.

Miss Crawford is making a fuss, asking why the bulk of the population left everything till the last moment, while she has been ready for two years. Agnes has also a grouse, about people not paying their share, and then when the Blitz comes, they will want to use the stirrup pumps etc., that other people have paid for.

SATURDAY, 8 FEBRUARY

Ernest van Someren

Alternated my normal work with trying to mend a toy cinema apparatus for one of the electricians, which I finally gave up as too rickety. K and I went by bus to Hertford to do a bit of shopping, I bought a winter dressing gown and some collars. We bought L a magnet, very strong. Back by bus, just at his bedtime, and he was very pleased with the magnet. There is a painted iron fireplace surround in our sitting room and we can stick a bit of paper on it by means of the magnet.

SUNDAY, 9 FEBRUARY

Edward Stebbing

Changes in the Government led an Irishman to express his opinion that they were all 'too old-fashioned. They all ought to be kicked out'. A sergeant was not so extreme but said there must be changes. 'I'll tell you who is worth his salt – Anthony Eden.' 'Of course, Churchill's a good man.' 'No he isn't,' said the Irishman. 'He is no better than Chamberlain.'

Some of us have been detailed for fire-watching at night in different parts of the town until further notice. This has caused resentment, as we feel that this is a civilian's job (there are posters everywhere; 'Fall in the fire-bomb fighters'). 'What's the Home Guard for?' said one. Apart from this, Leeds has only had one alarm in several weeks and all think it crazy and unnecessary to wander about the streets in the middle of the night looking for fires when there isn't even a warning on. All the time one hears grumbles about the stupidity of the military authorities, the red tape, the habit of doing things in the most awkward and roundabout way, the silly, trivial things we are made to do, the shortage of food (tea today: one piece of bread and jam, a piece of cake and a cup of tea). If only people knew of the discontent which settles behind the façade of unity!

As a soldier said to me tonight, 'It's not aeroplanes and guns and munitions that'll win this war. It's food. No one can live without food.' And all the time, too, one hears soldiers saying they're fed up with the war, fed up with the Army, fed up with the filthy tyranny and will be glad to get out of it. 'If I'd had any sense,' said the same one, 'I'd have been a conscientious objector, but I hadn't the guts. I was too soft.'

Ernest van Someren
After supper we listened to Mr Churchill, who spoke too long, several times continuing after an apparent climax. We were all shocked at his blasphemous misuse of Matt vii,7.

Pam Ashford
I have given the day to the German correspondence course and get a fair amount done. One voice tells me, 'I shall be glad when the war is over and it is all for my own good'; another voice tells me that 'nothing will be the same after the war, and there never will be any more commercial correspondence with Germany. I can count all my pre-war German contacts as dead already'.

All the time I wish I had taken Spanish instead. It is a perfectly useless language to me, but always had a kind of fascination about it, possibly because I have been mistaken for a Spaniard so many times, and then when I repudiate that nationality, people say, 'It is your dark, expressive eyes. All Spaniards have eyes like yours.'

MONDAY, 10 FEBRUARY

Ernest van Someren
In the evening went with K to the movies in Hoddesdon, *The Great Dictator* and two shorts, both good, one Ministry of Information on police in wartime, the other a debate film on nationalisation of transport. We enjoyed the main film, both farce, comedy, and lesson. Afterwards I was struck by the clever mimicry of the mock-speeches. We walked home by moonlight, enjoying the evening.

TUESDAY, 11 FEBRUARY

Pam Ashford
There is a rhythm in everything into which life enters, and you see it in public morale too. There is a pulse and when the beat is strong you hear war talk everywhere, and when it is weak the war slips into the background.

We work under the most unpleasant conditions nowadays. Our managing director, Mr Ferguson, is modelling himself on the slave driver in *Uncle Tom's Cabin*, and in several quarters the same idea is emerging spontaneously, 'What would he be like in a Blitz? Firemen, policemen, soldiers, etc, would never put up with it.' Of course I work for the nicest man in the world, Mr Mitchell, and personally I am not affected.

Mother and I have gone over all our papers and locked them up in a deed box. I am determined to pack our suitcases, so that if we have to get away quickly there will be some system in what we carry away. I cannot but believe that the attempt at invasion will come, but Mother scoffs at the suggestion.

Edward Stebbing

Moving to Peebles in Scotland, on Thursday. I would much rather be nearer home, but it will be interesting to see something of Scotland for the first time.

Maggie Joy Blunt

I had not seen June and Kassim since before Xmas. It was pleasant to be in their familiar Hampstead flat again, within reach and sight of beloved London town. For, although I adore the country and have the greatest difficulty in uprooting myself from the cottage, London casts a spell upon me as soon as I reach its straggling boundaries. I have spent part of every one of the past 4 weeks in Hampstead: I have seen some of the damaged City buildings with my new friend DF, I have been to one or two of the short Ballet performances, visited the Fabian society and lunched at a new suburban Town Hall where Kassim now works.

Going round the City I have realised, as I realised during visits to London before Xmas, that report and rumour exaggerate bomb damage grossly. If we are ever to have a better capital I fear that a great and drastic number of more bombs must fall. I should think that this month has been one of the most normal since heavy raids began. The only town reported to have suffered badly anywhere in Britain was Swansea. There are of course in London many buildings and street corners in ruins – heaps of rubble and twisted, rusty girders, but life goes on as though these ruins had been there for years. Water supply, lighting, bus and train services, telephones, cafes – all are functioning again. Business continues at the Guildhall which was said to have been destroyed completely. The workers stream out for lunch at midday passing, as usual, with dull eyes the churches Wren built. Many of these little buildings will never flower again in their original grace; though walls remain, plaster work and wood carving of rare beauty have gone forever.

It is a lost city. A square mile of tortuous streets which the hand of trade has choked with its monstrous offices. Here and there in alleyways and dark corners a carved stone above a forgotten doorway, an old cobble in a gutter, or a spire seen through an unexpected opening against the sky speak in a whisper of a tradition the City workers have no pride in. Their lives are spent in getting to work and getting away from it to suburban retreats and cinemas and Corner Houses.

Not long ago a doctor broadcast on 'suburban neurosis' from which many women who have worked in such offices suffer after they have married and settled down in an instalment paid villa. After a while, he said, they found life in these cheap housing estates unbearably dreary; they had no interests beyond the meagre limits of their home; through shyness or snobbery they 'kept themselves to themselves'. They would not go to the local pub and there were no clubs. The war had at least opened up for them new ways of living, given them new interests, a new sense of comradeship with their previously ignored neighbours. But when the war was over and the ARP had become an entertaining memory – would they go back to their own reserve and false idea of respectability? The choice is theirs.

WEDNESDAY, 12 FEBRUARY

Ernest van Someren
Lunch at one, in the works canteen, a good meal for 9d. Then played snooker, not as badly as usual, and won. We had a new girl in the lab today, a junior to replace one who used to wash up for us who was not very clean and neat. Her name is Joyce, it is her first job, she lives about 2 miles away and went home to lunch. A nice looking kid. I moved my desk so as to get a better light for reading.

I tested L's magnet which weighs an ounce and will lift a pound. Before leaving I tied up a bundle of scrap wood which is being given away by the packing department and strapped it on to the back of my bicycle. We had supper, soup and steamed roe with caper sauce, and I opened a bottle of canary sac which we sampled, a good tasty drink.

Edward Stebbing
Was tired after doing fire-watching for three nights previous so did not bother to get up to go to breakfast. Got up about 7.30 dressed, rolled up my bed, and had a wash.

Today is my 21st birthday. At home it would have been something of an event, but here it is like any other day, and I forget for long periods that this is the day when one is said to have 'come of age' and assumes full adult status and responsibility. But to me it has no such importance.

After waking, I have to get ready for the adjutants parade, as I am leaving tomorrow and all men leaving have to be inspected by the adjutant. Preparations include polishing buttons and fixing up 'marching order' equipment. Putting this equipment on is a struggle and getting it comfortable a work of art of which not many are capable. Having managed the first part, but not the second, I walked up to the company office for the parade at 9.45. It would have to be raining. At the company office we have to wait about some time, so I went and bought a *News Chronicle* and read it while I waited. Not much there today, but was interested in the article on 'The Problem of Pain' in the 'God and the War' series. While I was reading it the sergeant major came and asked me if all had pay-books, identity discs, first field-dressings, and money. Most of us said they hadn't any money, in the hope of getting paid before leaving. I said I had a little, as I had quite a lot. The sergeant-major was annoyed with those who hadn't any. Then we fell in and the sergeant in charge of the parade found fault with everybody's dress, though he admitted that the rolling of my guns cape wasn't too bad, so we all fell out and adjusted our equipment, then fell in again, looking, in my opinion, no better than we did before.

Then we were marched down to the stores to make up one or two deficiencies in kit. Then we were marched back to the company office for further re-adjustments. 'I want you all perfect for the parade,' said the sergeant. Having made ourselves as near 'perfect' as possible, we were marched to the Medical Inspection room for examination for freedom from infection and had to take all our kit off again *before* the adjustments parade.

Then we had to rush it on again in a hurry. This is the sort of thing that maddens one. Then we went down to the depot orderly room and the RSM came out and said the adjutant wasn't there and told us to wait. At length he came and gave us a quick inspection and asked us all if we had any complaints. We all said 'No'. The complaint I would have liked to make would have been about being in the Army at all. Then he said he might pay us before lunch, so we waited but in the end he didn't so we were told to parade again at two o'clock. Went back to the billet and took off my pack. Found a birthday card from my sister and her husband. By now it was dinnertime, but I did not go to the company dining-hall, but to a little café along the road, and had a well-cooked dinner of rabbit pie, Yorkshire pudding, peas, and potatoes, a piece of tart and a cake and a mug of tea for 1s 1½d.

Went on parade at a quarter to two and at two o'clock the pay sergeant told us that we wouldn't be paid till tomorrow at twelve. We went to see the orderly sergeant for further orders but he didn't really know what to do with us, so sent myself and two others to the sergeants mess for fatigues. As we were allowed to walk down on our own and there was no check-up at either end, I didn't go and the others probably didn't either.

I caught a train into the town instead. First I went to the YMCA and had a cup of coffee and some cake and finished reading the *News Chronicle*. Then, about 3.15 I went into a newsreel cinema which was full up. Six features were shown: 'The New Britain', 'Think First', 'Scrambled Eggs', 'World News', 'London's Got Grit', and 'Heart of Britain'. The first was a film showing achievements in this country before the war (new roads, housing estates, holidays for all, television, better health services, etc.) but finishing each description with the words 'We forgot Germany' in a most sinister voice. It finished with the commentator saying that we would not let our children's lives suffer because of Germany. I was impressed by the glowing account of the improvements which had taken place in pre-war Britain, but felt that a list of the things which still needed, not only improving, but also abolishing, would have been still more impressive. The second film was one for the 'Crime Does Not Pay' series, about shoplifting. The third was a particularly childish coloured cartoon. 'World News' was simply a review of recent events including Roosevelt's recent speech to congress, Churchill's tour of two seaports, and Haile Selassie's return to Abyssinia.

The last two were similar, being accounts of how Britain is carrying on in spite of air-raids, on the note that you can't beat a people with such a spirit of courage and determination. I came out about 4.40 and had tea (sausages and beans) at a church canteen. Then I went back to the billet and made my bed. Then I went downstairs and found a letter and 10s from an aunt and a birthday card from my father.

As it was ten to eight and too late to go to the pictures or variety I decided to go to a dance-hall in the town. This was my second visit. The dance, however, was not very enjoyable. There were rather more women than men. Dances were not always announced and included too many difficult dances like rumbas, tangos and slow fox-trots. The girls didn't seem to be very good dancers and no attempt was made to draw out rather reserved people like myself. I only had a few dances and didn't speak much to anybody. Then I bought some fish and chips for supper (a frequent habit) and went back to the billet and got into bed about 11.15. What a dull, insignificant 21st birthday!

Pam Ashford
Another shipment to Iceland via Fleetwood, where a liner is due on Saturday, only it certainly won't be up to time. There are two

consignments, viz. window panes worth about £150 and aluminium pots and pans worth about £500; also many samples. Here are some of the items – cutlery and kitchen utensils (other than aluminium), bookkeeping books (samples cash books, etc.), dress material, textiles for quilts, curtains and net, two lots of packings and joints for machinery, twine, whisky, jewellery, Cremola, Lem-Lem, pickles, groceries, linoleum.

THURSDAY, 13 FEBRUARY

Pam Ashford
Mrs Stewart came in for 30 minutes to deliver a 3-page foolscap sheet (single space typing) of instructions from the Magna Committee. She fully expects an invasion soon. 'Some of the men who come to my house talk as they should not. They say that we know exactly where the Germans mean to try the invasion and the place is full of landmines.' I said, 'They would try several places simultaneously, and I myself would not be surprised at the East Coast of Scotland.' It turns out that is where the soldiers meant. Mrs Stewart said, 'Our men are longing for an invasion.' I said, 'I quite believe it. They must be sick of doing nothing.'

I have been much surprised to find how many, many ancestors have left us gold brooches, chains, rings etc., and have been sorting them out according to their intrinsic value, while Mother surveys them with nothing but their sentimental value before exclaiming, 'My grandfather gave me that when I was 7. Dad bought that at an exhibition in 1880.' There are quite a number of gold brooches with lockets of hair, but whose hair?

FRIDAY, 14 FEBRUARY

Edward Stebbing
Travelled by night and arrived in Peebles about 9 o'clock this morning. Got no sleep and had to sit in the corridor most of the way. Also had to carry four blankets – another of the Army's crazy ideas. We could really be issued with blankets on arrival so were pretty exhausted when I reached this unit.

Ernest van Someren
After four was livened up by a letter from the firm announcing a supplementary war bonus, which is in my case nominally £60 a year payable monthly and retrospectively from Jan 1st. This is a very good thing – it is our first war bonus, though in the case of junior staff it is

the second, they got one last summer. Cycled home, stopping to buy salted peanuts on the way, a minor luxury which has been unobtainable lately. K was very pleased about the bonus.

SATURDAY, 15 FEBRUARY

Edward Stebbing
Conditions here not so bad, but . . . not so good. Proper beds to sleep on, the first I have seen for six weeks, plenty of hot water, reasonably good food. Most of us are just doing ordinary training – squad drill, stretcher drill, gas lectures, fatigues, etc. which I thought I had finished with. One fellow said: 'I think they've got too many men in the Army and just send us here to get us out of the way.' How can one help being dissatisfied if one qualifies at a trade, as I have, and then after three months has not been employed in that trade. During that time I have done absolutely nothing useful connected with the Army.

Perhaps the best thing about this place is the splendid scenery all around. But it is lonely and cheerless to one who likes towns with their crowds of people, shops and cinemas. Peebles is about two miles away, but it's awkward to get to as buses only run once an hour. It is a small town, but rather attractive. Possessing only two cinemas its entertainments are soon exhausted.

SUNDAY, 16 FEBRUARY

Pam Ashford
Today I went to the fire station. The warden had counted the number of people carrying gas masks and found one in 40. The speaker was introduced, an AFS man called McEwen. He gave a 40 minute lecture in which he treated fire fighting both exhaustively and lucidly, and making it at the same time seem very easy too. Then we went to the yard where a bonfire was burning. It was extinguished by three members of the public using a stirrup pump. It was relit, with a big helping of tar, and extinguished again; relit again, this time with much tar and oil (this was a very big blaze) and extinguished once more. The audience certainly enjoyed themselves.

A question was asked about fires in lofts and the fireman said that probably the best thing to do was to break the ceiling with a broom, let the incendiary bomb fall into your room, then you can extinguish the burning ceiling with the pump and then you can attend to the bomb. Don't turn to a fire, if you are out of breath you will inhale twice as much smoke and might knock yourself out. If you feel the heat, turn the hose on yourself.

MONDAY, 17 FEBRUARY

Pam Ashford
The speaker at the Soroptomist Club was Madame D'Alroy, who lectures under the Ministry of Information. She speaks English (not broken English) but is typically French in everything else.

The subject was 'Keeping up Appearances' and it had attracted a large crowd. Her remarks were something like the following, which is anything but verbatim. 'Women are being praised for keeping the nation up, but they have always done that. Women always have kept the home up, their husbands up, everything up. We keep appearances up. In Appearances these are the three factors (1) Line (2) Colour (3) Material. Take each. Line, there are straight lines which indicate masculinity, conventionalism, conservatism, stateliness. Curved lines, femininity, grace, beauty. Diagonal lines – sophistication. Take colour. There are three colours – blue, red and yellow. What is your favourite colour? Red, that means life: blue, truth: yellow, love.' Then someone says 'My favourite colour is green.' Green is yellow and blue mixed, i.e. love of truth. Orange – red and yellow, love of life. Purple, blue and red mixed – truth and life. That is a difficult colour to live up to. Add white, and you make them more ethereal, add darkness and they become more material.

Madame D'Alroy said that in nature birds and animals are the colours of their environment. You see the same today. Soldiers – khaki, the colour of earth and sand: sailors, dark blue; airmen, sky blue. It is to avoid being shot at. In my mother's time to be a lady out of doors you had to dress in drab colours. The buildings were drab and you had to be dressed drably in order not to be shot at. We have changed now. Women are quite capable of coping with the situation of being shot at and they therefore wear bright colours.

TUESDAY, 18 FEBRUARY

Pam Ashford
Compulsory fire fighting for men is easier to arrange than voluntary fire fighting for women. Miss Smith in choosing who should and who should not be volunteers honestly did her best to interpret what she thought the person would wish (you might well ask why she did not ask). Agnes was missed out because she has had two serious operations in the last 12 months and is to undergo another this summer, and suffers from haemorrhage after exertion. Agnes's doctor confirms that Agnes is not fit, and thinks putting her on to fire fighting is much the same as setting the building on fire, but Agnes

has insisted on exercising her rights under the British Constitution and will fight fires with Margaret, office girl and hysterical. Margaret is now worked up at the prospect of having both Agnes's haemorrhage and a burning building on her hands simultaneously.

FRIDAY, 21 FEBRUARY

Pam Ashford

Madame D'Alroy said many things that I did not record, and one I have remembered since: 'In war, everyone is working on a bigger canvas, the selfish are more selfish, the unselfish more unselfish.' My impression is that this 'waiting to be invaded' period brings selfishness forward more than its reverse. I hate putting that down, and promptly remind myself that I am a notorious pessimist, I have a very limited circle, and don't know much that goes on outside it, and the cold weather makes me bilious. However it is, I feel irritable and querulous, and it seems to me that half the office is just the same.

SATURDAY, 22 FEBRUARY

Ernest van Someren

The town by train, shopping for the firm and myself and then at 10.30 to a meeting of the Rheologists Club in the City, at the lab of a research association. About 40 of us gathered for a discussion of certain types of apparatus, then went to lunch at a café in Fleet St. Sat next to an old acquaintance from my college, with whom I talked about music. A naval officer and scientist opposite explained that degaussing [neutralising the magnetic field of a ship] only caught on in the Navy because its name suggested an analogy with de-lousing – if they had prosily called it de-magnetisation it would have seriously prejudiced its chances of general adoption.

After lunch I went with three other men to a pub, then I left them and went to the Patent Office library and browsed in photographic periodicals for a bit. Left at 4.45 and went to my mother's home and collected a parcel of Japanese antiques.

Pam Ashford

The last day for forwarding goods to Fleetwood for the Icelandic liner on Monday. Two packages arrived this morning just in time, viz Bassett's sweets, samples of Liquorice Allsorts, Pontefract Cakes and four others: also a big bundle of stocks and crooks for shepherds – about 25 in all.

Quite often I hear people say that the war has broken down

provincial barriers, by which they mean city dwellers have gone to the country, men in the Forces have been transferred to places far from their home towns, etc. But side by side there is an increasing localism, brought about by ignorance of conditions outside one's own area. This week everyone is seeing motorcars in our streets with thick coverings of snow, denoting a blizzard somewhere near, but where? We in the coal trade know that the answer is the Lothians, where the pits are idle, but when I tell people (which perhaps I should not do at all) they mostly express ignorance. From mouth to mouth word passes that the alert has been sounded in Edinburgh several times recently, and also that lives have been lost in Aberdeen during an air raid there. But with nothing reported in the papers, Edinburgh and Aberdeen are becoming almost as remote as Abyssinia.

MONDAY, 24 FEBRUARY

Pam Ashford

Just as I was getting out to write today's entry the wireless put on a record taken a year ago of Gracie Fields with the troops in France. It was more like the last war than this one. It brought back vividly the emotional attitude during the 'phoney' war period when nothing was happening. The present moment became indescribably horrible in comparison. Here we are in another waiting period, with nothing much happening to the UK, but the expectation of things to be happening soon is detestable. I enjoyed the beginning of the war, and sometimes I still do enjoy the shaking up out of ruts, but for the most part I don't enjoy the war any longer.

Edward Stebbing

One of the fellows, looking at yesterday's paper, noticed a paragraph saying that the 19 age-group would be called up by the middle of next month. 'They're young to be called up,' he said. 'Too young,' said another. 'I was only twenty when I was called up.' 'And how old are you now?' 'Twenty-one.' 'I should have thought you were at least twenty-seven.' 'It's the Army. It's put years on me. How old are you?' 'Twenty-one.' 'Oh you look about thirty.'

TUESDAY, 25 FEBRUARY

Maggie Joy Blunt

It has been a month of doubt and waiting. Our victories in North Africa have been spectacular though there has been no rejoicing for them in this country. In fact A.J. Cummings has been moved to warn

71

against a tendency to underestimate their moral and strategic value. They have strengthened the confidence of our friends; they have silenced the waverers in France and America; and they have upset the Axis in the Balkans. We had an appeal by Greece to America for arms, growing alarm in Australia and America at the attitude of Japan, repeated warnings of the possible invasion of this country, Hitler's threat of an intense submarine offensive, Lord Woolton's speech on the food situation – from all these things and more rise enormous shadows to cloud our confidence. Gas attacks, intensified bombardment, war in the Far East, America mobilised, Russia joining the conflict, German troops on British soil, heavier and heavier shipping losses, inflation, starvation – these are the shadows. I sympathise with June's gloomy view of the future ('How much grass,' she asks plaintively, 'can one eat before one's tummy begins to swell?').

Yet I do not believe it will happen. That we shall suffer increasingly and terribly, yes. That the war may be a very long one – yes. But I am possessed of an optimism I find it difficult to defend. We are in the grip of forces few of us really understand. But there are straws. Churchill's magnificent speech at the beginning of the month which cheered even the weather; our North African successes; the Fleet's attack on Genoa; the RAF's attacks on Nazi bases in Sicily and its activities all over the continent; the leaflets dropped on tortured Poland; the astonishing courage and foresight of Churchill and Dill planning the Middle East campaign last June; the recognition of Abyssinia as an independent state under Haile Selassie; Eden and Dill's visit to Turkey and the meeting with Cripps; the still fairly wide freedom of our Press; the discussions on reconstruction with leading progressive thinkers; Priestley's continued broadcasts . . .

June, who under the influence of John Middleton Murray tends to think we could come to terms with Germany under an armed truce, is appalled by the growing hate for the German people in Conservative circles and dreads a victory that will impose the same fearful penalties on that intelligent nation that it suffered in 1918. But the military might of the Nazis must be broken. It is the aggressive element in the German character we are fighting.

Meanwhile it freezes and thaws and the sun grows warmer. Yellow crocuses are out on the rockery. The Army which had possessed our woods all the winter is now wiring them in. Huge lorries, like futuristic elephants, are parked right to the edges. The air is poisoned with the smell of heavy engine oil (I realise now what makes me seasick). The soft ground is torn by heavy tires. Lady A, who has a permit to walk her dog through the woods daily, says there is no joy in it. Every few yards one comes upon a lorry and the ground is a quagmire. How long before we can walk freely those lovely ways again? Must they be bombed before this perplexing war is over? And why *our* woods? The local people are grumbling fiercely. Summer bought them a good tripper trade. Hundreds and hundreds of Blitz-weary Londoners will be denied their treats now.

We did not know how well off we were before the war. The local cigarette and sweet shop is a depressing sight. Empty cartons in its windows, empty shelves within – a few boxes of chewing gum, a few boxes of Woodbines and other half-size cigarettes so weedy and cheap they are only an irritation to smoke. Yet people go on smoking. The owner of this shop thrust a deeply stained forefinger at me and said he was smoking more than ever.

Chapter Three

LO HERE, LO THERE

I thought testing was a formidable process: a rattle heralds a practice gas alert in Brighton.

27 February–3 May 1941

1 March An earthquake in Greece leaves 10,000 homeless; Himmler visits Auschwitz to oversee an expansion programme.

7 March Ernest Bevin, the Minister for Labour, announces the Essential Work Orders, preventing staff engaged in work of national importance either leaving or being dismissed without official approval (two days later he appeals for more women to join the war effort); the first British troops land in Greece.

8 March 34 people are killed in the bombing of Piccadilly's Café de Paris.

11 March Roosevelt signs the Lend-Lease Bill, essentially bringing the United States into the war with the Allies.

19 March The Luftwaffe resume heavy bombing across Britain.

27 March The battleships *Warspite*, *Barham* and *Valiant* set sail to engage the Italian fleet at Cape Matapan, Greece; the anti-Axis powers coup occurs in Belgrade.

5 April Rommel launches his African offensive.

7 April The basic rate of income tax in Britain rises from 8/6 in the pound to 10 shillings, a new record.

8 April Germany begins assaults on the Balkans.

11 April French Lieutenant Alain le Ray is the first prisoner to escape from Colditz.

15 April 758 people killed in air raids on Belfast.

16 April Churchill agrees to evacuate mainland Greece; the last tower at Crystal Palace, south London, is demolished to end its use as an enemy signpost.

20 April Britain suffers attacks from a new German weapon – landmines dropped by parachute; London and Plymouth devastated by Luftwaffe raids, and a week later Liverpool suffers a great loss of life and landscape.

THURSDAY, 27 FEBRUARY

Ernest van Someren
The hens laid us 5 eggs today, in spite of their trouble due to disagreements (we have mixed two generations and they scrap a bit). We have 4 young and 3 older ones, and have started preserving the eggs. Yesterday K made marmalade.

Went to one of the neighbours this evening to leave a notice of a concert, and found that he has been called up and was packing ready to leave the house. He is a commercial artist aged 35 with a wife and young child, very unhappy about having to go, as he will obviously be a misfit.

SATURDAY, 1 MARCH

Ernest van Someren
The county library have just responded to my request for two books by buying new copies of them, one on Sweden and one on psychoanalysis, 14/- each. I feel very pleased with their service.

Edward Stebbing
There is no canteen here, only a little kiosk which opens at midday and tea-time for half an hour, where we can buy cigarettes and chocolate. One person is allowed two pieces of chocolate.

There is little to do in the town. My evenings are spent chiefly in reading (Lawrence's *Seven Pillars of Wisdom*). The days are more or less the same, equally dull. The recruits do their training and the trained men have to join in, but I being on the sick list, waiting to go into hospital, avoid most of the drill. In peace-time, going into hospital would have filled me with anxiety, but now I look forward to it, to escape for a little while from the Army's tyranny, and hope for sick-leave.

Pam Ashford
Women's columns, shop windows and talk are all emphasising the new shoes with thick rubber unders, brightly coloured laces and leather inset in very odd shapes. I said, 'It is obvious that leather is becoming scarce,' but apparently that was not the right line to take. Everyone thinks of them as fashion pure and simple, utility never at all. My feeling is that I don't want the wheels of production to make one unnecessary turn on my behalf, but where women's fashions are concerned it is useless to counsel one's neighbours thus. Miss Smith, 'If you are not in fashion, where are you?' Miss Carswell, 'You could not wear square shoulders if sloping ones came in.'

If Irving had wanted a model for tragedy, he could have found one in Miss Bousie. The shock of the collapse of France was mild, but the shock this morning from a [newspaper] board on her way back from the Bank was worse. She walked into the office with a steady, slow, solemn gait, declaiming, 'France bows the knee to Japan.' The general office was completely bowled out by the horror of the situation. I scoffed openly. Miss Bousie: 'One disaster after another disaster. One defeat after another defeat. Never a ray of hope anywhere.' I: 'Hold on there. The British are doing jolly well.' Miss Smith: 'Only in Africa. Every new step strengthens Hitler's hand.' I: 'Every new step shows how shaky his position is.'

MONDAY, 3 MARCH

Pam Ashford
Everything indicates that terrible happenings are imminent in the war, but this wonderful Iceland 'merchant adventuring' takes up my thoughts so much that I have little thinking power left for the war. If these pages should happen to survive and one day come to be read by someone who would of course know the denouement of the mighty drama in which we are actors today, perhaps that someone will wonder at such indifference as to the future, but that is so. We live for the day, and as to tomorrow, sufficient until the day be the evil thereof. I don't think I am unique by any means, though that is not, of course, to say that there are not people who have already worried themselves half way into their graves by now.

Ernest van Someren
A mixture of ups and downs. At breakfast I had a letter from Mass-Obs with a book-token for 3/6, a welcome gift. My coach to town was late and I had no luck at my library task. But I dropped in at the Eric Gill memorial exhibition at the Vic. and Alb. museum and enjoyed it for nearly half an hour. Went to the V & A Library where I hunted out the identity of the painter of some pictures on the ceiling of a Castle in Denmark, this took a long time as I only read Danish slightly and slowly. I want to sell photos of the paintings to an American magazine. Coming home in the coach I talked to my neighbour after a while, a WATS girl. I opened by asking her if wearing that uniform made her feel rather cut off from people, especially men in mufti. She admitted that it did, and talked a bit about the first performance of *Applesauce* which she had been to see.

TUESDAY, 4 MARCH

Edward Stebbing
Boredom relieved a little by the first ENSA concert to be held here. As we have no concert hall it was held in the dining hall, admission free, and drew a large audience. Perhaps because it was the first entertainment of its kind to be given here it received a better reception than it might have done, but nevertheless it was a very bright and lively show, which we must consider ourselves lucky to get.

By far the majority of the jokes – about 80 per cent – dealt with sex, the idea being apparently that any allusion to sex, however 'blue', would get a laugh from the troops (which it invariably did). Of the rest most were cracks at Mussolini and the Italians, some even working in a sex angle as well, e.g. an Italian comes home and says 'Where is my Bianca?' His wife replies, 'In bed with tonsillitis.' The Italian says, 'Good heavens, these Greeks are everywhere.'

Most of the programme consisted of this kind of thing, either in straight cross-talk or worked into short sketches. There were also some popular songs, not very well sung by a soprano or rendered on a piano accordion, and a couple of tap-dances. At the end there was a little community singing. Most popular song was 'Bless 'em all'. A few months ago I said I thought 'Roll Out the Barrel' was the song of the war, but I think this beats it. Incidentally, there were cheers and roars when the words 'This place is run all wrong' came into one of the sketches. Next day opinions were very favourable – 'Marvellous show', 'Bloody good'.

Pam Ashford
Mother went to the English Society and says Mrs Robinson has been given a knitters medal. She has knitted more than 200 pairs of socks and 16 pullovers. On Saturday night last she knitted three pairs of socks. The speed with which she does them is a byword. Her gunner son is at Salisbury Plain now and said his men were made to sleep in wet beds and many contracted pneumonia.

Table talk at the English Society is that Mr Churchill was in Glasgow visiting the shipyards today and that the King and Queen are coming tomorrow. Later in the evening the BBC described some of Mr Churchill's actions today so that yarn was soon disposed of. About tomorrow, special constables are to be on duty.

80

WEDNESDAY, 5 MARCH

Pam Ashford

Charlie left the house at 8 this morning (instead of 9.30) which suggested no more to me than that of going out of town, but Mother with royalty in her mind twigged what was happening and demanded to know if he was going to meet the King and Queen, and this was the case. Everyone in the office knew of the Majestic visit today, claiming the testimony of a friend who knew someone who knew etc. Having an irrefutable witness of my own, I was afraid to say anything at all! In fact, before going to work I impressed on Mother the necessity of keeping her lips tight. 'You don't want the King and Queen to be bumped off as a result of an indiscreet word of yours.'

THURSDAY, 6 MARCH

Ernest van Someren

A busy day, helped my colleague Dr R to interview a few candidates for a job, replacing his assistant who went away to sea. I tried a little test for visual memory and neatness, suitable for a boy, which is to ask him to draw the frame of a bicycle. It seems easy, but shows up the type who makes mistakes which would leave the bicycle mechanically unsound. I don't ask for wheels on it, as that would be a test of drawing.

FRIDAY, 7 MARCH

Pam Ashford

The Saxone Shoe Co have appointed us their agents for Iceland and Faroe and by the next steamer we are sending between 30 and 40 pairs of shoes as samples.

We are handling so many things now. I said to Mr Mitchell that 'Jane Seymour' should be a good brand of beauty culture and we wrote two days ago. An enthusiastic letter came back this morning. There is no such person as Jane Seymour, the show is run by four men, and the Managing Director was in the Glasgow Shipping Trade for many years and knew us well.

Ponds are enthusiastic too. A number of cosmetic makers are represented already – Yardleys and Elizabeth Arden, for instance. There seems to be a tremendous demand for the beauty culture in Iceland.

Miss Crawford was saying that someone at Bridge of Weir who had lost a son in the war had a call from a 'soldier' who said he was her son's pal. He wanted to stay overnight, but that was not convenient. However, he turned up at 9am again. A neighbour came in and the soldier was left alone in the kitchen while the lady was showing the neighbour out. The man immediately thereafter took his departure, which struck her as so strange that she watched him from the window and saw him running away. She immediately sought her purse and found it had been stolen from the dresser, with 30/-. She reported it to the police and she was the man's third victim. He had got someone to take him in for the first night and robbed them, and he had got a ham and egg breakfast from someone else.

SATURDAY, 8 MARCH

Edward Stebbing
Of the little news read in the last few days the most interesting to me is the BBC's notice to performers whose political views differ from the Government's, and the protests which this has aroused. I am glad that MPs and other prominent persons have voiced their strong disapproval of the BBC's action, for this is indeed the very thing we are supposed to be fighting against.

I danced at the drill-hall tonight, after a haircut for which I had to pay the excessive price of 9d. After being in Scotland for three weeks I can understand the Scottish reputation for thriftiness, though I think it is very often exaggerated. Scottish people are not really mean, but very careful in money matters, and they are colder, more puritanical than, for instance, the people of Yorkshire. Yet, I should think, once one has made friends with a Scot he would be as sincere and generous a friend as could be found anywhere.

SUNDAY, 9 MARCH

Pam Ashford
Mother was at a whist drive yesterday at the Burns House. It was something to do with a Burns Club, the tobacco trade, the Red Cross and war comforts. Mrs Robinson got her knitting medal presented. She said to mother that she knitted so much to keep herself from brooding. When she was not knitting she got depressed. She carries knitting to the whist drives and even knits between the hands. It seems to be an obsession.

Edward Stebbing
Snatch of conversation after dinner: 'They say this lot'll be over by June.' 'Who says so?' '*Old Moore's Almanac*, and it's never been

wrong yet.' 'Well, I don't think it can last through another winter. You don't know how bad it is in civilian life. They're having meatless days up North.'

MONDAY, 10 MARCH

Maggie Joy Blunt
Today I go to Hampstead again, for a week I hope. Raids are intensifying and incendiaries have been dropping near here, so I have been taking all precautions. Last night wrote a moving 'last letter' to Ella, who, poor darling, would have the fearful task of sorting and clearing up my possessions. I was so overcome by the end of it I felt I had already died, and so fascinated by the spectacle of scenes in the cottage after my decease I could not sleep for hours. Today I feel very alive.

TUESDAY, 11 MARCH

Pam Ashford
Miss Bousie has her grouse. She has read proposals that excess profits tax should be reduced. 'The Government are contemplating doing that and yet they leave income tax at the present level.' She had an apt listener in Miss Carswell, and both of them began to object strongly to being asked to pay for the war. 'The whole thing is due to Mr Chamberlain's blundering, and the inconvenience we suffer is quite enough without wanting us to pay too.'

She is a queer woman. She never comes back from the bank without something 'horrible', and then goes on with 'I cannot understand it'. Yesterday it was a board saying 'Bulgarian soldiers enter Yugo-Slavia'. Today at one o'clock mother and I heard that recent shipping losses had been severe and Miss Bousie came back at 2.30 having heard this from her sister who also listens at one, dramatically declaiming, 'The U-boat campaign has started. Our number is up. Our mercantile fleet is practically eliminated.'

In the early days of the war I built up a magnificent reserve of tinned soup. As ever Mother has used it without replacement and on Sunday made the discovery that the cupboard was bare. So I am told to buy fresh, and this week I have been watching for Heinz's soups. Craigs have two brands (vegetable and celery) but only sell to customers. Peacocks have chicken, celery, vegetable and kidney, but as today is their grocery department half day they would not sell.

WEDNESDAY, 12 MARCH

Pam Ashford
I have been watching the tinned soup situation with alertness. There are piles of Noel & Poulton's and of course Jean McGregor's Scotch Broth. We know from Charlie that Jean McGregor's is not allowed outside the Clyde area, and I have always supposed Noel & Poultons must be the same. Frankly, Noel & Poulton's (of whom I never heard before the war) is awful! But the good soups are scarce! I think we ran out just in time, for very soon there won't be any soups at all with which to replenish the larder. Cowan's under the bridge have Campbell's julienne in the window and would not take it out (possibly it was a dummy tin). They let me have a tin of Campbell's mulligatawny, however.

The news that Buckingham Palace has been bombed has caused many spontaneous outbursts of resentment.

Ernest van Someren
Our daily help thought the fires last night were at a children's hospital at a country house near Ware, and there were lots of children there and probably all burnt up. (Later we hear that it was 2 haystacks.)

Haircut after lunch, barber has put prices up, also keeps a sweet-shop & 2d library, with not much profit altogether.

In the evening I went to the listening group which was held in Hoddesdon this week. We had some modern music, Lambert, Ravel and Berg on records, and then a little Bach to finish with. One of the members (D.B) gave me a lift back in his car, and surprised me by using it to go one mile each way on a fine night, when he also has a cycle. He is an odd chap.

THURSDAY, 13 MARCH

Pam Ashford
Charlie has been taking pickles for supper in lieu of cheese, and Mother has included this in her grocery order to the Hyndland grocer, but now Hyndland is out of pickles and Mother has commissioned me to get some. But where? Most shops have Heinz's pickled walnuts, Cooper's have Rosella fruit chutney and something called sweet pickles (very suspicious).

At 11.30 there were two intensely vivid flashes, and I thought, 'Crikey me, this one's ours.' And then there was a din and the house swayed to and fro, and fro and to, and this way and that. And what a crashing of glasses somewhere outside. I jumped off the bed and ran in Mother's direction, and we met in the hall, for she was running towards me. She had at last come round to the idea that bombs were falling, and looked a bit taken aback. I put my arms around her and said, 'That one was not for us,' and then the second one went off, just a shade further off, but pretty bad.

In the light of subsequent knowledge I can say that these were landmines, one falling on a garden 80/90 yards away, and the second on a tenement building at Dudley Drive, about 300 yards away.

Mother said she would like to put on her shoes, instead of carpet slippers, and get her hat and coat, so we got Mother togged up to make a dash for it. Then we thought of the wee birdie in the dining room window, and fetched him into the hall, and also the deed box and the cash box, and of course, our handbags. So there we were all dressed up and nowhere to go.

FRIDAY, 14 MARCH

Pam Ashford

At 1.30am I thought things better and we went to bed, fully clothed, but under the bedding.

At 8am Charlie turned up to shave and have breakfast. It was as I divined. The Ministry of Aircraft Production expects trouble and he remained in their premises on purpose. Every bomb that falls on Scotland is, of course, reported to them at once, and he knew about the Hyndland landmines. I am sure he was anxious, and our welcome did him good.

All the staff, but Helen, arrived. Mr Mitchell – at Bridge-of-Weir, 14 miles out – had spent the time watching the Blitz over Glasgow, and said, 'It was a beautiful sight to see the lights in the sky.'

Helen came in the afternoon, very nervous and low-spirited. She had had a terrible experience at Maryhill. A tenement opposite them had a direct hit, and many people have been killed and injured. She had spent the morning looking out of their window seeing the bodies being taken out, and dismembered limbs. Her brother had tried to get two wee boys out and their heads had been severed.

Everyone, of course, expected the Jerries back again tonight, and sure enough we had our second night of Blitz, this time starting at 8.30 and much less intense.

Mother sat beside the fire knitting. Most of the noise sounded at a distance, though at 11.30 there was a whizzing through the air and the place shook all over. I went to Mother and said, 'This is very close now. You are not safe beside those big windows.'

Believing wholeheartedly that this nation must stand firm and being willing to pay the price goes a long way to cast off from you the fear of suffering.

Edward Stebbing
Last night and tonight alarms have been sounded for the first time since I have been here. We were ordered to sleep fully dressed, including boots – an order which everybody thought ridiculous and, needless to say, was not completely obeyed.

SATURDAY, 15 MARCH

Pam Ashford
Miss Carswell's fiancé was with them last night, much depressed. He lives at Scotstoun and last night two shelters beside them got a direct hit and 50 people were killed. The bodies were laid out on the waste ground opposite them. A neighbour has lost two daughters, 12 and 16. (This shelter that got a direct hit is the subject of widespread tales, the numbers vary between 50 and 80, the people concerned are given as neighbours in some stories and workmen in Yarrow's yard in others, and later in the week the accident was being explained as due to a bomber being brought down, loaded with bombs which all went off simultaneously.)

Miss Bousie seems utterly exhausted from two nights sitting up in a chair.

At one I went to see *Pagliacci*, with Tauber at the Cosmo – rotten. As usual after the feature film (3.15 today) I went out, missing the shorts. While on the bus from the Cosmo to the Academy of Music, I found the back stacked with attaché cases and everywhere in town people were staggering under cases – and caged birds. It might have been a holiday weekend. I began to wonder how many scores and scores of people were clearing out.

I reached the Academy of Music at 3.30, and heard one side of a disc, when the siren went. Down to the basement. All clear. Up to the Lecture Room. We had a Mozart Trio. Siren again. Down to the basement again.

SUNDAY, 16 MARCH

Pam Ashford
The Jerries never came!

Every piece of furniture is coated with dust so thick that you could write your name on it, and when you have dusted it, you go back in half an hour and find it as bad.

MONDAY, 17 MARCH

Pam Ashford
Tongues have wagged today as you would never believe possible in this land of the dour Scots. Everyone is talking about experiences that have befallen a victim they know, or of some they have heard from a friend. The stories are not the rumour type, but genuine enough. During the day I heard that Broomhill laid in ruins, Jordanhill laid in ruins, Victoria Park Drive North laid in ruins. Coming back from work I stayed on the bus as far as Jordanhill College, walking across to Victoria Park Drive North, which I traversed from end to end, and then round Broomhill – and I saw nothing whatever. I told Mrs Stewart in the evening and she said, 'You need a guide. If you had stayed on the bus a minute longer you would have seen a terrace in South Brae Drive laid flat, and if you had made a detour around Mitre Road you would have seen yet a third terrace laid flat.'

TUESDAY, 18 MARCH

Maggie Joy Blunt
A growing feeling of optimism. Lady A thinks it will all be over by the autumn. June's Mrs R thinks that the worst is over. Or is it the sunshine? American help very important.

Lady A was given an onion yesterday for her birthday. Her cook flavoured bread sauce with it and then used it for something else.

WEDNESDAY, 19 MARCH

Ernest van Someren
Lots of people complained about the noise in the night. The Rowes went off for the day to clean up in their home, left their baby in our charge, she was good and L was too. His chief fault now is that he sometimes says 'I won't' when asked to do something, and if we insist he gradually works up a row. We can sometimes side-track him by indirect persuasion, and we get our way in the end whether there is a row or not, but we try to avoid rows. Occasionally a fuss finished by a spank will sweeten his temper for a day or two, more often he is punished only by being shut out of a room and left to cry alone, which annoys him deeply.

It was a noisy evening. At bedtime we moved his cot into our room so that we could reassure him if bombs woke him in the night – he slept through the evening ones well. Actually he only woke spontaneously, bounced a bit and went to sleep again. On Wednesday morning when the two nearest bombs woke him, he promptly talked to me about a train stopping and filling up with oil, a fragment of a dream which had been broken by the explosions.

Pam Ashford
At 9pm the wireless gave out the official figures for Clydeside, viz. 500 killed, 800 seriously injured. (I suggest 250 Glasgow, 250 Clydebank.)

Reaching work I found everyone rejecting the official figures. Mr Ferguson knew for a fact that 5000 (yes, five thousand) had been killed in Clydebank alone. Someone else said that the SCWS coffin department had had to supply 1000 coffins for Glasgow.

I had read that 38 cows had been killed at a farm and today the Bulletin gave a photo of the farm. I recognised it as the Peel of Drumry, near Knightswood. I could have cried. One lovely Sunday last June I went out that way. The grass was so green, the trees so leafy, how fresh the breeze and clear the sky. Everything evoked joy, and yet pessimism was eating into my heart. The meadow of Drumry was full of cows and calves, and as I stood watching, a calf came up to the gate, and over the bars I tickled its chin and stroked its brow, while our eyes gazed into one another's soul. How well I remember it, for the world of nature and the world of men were in such vivid contrast with one another. And that is the herd that was lost.

THURSDAY, 20 MARCH

Pam Ashford
Miss Bousie (with the active encouragement of most of the staff) talks of writing to Mr Churchill demanding that Glasgow should be told the truth about the Blitz. 'The figures are ridiculous!' Miss Carswell says that the SCWS alone had to supply 1500 coffins (which is only 500 over yesterday's figure). Along with this goes another annoyance, viz. that Glasgow University was mentioned at all: 'They put property before lives!'

I feel that I must keep up the morale.

FRIDAY, 21 MARCH

Ernest van Someren
Went to bed at 6 but didn't sleep any more, got up and had a bath. L came to watch me and was pleased at being allowed to scrub my back. At work did some reporting, knocked off at noon and went to town by coach, and lunched with an old friend Jean R. and her new

mate. Jean interrupted her second university course to marry a scientist, who proved a very bad husband, and she managed to divorce him for desertion last summer. Now she has found a better man, an ex naval officer (of last war) working for the Min. of Supply. Like me he is ex Plymouth Brethren and now almost Quaker.

SATURDAY, 22 MARCH

Ernest van Someren
K and I went to Hoddesdon and to the movies in Hertford, our last outing before the baby. We saw *The Thief of Baghdad*, a bourgeois fairytale in colour, technically excellent. One could criticise it for departing from tradition, or for trying to get too much into one film, but there are worse faults in films and it was never dull.

Maggie Joy Blunt
I can't help it, but a feeling of optimism increases and increases. I cannot share June's gloom – she seems to see nothing but disaster and privation ahead. But I am singing. Inside I am full of song. It comes out in funny squeaks and croaks, but it is there, a swelling tumultuous volume.

I want to work for the National Buildings Record just recently formed and have written to the Director. Have not wanted anything so much for a long time. The possibility only occurred to me last week. Have no idea if they want assistants or would consider me if they did.

Edward Stebbing
Looking at this week's *Picture Post*, with its articles on the German terror film, J.B. Priestley, and the BBC ban, set me to thinking about the principles at stake in this war. For a long time I have had a grave suspicion, rapidly becoming a conviction, that we are not fighting for freedom and democracy at all, but that we shall have to fight harder still against Fascism in this country when the war is over. We may defeat Germany, but we shall not defeat Fascism at this rate; instead we seem to be making its continuance ever more sure. The *Daily Worker* is banned, while some other papers become more Fascist in flavour. Pacifists and Communists are victimised by the BBC; an attack is made on the progressive voice of Priestley.

Later in the evening I went to a dance, crowded out with young people, and forgot all about the war.

MONDAY, 24 MARCH

Pam Ashford
At the Soroptomist Club today the speaker was Dr Macgregor, the MoH for Glasgow. He must be a very good doctor, for it could not have been by his after lunch speeches that he came to office. He reviewed three illnesses, the incidence of which it had been expected would rise in wartime, but this dread has not materialised, viz. diphtheria, pneumonia and neurosis, the latter having actually declined markedly. He got on to rickets and urged everyone to register under the Free Milk Scheme (who could), it was not charity but was to assure that those who needed milk had it. And then on to food. He wanted the rationing to be related to physiological needs, and was glad that miners and agricultural workers are able to get more cheese. He is a most dreary speaker.

Ernest van Someren
In the evening several people called in to wish Kay a good time, and good fortune, and others telephoned, so that we didn't do much except talk to people all evening.

TUESDAY, 25 MARCH

Ernest van Someren
In the evening came home to high tea with the family, then got the movie camera out and took a short shot of L and K making their farewell. Then took K off to hospital by bus which goes right to the hospital entrance at the other side of Hertford.

Kay has a cubicle in the private maternity ward, one of a set of four which form a large room, it's the end one and the next is vacant. The bed is comfortable and the room well-equipped but small. I stayed till she was in bed, then came away. Stopped for a drink at the nearest pub, the Cold Bath.

Edward Stebbing
Went on a long route march today, over hills which may have been beautiful, but were heartbreaking to anyone with a pack on and other impedimenta to carry and few stops for rest. I almost collapsed on the way home – I was not the only one – and all cursed the Army.

WEDNESDAY, 26 MARCH

Edward Stebbing
Read in the paper that J.B. Priestley's talks have again been stopped. It is now obvious that the BBC – in other words, the Government – wants only one point of view to be expounded.

Ernest van Someren
Miss Hill, the surgeon who has operated on Kay before, did a Caesarean section at three and duly extracted a baby girl, Julia – we have been referring to her provisionally by that name for months. Kay was also sterilised to prevent any further conception. Our doctor was there as anaesthetist, and telephoned me when Kay had come round, a bit before five, announcing the birth. I felt very pleased and relieved, and wrote a card to Kay before leaving the works as the post goes very early now.

On the way home met L out for a walk with a neighbour, told him the news and he told me that they had been to see a 'crane that worked by steam'.

Towards eight about a dozen people began to arrive for our listening group. A member who was to have given a talk did not come so they listened to the broadcast of Carmen or talked till 9.00. After 9 I played them gramophone records of ballet music for an hour or so.

THURSDAY, 27 MARCH

Pam Ashford
I have got over my state of shock: this morning a slater found the remains of an incendiary bomb on our roof which had smouldered on the slates till it went out.

Ernest van Someren
A fine mild morning, cycled to work, had a lot of phone calls to make about some enquiries for a German publication which I am trying to trace. Rang the hospital before lunch and was told only that Kay was very well. Left work a bit early, came home, fed chickens and had tea. By bus to Hertford and saw Kay, who looks as well as can be expected. She has to sit up all the time and so slept very little, is very pleased and quite satisfied with Julia, who is in a room with 15 other babies and looks very much like most of them. Kay had the energy to write postcards to L and to her mother today, she reads with a good bed-table but does not listen in because it's always 'The Forces'

programme on the hospital headphone system. I lent her my watch as she has not one available, and spent about an hour with her.

FRIDAY, 28 MARCH

Pam Ashford
It turns out that Mother, whose mind is made up that she's going to run for it, has taken to going to bed in her clothes.

I enjoyed Mr Brown's postscript. How true it is that the fifth columnists try to turn the Scots against the English. The yarn going about now is that all the RAF was centred at London to protect London, and on the 13th and 14th they didn't care a damn what happened to Scotland. In fact, as a representative of England, I have been cursed four times this week. I say nothing, for I have not the slightest intention of helping on the fifth column by telling the speakers (always people of feeble intelligence) what blithering idiots they are.

Edward Stebbing
Received a parcel from home containing tobacco and cakes. I do not expect much in the way of parcels now, as letters from my sister show that many things are hard to get. In a previous letter she says: 'I think we are in for a hard time. It looks as though I shall be conscripted. I am 25. Still, if it will help us to win we must do it.' The last part of this distresses me beyond words. I never dreamed that my sister, now married, might be called upon for war-work.

SATURDAY, 29 MARCH

Pam Ashford
It seems to me that the whole community is desirous of seeing the RAF bomb German civilians, 'give them what they give us', and my voice to the contrary is a lone one in the wilderness. Mr Mitchell went down to London with a Canadian airman, and expressed strong disapproval of our bombing only military targets. The airman said, 'Don't you believe it. When I was over Berlin last time, the anti-aircraft fire was very hot, and the pilot said, "We'd better get out of this. Open the bomb clutches." And we dropped everything we had plump on a residential district – a heap of high explosives and incendiaries.' Life is very cheap nowadays.

Mr Mitchell walked from Euston via Russell Square and Charing Cross Road to Whitehall. He saw that a two storey building at the Horse Guards was knocked down, but very little else. He was most surprised to find how normal London was, compared with the yarns we hear. (That is a point Charlie stresses again and again, viz. that the people who come up here are all the jitterbugs who've run away). There was damage round about Russell Square and the grass square was covered with debris. He saw however that crocuses had come up from beneath it all, and the daffodils too. So he wrote a sonnet about Russell Square and its crocuses, and I enclose a copy.

March 1941

Amid the debris of a London Square
I saw a crocus smiling at the sun –
A golden shaft to make earth's sadness fair
And light the way to triumph sorely won.

Lo here! Lo there! Such devastation reigns
And bares the cloven-hoof of devilry
High in the blue, along the chosen lines
The Hun delights in making revelry!

A troubled people sing their psalms to God
The while their sons are fighting in the blue,
Knowing that triumph is their sure reward
– Their triumph ours – those fleet-winged Glorious Few
Who fear not Death, nor hold their all to give
That we may freedom breathe and gladly live.

Ernest van Someren
A cold windy morning, to dentist by cycle at nine, for a little job of grinding a rough edge to a filling. Went on to Hertford by cycle, to the county library to return some books and borrow some others. Then I went to the Registrar's Office and registered Alison Julia. At about 11.30 I went to see Kay with some books and a jar of fruit salad – it's a nuisance not being able to get her fresh fruit at all. She was better again, and had started feeding Julia a little. I cycled back at 12.15 and left the registration form at the local food office to get Julia's ration books.

SUNDAY, 30 MARCH

Ernest van Someren
Up at about eight, after breakfast tidied up a bit and then took L with me to Hertford to see Kay. We sat on top of the bus in front and

enjoyed the five-mile ride, then found K sitting up and very glad to see us. We took her a picture to hang on the wall opposite her bed, and we took biscuits for our own elevenses which we ate soon after arriving. We looked at Julia. L was not at all impressed, and we looked at all the other 8 babies and decided she was not the worst-looking. I went to another ward to see a man from our lab who was in for an abdominal operation.

MONDAY, 31 MARCH

Ernest van Someren
In the evening had a quick tea at home and went by bus to see K, who is making good progress. I kept from touching her as I seem to be starting a cold.

Pam Ashford
The fifth column is no myth. There are times when I feel like saying, 'Why don't you allege that Glasgow was blitzed by the English?' People are coming up to me in subdued tones and saying, 'Is it not shocking about the King and Queen?' I in my innocence say, 'Good Lord! They have not been hit!' And then it turns out that whereas they invariably send a message of sympathy to English towns they have given Glasgow the cold shoulder.

This man Lord Haw Haw is alleged to have said that German airmen have instructions not to drop bombs on Shawlands, Glasgow, as he had a dear aunt living there. And now the jitterbugs are searching for accommodation at Shawlands!

TUESDAY, 1 APRIL

Ernest van Someren
Stayed in bed to check the cold in my head.

L came and sat at the other end of the bed and watched me do some writing, and some work on sand-papering the bed-table. I had a nap after lunch, then a good sweat in a bath, which L came and watched.

Pam Ashford
Quite pre-Blitz like conditions in the office. People are disposed to believe that 'Hitler has his hands full in the Balkans, he won't attack this island now.' I do not concur.

In the evening I said to Mother, 'I am determined to mention the subject of fire watchers,' and then Mother and I clashed so violently that we argued from 6.30 till 9. Her argument is, 'Fire bombs may fall on other people's tenements but none will fall on ours. Therefore why watch?' My line is, 'Incendiary bombs should be tackled in their early stages. It is unfair to the fire brigade to leave it to them, and it is unfair to the neighbourhood to allow a burning building to illuminate everything, and in any case I should strongly object to our losing our home.' Her argument is, 'There are no able-bodied men in the tenement and that is all there is to it.' Mine runs, 'If we have no able-bodied men we have got to make good with what we have.' Hers: 'I am ready to die any day. I don't mind going that way.' I reply, 'You speak like that because you have had a long life.' I go on, 'This tenement is a danger to the community. If anyone has diphtheria he is put into isolation. It is a pity they can't put this tenement into isolation.' She: 'Don't you waste your thought on fire fighting. Leave it to those who are physically fit.' I: 'If there is no-one physically fit, then I will fight the fire.' She: 'If the place goes on fire, you are clearing right out.' I: 'If the place goes on fire, I stay on the top floor till the last moment.'

WEDNESDAY, 2 APRIL

Ernest van Someren
In the evening went by bus to see K although it was raining again. She is getting on well and had a lot of letters, which we talked over. I took her another bottle of wine and had a drink with her. The husband of one of the other patients in the same ward gave me a lift back in his car. He is a tomato grower in this neighbourhood, and says it's a poor business now. He has had no direct bombing, but has lost about 2000 pieces of glass by shrapnel and splinters.

Edward Stebbing
Went out to a dance, and when I got back to camp at about 10 o'clock found a note to say that I had to catch the 10.30 ambulance to hospital the same night. The ambulance was late and I didn't get to bed much before 12.00. As usual, the Army keeps you waiting (I had been waiting about five weeks for a hospital bed) and then acts without warning at the most inconvenient time.

THURSDAY, 3 APRIL

Edward Stebbing
Had my operation, not a very serious one, in the morning. Just before I went in to have it I heard a patient who was going on sick leave telling another that he had 13 bars of chocolate to take home!

After the operation I felt fairly comfortable and lazily thought how content I would be to remain in the luxury of a spring-bed with sheets, good food, being waited on, and having nothing in particular to do, and never go back to the boring, futile routine of Army life, which I hate. I look forward to having the most pleasant time I have had since being in the Army. It may be wrong to feel like this, when thousands of people have suffered much more terrible experiences from air raids than I have had to put up with. Yet the feeling was inevitable, and sometimes I think I would rather share worse experiences and be free than safe but imprisoned. (In my unit the camp is often referred to as a 'concentration camp' and ourselves as already being 'prisoners of war'.)

FRIDAY, 4 APRIL

Ernest van Someren

After tea was taken to Hertford in a car by Mr H, the husband of one of the other maternity patients, who had an operation like my wife's a week earlier. He and I reached the ward a trifle early and found the babies still with their mothers. Julia looks more human now and is rather a greedy feeder, takes too much and has thrown it back violently once. Had a talk with K and a scrap of her supper (milk pudding) and Mr H took me back. He says if tomatoes retail at only 1/- this summer it will hardly pay to grow them under glass.

I was inoculated against typhoid. My mother came before lunch to stay with us, she is very tired after influenza trouble with my grandmother, who is rather crazy and has also taken to bed-wetting. The cousin who lives with them has pneumonia. My arm was very stiff as a result of the inoculation, and rather painful.

SUNDAY, 6 APRIL

Ernest van Someren

K will come out on Wednesday morning, sharing an ambulance with Mrs H. In the evening we talked, and had a leisurely supper, we discussed pacifism a bit. Poor Mother must cope with her mother again tomorrow, and can't see how to get her looked after tolerably well. Grandma says she would rather die than leave her (daughter's) home – unfortunately she is in quite good condition physically and won't die by inclination. She is bored, selfish and certifiably feeble-minded, that's all.

Pam Ashford
Today has been made lovely by the second part of St Matthew's Passion on the wireless. The first half last week has rung in my head for seven days and now the second half is added to ring in my ears. I expect this is a funny opening of a day in which Germany has elected to attack Yugoslavia and Greece, but of course this time there is no element of surprise as there was in the incidents last April. My belief is that Germany will make it hot for this country so as to endeavour to persuade us against sending large resources to the Eastern Mediterranean.

MONDAY, 7 APRIL

Ernest van Someren
Home to a light supper, and news of the budget, with its properly serious taxation. I approve in principle of high income tax, but mine will be about doubled after being trebled last year.

Pam Ashford
The expectation is rife that 'it' will come again one night this week. Often I have thought I would like to have our belongings packed in cases, but have always been very lazy about it. The large suitcase used at holidays has been the depository of the lingerie I collected between Munich and the 3rd September 1939, and I have always drawn consolation from its presence under the bed. One difficulty is 'Who is to carry the cases?' We have a cane hamper. This evening I packed it with clothes (frocks and costumes). My tests are intrinsic value, lightness of weight and unrushability (or ironability). It would all depend on how many journeys I could make up and down the stairs with the cases. The bird, cash box and deed box of course take priority.

I went to bed at 9.30 and at 10 the sirens went. That was the sign of a spurt of unusual vigour on my part. First to dress, of course. Then there were the windows. Charlie is most insistent that they be open, and we have had them open for three weeks. It seemed to take such a time climbing on chairs to unfasten them, and then getting the black-out adjusted. Meantime the bath was filling up, and Mother, at my urgent request, was filling everything we had with water.

Never have I gone through such a night of hell – oh, no, not the bombs, they don't worry me, but the sofa. No springs and stuffed tight, my body is black and blue. Too narrow to turn on, too short, feet out in space and such difficulty in keeping the blankets from slipping off.

WEDNESDAY, 9 APRIL

Ernest van Someren
Bought a small azalea in a pot and some violets at Kay's mother's request to give K on her return. She is glad to be back in her very comfortable bed. Nurse W and Julia sleep downstairs in the room where we all slept last autumn, now to be called the nursery.

People talk about the budget a little, soberly and not resentfully, people with the good salaries such as myself feel that the really rich have got it much harder than we have, but we have been taxed hard enough this time, and that the extension to the lower income-classes is vaguely a good thing.

THURSDAY, 10 APRIL

Pam Ashford
After work I bought a whistle. They had only three in the shop and would not sell more than one. A month ago I had thought quite independently that a whistle would be a help to anyone buried under debris, and Mother having read the same suggestion in a newspaper has urged me to buy her one.

Mr Mitchell came back from the Exchange saying that we had dropped these new, very powerful bombs on Berlin and I don't know how many thousand houses had been destroyed. So many people say Berlin for Belgrade, an eye for an eye and a tooth for a tooth. I said, 'It is to be hoped that the Germans won't get hold of the composition of that bomb and give it back to us.' Miss Bousie is quite sure they will, also that we shall get both gas and bacteria bombs.

Edward Stebbing
News very depressing this morning. It is not a question of who is going to win that worries me, although of course I do not want Germany to win, but a question of how much more misery and destruction there must be before it all comes to an end. When Churchill speaks of the war in 1942 I become utterly weary of the whole business. Later in the day the depression wore off, but after 6 o'clock I asked a sister what the news was; she said, 'Oh, I don't know. It's too depressing.'

Later there was an ENSA concert in the dining-hall and this dispelled all gloom. It was a really first-class show, with a conjuror, two comedians, a soprano, a pianist, and two soubrettes. At the end we were promised a similar show every week.

FRIDAY, 11 APRIL

Pam Ashford
I got the gas-masks tested tonight. I thought testing was a formidable process, but it only means the ARP office puts the mask over your head and asks you to breathe with a paper in front. I also got Mother's and my own earplugs. This afternoon I got a whistle at another shop and Mother and I are going to bed wearing the things. Also I packed a hat box with 'the first line of defence' which Mother is to carry, namely deed box, cash box, the memorial album (a tribute to my father), two packets of bird seed, bandage, lint, burn cure, boracic ointment, sticking plaster, scissors . . . Mother *must* carry it, along with the bird.

I have explained to Mother what to do. Get everything on to the opposite pavement; next, hide the suitcases in the garden of the Admiralty hostel opposite; then take cover at Middleton School (carrying the bird and the 'first line of defence' case). When the raid is over, Mother is to sit in the shelter and I return to wait for Charlie. Two pairs of strong arms could cope with the three cases and the hamper. I try to school Mother in the procedure, but she is merely amused.

SATURDAY, 12 APRIL

Ernest van Someren
For two days my inoculated arm has been sore (it was OK on Wednesday) and I took it to the works doctor to see this morning. He said it would get better and recommended hot water. In the afternoon I shopped, had a long list, and only next day remembered I ought to have registered for military service. Neither the *Telegraph* or *Chronicle* printed a reminder of this today.

After tea I got the room ready for movies, and we had some films of L's early life. After L was in bed we had our 1939 summer holiday film of the Mt Blanc region, partly in colour, which made us long for the Alps again.

SUNDAY, 13 APRIL

Ernest van Someren
Boiled eggs and dyed them, with initials left blank for L and for the two children next door. We took them the eggs hot at breakfast time. L also had two chocolate Easter eggs and a third was brought him later. I enlarged the hen-run and got a headache in the morning, so

lay down and listened to orchestral music after lunch, while K took her rest too. L had to be put to bed soon after tea very sleepy and a bit cross, so I cheered him up a bit with a shampoo before his bath. For supper we had soup and then a zabaglione which I made for a treat, with 5 eggs and some rather stale white wine and about ½ lb of sugar, it was very good.

This morning after breakfast I got the still and movie cameras to take the first pictures of Julia, aged 17 days, at her morning feed in our bright bedroom.

MONDAY, 14 APRIL

Edward Stebbing
Germany invades Egypt. This headline alarmed me when I saw it, but reading further I saw that somebody had said the situation is not alarming! Surely it is alarming when all the gains of the last few weeks are being lost more quickly than they were won.

Ernest van Someren
In the afternoon I went on tidying out and found the nest of mice who have been eating our hens' meal. It was in a box of rubbish. There are two suckling mice, which I caught in a pot, their mother escaped, I got annoyed and found two older mice and killed them after a wild chase.

After tea L and I went out and collected some frogs eggs from a stream and brought them home, to develop in a pot in the corner of his sand-pit.

TUESDAY, 15 APRIL

Pam Ashford
Agnes was full of the terrible destruction at Knightswood. Many times I visited the Peace Pavilion at the Scottish Empire Exhibition and their walls were decorated with pictures of Guernica. I think I took Guernica as typical, and by that standard estimate Glasgow's damage as slight. Here is a flower from Agnes: 'I have no patience with people visiting bombed areas. It is morbid curiosity. The police should be empowered to shoot at sight.'

Elsie came to lunch today from Kilmarnock and then went to an English Society whist drive with Mother. Evacuees are going down her way now. 1500 from Glasgow turned up the other day, and Elsie's First Aid Station was all ready for service. 25 of the children were rejected by Kilmarnock medical authorities because of vermin.

Edward Stebbing
Last night I dreamed that I had my hands splashed with mustard gas, causing red blisters. Yet no one else had been splashed, no one knew blister gas had been used.

Ernest van Someren
Today L decided that our tadpoles might feel a draught, and has protected them with hay in and on the water – this is by analogy to the protection of young rhubarb-shoots with hay which he noticed in a friend's garden.

In the lunch-hour I went to register, which I ought to have done on Saturday, and am provisionally registered as a Conscientious Objector.

THURSDAY, 17 APRIL

Pam Ashford
On one bus journey the conductress did not punch my season so I took advantage of the extra journey to go out to Jordanhill, or rather to walk there and ride home in the evening. Dudley Drive is now clear. I stood on the site, my heart full of pity. A number of relics were lying about. I looked at two books, *The Lost Horizon* and another book opened at a chapter headed 'The Farewell Message'. Quite a number of good boots and a fur collar lay there and two shaving brushes. I thought sadly of the probable fate of their owners.

Ernest van Someren
People are all talking about the bad raid in town. People are quietly depressed about it, but realise it's inevitable now, and it rather takes their minds off the Middle East, which was worrying enough for a week or so.

FRIDAY, 18 APRIL

Edward Stebbing
In hospital here the war has still not touched us directly, but letters from home reveal how it has affected life there. My sister, for instance, says in a letter: 'Things are very difficult, and I get tired out when I go shopping, what with queuing up for this and that and then when you get it home you have to scheme and think how to make it last a week. I suppose we ought not to grumble, but if we could see an end to the war we would not mind these small hardships.'

Today, too, I read about London's worst raid and it makes me realise what a comparatively easy time I have. But though I have not suffered bodily – at least, while I have known some discomfort, I have not received any injury – I have at the same time suffered mentally. Apart from my general views about the war, I have been more anxious lately about my family, who live near to London. In my imagination I see all the hardship and worry which people in the bombed towns, especially London, have to bear.

SATURDAY, 19 APRIL

Pam Ashford
Mr Mitchell does not seem at all well. His nerves are bad and I cannot for the life of me decide whether it is his health or the war. I certainly know that I am half-carrying him through his day's work. The Blitz has made him cynical and he sneers at humanity (always remembering that he is one of the kindest, nicest men in the world). He says that a Glasgow factory has gone on strike because the workgirls objected to the manager objecting to the way they did their hair.

We sat up when we heard the list of buildings seriously damaged in the recent raids on London. Most of us at times I think speculate on the wonderful opportunity the architects will have after the war (I myself think that Town Councils will do their best to damn the architects). I was, however, not prepared for Miss Smith's summing up for the fire at Christie's. 'This will give the modern artists a chance to show what they are worth.' Staggered, I said, 'What crowds the modern artists out is not the dead "Old Masters" but the "dead" general public living at the present moment.' That started an argument in which everyone contributed a brickbat and all manner of vituperation was hurled at modern art. In endeavouring to find out what the evidence was, I learnt that not a soul in the office has in her life set foot inside an art dealer's shop, no one goes to the Fine Arts Institute or shows at the McLellan Galleries (Miss Smith and Miss Bousie have not set foot in it since 1911).

MONDAY, 21 APRIL

Maggie Joy Blunt
Are we really going to lose this war? The Nazis sweep from triumph to triumph making no mistakes while we make all the mistakes.

N says, 'I would rather die than live under Nazi rule.' The next few years are of importance to us. Potentialities for a good new social order are so great, but Nazi power so terrific, well organised and efficient. Will it crush this hope of a new world? The forces of progress seem immature, scattered, though well-intentioned, and are having to fight two battles – one against Prussian military might, the other against vested interests: the millionaires who have used democracy for their own ends and now exploit the democratic peoples to maintain an order that suits them.

God alone knows what we shall be called upon to endure these next few years but as others wiser than I have said, it is not what one endures but how one endures it that counts.

Spring has been long delayed again this year. The hawthorn came out only this last week with willow and a few early chestnuts. The other trees are still doubtful. Gardens are full of daffodils and the garden here is alight with primroses, the currant bush drips with bloom, is alive with bees – is alive indeed with its own bloom and leaf but to stand near it is to hear a happy, droning chorus so that the bush seems to vibrate with bee-song of its own. Grape hyacinths, aubrietia, forget-me-nots are pools of colour in odd places. Tulips are in bud, waiting.

There were bad raids again on London last week. Planes overhead again tonight. The horror of that sound has become dulled by familiarity and resignation.

N and I have been reading Hemingway's *For Whom the Bell Tolls*. Grim but magnificent.

I HAVE NOT – Done any work on Jules'
'WIDOW' play for months
Been to the Fabian Society since Feb or early March
Taken any Red Cross exam
Done any more articles on London City
Read half the books bought or borrowed
Obtained work with the National Buildings Record . . .

BUT I HAVE – Done an article for COUNTRY LIFE
Received £8.8 from the BUILDER

Pam Ashford
Elsie went to the Soroptomist Club today. The feature was a musical programme, when Miss Agnes Dick sang some songs Mrs Smart (our poet representative) had written. I thought it was a pretty poor show. Conversation at the table turned on the bombing of civilian populations in Germany and practically everyone was opposed to it on the grounds that it would stiffen the Germans. The argument was this: The Germans are no different from us; bombing civilians here

has stiffened the nation and it would do the same there. Miss Weir thought (and everyone agreed) that what was needed were mass attacks on Germany.

TUESDAY, 22 APRIL

Pam Ashford

'We are passing through terrible experiences and our loved one is at rest and at peace.' Thus runs a letter from Penzance in reply to a letter of sympathy on a death of an old friend (65) from natural causes. That is a common attitude towards bereavement nowadays. If people take to thinking that the dead are better off than the living they are half way to suicide already.

At 12.30 I came home promptly, only to find that the wireless set in the dining room had been put out of action by the woman who cleans. I took my lunch plate into the drawing room and heard that part of the Greek Army had capitulated.

I have been reading about the Government leaflet on Poison Gases and wondering when our copy would be delivered. It turns out it came some days ago and was put on the pile of unpaid bills along with the gas account. 'What To Do About Gas' was of course its title.

FRIDAY, 25 APRIL

Pam Ashford

I do not know what to do with Mr Mitchell, his nerves are so bad. His irritability is such that every one perceives it. He is alright when he is packing boxes of samples, and he likes going out. But he does not seem to be able to concentrate on anything that requires sitting down to. This afternoon he would only say that we were on the brink of defeat. The Germans will be here in no time. Miss Bousie is every bit as despondent. I myself can see a lot of the country in ruins before the war is won. I said to Miss Bousie, 'Right always triumphs in the end.' She said, 'That is our sole hope.'

SUNDAY, 27 APRIL

Pam Ashford

From 2.30 till 5.30 I struggled with my German correspondence course, a composition on the Commercial Importance of the Telephone and Telegraph. Can you imagine a more desultory theme?

Mr Churchill comes on the wireless at 9 and we are all on tiptoes of expectation.

Edward Stebbing

Listened to Churchill's speech on the radio – the first time I had listened to the radio for a very long time. His statement that morale was best in the worst-bombed areas took some swallowing. 'You liar,' one of the other patients said. The news that Wavell had only two divisions at any one time to use in Libya was also a big surprise to me. I was under the impression that he had an army of about 300,000. On the whole, Churchill's speech did give new hope.

MONDAY, 28 APRIL

Maggie Joy Blunt

Churchill's speech last night – well, everyone at the Canteen this morning pronounced it excellent so I suppose it was. But the division of aims among our own people and our maddening inefficiency threaten, I think, to lose us the war. There are people who want a new social order, but not Hitler's. There are the powerful sets, apparently in control of the war and trying to preserve 'democracy' for their own ends. The confusion is terrible. Germany solves it at the moment by liquidating all opposition to its one ideal, ruthlessly. It is not the right way, but it appears to be the quickest. We shall discover in time, but how long, O Lord, how long?

Our troops are evacuating Greece. We still hold Tobruk.

Pam Ashford

Mr Churchill's remarks were sober, but did not strike me as depressing. Mother in fact thought that his speech was a tonic. All the jitterbugs however take it to be the final proof that the British Empire is on the point of elimination. I say to them, 'Do you know how many German submarines have sunk?' They don't. I say, 'Then on what grounds do you set up as a judge? The English have never been defeated, simply because when other people thought they were defeated they failed to see the point themselves and continued the fight.'

Ernest van Someren

In the evening took L to see neighbours and collect tadpoles from a nearby channel which L has christened 'Stinky Water'. We brought home a jam-jar sample of its crowded life, with 3 tadpoles, to replace the frogs eggs which L coddled to death with hay and sand.

After we went to bed we were roused by a policeman protesting at inefficient black-out in a front bedroom, but examination the next night failed to trace the source of his complaint.

TUESDAY, 29 APRIL

Pam Ashford
A month ago Mother gave the Burns Club some sugar and they raffled it for 30/-. She offered the English Society 4 lbs to be raffled a fortnight ago and on the morning of the raffle a lady was sent round to say it was illegal. Mother took it to today's whist drive and it was raffled as a 'mystery parcel' and raised only 16/-.

WEDNESDAY, 30 APRIL

Ernest van Someren
I am preparing a report on the photography of welds, which is to be a fairly big piece of work.

Pam Ashford
There was a board today saying that thousands of Germans were marching towards Finland. Miss Carswell regarded it as a German desire to get a base from which to invade us.

The news that Plymouth has suffered yet again is shocking. Mr Fuller was wondering if the Hoe was still there. I said, 'One thing they cannot destroy is the view from Plymouth Hoe.' Of course that was said literally, but writing it down it takes on another meaning, the memory of the view from Plymouth – and lots beside – are a part of my being, that nothing can take from me.

Edward Stebbing
Went to the weekly ENSA concert, which was good of its kind. It was nearly all songs and comedy – no political jokes. One song they sang was 'When This Blinkin' War Is Over', a sort of unwritten theme song which has been in circulation wherever I have been, but which I have not heard on the stage before. Some of the words were altered tonight – 'blinkin'' for 'bloody' for example. It starts off:

> *'When this bloody war is over,*
> *Oh, how happy I shall be.*
> *When I get my civvy clothes on,*
> *No more guards for you and me.'*

Unfortunately they played the wrong tune.

THURSDAY, 1 MAY

Edward Stebbing
The news that the whole US Atlantic fleet is out on patrol seems to bring America another step towards entering the war. I expect it any day now. As another patient said the other day, 'America and Japan will be in it soon. It will be a world war before it's finished.' I am not sure about Japan, though it would not surprise me if she did come in.

Ernest van Someren
In the afternoon I had an interesting time trying to design a new piece of apparatus. It's only these spells of inventiveness on strictly practical lines which justify my firm in paying me well. A lot of my work is just routine, but I have a good head for gadgets, the kind that work.

Pam Ashford
May Day and the world of nature just as it should be; trees in various stages of opening, waste ground with silverweek unfolding, colts foot fading, dandelions in bud, and the gardens of our aristocratic Kelvinside neighbours cloudless and blue. And here are two reflections from Miss Craigie with whom I came home: 'This cloudless sky frightens me. It makes me think they will be over tonight.' And: 'The winter does not depress me. But this fine weather does. I think of all the young men who won't be playing tennis and golf as they did before the war.'

Some little time back I wrote that at a big conference of astrologists someone had given the precise minute in the early hours of 11th May when Hitler was going to do something particularly dreadful, and I wrote it down to disprove the astrologer. The farcical point is that I am now watching the date as if it were really going to be so.

SATURDAY, 3 MAY

Maggie Joy Blunt
I am glad to see this week's *New Statesman*'s Critic's comments on the Prime Minister's speech. I could not myself state what I felt to be wrong about it . . . 'It is plain fact and not propaganda that people bear severe bombing with astonishing fortitude. Before congratulating our local authorities on their response to demands put upon them, Mr Churchill should surely have enquired about the actual grievances of the homeless, the problems of compensation, of food shortage, of separation of families and all the other questions of daily

routine that actually fill the thoughts of the vast mass of people most of the time. A gardener who listened to Mr Churchill remarked, "He talked like a War Lord and the Germans could do that better . . ."'

Among people with still sufficient means to meet increased cost of living the war has not yet made drastic material difference. We have enough food and it is of good quality, though choice is limited. Our normal lives are very little interrupted and we have now adapted ourselves to such things as restricted entertainment in the evenings – though the extra hour we are grabbing tonight will mean daylight for us until 10 o'clock and later 11 o'clock.

Ernest van Someren
I did some small shopping in Hertford: toffee and a tie.

Pam Ashford
Yesterday afternoon I turned more sick than ever before and could not go to work this morning. I went around to Dr Middlemiss at 2, but he had been called to a Medical Board. Mrs Middlemiss has lost her voice 'because of all the draughts'. A talkative person with no voice is hard to follow, but she did wonderfully well in the circumstances. Despite a lot of 'terribles' and 'awfuls', she gave the impression of thoroughly enjoying talking about the Turnberry Road landmine. The back of the house lost all its windows, including one frame, all its blind rollers, all the inside doors, a fireplace shot into a room, all the soot came down. An ARP man told her he saw the landmine with parachute leave the plane apparently over Lennie's (157 Hyndland Road). It drifted westwards, just avoiding the roof of 168, and on down Turnberry Road till it hit the ground in the garden of the house that fell down.

The two people killed were Mr and Mrs Stack.

Chapter Four

THE BIRMINGHAM JEWS

The INCREDIBLE STORY of RUDOLF HESS

And His 900-Miles Flight from Augsburg to Scotland

THE DEPUTY FÜHRER AS A PILOT; WITH THE WIFE HE HAS LEFT BEHIND IN GERMANY: It has now been denied by the German authorities that Frau Hess has been arrested

FROM AUGSBURG IN SOUTHERN GERMANY TO SCOTLAND—TWO POSSIBLE ROUTES TAKEN BY RUDOLF HESS:
From Augsburg to the point at which Hess landed by parachute near Glasgow is a distance, as the crow flies, of 825 miles—or about 3 hours' flight in the fast aircraft the Deputy Führer had selected for the journey. It has been suggested—although this view is without confirmation—that Hess may have flown by way of Kiel, re-fuelling at that point: if this were indeed the route followed it would represent a distance of nearly 1,000 miles

The headline was a breath-taker: Rudolf Hess parachutes in near Glasgow.

4 May–10 July 1941

9 May An Enigma cipher machine seized from a German U-boat and sent to Bletchley Park for code-breaking.

10 May Rudolf Hess lands near Glasgow by parachute on a 'peace mission'; 500 German bombers hit London in the worst raid of the war; approximately 5000 houses were destroyed, including the Chamber of the House of Commons.

11 May Former President Herbert Hoover urges the United States to stay out of the war.

14 May The Home Guard celebrates its first birthday; some 1.5 million men have enlisted in 1200 battalions.

20 May Goering mentions his 'Final Solution' for Europe's Jews.

22 May German paratroopers land on Crete.

24 May HMS *Hood* sunk by the *Bismarck* off the coast of Greenland; three days later the *Bismarck* is sunk by the *Ark Royal*.

1 June Clothes rationing starts in Britain; each adult and child will receive 66 coupons for a year: a woollen dress requires 11 coupons, a man's jacket 13.

17 June The British public learn for the first time about radar and of its role in the Battle of Britain.

22 June Germany attacks the Soviet Union along an 1800-mile front from the Baltic to the Black Sea; the subsequent Panzer attack Operation Barbarossa makes swift inroads deep into Russia.

2 July Japan conscripts one million men as it recalls its merchant ships from the Atlantic.

3 July Noel Coward's *Blithe Spirit* opens in London's West End.

SUNDAY, 4 MAY

Edward Stebbing
Was reading the *News of the World* and saw for the first time the official advertisement on precautions to be taken by the civilian population in the event of a gas attack. As far as it goes I thought it quite a good poster, but it leaves out some very important points. It does not explain that if a person gets a breath or two of vapour gas before he has put on his gas mask, he will at first feel *worse* after he has put it on, but that this will wear off if he keeps it on. Some people may think the 'discomfort' refers to the ordinary discomfort caused by wearing a gas mask. It does not explain why collars should be turned up and hands kept in pockets, does not say how long clothes will give protection against blister gas (which would not be very long), and puts what is consequently the best precaution – 'Take cover' – in small letters, so that I did not see it until re-reading. Also it omits the most important warning not to look up at the sky, since a minute drop of blister gas in the eye would mean total blindness.

Ernest van Someren
Made curried beans for supper. We listened to Mr Churchill's speech and thought he was speaking very well – about a year ago I remember thinking that the one thing he feared was the German blockade because he did not mention it in his broadcasts, but his tone is franker now.

THURSDAY, 8 MAY

Ernest van Someren
K and I went to the movies to see *Quiet Wedding*, which we much enjoyed. I usually like an Asquith film. We walked home just at dusk, Kay's first outing in the evening since Julia was born 6 weeks ago.

I stayed up till 2.00 fire-watching. Now that warnings are less frequent Laurie is usually awoken by the siren, to my intense annoyance.

SUNDAY, 11 MAY

Maggie Joy Blunt
Time waits. Clear bird notes fall through the quiet woodland. Leaves and branches are moved by a light, cool current of air. The clock is now two hours ahead of the sun and spring is a month behind.

And I wait . . . to hear from MP (another possible source of work), to hear from June . . . pausing between last week's orgy of spring cleaning when decorators repainted the kitchen. I want to write poetry and cannot. A neighbour's radio lets forth a Forces Programme. A bad blitz on London again last night, much damage done and casualties feared heavy. One's heart tightens with anxiety for friends one knows who were there. One cannot grieve any longer for all the wounded and bereaved; there are, inevitably, too many.

Ernest van Someren
We found one pane of the greenhouse blown in and broken. I went to the neighbours and borrowed a ladder, and I spent part of the morning and of the afternoon mending the greenhouse roof and securing much of the glass more firmly. My mother came over for a bit in the morning and in the afternoon. Laurie enjoyed climbing the ladder, and I photographed him peering over the top of the greenhouse roof.

MONDAY, 12 MAY

Ernest van Someren
Went to town by train, found Liverpool St Station still dripping from a fire. I had to stop at a shop to call for a watch which Mother had left there to be repaired for a present to K. The glass was blown in but the shop was still whole, the assistant and I both arrived at about ten, the streets were full of little groups of people discussing what to do now that their office was gone. I went also to an insurance agent to discuss some insurance for Julia under the War Damage Act, for which I am taking out supplementary cover because of the value of things in the house which people have lent us, and the Japanese things we have from my mother.

TUESDAY, 13 MAY

Pam Ashford
The diary recovers to full consciousness. Nothing could restore it like today's news. I am sorry there has been a break, but I knew that my gastric condition was due to working harder than my strength can comfortably stand and last week I 'lazed'.

Please do not blame the war (however much Plymouth may distress me) as for at least 20 years I have been out of sorts in the spring, and even if ear ache was the trouble for two or three years past, gastric trouble is only a reversion to 1934 and 1938.

Last week Glasgow had the sirens five nights. Paisley and

Dumbarton were raided, and Greenock suffered severely. There were also harrowing stories of people fleeing to the steep braes overlooking the town being the objects of machine gunning and incendiary bomb attacks. Everyone will tell you that Glasgow escaped, and yet on Sunday afternoon at Knightswood I came on three houses knocked down that had been standing the previous Sunday.

Some days the papers come very early and then I am able to read the *Herald* before I get up. The headline 'Rudolf Hess in Glasgow' was a breath-taker!

Feelings were confused today. During the morning many people (including myself) anticipated that Rudolf Hess in our midst would bring about some first class blitzes on Glasgow, and we sighed with relief when the 1 o'clock news gave out that he had been removed to an unknown destination.

I myself feel tremendously tickled. I keep on thinking of what Hitler said when they told him. It dawned on me too that it was probably the early hours of the 11th when they told him, so that perhaps it was Hitler's bad language that the astrologer foresaw.

The motive? That is the question that holds all minds. I have been saying, 'He knows his name is next on the list. He remembers what happened to Roehm and has cleared out while the going is good.' That seems to be the Ministry of Information view judging by their announcement that he is a refugee. But many people will not accept anything so simple. It may be that his better nature has revolted against the atrocities. That is generally discredited on the grounds that no Nazis have better natures.

Another view is that he was flying to Ireland to stir up trouble, and crashed. Fantastic as his appearance is, I feel that motive is even more fantastic.

Miss Bousie and Mr Mitchell are obsessed with the idea that it is a peace move arranged by Hitler. I differ, with the qualification that if there is a peace move in it, it is his own. There is a prevalent idea that Hitler, that cunning and crafty creature, is at the back of it, whatever it is meant for.

Maggie Joy Blunt
Hess's flight to Scotland gives rise to all sorts of intriguing implications and guesses as to the reason for his flight. It is best, however, not to try to guess, or one would soon be indulging in the most fantastic wishful thinking. It is best just to wait and see. But whatever the motives for it, it is surely an event of the greatest importance for one of Hitler's staunchest supporters and most

important leaders to come over here. He has flown in a ME110 from Augsburg and landed by parachute on farmland in Scotland, without arms, or ammunition, and is now somewhere in GB recovering from a broken ankle. If it is not part of some deep laid Nazi plot, the implications are tremendous . . . and the romance of it! It is the best piece of news we have been given for months.

Perhaps the most fascinating aspect of Hess's escape was put into words this afternoon by another patient (a Jew) who said, 'He knows all Germany's secrets; he knows everything about Germany. He's a man behind the scenes.'

In capable hands, this event can be used to great effect in our propaganda. But is our propaganda in capable hands?

WEDNESDAY, 14 MAY

Pam Ashford
We keep on saying how glad we are he is gone. Mr Mitchell is insisting that it is an arranged affair and part of a peace plan. This makes me angry, 'Do you think we would make peace with that gang?' and he goes on, 'I only said part of a plan, not that we would agree. I should hope not.' Mr Mitchell expressed wonder that the plane had not been shot down.

THURSDAY, 15 MAY

Edward Stebbing
In the afternoon there was a concert, of which the star turn was Sir Harry Lauder, who was in good form and was enthusiastically applauded. At the end Lord Elibank, in thanking him, began to talk about Rudolf Hess, whose plane had landed not far from Sir Harry Lauder's house.

Pam Ashford
People are interested in the precise spot. 'Everyone' in Glasgow knew about the Carmunook plane last weekend and connected it with Hess. The papers now speak of Mearnskirk, Newton Mearns and Eaglesham – in other words, the spot shifts about within an area of 5/6 miles. Mr Mitchell has discovered the place is called Floors Farm, Newton Mearns.

Ernest van Someren
Spent most of the morning patching up the frame of someone's spectacles with shellac cement.

115

FRIDAY, 16 MAY

Ernest van Someren
I cycled to work and stayed to do some enlarging afterwards, of some pictures of a little half-caste boy who was brought to see us on Sunday. His father is Hindu, mother Lancashire, his father used to run a hostel for lascars and has been doing relief work in the East End. Their first son is called Krishna and is to be brought up as a good Hindu, the second is 3 weeks old, called Mohammed and is to be brought up Mahommeddan, the next child may be brought up a Christian. This is the parents' contribution to solving the problem of religious differences in India.

SATURDAY, 17 MAY

Maggie Joy Blunt
HMS *Hood* has been destroyed and intense fighting between British and German forces is going on in Crete. The whole Mediterranean situation seems to depend on the outcome of this battle.

And rain has come at last, the dry cold spring has broken.

TUESDAY, 20 MAY

Pam Ashford
The Executive of the Glasgow Association of University Women met this evening. There was much discussion about the coffee morning which Miss Cunningham is giving on 14th June. This used to be a bring and buy sale, to which you obtained entrance by buying a 6d ticket for a cup of coffee. Great doubts are expressed about people's ability to 'bring' and it was thought that donations would balance the consequent inability to 'buy'. Many people thought that if entrance was by donation, instead of the customary 6d, people would be scared away. There will be three stalls, viz books, provisions and work stall. We hope for the best.

Dr Schukoff, the foreigner (and from her accent I should say Pole) who has always mystified me, has been awarded a fellowship to do cancer research.

We tackled next year's syllabus and the speakers marked down tentatively for the luncheons were Prof. Winifred 'Port' Cullis, Miss Hilton and Miss Barbara Ward.

WEDNESDAY, 21 MAY

Ernest van Someren

Cycled to work again, a misty morning. Spent a bit of time gossiping with the other new fathers – there are now four at our end of our lab building. All four are daughters, in 8 weeks, and at Hertford hospital 20 out of 22 recent babies are girls. The other three live all within 500 yards of each other and of a battery of anti-aircraft guns near the works, a miserable spot in my opinion even without the guns, as it's a new lot of houses on an arterial road.

One of the four, Dr R, came to supper with us on his way to visit his wife in hospital, they have been unable to decide on a name for their girl in the first week. His wife is superstitious and much regrets that the child was born on 13th. She is trying to find a name that has no unpleasant associations at all.

Pam Ashford

According to Mr Mitchell the Americans are giving out that the British have murdered Hess. There is great resentment about German paratroops wearing New Zealanders' uniform. Mother says Mr Churchill has given out that they were wearing our uniforms too. Dirty dogs.

FRIDAY, 23 MAY

Pam Ashford

Mr Tom Bell, the Warwickshire Coal Selling Scheme man, has written Mr Ferguson that for 20 miles around Birmingham Jews have been buying up all the houses they can, getting holus-bolus remote villages. They furnish them with furniture purchased from blitzed houses in London, and then they let them as furnished houses at exorbitant prices. Many people in the office registered indignation, and clamoured that the Government should put a stop to it. My own thought was that the defence of Jewry is one of the many causes for which this war is being fought.

Mother says that the 6 o'clock news said that the U-boat commander who sank the *Royal Oak* has been drowned. I want to say something but only trite phrases come to my mind: 'Poetic Justice', 'Revenge is sweet', 'Vengeance is mine, I will repay'. Be it what it will, I am satisfied.

When Mr Mitchell sees a soldier with a polar bear on his shoulder he contrives to get into conversation, thus ascertaining the Icelander's needs. A man today was saying that the population by no means liked the British troops, and Icelandic girls sometimes refused to dance with our men.

SATURDAY, 24 MAY

Edward Stebbing

Listened to some conversation on the situation in Crete. One patient said, 'Reading between the lines it looks as though – trying to break it gently, you know – as though they're preparing us for the loss of Crete.' (It seems like this to me, too.) But another was confident that the Germans could not hold out without tanks and heavy artillery. I have a feeling of impending disaster.

Ernest van Someren

Up at 6.30 and after breakfast by bus to near the works where I met my colleague Dr R and went in his car up to Birmingham. I went by bus through Dudley to Sedgley, in the rain, and got to the Vicarage just in time for lunch. Trevor K (the Vicar) and his wife Elizabeth and their son Indigo aged 2 live there. They used to work in Enfield.

A young couple about to be married came in for a consultative call. Trevor finds the people depressing, he says he could entertain all the intelligentsia of the parish in his sitting-room without bringing in another chair.

Pam Ashford

As Fate would have it, the same page of the diary that contains an unethical feeling towards the U-boat ace, must also bear the loss of HMS *Hood*. When we came to Glasgow in 1917 that boat was being built at Clydebank.

Charlie was an apprentice at John Brown's then, and the building of the *Hood* was a subject on which I heard much, in contradistinction to subsequent constructions – say the *Queen Mary* and the *Queen Elizabeth*, which came at a time when I had no links with Clydebank.

This afternoon I went to see *Escape to Happiness* at the Cosmo, with Leslie Howard. Everyone has been saying how good it is, and of course it is good, but far too slushy for my taste.

SUNDAY, 25 MAY

Ernest van Someren

Up at about 8.30 and had a bath in soft water for a change. After lunch I had to leave, by bus to Dudley where Dr R met me with the car and motored into Birmingham. I asked him to stop at a friend's house, and we were shown round an old Edgbaston house beautifully redecorated by a couple whom I introduced to each other in 1932. They now have two children. She is an artist and he is musical but a lawyer. We had some brandy to drink and admired the house a bit, and heard that he is working in the Food Control office on the investigation side. He says they track down profiteering rackets fairly easily but have great difficulty in getting adequate sentences on conviction from the magistrates.

MONDAY, 26 MAY

Edward Stebbing
Moved to a convalescent home for a month, and here the war seems farther away than ever. The only recreation consists of a few games, some books, and a radio. It looks as though boredom will soon set in.

Pam Ashford
At the Soroptomists I was at a table that was wrapped in deep gloom all the time. It was unanimously held that we should have to evacuate Crete and that the reports were designed to lead us up to this point by easy stages.

The address was given by Mrs McKenzie Anderson, who people were saying has lost three children in this war, viz. a son in a submarine, a son in the RAF and a daughter. She is a secretary of the Glasgow Society of Treelovers, and began by saying that it may seem incongruous that at a moment when such tremendous happenings were in progress, people should talk about trees, but there were many people who found the contemplation of trees beneficial relief. (Which I endorse.)

TUESDAY, 27 MAY

Edward Stebbing
'I shouldn't be surprised if America declared war today,' said another convalescent. Later one came in and said, 'Heard the latest news? The *Bismarck* has been done in. The Fleet Air Arm finished her off.'

Pam Ashford
Mr Mitchell was downstairs when he heard someone in the *Daily Mail* say over the telephone that the *Bismarck* was captured and he went right through the building telling all the offices. Everyone accepted the news without a question. A quarter of an hour later Mr

Mitchell, on enquiring personally at the *Daily Mail*, was told it was not authentic and went right through the building telling everyone that. Then someone came into the office saying it was authentic. When I left at 12.30 on a board opposite was chalked 'Biggest Naval Battle in History – Bismarck captured'. On getting home at 12.58 I said to Mother, 'There are wild stories going about regarding a battle in the Atlantic. I want to hear the news.'

It *was* a thrill to hear she was sunk. Mother exclaimed, 'Thank God,' three times, almost beside herself with joy. It is great news, the best news, and it helps to keep the news from Crete from bearing us down. What an ugly situation! What a list of ships lost!

This afternoon there was a flash of lightning and a clap of thunder with a bare second between. A second later Miss Carswell said, 'Oh look at the ball of fire.' Sure enough a barrage balloon was blazing and falling slowly down. Miss Bousie began to bewail the people caught underneath it, but its passage down must have lasted quite three minutes, and if it fell in a street people could surely get out of the way. It was one that protects the river. All around the office the same comment went up that: 'Things that would have thrilled us all over before the war, only stir us mildly now. We have got used to the unusual, and dear knows how we should ever adapt ourselves to quiet times if we were switched back to pre-war days.'

WEDNESDAY, 28 MAY

Maggie Joy Blunt
How big little moments can sometimes seem. Ella has just left. I saw her off at Beaconsfield and have just returned to a mournfully empty cottage. Am in a suicidal mood today. No word from MP although I left a phone message at his office. Everything seems to be going wrong and I don't know what to DO. Have put a call through to June – there is a delay to London. Want to sink into a comfortable coma and emerge to find all the kinks and mountains removed. War news is very critical. Shall I go for a long bicycle ride, rain or no rain? How lonely I feel at this moment . . . in a fog all by myself and only myself to find the way through it. I hate the feeling of restriction when people are here with me and hate the emptiness when they are gone, as though with them have gone opportunities I didn't use, things I never saw or understood that I should and could have understood. Like having a book in my possession that I didn't bother to read properly.

Pam Ashford
The dandelions are in fruit now and I have collected two big bunches of heads to be dried for Dick's use in the winter.

Miss Bousie came in saying 'a transport down and 3000 lives lost'. We were knocked all of a heap, and then after a couple of minutes it turns out she was referring to a Nazi ship. Why do these people with pacifist tendencies handle things in that manner? The place was changed to smiles. There were also a number of comments on 'how bloodthirsty we have grown'.

Ernest van Someren
In the evening after an early supper cycled to Hertford for a small committee meeting of the two WEA branches. Six of us met in the rooms of the secretary there. We found that we could not imagine how this country could win the war, in a military sense of the word, though we can believe that the ideals for which we stand will survive. Military invasion of Europe seems absurd, considering how difficult invasions are now. I personally think that Hitler will not try to invade here until he has either weakened us physically by the blockade, or morally by dividing us over a peace offer.

FRIDAY, 30 MAY

Pam Ashford
This was Miss Carswell's last day with us. She gave a tea party in the office in the afternoon – the collection of the cakes (3 jam and cream (synthetic) sandwiches and 15 French cakes) being a major problem, involving booking things in advance at half a dozen shops. We had piles of confetti, manufactured from scrap paper with the puncher. Riot ran high. Her presents from the office were: canteen of cutlery from Mr Ferguson, coffee set, silver napkin rings, marmalade jar, china flower basket, china vase, crystal vase, lace table cloth, linen table cloth, pewter bowl, wine goblets, sandwich dish, barometer.

Edward Stebbing
It looks like another withdrawal for us, this time from Crete, though one must not give up hope yet.

We talk a little about the news, of course, but more about other matters, such as getting one's 'ticket', in other words, being discharged from the Army, for which almost everyone, both here and at the hospital, hopes. How we envy those who are ordered to send home for their civvy clothes!

I have been reading Pepys' *Diary* since being here. I wonder what that famous diarist would have written today. Altogether I have read 18 books in just over eight weeks while I have been in hospital.

SATURDAY, 31 MAY

Pam Ashford
This morning at 8.50 I thought how lovely Peacock's window was with 20 large chocolate cakes and three birthday cakes (say 3/- and 6/- per cake respectively) and trayfuls of French cakes. On looking inside I saw a queue which I counted as 50. I have seen a queue of about 50 at Cooper's biscuit counter, but did not know what biscuit was the draw – possibly Carr's cheese club biscuits.

Ernest van Someren
Cycled to work, took an old dry-shaver with me and fixed it on to my new testing apparatus, with amazing results.

SUNDAY, 1 JUNE

Edward Stebbing
The rationing of clothes is certainly a big surprise to me, though as a member of the Forces I shall not have to worry about it personally. At first glance the rationing seems severe, but I don't know how it will work out in practice. It seems rather a confused scheme and I think there will be many difficulties, people not knowing exactly what is rationed and how to use their coupons to the best effect. Also, children will probably not need as many coupons as adults, so that people with children will be able to use some of their children's coupons on themselves, while people with no children will have only their own. The fact that margarine coupons are to be used at first (until proper clothing coupons are issued) makes it all seem a little ridiculous.

Maggie Joy Blunt
We have lost the battle of Crete with very heavy losses. Clothes are to be rationed. MP cannot accept my offer of assistance on this new RIBA committee.

Pam Ashford
Rationing of clothes! None of us dreamed of listening to the President of the Board of Trade at 9 and when the papers came at 10.30 Mother, all excitement, came to me saying, 'You are a lucky

girl with your hoard of clothes.' This hoard has been mentioned before in the diary. I am a lucky girl, but all the same, even if there were no hoard (and remembering it was gathered between December 1938 and September 1939, and has begun to shrink already) 66 coupons are sufficient for my needs, though it eliminates the possibility of variety. Mother says she is delighted, for it means we (she and I) won't look shabby now as against other people. I feel the same way too. I am absolutely determined that the wheels of industry shall make no unnecessary turns on my account but that does not mean I don't have my feelings when I see the better appearance of people who don't think the same way. I have heard their arguments many times, viz. 'But a new frock is a *tonic*.' 'A new frock does your morale good.' 'The clothing industry has to be kept going, or else what is going to become of the workers else?' 'But if I were not in fashion, I should not feel life worth living.'

MONDAY, 2 JUNE

Pam Ashford

Miss Bousie returned in the afternoon much distressed to say that 'Crete is worse than Dunkirk. And while it is going on, what do the BBC do? They gave out the sinking of the *Bismarck*, and the sinking of the *Bismarck*, and the sinking of the *Bismarck*. Crete was pushed into the background by a trivial incident like the *Bismarck*. I was so angry that I could have smashed the wireless set.'

TUESDAY, 3 JUNE

Maggie Joy Blunt

For five weeks this ad has been appearing in the *Architect's Journal*: 'Vacancy exists for woman architect or architectural student on the editorial staff of an architectural publication. Candidates must be able to write easily and well. An interest in the presentation of buildings illustrated in architectural journals and general knowledge of our current events in the profession and building industry are also desirable.' The last one appeared on May 22nd and I have to see it NOW. Have written, but of course it is much too late. Am frantic.

WEDNESDAY, 4 JUNE

Pam Ashford

The ex-Kaiser died today. I was most surprised by the tone of the obituary notice that the BBC gave at 1.10, as my own store of memories consists largely of the insulting things said about him in the last war. However, among the staff in the office all that seems forgotten and forgiven. We have certainly seen a worse villain since.

THURSDAY, 5 JUNE

Pam Ashford
Miss Smith spoke to the mannequin at Macdonald's today saying, 'It is a shame for you to show us these lovely frocks when we cannot buy them.' The mannequin said, 'We are selling many frocks. There have been people who have used up practically all their coupons already. Personally I don't think it is wise. I intend to keep some of mine for the winter.' Miss Smith cannot think why people should act like that. I said, 'Probably they think good clothes will become scarce and they are buying up while they may.' Miss Smith said, 'That policy will make clothes scarce,' and then she launched into a tirade: 'It makes me disgusted with my own sex. They are out for themselves. Just selfishness.'

FRIDAY, 6 JUNE

Ernest van Someren
There is a good deal more talk this week about the trouble in Crete and what it betides than about clothes rationing. Yesterday K went to Enfield with a friend in her car to do some shopping and bought clothes for herself and Laurie.

Edward Stebbing
I had a talk with another patient about how much longer the war would last. He said, 'If Germany is going to win it might be over quickly, but if we are going to win it will take a long time.' He thought it might last another five or six years, or even longer, but I said I did not think economic circumstances would allow either side to hold out so long.

SATURDAY, 7 JUNE

Ernest van Someren
For the first time L climbed over the garden wall (about 5 ft high) and down the other side, to play with the boy next door. I took out on my cycle for a little shopping, hurried home to dodge a thunderstorm. It's a shocking fact that we should have to explain to L that thunder makes a noise like guns, instead of vice-versa.

MONDAY, 9 JUNE

Edward Stebbing
My father mentions clothes rationing in his letter today: 'But I don't think I shall feel that as much as the food business. I miss the cheese more than anything . . .'

WEDNESDAY, 11 JUNE

Edward Stebbing
I read Churchill's speech in the paper and, as has been the case before in his speeches to Parliament (but not in his broadcast speeches), I felt some dissatisfaction with his attitude. He drew attention to the fact that Hitler had not had to account for the loss of the *Bismarck*, nor Mussolini for his defeat in Libya, as much as to say that he should not have to account for our loss in Crete, ignoring the fact that in this matter of public debate lies the very difference between democracy and dictatorship. Again, Churchill concentrated on disposing of the argument that we should not have defended Crete, which was, I am sure, the opinion of a small minority, in order to distract attention from the question as to why Crete was not *better* defended. He seemed very vague on this point. And although he often says that he wants to give the public as much information as possible, he seems to find numerous excuses not to do so.

FRIDAY, 13 JUNE

Ernest van Someren
Woke at 4.00 with sound of planes about, found the electric clock was 12 hours wrong so that the alarm would ring in the afternoon. Got up and wrote diary, there was no warning but some patrol flying in the bright moonlight. At about six I made a cup of tea for Kay and took Julia up for her feed, then went to bed and slept a bit more. Another cool day, I cycled to work and the bike developed a groaning noise in the back hub.

SUNDAY, 15 JUNE

Edward Stebbing
The march into Syria proves unexciting and slow, and causes hardly any comment. The papers are making a lot of fuss about relations between Germany and Russia, but I think it is mostly propaganda, designed partly to raise morale by giving hopes of a war between

Russia and Germany, and partly to try and split the two countries. Personally, I do not think Hitler would be so stupid as to involve himself in a war with Russia and I do not think Russia wants to help us.

Ernest van Someren

Julia didn't wake till 7am for once. She has gained 8oz this week and weighs 12½ lbs at 11 weeks, which is on the fat side. The boy next door who plays with L asked him what Julia has to eat.

Just before 10 a woman fell off her cycle outside the house, she looked hurt so we asked her in, with her husband. She had two cuts on her legs and a very bad bruise, Kay washed them and I bandaged them and we gave them a pot of tea, and she rested on our sofa till she felt better. Her husband was very grateful but a rather helpless chap with no idea of first-aid.

MONDAY, 16 JUNE

Pam Ashford

At the Soroptomist Lunch today the speaker was Miss Andross, Lecturer on Dietetics at the Dough School, on 'Food Preservation'. She described how to make 7½lbs of marmalade from three sweet oranges; also various ways of bottling (cold and hot) fruits and vegetables, of preserving vegetables in brine, and in dry salt, and of drying green vegetables. There were many questions and the meeting did not break up till 2.25. It must be remembered that Miss Andross is a most entertaining personality quite apart from the appeal of her subject.

The Oklahoma (U.S.A.) Soroptomists have sent us 24 bars of chocolate and it was decided to raffle them (6d ticket) and to give the proceeds to the Coastal Battery Fund. As there were 40 persons present there was a good chance of getting a bar, though I for one was among the 16 unlucky persons.

WEDNESDAY, 18 JUNE

Edward Stebbing

The system of radiolocation by which enemy aircraft are detected, revealed by Lord Beaverbrook, was no secret to me. I had heard of it some time ago, even before I was called up, although I only believed it in a half-hearted way.

THURSDAY, 19 JUNE

Maggie Joy Blunt
The cigarette problem is acute. Have failed to get any in Slough these last 3 weeks. The village tobacconist had yesterday a few Woodbines. In London last week I managed to get 100 and Verrey had collected some tens and twenties for me which I am trying to make last but with the greatest difficulty. I cannot do without them. It shocks me to find that they have such a hold on me. Verrey tells me it indicates a craving for sex but frankly at the moment I would rather have the cigarettes.

SATURDAY, 21 JUNE

Maggie Joy Blunt
Really life strikes me as so pleasant at this moment – must say so here. After a long winter and a frozen spring the weather has swept into a train of royal summer days. Roses and lupins and foxgloves, oriental poppies, purple and yellow iris bloom in the garden. The heat is Mediterranean. At night a sheet on the bed is too much. But the surrounding trees grant us coolness day and night and a luscious restful green to look upon at midday.

Only the constant passing of airplanes reminds me of war. I have more than enough food for my needs. I have clothes enough, money in the bank, interesting work, a lover, books, papers, radio, a few very good friends and many agreeable acquaintances, two cats and a kitten, a heavenly garden and cottage . . . What more could a woman want? (Cigarettes. 20 or even 15 a day would suffice.)

Ernest van Someren
I set out on my cycle with weekend rations to Welwyn Garden City, where the British Rheologists Club was to meet at an Inn. It was very hot, I wore a white shirt with a red tie in my pocket to put on when I arrived, and strapped my coat on the carrier.

We had a discussion on the terminology of rheology, in a nice little restaurant next door to the ballroom in which someone was holding a very audible dance lesson for children. Then lunch in the larger room. Our hosts, the British Rubber Producers Research Association, have no central building, only three small labs in different buildings, which we visited in turn in parties after lunch. I got bored by 3.30 and set out to cycle in the heat of the day to Bricket Wood, about 15 miles.

Arrived in time for a swim before tea, in the swimming pool which my host shares with a nudist club. It was warm but fresh.

SUNDAY, 22 JUNE

Ernest van Someren
Woke early and practised the recorder a bit before going for a swim at about 8. Most people were sleepy but kindly said they had liked being waked by music. We had a huge breakfast on the lawn from 9 to 10, with porridge, bacon and sausages. Heard the news about Germany and USSR. The chap who told me, Bert S, an engineer of the Left, gloomily announced that Churchill would make a speech this evening, probably to announce that we were switching to a war against Russia. This seemed to me unlikely, but I felt apprehensive about the new turn of events.

After lunch I played the recorder with one girl who borrowed another from a boy in the house, we tried rounds together and with voices.

There were two girls who did not bathe, probably because they weren't used to nudity, and one who defied convention by bathing in a costume where everyone else was naked.

Maggie Joy Blunt
On the hottest day of the year we hear at 9am that Germany has invaded Russia and at 9pm that the declared policy of the British Government is to aid all nations who are victims of Nazi aggression.* WE ARE GOING TO HELP RUSSIA! Churchill made one of the cleverest speeches of his career. I smoke my last cigarette to him. I think this is the most important day of the century . . . we ally ourselves with the USSR at last.

Edward Stebbing
At breakfast someone said that Germany had declared war on Russia. One of the nurses said that Rumania was going to help us, though how that can be when Rumania is already occupied by Germany I don't know. 'The war will soon be over now,' said someone else. I still hardly know whether to believe it and shall not completely accept it until I hear it on the radio or read it in the papers. If it is true, then I think Germany has spoilt her chances.

Listened to the one o'clock bulletin and learned the news beyond doubt. Like several other things that have happened in this war, it is

---

*Accurately, Churchill said: 'Any man or State who fights against Nazism will have our aid. Any man or state who marches with Hitler is our foe.'

extremely difficult to understand the circumstances that have led up to it. There is nothing straightforward about this war. In the maze of lies and treachery it is almost impossible to find the truth. The only conclusion that one can come to is that it is favourable to us. 'The Russians will slaughter the Jerries,' was one opinion. The comments on the radio have noticeably showed no warmth to Russia, no welcome to her as a new ally. The announcer spoke of Germany's move as being directed really against the democracies, hinting that Russia is not a democracy and not really one of us. I suppose this is all one can expect from our Conservative leaders, but if our attitude to Russia continues to be distant the war may still take longer to finish than it need. Collaboration with Russia and America would give us a marked superiority over Germany.

Pam Ashford

Three comments. Charlie: 'Quite the most interesting news we have had for a long time.' Mother: 'It is just what Pimpernel Smith said. He said the Nazis would fall on the Russians. The Nazis could never make peace, they must go on making wars or perish. Russia would be their undoing. Germany is a doomed nation.' I: 'The Hess secret is out. He wanted to impress on us that Russia was our foe and we should back Germany, but that in any case if we did not, Germany would destroy us after she had finished with Russia.'

MONDAY, 23 JUNE

Pam Ashford

Miss Bousie disliked Mr Churchill's bloodthirsty speech, though as a great admirer of Russia she applauded our association. Agnes is convinced that the Russians are going to murder 'every German'. Mr Mitchell wants, when we have won the war, for all the Germans, 80,000,000 odd, to be put in camps and gassed like vermin.

A Soroptomist living near Hampden Park said that when there was an international football match there recently every cake shop on the road was laden with cakes 'apparently to impress the visitors'.

TUESDAY, 24 JUNE

Ernest van Someren

We had supper in the garden, and afterwards the Hamiltons came to see us, Mrs H was in hospital with K and also had a girl baby Caroline. We talked, had olive sandwiches and some white wine – olives from Woolworths. They waited to see Julia at about 10, then went home by car. Mr H is a man of action, a small tomato-grower in this valley, aged about 30.

WEDNESDAY, 25 JUNE

Ernest van Someren
Cycled home and stopped at a pub at closing time. Heard two people coming out and saying, 'What sort of climate have they got in the Ukraine?' and the cautious reply began, 'Let me see . . .'

THURSDAY, 26 JUNE

Ernest van Someren
Fire watching from 2.00 to 5.00, did diary and read a bit, then got some sleep. Took a half-tablet of Benzedrine. It just tides me over the afternoon drowsiness if taken at breakfast time, and does not interfere with night's sleep later.

SATURDAY, 28 JUNE

Pam Ashford
My summer holidays began today. We brought our rations with us, including 23 eggs.

During recent months I have had abundant testimonies that Glasgow's food supplies are better than those of other towns, and five minutes in Ayr brought that home to us. Believe it or not, at 2.30 there was not a single baker in Ayr that had so much as a crumb of bread or anything else. I urged mother to draw liberally on her store of tins, and we shall need them.

SUNDAY, 29 JUNE

Pam Ashford
We spent the morning reading the papers on the seafront.

The Russo–German battlefield will take up many pages in future history books, as against the much more limited space they are likely to give to the British in Iceland, while this diary is quite the other way round. But I am sure very few people take a 'bird's eye view' of the world, that is to say the historian's standpoint; things in which we are actively participating loom large in our thoughts, and other things – however terrific in themselves – fail to hold the attention long.

Ernest van Someren

After breakfast in the garden I cleaned the henrun and did some gardening, then set out with some sandwiches and my cycle by train to Bishops Stortford and north by road, looking for holiday accommodation. I went through Barkway to Barley, where I sought out John Radham, an old friend of mine whom I rang up last June and have not seen for 9 years. He has a lovely cottage and garden, is good at carpentry, gardening, cooking and writing. *Good God* has sold some 90,000 copies and his other book *God in a World at War* is in the second edition. Besides the distinction of writing religious best-sellers he paints and does embroidery and is an authority on anti-semitism.

We had tea in the garden. He grows strawberries of the Alpine variety and I tasted them.

MONDAY, 30 JUNE

Pam Ashford

We hastily booked seats for the Stinchar valley this afternoon.

The heat was intense at 2 when we sat in the coach waiting for it to start at 2.15. Looking up I saw a mackerel sky and recalled the lines 'mackerel sky, mackerel sky, not long wet, not long dry'. And so it was.

In July 1939 at Scarborough we kept saying, 'Thank God, we have our holiday before the war starts.' In July 1940 at Helensburgh we kept saying, 'Thank God we have our holiday before the invasion starts.'

TUESDAY, 1 JULY

Pam Ashford

Does the war continue? It is not much in evidence here, or are the things that used to shriek war now become commonplace? I refer to the poles on the Low Green, wooden barricades on the sands, barriers across the roads leading to the sea (which now have heavy railway lines lying beside them with which to block the causeway no doubt), and the airplanes constantly flying overhead.

Accommodation in Ayr is, of course, completely used up and wherever we go there are people. The proportion of children is very high indeed, with a good many middle-aged couples. But there are many more women than men – holidays bring home to me what the City does not, viz. that the young men are away in the Forces.

Edward Stebbing

An old soldier's opinions: 'There'll be some happy homes broken up after this lot, with all these women in the ATS and the WAAFS and that. All the women ought to be put in munition factories, instead of soldiering with all these different soldiers. There'll be a lot of divorces after this war . . .'

WEDNESDAY, 2 JULY

Ernest van Someren

At work did some making-over to improve an old bit of home-made apparatus. In the evening went with K and L to bathe in the river from a friend's garden; only I bathed. The river is a bit weedy and last week a boy aged 19, swimming well, was drowned near the boathouses. The wife of our Hindu friend went in to try to rescue him and swam under water a lot for the first time this year, now she is in bed with acute rheumatism in consequence.

THURSDAY, 3 JULY

Edward Stebbing

Apparatus has now been installed in the hospital so that a person's voice can be relayed over the radio-relay system. This evening the padre 'broadcast' a lecture on why we are at war. It contained a lot of truths, but missed out a lot too. Much of it was Empire propaganda. Although I hate the Nazi regime as much as anybody, I cannot understand how any clergyman can fall for the notion that this 'is a fight of good against evil, of God against the Devil, a crusade'.

Pam Ashford

There is one view of the military situation, and only one view, you hear it everywhere, viz. that Hitler has taken on more than he can chew. The war is as good as over, we have nothing more to worry about. Personally, I don't agree, though I find it marvellous that this breathing space has coincided with our holidays.

SATURDAY, 5 JULY

Ernest van Someren

On the way home bought strawberries, these being now controlled and curiously scarce. I stopped at a shop where I had enquired on the way to work, was taken into a side passage where they had a few baskets and after a short conference between the shop staff they consented to sell me a 2lb basket for 3 shillings. My mother has had my grandmother moved to a 'Home for the Aged' this week and feels much relieved, but apprehensive that she may be too difficult a patient for them to keep.

SUNDAY, 6 JULY

Maggie Joy Blunt
Jules and Mavis have just left. They belong to a class and age I just missed being born into. That their class and age are dying doesn't make any difference – I am filled with wistful envy. I adore them both. Why they should be so sweet to me I do not know – coming that vile journey from London on a blistering day to see me. I am very touched, very flattered. Mavis bought me 300 cigarettes, chocolate, a jar of jam, Parmesan cheese. That this is a class war and that nothing they can do will stop the advent of a social revolution they accept as inevitable and with such good humoured dignity. They belong to the 'privileged' classes, to an age when aristocracy mattered and had real influence, but they are workers – they are privileged but not leisured.

During the last blitz on London, about 6 weeks ago, Marylebone 'got it'. Druces in Baker Street has been obliterated. Jules and Mavis' flat is in Gloucester Place, just behind. Fires raged round them all night. Their house was one of the only four in the block which was not burnt. A sudden change of wind favoured them. They were up until 7.30am helping to quench fires. Sheets of flame blew over their roof. It was the worst night they had ever known. But they describe them, these bad nights, with great gusto. They laugh about it. They would. They face danger magnificently. I shall never forget the Blitz I watched with Jules from S's flat in Marylebone High Street. One has no sense of panicky, cringing, let's-run fear with him. It is a great, dramatic adventure. IF you are hit, well that is just too bad. Fires one can help to put out. So let's just enjoy the drama of it while we can.

MONDAY, 7 JULY

Ernest van Someren
Breakfast in garden. During the day we had a letter and parcel from my sister in Florida, she sent honey and kumquats in jars. A hen died mysteriously, possibly sunstroke as she was rather bald from being hen-pecked.

TUESDAY, 8 JULY

Pam Ashford
We spent the morning reading on the front. We certainly enjoyed the three hours on the esplanade, though we could not but remark on the absence of gaiety, as in other holiday resorts. The lack of pierrots and bands accounts for a lot of it, and while ice creams are available at cafes, the 'stop me and buy one' boys are all gone. You feel like asking the question, 'Where are the lads of the village tonight?'

WEDNESDAY, 9 JULY

Edward Stebbing
The welcome given to the Russian mission – people giving the Communist salute, singing the Red Anthem – seems almost comical in view of the recent outcry against Communists and the banning of the *Daily Worker*. Of course, the Communists have changed their tune too. But everyone agrees that Russia is giving the Germans a lot of trouble and the general feeling seems much more confident than it was a little while ago. This is true for myself as well.

Pam Ashford
This morning's papers were headed '100,000 American troops for Iceland' followed by reports of British withdrawal. Mother thinks, 'This will mean a big increase in your trade,' while I wonder if it will give American exporters a pull over us. However, this evening's papers have Mr Churchill's statement that the British forces remain. I am afraid that personal considerations come first and national ones second.

THURSDAY, 10 JULY

Edward Stebbing
Most important news for me today is that I am to be discharged from the Army on medical grounds. Nothing could please me more than this. Civilian life may be harder than Army life – food rations will be less (but better prepared), clothes rationed, air-raids more disturbing, and there will be none of the soldier's privileges. But I shall have more personal freedom. I shall not have my life controlled for me to such a degree, I shall be with my own people, and I shall probably be able to do more useful work as a civilian than as a soldier. My service in the Army has seemed to me a sheer waste of time. Now, paradoxically, I am going to see what the war is like.

Chapter Five

NEW WORLD AT RALSTON

Don't think that the war is over: a stark warning from 1941.

12 July–1 October 1941

12 July Anglo–USSR pact signed after almost a quarter century of distrust.

20 July The 'V For Victory' campaign begins; Britons were encouraged to paint V signs wherever they could to demonstrate determination and invincibility.

28 July Japanese troops advance into Indochina.

12 August Marshal Petain imposes Fascist rule on France.

14 August Roosevelt and Churchill sign the 'Atlantic Charter' after meeting at sea off Newfoundland.

3 September Allied forces take control of Spitzbergen, the Nazis' most northerly outpost.

8 September The siege of Leningrad begins.

19 September The German army capture Kiev, the capital of the Ukraine; British troops enter Tehran.

23 September In London, General de Gaulle announces plans for a committee to be the French government in exile.

SATURDAY, 12 JULY

Edward Stebbing

Travelled overnight from Scotland and arrived home this morning. Outwardly everything seemed the same, and I was glad to be back among familiar things and people. I think it will be easy to slip back into civilian life; already the Army life is sliding rapidly into the past. The chief element of which I shall have to get accustomed is the rationing of so many articles. I have a month's leave during which I shall be paid by the Army, so I have no need to hurry into a civilian job.

Pam Ashford

Our landlady Mrs Hay mentioned a family of 4 adults who were staying with her in May. They brought with them from Glasgow 7 double loin chops and 4 eggs which they had for tea on the Saturday. Next morning they produced for breakfast four large fillets of steak. For dinner they produced a 4lb joint of beef. In the morning the man went out and returned with 7 more double loin chops and 4 eggs for breakfast and a large steak and kidney pie for lunch. Each day the man went out and returned with equivalent purchases. When Mrs Hay said to him that she had had no butcher meat for a week, he thought she was daft. He said he just went into the butcher's shops and talked to the butcher. No coupons were given. He was a butcher in Glasgow, but he denied that he had any influence with the Ayr butchers on that account. In fact, he said they did not know he was a butcher.

During our morning shopping I have seen people buying for boarding houses getting things that I thought were now off the market, such as tinned milk, tinned fruits, salmon, chicken soup and tomato soup. Mrs Hay's grocer said to her, 'We have privileged customers to whom we grant privileges that we are not prepared to grant to ordinary customers.'

In the afternoon we went to see *Comrade X* with Hedy Lemarr and Clark Gable. I have never seen Clark Gable before. Mother was bored by the show but I quite enjoyed it.

SUNDAY, 13 JULY

Edward Stebbing

When the radio announcer said there would be a special announcement at 2 o'clock, we all wondered what it would be and most of us thought it would be something to do with America. When it turned out to be a treaty with Russia it was rather a disappointment. 'They could easily have included it with the news,' said my brother-in-law.

The *Sunday Pictorial* ballot on who should be removed from the Government was of interest, and I agreed with the results. The paper emphasises the fact (as other papers have) that Churchill needs better men behind him if he is to conduct the war successfully. What the papers seem to overlook (deliberately, I expect) is that Churchill chooses his men and is really the one to blame.

Pam Ashford

All the Sunday papers are still to be read, save for the leader by Garvin in the *Observer* which I devour as early in the day as I can get hold of it. He begins by saying that the present struggle makes small the mythological struggle between the gods and the titans. I remember in my record of the Munich crisis wondering if a clash between heaven and hell was coming. The war has gone on for such a long time now that I have passed that kind of talk. I give Mass-Observation food queues instead.

MONDAY, 14 JULY

Ernest van Someren

L shocked K after lunch by depositing a large nail (about 2 ins long) in his pot. When asked about it he said he had pulled it out of the fireplace in his bedroom and swallowed it yesterday. It hurt going down, but not coming out. K is now glad she didn't know about it all the time, as such things are a bit disconcerting.

Pam Ashford

Back at work again. The war has dropped right into the background. Holidays are the subject. Everyone (literally, and not an exaggeration) is having their full holidays this summer – 'we need it' – and doubts that weighted us down last year are absent. Not only are the West Coast towns filling, but the East Coast ones are getting full too.

Here is an amusing evacuee story. A prim, elderly maiden lady at Uplawmoor at the first evacuation had a verminous 8-year-old girl. She cleaned her up and they lived happily together for some months, and then the child went home. At the evacuation following the March blitz she said she would like the same child again. The child arrived, just as dirty. The mother seems a flighty type who haunts dance halls. The child asked the hostess if she had ever gone to dance halls. The hostess said she did not fancy it, and the child said, with sympathetic understanding, 'Ah, well, perhaps that is just as well. I don't think anyone would ask you for a dance.'

THURSDAY, 17 JULY

Edward Stebbing

As I expected, the rationing is the most difficult thing to get used to. Besides the many articles which are rationed, there seem to be various others which are scarce, although unrationed. One of the biggest surprises to me was to see a notice on the door of a pub, saying 'No Beer', though this does not affect me personally.

I think the papers are making too much fuss over the Victory V campaign. What good the campaign, if there really is one, will do, I don't know. I don't believe half the newspapers say about the extent of it. The way they write about it, it sounds like a cheap thriller.

FRIDAY, 18 JULY

Edward Stebbing

Spent the day in London. It still seems the same to me, in spite of the damage done. Its streets were as busy as ever, and the cinemas and theatres seemed to be in almost full swing again. The theatre which I visited in the afternoon (Victoria Palace) was packed. However much London is bombed it will always be the same.

MONDAY, 21 JULY

Pam Ashford

Two of mother's cronies arrived. Mrs Heddon (a widow) has spent 3½ weeks writing out the covers of the ration books. There were 300 women in the banqueting hall of the City Chambers, working under electric light all the time as the hall is blacked out. The hours were 9.30 to 9.30, 7 days a week, except Saturday, when they stopped at 5.30. Mrs Heddon was so tired that she could not sleep sometimes. She could not have held on much longer, but was very glad to get the money. While there she heard that the women at the Food Controller's office have to work very hard under a martinet, who keeps them at it all the time. The workers there called the Food Office 'The concentration camp'. One girl Mrs Heddon knows needs a bottle of Hall's Wine to keep going.

The other crony, Mrs Saddleton, had arranged with Mother to swap fruit for sugar. Her brother sent her a parcel of 12lbs of cherries and only 2lbs arrived, 10lbs were pilfered on the way. The box was wrapped in wire netting with paper outside. People tore the paper away and got their fingers through the wire netting.

TUESDAY, 22 JULY

Ernest van Someren
Noticed in the factory a number of V signs about, for example chalked on odd screens and girls with little Vs cut out of brown sticky paper on their overalls.

When I came home had some letters to read, and L disappeared. He came back and said, 'Don't you know what I've been doing in the scullery? You go and look and I'll be right at the bottom of the garden.' I went and looked and found only some starch spilled on the floor, which we made him clear up after we had got over laughing at his caution.

Pam Ashford
Heinz's soup has come on the market again and many shops have supplies. I bought two vegetable soup tins at the Buttercup dairy on Saturday and a tin of chicken and one of celery at Massey's today. Crosse & Blackwell's made nice soup before the war, but what they were selling in January/March did not taste nice. One day their kidney soup made me vomit.

Edward Stebbing
Vs have appeared all over the place.

FRIDAY, 25 JULY

Maggie Joy Blunt
Tomorrow I join N at St Bees for 10 days' holiday in the Lakes and am now suffering a bad bout of disinclination. I want to go but do not want to undertake that frightful journey. Weather is warm again. Cannot get on with packing and arrangements here, do not want to leave the cottage and the cats, it is all too silly. Suppose I shall be up very late finishing and then have to scramble for 9.20 bus in the morning and arrive at destination exhausted. What will I do if I have to leave here to do war work? It won't be long now before my age group will be registering.

Ernest van Someren
A busy day at work. After lunch had an announcement of an increase of salary of £30 p.a., the first rise since 1931. All intervening

increases have been obtained by changing jobs. Had supper in the garden, talked of an idea of mine for a job in the USA.

SATURDAY, 26 JULY

Ernest van Someren
Went to meeting in the morning, sat behind a stranger who wept quietly a good deal of the time. It turned out that she is a German schoolgirl visiting people locally.

Pam Ashford
This entry is being written on the banks of the Canal at Knightswood. It is such a lovely summer day. If I say that there are many more wild flowers this year I am making a scientific, statistical observation and not indulging in poetic fancy. And the explanation is not far to seek. There are fewer people to tamper with them. During the last 20 years housing schemes have been spreading out in this direction and the uncultivated ground began to be trampled down by children playing and lovers lying about everywhere. With children being evacuated, young men going into the Forces, and the Blitz having rendered much of Knightswood uninhabitable and frightened the tenants still more, the tide has turned in the other direction.

SUNDAY, 27 JULY

Pam Ashford
A firm who specialise in novelties has offered us loving cups in which one handle is a reproduction of Mr Churchill and the other of Mr Roosevelt. Iceland might like that.

Tchaikovsky's Pathetique Symphony at the Prom tonight. It is like the old days to have the Proms again. I enjoyed the Eroica so much last Friday.

MONDAY, 28 JULY

Ernest van Someren
K's birthday (31). K tried to get a trunk call to her sister, we cancelled it at bedtime, were rung up later without any subsequent connection and cancelled it again.

TUESDAY, 29 JULY

Pam Ashford

Miss Smith left a stocking with a ladder at a shop for repairing and it will take five weeks.

I went along to the allotment and brought back a big bag of dandelions. Settling down to seed them, a huge beetle, black in colour, walked out of the bag, involving an exciting hunt, rendered a bit confused by Mother not knowing whether the quarry was a moth or a mouse. That is what the suppression of birdseed imports has involved bird owners in. I have told Miss Bousie what efforts I am making to get wild seeds stored for Dick in the winter. She has enough to last her budgie till November and is convinced that the war will be over by then.

Mr Churchill's speech to the Commons was good. The newspapers were out at 4.30 with huge headlines: 'Invasion expected on 1st September.' It caused extreme amusement in the office, the jokes particularly centring on the people who will be on holiday then. Miss Smith: 'Mr Churchill just said that because he knew that people were getting slack during this lull.' Probably. I too am enjoying the lull; it is wonderful to look at the blue sky and to know that a bomb is not going to fall from it just yet.

WEDNESDAY, 30 JULY

Pam Ashford

Mother says at lunchtime, 'I was asking Charlie about the invasion and he says there is not the slightest possibility. I said to him, "Why does Mr Churchill talk about an invasion on 1st September then?" and Charlie said that Mr Churchill did not know what he was talking about.'

Miss Bousie came back from the bank, aglow with excitement and in the front door. She began, 'I only come in the front door when there is news.' The whole office stopped and gazed expectantly. 'Goering and Hitler – sensation.' Everyone waited for her to go on, but she did not. That was the big news. Everyone began to say that it was just the newsboys chalking things up again. She said, 'No. There is a rush for papers. It is something. People began to point out that this story of a quarrel between Hitler and Goering had been put out several times before and is just meant to weaken our war effort. Everyone repudiated the idea that it was sensation. I said, 'Tell me that Goering has shot Hitler and committed suicide – that would be a sensation.'

Ernest van Someren

Woke with indigestion, which recurred frequently during the day. Busy with calculations again, interrupted for an odd job of glass-blowing as a welcome break. The evening was disturbed by L being sick five times.

THURSDAY, 31 JULY

Edward Stebbing

News of the war in Russia is encouraging. Perhaps the die-hard Tories, who said Russia would not last more than a week or two, will not despise the 'Reds' so much now. At the cinema last night people clapped Stalin and news of how the Russians are resisting.

FRIDAY, 1 AUGUST

Edward Stebbing

Was interviewed for a job at a factory, but as it would mean a lot of overtime I shall not accept it. Instead I went to see about a post as a laboratory assistant in a hospital, which would mean more travelling, but more reasonable hours and more interesting work.

A lady on the bus remarked, 'I don't believe the papers. I think they make the worst of things.'

Pam Ashford

Miss Bousie was saying she had not had a sound night's sleep since the war. Having given her the benefit of my advice (relax the muscles, plenty of bedclothes, hot milk and biscuits, and realising that it does not really matter whether you sleep or don't), Miss Bousie expressed consternation. 'But if you sleep as soundly as that you might not hear the siren.' I said, 'That would be all to the good,' but she did not look at it that way.

The Emperor Concerto tonight. It is good to have the Proms back, though it was a terrible transmission.

SATURDAY, 2 AUGUST

Ernest van Someren

L is still a bit irritable, and today K has digestive trouble and felt very limp. After L's rest I took him out to the library and shopping, we came back to tea in the garden. After tea I took L out again, we called on a neighbour who kept rabbits to see them, and on another who has two goats in a paddock to see them, then we went to the station and watched a couple of trains. It sometimes seems funny to me that I who have travelled about so much should now spend weekends pottering about in a mile circle like this. In my life I have had 25 addresses apart from holidays and have probably averaged 600 miles a year of travel in Europe.

Edward Stebbing
Succeeded in getting the job.

In the market of this town where I shall be working the biggest crush was at the sweet stall, which had a very large supply of chocolate and other sweets. People were spending up to £1 on sweets (some were perhaps owners of shops themselves).

SUNDAY, 3 AUGUST

Edward Stebbing
Was very interested in Beverley Baxter's article in the *Sunday Graphic* on Churchill and his critics. I usually dislike his articles, but this time I was more or less in agreement with him. Churchill's attitude to critics who are only trying to help is most unsatisfactory. On one point, however, I disagree with Baxter: he says 'the country at this moment would prefer Mr Churchill's absolute dictatorship to any possible government of which he was not the head'. This I do not believe and I, at any rate, would be definitely against it.

Ernest van Someren
I had twinges of indigestion but K was better, L fair. Had the hammock out (one of Grandma's) and Julia was very charming. She can roll over, but we have not yet seen her doing it. She kicks and coos a lot. In the evening K did up our lavender crop in bunches, and also our shallots, and we got nearly 9 pounds, which will last us all winter in case onions are scarce again. We had supper in the garden, omelettes from our own eggs flavoured with 'cheese', a soapy wartime product with no consistency and poor keeping quality, unfit to eat raw.

MONDAY, 4 AUGUST

Pam Ashford
The small band of Soroptomists who attend faithfully during the off season don't have to wait till they get to heaven for their reward, they get it right now, in a most marvellous lunch. Imagine today: broth, a big piece of fresh salmon, cucumber, lettuce, hard-boiled egg, peas,

followed by high helpings of trifle. Meals at home are dreadfully monotonous. Dr McLean said she had lost a stone and was well pleased as she could afford to lose it.

TUESDAY, 5 AUGUST

Pam Ashford
It was lovely to hear the Enigma Variations from the Prom tonight. Sir Henry Wood is far inferior to Adrian Boult, however. There is nothing in the field of music that penetrates so deeply into my spirit as the Enigma. I bought the three discs three years ago and have gone over it again and again on the gramophone. But now the gramophone is out of service. Charlie uses it for his dance records, despite there being something wrong with it. Charlie says that the gramophone needs to go to London for repairs and must wait till after the war. He evidently does not think this will be long.

WEDNESDAY, 6 AUGUST

Pam Ashford
Margaret is back from holiday at Hunter's Quay. Margaret's life revolves around her dog. I asked how he survives the absence of liver that used to be his staple food. It turns out that the dog now lives off the family's meat ration, 'though we get some of it ourselves'. His corners are filled in with brown bread soaked in Oxo. There is some biscuit called Stamina that he is willing to eat also. This is, of course, the dog that used to have milk chocolate every lunchtime and insisted on Cadbury's, resolutely refusing Rowntree's. (Or was it the other way round?)

SATURDAY, 9 AUGUST

Edward Stebbing
Comments by two men on the Russian raid on Berlin. First man: 'It seems as though the Russians are not so backwards as we thought.' Second: 'If we could arrange with the Russians to bomb Berlin together, or on alternate nights, we ought to be able to shake them up a bit.' First: 'Yes, they know which way our bombers come from and they've been able to concentrate their defences on that side. Now they won't know which side the bombers will come from.'

This weekend a contingent of tanks is to be on view in various parts of the district, to build up the tank campaign. Posters all over the town announce the coming of 'Waltzing Matilda and her family

146

of tanks'. This propaganda campaign seems to have captured a good deal of attention.

Pam Ashford
In the afternoon I went out to see the tanks. I took my stand in Sauchiehall Street, a little east of Radnor Street, and at 3pm along came a Bren gun carriage, Waltzing Matilda, two light tanks, a Corporation salvage vehicle advertising the anti-waste campaign, 10 buses, 3 trams and miscellaneous other traffic. The tanks stood at Radnor Street for 30 minutes and the police had their hands full getting the traffic through the dense crowds. Little boys swarmed over the tanks until they looked like human anthills.

SUNDAY, 10 AUGUST

Edward Stebbing
The tank display this afternoon attracted a big crowd of people, but I did not consider it very impressive, there being only three small tanks which drove around and climbed a few bumps, sometimes slipping back or getting stuck.

MONDAY, 11 AUGUST

Pam Ashford
The Soroptomists! And what a lunch! Two big pieces of chicken, a large piece of an accompanying bread pudding and as much cauliflower and potato as one liked; a blancmange, gooseberries and a jelly sauce, with coffee to finish. However, my stomach has got unaccustomed to delicacies and on returning to the office I needed milk of magnesia.

Miss Allen is in hot water. She is an optician at Trotter's and a director too it turns out. She leaves the shop normally before locking up time. Recently she returned after business hours for a parcel and left a light in the shop. The noise of the police battering on the iron could be heard over a wide area, a tremendous crowd congregated and there was much excitement. The man with the keys was eventually unearthed. The police then took to measuring the distance that the light was from the street, and it remains to be seen whether the mathematical calculations at present being worked out necessitate a prosecution or not.

TUESDAY, 12 AUGUST

Maggie Joy Blunt

It was a good holiday. We stayed on a farm at Crossdale, near Ennerdale. We fed on butter and cream and large starchy meals and became liverish. No fruit, few greens or salads. Farm people have no excuse for these sort of shortages but they were the type who do not consider greens or brown bread important. Kind people. Mrs E, ridden with arthritis, ruled the household from her chair by the kitchen stove. The domestic help Maggie did all the work, clattered about with Cumbrian clogs and seemed never to rest. Assistance was given by pale and pretty young daughter Annie. There were 5 dogs, 10 cats, cows, a bull, pet lambs, chickens, every farm animal you can think of. The dogs were much beloved. We borrowed bicycles one evening and visited Loweswater and Crummock. Some days it rained heavily, others it was showery, and for two days it was too hot to do anything but idle by the lake. We returned to London by the night train last Thursday.

I hear planes in the night outside. Though we have had no enemy activity over this area for many months, that sound still spells a dread – I wait half-consciously for the siren and the noise of gunfire. The clocks went back an hour this weekend. We have enjoyed two extra hours of daylight for three of the summer months. During June it was not dark until after 11.30 and has saved me all the bother of blacking out. My home-made black-out frames are falling to pieces, and I want to find a handyman to make me new ones.

In October we are to be rationed to half a pint of milk per adult per day. I can manage with this but with three cats it will be a watery half pint and there will be no milk puddings. We look forward to a lean winter – more and more food rationed, fuel rationed, clothes rationed. Oil for lamps is difficult to get now and has been for some time.

Saw Greta Garbo in *Ninotchka* this afternoon, but somehow it failed to entertain me as it might have done had I seen it before Russia entered the war – and before our eggs were rationed. It seemed in rather bad taste to be laughing at the Bolsheviks now.

Ordinary fruit cordials unobtainable. Bought some orange and lemon wine essence for summer drinks today but they are horribly synthetic. I lunched in Slough at Williamsons – steak and kidney pudding (rather much pudding and rather much gristle but eatable and filling) with greens, then tinned pears and thick custard, and coffee – 1s 8½d. Bought one of their cream sponge cakes – their cakes are still good but do not keep.

148

Pam Ashford

Mr Mitchell introduced me to Mr Wilkinson who took us all over his warehouse. He said before the war he never had less than 22 pianos there, but today there were none. I said, with childlike innocence, 'When the war is over I want a new piano,' and nearly got involved in a sale on the spot. Mr Wilkinson said, 'Pianos are going to be much dearer after the war.'

For one wireless set there today, he had 100 before the war. He thought a make called Rogers the best, ranging from £16 to £120. Their factory has been bombed out and there will be no more Rogers sets till after the war.

It surprised me the range of instruments there are that the soldiers in Iceland would enjoy. There are banjos, guitars, concertinas and all sorts of things whose names I don't know. We have already sent Jaw Harps (formerly Jews' Harps).

Ernest van Someren

Cycled to work, spent most of the day drying a piece of specially treated string, and calculating the surprising implications of the results. It was a new experiment which threw light on a lot of work I have been doing lately.

In the evening Mr H called to see the hens, as he is going to look after them while I am away. He killed the sick one for me. After some hesitation I decided not to pluck and draw it, a thing I've never done yet, and would not enjoy.

WEDNESDAY, 13 AUGUST

Ernest van Someren

At work we had a sample of vinegar in from the canteen which was full of visible wriggly objects. With some trouble I found out from an old book on microscopy that they are called 'vinegar eels', and although a kind of worm are not parasitic.

Maggie Joy Blunt

All day a drizzle. I spent the morning, after breakfast in bed as is my custom, pottering about the house, sucking barley sugar (1s for ½ lb), preparing a vegetable stew, French beans picked from the garden and rhubarb and bread steamed pudding. The stew and beans I served with a thick Parmesan sauce for my lunch. Pudding was not cooked in time so ate two pastry cases (bought for 1d each) filled with cherry jam. Afterwards dozed until 3.30pm over the last volume of *Tom Jones*, sucking more barley sugar and feeling very ashamed of my gluttony and idleness. So made tea, finished a scone and had two slices of Williamsons' cream sponge and now feel sick but determined to do some work.

Matches, I note, we are now getting from India and Thailand. They have a lean, brown, oriental look.

THURSDAY, 14 AUGUST

Pam Ashford

Opening the papers this morning we read that Mr Attlee was to make an important announcement at 3, and the 8 o'clock bulletin gave this publicity too. It was, of course, something to do with America, but what? My own reaction was this: 'The Sunday on which we concluded the alliance with Russia the BBC made a similar announcement and then when the news came, the obviousness of it produced an anticlimax. It will be just the same again.' So much for me. Mother was emphatic both at 8 and at 1 that 'Great Britain was going to declare war on Japan.' Mr Mitchell: 'Great Britain and America are going to give Japan a warning that if she does any more monkeying about, they will attack her.'

Miss Bousie: 'America has declared war.' I: 'No. If it were that, Mr Churchill would be the speaker.' Miss Bousie: 'But where is Mr Churchill?' I: 'There is something mysterious about that.' Miss Bousie: 'He is with Roosevelt.' This view astonished me and I said, 'Do you think Roosevelt's cruise has taken him across the Atlantic?' Miss Bousie: 'No, Mr Churchill has gone over to America.' Returning from the bank later Miss Bousie reported that all the chalked notices ran, 'Where is Churchill?'

Later Mr Mitchell told us how Mr Churchill and Mr Roosevelt had met in the Atlantic.

Maggie Joy Blunt

Attlee announced today that Churchill and President Roosevelt have met at sea and declared certain rather nebulous war – or was it peace? – aims. What is astonishing, daring and delightful about this news is that these two important people have met *at sea* . . .

Red Army has abandoned Smolensk. Paper today is full of the exploits of the RAF during recent raids on Cologne and Berlin.

My cigarettes are still limited to 10 a day.

Edward Stebbing

I did not hear Mr Attlee's broadcast this afternoon, but two of my superiors did and afterwards I heard them talking about it. 'Well, it wasn't half so drastic as I expected. I expected at least that America had declared war,' said one.

If the resulting statement, as given out by Attlee, was not dramatic, the meeting itself (between Churchill and Roosevelt, at sea) was. I asked my sister if she was disappointed or not; she said she was. My father was too.

Ernest van Someren
Indigestion worse, went to work by train. I wonder if it was started by a little vinegar I had on Tuesday, or by some war-time cheese we had that day at home. In the evening K made a delicious soup from our dead hen, which I took to the butcher to have 'dressed' yesterday. Thickened with rice I ate a lot for my supper. After supper drafted a letter of application for a rather unlikely job.

FRIDAY, 15 AUGUST

Maggie Joy Blunt
Have begun to use cold boiled rice for breakfast and with salad for lunch. A success. Cooking and eating apples fairly plentiful at controlled price of 8d – but such miserable specimens. We would not have paid 2d for them before the war. Still 'No Sweets, No Cigarettes' at our tobacconists. I have cigarettes to last me 28 more days at 10 a day. But Mavis and Jules have promised to collect more for me and I will tramp round London again myself soon.

SATURDAY, 16 AUGUST

Ernest van Someren
Started my annual holiday of one week. Our daily help Hilda came too. At Newbury we got a taxi to Alderwood House Community School, which is on the edge of a common nearly four miles out of the town, about 450 ft above sea level and commanding a lovely view of the Hampshire downs.

We had a cup of tea and slice of cake on a porch with other guests.

SUNDAY, 17 AUGUST

Ernest van Someren
I slept poorly, partly because Julia was in our room. Hilda and L shared the next room, in fact I lay awake at night worrying about the threatened reduction in the milk consumption of the nation and its implications, which are very grim.

Poor K was bitten on the eyelid by a mosquito. They are so active here that the school provided a bottle of citronella in every room as a preventive measure, and each night at bedtime I went round the room killing them while Julia had her last feed.

After that L and I went out to the post, about 10 mins walk, which took a long time as we met a convoy of light artillery and stopped to stare a lot. One of the men was convalescing from broken ankles (he had been run over by a farm implement).

Pam Ashford

One always seems to enter a new world when one goes to Ralston.

Lil overlooks the golf course. One time when I was there she was full of the Home Guards practising there and the way they dug trenches into which the golfers' balls rolled. Now there is the additional complication that the army is encamped there too. Lil enjoys watching the soldiers fetching big mugs of tea from a canteen and gave me field glasses to watch the operation, but it seemed to me that what I was watching was them forming fours.

MONDAY, 18 AUGUST

Maggie Joy Blunt

Am reading *I Came Out of France* by Cecily Mackworth – story of a young woman's escape last year when France capitulated. Written quietly, easily, it gives a vivid picture of the fantastic horrors the refugees went through. One can hardly believe it. People swarming from the north, from the south, over-running country towns and villages; no food, no medical attention, no petrol; wild rumours, contradictory orders; suspicion, mistrust, hunger, illness, death.

One feels one had no business to be sleeping comfortably and eating well when the French nation was suffering so much. They expected then that it would only be a matter of a few weeks or possibly days before we capitulated. But we didn't. The Germans haven't conquered us yet – nearly 15 months later. But what will their tactics be when they have had enough of their bloody push into Russia? They are gaining ground in the Ukraine. They are making tremendous efforts to win this campaign before the seasons change. And if they do win . . .?

Age groups of women to register are creeping up. The sooner I get myself into a really useful job the better.

Pam Ashford

There was no end of talk today about preserving fruit, etc. It was said that fruit growing districts have their fruit rotting on the bushes through lack of pickers. Mrs Tucker got raspberries and gooseberries given her that way. She made raspberry jam, took off the scum of course, and then she put the scum in with the gooseberries to sweeten them. It works. Wild fruits were discussed too. Whortleberries make good jam though most people only know them in tarts.

TUESDAY, 19 AUGUST

Ernest van Someren

My 38th birthday. L gave me a birthday postcard with a picture of a train on it, his own choice. We took him to Newbury by bus, and wandered round the main streets shopping. K tried to buy me a safety-razor-blade sharpener but could not find a good one. We went to a café and had large fills of coffee and buns and ices. It's a nice small town, peaceful except for convoys of armoured vehicles.

After supper K and I went for a walk, round the common and to the nearest pub, which was shut.

SUNDAY, 24 AUGUST

Ernest van Someren

Spent most of the day in the garden, picked 7 lbs of French beans. Laurie was rather rackety and at various times broke two cups and a window, spread over the day.

After supper we listened to Churchill's talk, good and not as depressing as sometimes, in fact a very good speech.

MONDAY, 25 AUGUST

Edward Stebbing

I asked a man I work with what he thought of Churchill's speech. 'Well,' he said, 'I've heard more fiery ones.' I said, 'I prefer them when they're not so fiery.' On the British invasion of Iran, he said he thought we were right in getting in there before Germany.

Two women on the bus were talking about milk rationing, remarking on the smallness of it. 'If they increased the butter ration it wouldn't be so bad. I don't mind about the cheese, but I do like a bit o' butter . . . And the beastly old marge is horrible, isn't it?'

TUESDAY, 26 AUGUST

Pam Ashford

It is eight. The BBC is just announcing that Myra Hess is to give a Beethoven programme.

8.30: it goes without saying that the diary halted for half an hour. Music soothes and encourages as nothing else can. I must hurry over this entry for Vic Oliver and Sarah Churchill are coming on now. That is the only humour to which I listen. BBC vaudeville annoys and bores me. So does Vic Oliver at times, for his jokes don't always pass with me, but all the same he is very funny.

WEDNESDAY, 27 AUGUST

Pam Ashford

Rumours are going all over the place about City office workers (girls) who understood they were indispensable and are now being whisked away to make munitions. I say rumours.

I am aware of the fact that men don't see why women should object to being conscripted, but you don't need to look or listen long to find that women look at it differently. The fact is that the young women who don't mind being regimented volunteered. Among the others there are a tremendous number of women who regard life in the Forces as just about knocking the bottom out of their existence. Emotional natures never did and never will take to regimentation and emotional natures loom larger among women than men. The fear of leaving home is outstanding too. If and when registration reached my age (38) I expect I shall be upset about it too.

THURSDAY, 28 AUGUST

Edward Stebbing

The attempted assassination of Laval is welcome news. It shows that all is not quiet in France and it may rid the world of one of its evil influences.

SATURDAY, 30 AUGUST

Edward Stebbing

Tried about 10 shops before I was able to obtain some tobacco. For some time I believed the Government assertions that supplies were low because people were smoking much more than they used to, but now I have come to the conclusion that this is merely their excuse for their failure to maintain supplies. There has been a shortage now for many weeks, so it is impossible for anyone to smoke more than previously, yet there is still no improvement.

MONDAY, 1 SEPTEMBER

Pam Ashford
I wear my hair (two long thick plaits) round my head in halo fashion but that style is getting obsolete, and I have been practising with a curl on the top and side combs. I have used Mother's grey combs, and decided to buy dark brown ones today to match my hair, and do you know, not only are there no side combs but there are no combs of any description. I go through combs (ordinary ones) more quickly than some people do – the teeth fly heavenwards over the thick tangles, and on occasions the comb snatches midships. This limitation of supplies is going too far. I knew that the limitation of hairdressers' equipment was forcing the shorthaired to grow long hair, and Good Lord! now the shortage of combs is to force the longhaired to – do what?

Edward Stebbing
I listened to the news at a friend's. I wonder why we have to register for onions and not for other vegetables.

WEDNESDAY, 3 SEPTEMBER

Maggie Joy Blunt
Two years ago, we are reminded by Press and BBC, war was declared. For two years I have been lucky, living so happily here. But the time is coming when I shall have to make sacrifices, like everyone else. There seems to be no hope of the war ending for years. The future appears dreary and incalculable. I cannot expect anyone to understand what it will mean to me to give up my indolent cottage life. The problem of what to do with the cats, for instance, seems appalling. They have become individuals whom I love, who love and trust me. If the worst happens and I am pushed into uniform (I don't WANT to be pushed into uniform) no one will want to feed and care for three cats for me. Stella might be persuaded to have Dinah or Kittyhawk, or perhaps M, or perhaps they would take one each. But that leaves Ginger. It seems inevitable that Ginger would have to go. But here I go, worrying about things before they happen.

Pam Ashford

There has been much talk about the mock invasion. Tear gas was sprayed in a number of Glasgow areas. Miss MacLean going to Helensburgh by bus had to wear her gas mask; it was so hot that she was almost suffocated. Miss Craigie tells me that she and her mother were in Byres Road just after it had been sprayed and they saw a girl who had no mask in a pitiable state. The mock invasion seems to have been thoroughly enjoyed by all the participants, though they have since been complaining of feeling tired.

Mr Mitchell has come upon an Austrian Jew who is making fancy leather goods and would like to do some export business. He was in a concentration camp in Germany and has been telling Mr Mitchell what an awful time he had, but Mr Mitchell has not given me details.

Miss Hall of Jane Seymour, Ltd.!!!! Not a sales representative, however, but the Managing Director's secretary. We knew she was on holiday at her hometown of Dunfermline and this morning she 'phoned to say she would like to come through to see us.

She and I are about the same age, and I took an immense liking for her. She has a very plain face, and did not look as if she had any make-up on at all, which I suppose is a credit to her skill in applying it; her face was, however, very pimply, though it is not for me to say whether there is any connection between that and the beauty culture.

Seeing Miss Hall, I said, 'Here am I pushing your products my hardest and never put a scrap on myself yet,' to which she said, 'Why should you? You don't need make-up. What a lovely complexion. If I had your cheeks I would not put on make-up.' She thereupon went on to explain I could do with cleansing lotion, Juniper skin tonic, petal lotion, petal cream, triangular patches of fuchsia colour powder on the cheekbones and my 'lovely red lips' could do with having the cupid's bow enhanced by Jane Seymour No. 3 lipstick.

Jane Seymour's factory has not been damaged, but it is in a very bad part of London and Miss Hall said it was estimated that only one factory in five had escaped. I said how many of the London firms we write have temporary addresses, and she said yes. In London you phone and get no answer and the Exchange tells you the connection is broken. 'It is all rather fun,' said Miss Hall.

Ernest van Someren

By train to town, and did a little shopping. Spent a gift-token at Boots and bought a view-finder for a camera, both presents for my own birthday recently. I wanted to go to see *Fantasia* but it would have made me very late home. Did some shopping in Soho which is sadly depleted but one still hears plenty of French and Italian spoken in the streets.

THURSDAY, 4 SEPTEMBER

Edward Stebbing

Was very interested in the article in *Picture Post* on astrology. It shows up the newspaper astrologists for the worthless impostors they really are. Pseudo-scientific, they exploit the credulity of the uneducated masses. There should be more articles like this until these misleaders of public opinion are driven from the pages of the Press.

FRIDAY, 5 SEPTEMBER

Edward Stebbing

Interesting piece of local news is the rejection by an urban council of a proposal to ban the works of P.G. Wodehouse from the local library. Most members took the broad view that they were works of art which had nothing to do with the writer's political activities. It was up to the public not to borrow his books if they didn't want to. The motion was defeated by 14 votes to 5.

Maggie Joy Blunt

I have no business to feel tired so often and so much. It is wearing me out. Even my passion for the garden is not what it was. This evening I layered the carnations but at the outset it seemed a task demanding more energy than I could summon. Apart from that little job I have done nothing important beyond chores all day. Perhaps my mail this morning is responsible: the Publicity Department of the MOWB is full. There is no vacancy on the staff of *The Builder*. Yesterday I tried to crash into the Press Department of the British Council without success. It is incredible how a few refusals can depress one, make one feel unwanted, a meddling amateur or a tiresome pusher. Shall I put an ad in the *Architectural Journal* or write to other journals or do both? What about the local papers – should like to work in Windsor.

SATURDAY, 6 SEPTEMBER

Ernest van Someren

In the afternoon out with K and L and Julia to call on my colleague Harry P. We ate a huge tea, his wife is a Yorkshire girl with a high standard of housework. We went home by crowded buses, a strange man took L on his knee and gave him a biscuit to eat.

Pam Ashford

The Viennese Jew I mentioned came up this morning and as Mr Mitchell was out I entertained him at the counter.

He has been in this country for two years and knew no English whatever before coming to us. He speaks very quickly – more quickly than I do in fact – but makes many mistakes and his vocabulary is limited. I found it hard work following him. He was extremely nice, full of smiles, and good spirits. He got into trouble when the Nazis invaded Austria. He showed me his photo from three years ago and he had certainly changed in that time. 30lbs lost in weight he said.

He was at Dachau Concentration Camp and escaped nine times (if this figure is wrong, excuse me, his English was so poor) into Romania, Poland and Czechoslovakia, and time after time the Gestapo hunted him down. He at last got away to this country. He did not describe the torture (which I did not want to hear – at any rate not at the counter) but he held out his hands and said, 'See what they did to me.' I think they must have torn his nails off, but I was afraid to look closely or answer. How he loves Vienna and Austria – the music, the countryside, the wine, the kind natures of Austrians, their friendship for this country, of all these he spoke; and how he disliked the Germans and their militaristic strutting, which he imitated for my benefit. I said, 'It is the Prussians,' but he persisted in saying 'Germans'.

He is making leather goods here with girls whom he is training. Since he came to this country he has married a Viennese woman refugee, a furrier, also with a business of her own in Vienna, and also a former inmate of a concentration camp. They did not know each other before, and she is much younger then he, but they love each other deeply. They work very hard, last night they went on until 3am. I said, 'You need your rest, don't work as hard as that,' but he said, 'We have lost too much time and too many money, we must work hard to make up for it.'

SUNDAY, 7 SEPTEMBER

Edward Stebbing

My sister asked me if I would go to church with her, as it was a National Day of Prayer, but I said no. I think these prayers for victory are absolute hypocrisy. Carry on this war to the bitter end we must, but do not let us bring God into it. Why should God help us kill more Germans than the Germans can kill Englishmen? God is on neither side, or both, and if every day were a day of prayer I do not think it would make the slightest difference to the outcome of the war. We have not been so righteous in the past that God should be on our side. People may get some comfort from praying to God, but it is a false comfort, and they are really blinding themselves to reality. I do not say this because I do not believe in God, but because I do not believe in prayer.

MONDAY, 8 SEPTEMBER

Maggie Joy Blunt
One is living at an intense tension. This war – endless, vindictive slaughter, drama, heroics, destruction. While a serene moon shines full upon ally and foe. What does the future hold? Will Germany defeat Russia? Are we doing all, to the full extent of our power, or is effort frustrated by red-tape, ambition over-riding ability? There are hundreds, thousands of ordinary people anxious to do what they can towards winning this war, and on every side one hears of girls knitting in factories, the wrong man in the job, delay in the Civil Service departments, men and women everywhere badly organised, not given a chance to do the work they can and want to do for the community . . .

Ernest van Someren
This morning found a hen dead, she had been ailing for 2–3 days.

TUESDAY, 9 SEPTEMBER

Edward Stebbing
Left home at a day's notice to take up another post some distance away. My work is that of pathological laboratory technician, for which the RAMC gave me training, so that however much I disliked the Army I have something to thank it for.

On the way there our bus was stopped by the police and all passengers had to produce their identity cards. One woman had not got hers, so the police inspector asked her whether she knew she could be detained for it and gave her a stern warning, but let her continue her journey.

Ernest van Someren
Mr Holmes rang up and asked if he could stay the night. He arrived as I was burying the hen.

We spent the evening talking about Holmes' job concerning flax development in this country. It is odd work, and he thinks there might be an opening for me there.

Pam Ashford

As I was taking my evening walk I could not help comparing it with the ones I took at the beginning of the war. The fresh breeze was the same, the weak sunshine the same, and the vegetation had the same degree of fadedness (though the gardens are more neglected now), but two years ago there was a fire in my veins. When the war is over I am going 'to let my ego rip', which is a phrase I found in a psychology textbook and though never quite sure what it means, I have always longed to do it. At any rate I take it that it means you release all your inhibitions simultaneously. Would not that be grand?

THURSDAY, 11 SEPTEMBER

Ernest van Someren

Another hen is seedy and we have isolated her in case it's infectious.

FRIDAY, 12 SEPTEMBER

Ernest van Someren

Cycled to work, after lunch did some enlargements of a portrait of the canteen dog. After work I hurried home to supper, then cycled out to Watton (9 miles) to have my back manipulated again. Then I cycled back in the dark, quite a pleasant ride, the most winding section of the road had reflecting studs to mark a white line down the middle of the road. I had some cider in Hoddesdon.

Pam Ashford

It is plain that I shan't get side combs. I am quite unknown to the hairdressing fraternity, and there is not a dog's chance of any of them serving me.

SATURDAY, 13 SEPTEMBER

Pam Ashford

Today the Cosmo had *Tales from the Vienna Woods* and it was very enjoyable. I thought many times of the Viennese Jew as I saw it this afternoon. Last Monday I had got a complimentary ticket for this film, intending him to have it, but a member of the staff – I leave you to guess who – took it away from me insisting that the Jew could afford to pay for himself.

Ernest van Someren

The new gadget which I made at work is a special type of thermometer, it turns out to be very sensitive as I hoped and may well be quite useful. Home and found the sick hen had died.

Mr Hodgkin came in earlier, at my invitation, and did a post mortem on the hen to show me the way about. We concluded she had not died of an infectious complaint, but some ovarian trouble and then heart failure. This is depressing, as we are again down to four hens having lost two this week. L watched us at first, but soon lost interest in the messy body.

MONDAY, 15 SEPTEMBER

Ernest van Someren

It smelt like autumn for the first time. Worked on my new gadget, which is disappointing. In the evening went to a PPU meeting after tea, a debate on the subject of the pacifist's attitude to the move for a negotiated peace now. I took the line that it was now impossible, and that people were not ready for it, so that it was not a primary aim for us. This was disputed on principle, with a cheerful disregard for the impossible which characterises all religious movements.

WEDNESDAY, 17 SEPTEMBER

Maggie Joy Blunt

I worked in the garden all the afternoon until it was dark. Today, except for the flowers and the green leaves everywhere, is like a fine day in late October. I find autumn more moving than spring. It has a mellow, melancholy beauty that touches me deeply. A day such as this when a golden mist, very faint, very lovely is spread between the earth and the clear sky, is full of memories. Memories of events, momentous events, that ended an adventure or started me upon a new one. Wood smoke and chrysanthemums. Summer holidays over. First days at school, at my father's office, at UCL . . .

A feeling of dread, of loneliness, of being turned from a comfortable secure life into unknown paths, among unfamiliar faces, occupied with new, difficult tasks while the weather is burningly beautiful in gold and blue and beechen copper. Summer over and winter ahead – I do not know what lies ahead for me this winter (no one ever does) but I know what lies behind and I know that sooner or later that freedom and that luscious idleness will be over too.

Ernest van Someren

K and L made a bonfire. L was a bit naughty in the garden, cutting vegetable plants about. He is very defiant frequently. Had my income tax assessment today. I like the idea that nearly one third of it will be a post-war credit, and on the whole I favour high income tax partly because it is fair, partly because the increase in salary and war bonus awarded me this year just covers it. Have heard several people at work grumbling about their unexpectedly large tax demands.

Pam Ashford

Mr Mitchell is as nice as possible again now. The change was marked yesterday when he spent part of the morning writing an Ode to commemorate the eighteenth anniversary of his wedding, which is today. According to him, Mrs Mitchell had been very depressed about it on Monday and he was wanting to cheer her up. In it he commented upon her 41 summers, and I had to point out that Mrs Mitchell is only 40. This involved much discussion between us and when I had won my point, it turns out that to get the rhythm right she must remain 41, but he is going to explain he means 'in her 41st year'. I could not but think that if Mrs Mitchell goes through what I have to some days, it is no wonder she feels depressed.

THURSDAY, 18 SEPTEMBER

Pam Ashford

It is a nice clear evening and I got around to the allotment where the dandelions continue to grow to a size so immense that they must thrill Dick to the very marrow of his bones.

FRIDAY, 19 SEPTEMBER

Ernest van Someren

After a large tea went to the Friends Hall where we had arranged a WEA meeting for a MOI film show. A disappointingly small audience arrived and we had a very interesting show of 8 short films on the navy coal products, silage, Christmas 1940 and such subjects.

Pam Ashford

The allotment continues to produce its finest in dandelion kind. Tonight I was out the unprecedently long time of 60 minutes and when I got back Mother was worked up thinking that some allotment holder had been wanting me arrested for pinching vegetables. There certainly have been many times when I have wondered at the

162

complete absence of restraint with which I can walk around people's vegetables.

Last night I thought the ARP was out in rather large force, and this morning Miss Gibson told me that they were practising till midnight and were to start off again tonight on a 'gas-incident'. These civil defence workers enjoy themselves. I wish, how I wish, I could be one with them, but that cannot be, and Mass-Observation is really a great blessing to me. Although few people know about the diary, it helps to restore my self-respect and makes me feel I have a war job too.

Edward Stebbing
Conversation this evening included some comment on the war in Russia. Two of the men thought that a British attack in the West was necessary and not unlikely; they discussed where a landing might be made. One of them said he didn't think the Germans would ever vanquish Russia; they could not even hold what they had won through the winter.

SATURDAY, 20 SEPTEMBER

Maggie Joy Blunt
I HAVE GOT A JOB. Don't believe it, but there it is, beginning on October 2nd on an architectural paper in London. So much to do now in preparation and tidying up – don't know where to begin. Saw T yesterday too (another architect editor) and he thinks also that there will be a boom in architectural journalism after the war.

Germany claims to have taken Kiev but Russian communiqués do not confirm this. The fighting on Russian soil is terrible, *terrible*. We feel that our aid is tardy, we fear the weight of anti-Russian influences in power.

SUNDAY, 21 SEPTEMBER

Edward Stebbing
The capture of Kiev by the Germans comes as more of a shock because it was unexpected and carried out apparently without much struggle. It was almost too easy. If it had been Leningrad or Odessa, it would not have been such a blow. However, perhaps this will serve to speed up our help to Russia, which now becomes even more urgent.

Maggie Joy Blunt

Ella this evening on the phone spoke glowingly of 'The News'. I could only think of the struggle for Kiev but she was referring to our bombing sweeps over the continent.

Yesterday the greengrocer brought me two oranges. He said, 'Don't think that the war is over!'

MONDAY, 22 SEPTEMBER

Edward Stebbing

Talking about the Russian war this dinnertime, remarks were made on the way in which German claims are usually admitted by the Allies after being denied for about three days. 'It gets you down,' said one man, 'the way they deny it for three days, then admit it.' Someone else said he didn't like the way the radio announcer kept saying, 'these reports are of course unconfirmed'. Another said if you wanted to know the truth about the land (but not the air) operations it was best to read the German communiqués. Then the conversation turned on to the newspaper military 'experts', whose articles were unanimously condemned as utter nonsense. One man said it was sometimes impossible to tell the difference between some of the military experts and *Beachcomber*, and we wondered why they got paid for it.

Pam Ashford

The Soroptomist Club again. There was a wedding in the next room and Mrs Kenmure (minister) with whom I walked up the street said she had had at least one wedding every week for months past. What looks like a wedding cake nowadays is a cardboard cover which is lifted off and the edible part is underneath. Marzipan (very good too) is used as a sandwich with a slab of cake below and another above – apparently marzipan on the top is contrary to the law.

TUESDAY, 23 SEPTEMBER

Maggie Joy Blunt

5.30pm

I have worried myself into a fever over the prospect of this job. Temperature last night was 100.6 – am sure due to over anxiety! So terrified am I that something will happen to prevent my starting on October 2nd or that I shall do something foolish and irrevocable when I do begin. So stupid. A nasty head cold accompanies the fever

164

and makes me feel very miserable. Just when I wanted to be full of energy to put my affairs in order!

8pm
The story of advertising has yet to be told. It will be a long and dramatic one. Glancing through this week's *Radio Times* I see the names of commodities that are now part of the fabric of the nation, such familiar names but they may not be used in articles, stores, novels, plays and broadcasts – in any of the things that make familiar things more familiar to us. But they have their influence and place. In my life, for instance – Gibbs Dentifrice: a pink block in a silvery tin that I used when very young until something about it enraged me (I smashed the tin and have never used it since). Rothman's Cigarettes, first smoked in quantity when I was at UCL, introduced by friend Sarah, but now banned to me because I was never a 'regular' customer. Odol, toothpaste and gargle which I bought with enthusiasm when they first appeared because of their bright light blue and white packs. Halex toothbrushes, good, colourful, I buy them often. Kruschen Health Salts in a dark brown jar from which I carefully extracted the prescribed amount to cover a sixpence in my early teens believing with ardour that they would solve all my problems. Malteser chocolates, delectable, introduced to me by June at Hampstead but now seldom to be seen except at the canteen when I hand them over the counter to the Tommies. Hartley's jams, Bournville cocoa, Peak Freen biscuits, Sifta salt, Pepsodent toothpaste – which I was warned by a cousin-in-law's dentist against using as it scratched the enamel, but did use. Lux toilet soap, Kelloggs Cornflakes, Seniors fish and meat pastes. Carters Little Liver Pills – the name spread on huge hoardings facing railway tracks. Caley's chocolates, Grey's cigarettes.

All these things and so many more have been and are part of my material existence, and have their associations and value. But take away the proprietary name and what have we: cigarettes, soap, cocoa, chocolate, toothpaste . . . Do we need so many varieties?

THURSDAY, 25 SEPTEMBER

Maggie Joy Blunt
One's life does not move in precise, distinct sections, it moves all the time, a continuous movement of threads weaving this way and that into a pattern we don't know.

N has been warning me not to underestimate my ability, not to allow myself to be exploited by a Tory editor, to stick out for my own work, not to sign away my liberty, to insist on a rise at the end of 6 months, and so on. I am starting at £3. 10s.

MONDAY, 29 SEPTEMBER

Edward Stebbing
The two papers I have read today both give a good deal of space to H.G. Wells' speech to the British Association. One recognises the need for planning a better future, but now I am getting rather fed up with all the new World Plans, World Brains, World Encyclopaedias, charters, declarations etc., when in reality there is no worldwide feeling in favour of any one of them. What good are all the rules and regulations if the spirit is not there?

WEDNESDAY, 1 OCTOBER

Maggie Joy Blunt
My last day of freedom! There have been irksome domestic responsibilities I shall in future escape. There won't be so many meals to think about and prepare, and Fanny is coming in every day except Friday and the weekend. It is odd to think that so long as I was here, alone and 'free', I submitted to do so much household tyranny – shopping, cooking, pottering. It seemed to fill three quarters of the day. Now it is to be reduced to one quarter. I could not discipline myself sufficiently to reduce it to that on my own.

Yesterday ordered a coat and skirt at Peter Jones for 13 guineas. An appalling price and 18 coupons, but I look on it as an investment. I can manage now with the clothes I have for at least a year. Stockings will be the only problem. At present I have six pairs and shall be able to wear one pair a day through the week, washing each every night when I take them off which should help to make them last. But I am very hard on stockings.

Letter this morning from Cousin M in Russia with RAF. He says that the Russians have obviously been concentrating on armament production for a long time, that they are supremely confident of victory, have not even yet fully mobilised the Army and that the British have been well and very efficiently received.

Army manoeuvres in South and Aldershot areas all this week against a mock invasion.

Chapter Six

THE *ARK ROYAL* HAS GONE DOWN

Got my clothing coupons: a non-woollen dress in Selfridges goes for 7 points.

2 October–8 December 1941

2 October Hitler launches Operation Typhoon, the concentrated assault on Moscow.

12 October The British begin another operation to relieve the Australian garrison in Tobruk.

20 October Stalin declares a state of siege in Moscow, urging Russian citizens to hold firm until the winter comes to their aid; a few days later he strengthens calls for the Allies to establish a Second Front in Europe.

5 November In Tokyo, Admiral Isoruku Yamamoto gains support for his proposed attack on Pearl Harbor.

14 November The *Ark Royal* sunk off the coast of Gibraltar.

21 November Roosevelt rejects Japanese peace terms, claiming they would provide unacceptable control of the western Pacific.

22 November The British cruiser *Devonshire* sinks *Atlantis*, destroyer of 22 Allied ships, but HMS *Barham* is destroyed three days later.

27 November Britain gains final victory over Italian forces in Ethiopia.

4 December Conscription regulations in Britain are extended to cover men over 18 years and six months, while unmarried women between 20 and 30 are required to work for the emergency services.

6 December Soviet forces gain ground in Moscow as winter takes hold.

7 December Japanese planes attack US Fleet at Pearl Harbor, bringing the United States into the war.

THURSDAY, 2 OCTOBER

Maggie Joy Blunt
An incredibly casual office. It does not matter if I do not get there until 10am. Everyone clears off by 4.30pm. We do not work on Saturdays. No one pays any attention to the contract one has to sign. Most of the work seems to be done by Assistant Editor M and Ed's secretary Miss St, aided by P. Ed seems to be away. So far I have read papers for 'news' and have been given a series of articles on roof construction to sub. Am not at the moment threatened with overwork . . . I catch the 8.20 Green Line bus in the morning which takes me to Hyde Park Corner by about 9.30, and a bus home from there about 5pm so that I am back here about 6.30pm. Fetter Lane – there is hardly anything left of it. Must have had 2 or 3 landmines. It looks terrible. No matches anywhere. But food situation and imports generally appear much brighter.

FRIDAY, 3 OCTOBER

Maggie Joy Blunt
Miss St knows some manufacturers of chocolate biscuits who are still making enough profit to buy a boat they intend to convert into a houseboat. Their chief trouble at the factory is to get and keep staff, as they fill their gas masks and pockets with biscuits but employers dare say nothing lest they walk out!

Sat for part of my lunch in Lincolns Inn. Heavenly spot. A bed of dahlias near the tennis court.

Edward Stebbing
I drew attention to the ludicrousness of the Anglo–German agreement to cease hostilities over the Channel for two days while sick and wounded men are exchanged. My landlady's daughter said, 'Isn't it daft? What do they keep on fighting for, then? That's what they send the bombers out for, to kill each other.'

SATURDAY, 4 OCTOBER

Edward Stebbing
Having got my clothing coupons, today I used 18 of them, together with ten emergency coupons. These were spent on a shirt and an order for a new suit without waistcoat. At the pictures tonight, the audience had claps for Churchill in his RAF uniform, but bigger claps for Russian troops.

SUNDAY, 5 OCTOBER

Edward Stebbing
In yesterday's *Daily Express* and today's *News of the World* the most important items, I think, were the appeals for a relaxation of the black-out, lights to be controlled by a master-switch. The black-out is undoubtedly a dominating factor in most people's lives. It weighs down tremendously on public morale. If the lights were to go up again I am sure people's spirits would soar enormously.

Mrs H said she reckoned the reason for the delay in the exchange of British and German sick and wounded was that the Germans wanted us to hand over Hess, but of course we shouldn't be such fools.

MONDAY, 6 OCTOBER

Maggie Joy Blunt
The exchange of prisoners between us and Germany seems to me fantastic. In the middle of the bloodiest, the most hot-headed of wars, the two governments pause, bow to each other at a polite distance above the heat of battle, command a truce over an area of the channel so that the wounded, the women and children of each can return to their own countries. If they can do that why can't they agree to stop the war altogether?

(These ships did not sail. All arrangements were cancelled and the prisoners sent back to their camps on October 8th. That MONSTER Hitler.)

WEDNESDAY, 8 OCTOBER

Pam Ashford
The Royal Philosophical Society started off tonight with Sir William Whyte on 'Replanning Towns'. I am quite sure that his paper will read well in the printed proceedings of the Society. But as a speaker, he is the world's worst. Everything is read, everything monotonous, one page audible for two inaudible. But I got a good laugh (when I got home that is to say). Sir Daniel Stevenson sitting in front of me, and said, 'Do you think he would go away if I gave him twopence?' Incidentally I am delighted to be able to bring Sir Daniel's name into the diary. Sir Daniel ascribes his great age to playing croquet, and only the other day I saw him at it, I will not say as active as a two year old, but marvellous for 90.

171

THURSDAY, 9 OCTOBER

Pam Ashford
It is my birthday. Last week I ordered one red and one blue fleecelined pixie hood from a Birmingham wholesaler from whom we have purchased goods for export, the intention being to get Charlie and Mother to donate one each, but this morning a letter came that under the Limitation of Supplies Order they could not spare them. I walked around Arnott Simpson's at 5.30 and there are some wretched things. I don't know what I want. Before the war a gramophone record was a sure winner, but I am determined not to buy luxuries in wartime.

Edward Stebbing
Today's news is grave. Perhaps I have overrated the powers of the Russians, but I do not attach any blame to them; I feel rather sorry for them. But my main feeling is one of bitter, flaming anger at the inertia of our government. I may be prejudiced in this respect, but I do not think I am far from the truth when I say I think that our help to Russia has been almost negligible. My landlady, however, said, 'Oh, I think we're sending help as fast as we can.' I simply do not agree. I feel as though I want to say, 'Kick out the whole present Government and let's have a new one.' Whether I should be justified in saying this I don't know. But our lack of action of any description is almost beyond belief. Are not our leaders sufficiently alarmed even now to take action? Complacently to condemn ourselves, and whoever else may still be in the war, to heaven knows how long a struggle, when some offensive action might prove decisive, is criminal.

FRIDAY, 10 OCTOBER

Edward Stebbing
The *News Chronicle* today says, rightly I think, that public anger is mounting higher than ever over the Norway fiasco. I have hardly any feeling of disappointment or despair, only anger. The public has had enough of this war; to let it drag on, always to our disadvantage, is maddening. The cry, 'Why don't we do something?' epitomises all the ordinary person's feelings.

THURSDAY, 16 OCTOBER

Ernest van Someren
Spent a good deal of the evening trying to make candied orange-peel, with inadequate instructions in two books. It didn't turn out very well, but we don't like wasting any part of an orange nowadays.

Pam Ashford
It is simply awful propping Mr Mitchell up. My nature is not unsympathetic, and I could cope with grief (I had that when his little boy died of diphtheria, so it is not an empty phrase), but what happens is that he harangues me at a speed of about 200 words a minute, sometimes for as long as three hours, and I cannot get a word in edgeways. Anger, pettiness, egotism, self-pity come down on my head like an avalanche. I know the man well enough to know he benefits from this sort of catharsis – there is every possibility of him being quite pleasant the next day, but so far as I am concerned, it takes all the philosophy I have to hold out at all. It seems to me that in the last month I must have spoken about Mr Hutchison's kindness half a dozen times, but I do appreciate it in that sadly storm-tossed export department; in fact, I don't think I could ever bolster Mr Mitchell up, if there were not someone bolstering me up on the other side.

FRIDAY, 17 OCTOBER

Edward Stebbing
Mr H: 'It looks as though Japan will be in it in a week or so.' Myself: 'I expect that will bring America in too.' Mr H: 'Yes, I think America will have to come right in before it's finished. I don't think we can finish it on our own.' He did not think invasion likely, however, unless Germany conquers Russia, which he also did not think likely.

SUNDAY, 19 OCTOBER

Pam Ashford
Conversation in Glasgow continues to be about personal affairs and not about the war, but now and again someone does mention Moscow. The holocaust that is opening up there does not appal us, not because of any emotional deficiency, but because of an intellectual one, simply that the vastness of the operations and the remoteness of the scene are more than we can easily grasp. The remoteness of the scene! Just as a new world was revealed to astonished

European eyes after the discovery of America, so it is as if a new world were being revealed to us now, far to the East this time. The inhabitants of Russia might have been brown bears for all we used to know of them, and the discovery that they are not calls for an extension of one's world outlook, which we are making readily enough but with great surprise to ourselves.

TUESDAY, 21 OCTOBER

Pam Ashford

During the day in the office conversation turned on what we will do after the war. We heard about gorging ices, chocolate and cakes, about orgies of spending on clothes, about dancing till the small hours. All the wishes were of a pleasurable nature; all presumed victorious conclusion; all presumed a reversion to pre-war conditions. Sometimes one hears another view – a persistent belief that because unemployment began in 1920 unemployment must follow this war also. I say often, 'Reconstruction will give enough work to every pair of hands in the world,' but one comes up against that obstinate reply, 'We are not going to work hard unless we are well paid for it.'

I think the crisis that will precede the (successful) conclusion of the war will be titanic and I shan't know whether I am standing on my head or my heels. I am quite sure that if not on the armistice day, then some time in the following week, I shall go into hysterics and cry like a watering cart.

Ernest van Someren

One of the neighbours who is a Conscientious Objector has recently had his appellate tribunal, and can go on with his work or do relief work. He is a journalist, and in July was refused registration as a CO, so his wife found work this term as a teacher at a school a few miles away. They found a neighbour to look after their little boy, and Mr C was prepared to go to prison rather than into the Forces. Now they find themselves with a larger income than ever before. Harold Rowe, who lived here for some months, was only allotted non-combatant service by his tribunal, and is also appealing.

WEDNESDAY, 22 OCTOBER

Ernest van Someren

Another slightly frosty morning, cycled to work, enjoying the autumn smells and sunshine. Bought a pair of scissors for the lab on

174

the way to work – these are getting scarce. Our previous pair have got lost after being detached from the chain which I provided for them, so these have been soldered on to the chain, and on the other end I have had a wire hoop 8 inches across welded on, so as to be awkward to put in one's pocket.

SUNDAY, 26 OCTOBER

Edward Stebbing
I had rather a heated argument with my landlady over our help to Russia. She thinks our leaders know what they are doing and we should leave it all to them. My point is that it is not wise to leave everything to a few experts who do not necessarily know what is the best thing to do every time. Criticism is essential. I would not mindso much if the Government would consider all reasonable criticism before rejecting it; it is their obstinate refusal to take any notice at all of what is being said and thought by other people which I dislike.

MONDAY, 27 OCTOBER

Pam Ashford
I have spent all today doing accounts for Iceland. A boat should be loading soon. Doing these Icelandic and Faroese transactions sometimes reminds me of the scenic railway at the 1938 exhibition. The angles at which our prospects rise and fall are so steep, and there are the most startling changes of front.

Today a Mr Gudmundsson of Reykjavik presented himself at 10 and spent the day with Mr Mitchell, talking and visiting warehouses. He says the pilfering at the docks and on the liners is dreadful. People bore holes in wooden boxes, extract goods, and stick back again the piece of wood removed.

WEDNESDAY, 29 OCTOBER

Pam Ashford
Where do rumours come from? Mr Mitchell came in at 12 saying Canadian and British Forces had landed in France. Miss Bousie returned from the bank deeply moved by the news. The BBC have nothing to say on the subject, even as late as 9 pm. Telling Mother at 12.50 (prior to the 1 pm news) she said, 'It is a lie. We are not such fools as that.' Personally I was prepared to hear that a raid had occurred. The news filled Miss Bousie with a belief that peace would

175

be declared by Christmas. I said, 'The Germans cannot be licked as quickly as that.' But she is all for compromise.

THURSDAY, 30 OCTOBER

Pam Ashford
This is a different war from the last one. Now no one wants to give up civilian status and no one disguises the fact. That holds good for male and female. More and more we feel ourselves being moved by powers we cannot control.

Peacocks have a window full of Hallowe'en cakes (about 2/- each), chocolate covered with the usual decorations, and of course, a queue to buy them.

FRIDAY, 31 OCTOBER

Ernest van Someren
We had another parcel from Tessa a day or two ago, containing some chocolate and some guava jelly and a paper on spectrochemical analysis from the US Bureau of Standards, sent in exchange for one I sent them through her. I sent off an answer by air-mail today. After work went to a meeting of the Hoddesdon Hospitality Committee, the first for many months, to decide what to do next. Two girls were brought over and supported by this committee for two years, and went to school near here. One has started her training as a nurse, and is doing well, she is now 18 and we are no longer responsible for her. The other, although she came over allegedly wishing for training as a nurse, had no desire or talent that way at all, she is useless and unreliable, but fairly ornamental. We helped her find a job after she had left school at the request of the headmistress. Now she has gone off on her own in London, with no mentionable means of support. Although it isn't our responsibility now, we can't help wondering if there is anything we could do. Her obvious type of job is hostess in a dance club, and we hear she tried that and was stopped by the London police.

Home to supper, then three neighbours dropped in to listen to a BBC talk with us. We discussed education and schooling for a bit, and then one went and the other two stayed to look over our collection of Japanese lacquer cups.

SATURDAY, 1 NOVEMBER

Ernest van Someren
To a sort of club in Cavendish Sq where the Rheologist Club were gathered for our AGM and a discussion. Oddly enough as the president was absent they nominated me to the chair.

It was quite a job to steer the meeting to some measure of agreement on a policy before the advertised closing time of 3.30, but I managed it. One of the questions was 'What is a solid?' We must have been feeling very precise not to be able to settle it at all. In the end we compromised on agreeing to define how a solid should behave, and supplement it with examples of substances suggesting solidity.

TUESDAY, 4 NOVEMBER

Ernest van Someren
To work by train, billiards at lunchtime with a partner who only scored 6 in half an hour. Luckily our opponents were weak and I made about 50, which is unusual for me. Home to tea and massage and then to my doctor for manipulation.

SATURDAY, 8 NOVEMBER

Edward Stebbing
I have been reading Aldous Huxley's *Ends and Means* and my agreement with most of his ideas contrasts strangely with my desire for stronger assistance to Russia. For there is so much truth in Huxley's book that no one with an honest mind can ignore it. One of the key passages of the book is this: 'The world sanctions two systems of morality – one for private individuals, another for national and other groups. Men who, in private, are consistently honest, humane, and considerate, believe that when they are acting as the representatives of a group they are justified in doing things which, as individuals, they know to be utterly disgraceful.' This is a great truth. Men condone cruelty and injustice and dishonesty when it is the policy of their country, but condemn it in the lives of individuals.

Last night we were talking about 'after the war'. I said that really nobody would 'win' the war, as all concerned would come out worse off than they were before. My landlady said that after the war would be the time when our troubles really would start. She did not think people would be content with things as they were before the war. 'Besides, they know too much about Russia now,' she said, a remark which I think highly significant. On another occasion she said she thought it quite possible that there would be a revolution in this country after the war.

Ernest van Someren
We all went for a walk up to the edge of the woods and back across the former golf-course, now ploughed for oats and potatoes. Laurie was interested in everything as usual but he has been a bit of a nuisance today, in the morning he upset a cupboard and broke ten assorted glasses.

SUNDAY, 9 NOVEMBER

Edward Stebbing
Man's comment on Churchill's statement that the RAF is now as big as the Luftwaffe: 'That's the best piece of news I've heard for a long time.' Regarding after the war, he said, 'When we have won this war there won't be any half measures this time' (meaning in connection with our treatment of Germany).

TUESDAY, 11 NOVEMBER

Ernest van Someren
Cycled to work, was in the Drawing Office at 11 and no one took any notice of the Silence – I was reading and forgot it. I don't think it was observed in the factory either.

Edward Stebbing
Armistice Day. This has never had much significance for me, and today it has had less than ever. It is just a remembrance of futility and horror, but not as such: they call it heroism.

THURSDAY, 13 NOVEMBER

Pam Ashford
The agent who has sold us office supplies for export was in today and was speaking of the extreme scarcity of practically everything. He has finished his blotting paper quota until January and says blotting paper is going to become rare. HB pencils too – more than HH and BB.

The *Ark Royal* has gone down. 'That much-sunk ship!' is the first comment on everyone's lips. Next people ask about the loss of life; then come such remarks as 'This must be expected in wartime', and 'It is nothing to what we have done to the Italians'. Mr Mitchell says,

'The Germans will say she has been sunk all along and the British have only now admitted it.' Miss Bousie: 'And that will be the truth. The Germans did not ask "Where is the *Ark Royal*?" without a reason.'

FRIDAY, 14 NOVEMBER

Edward Stebbing
The first thought, or if not the first, the most serious, that comes to people when news such as the sinking of the *Ark Royal* is announced is of the number of lives involved. (It was the same when 37 of our bombers failed to return; people were reckoning up how many lives lost that meant.) When someone told us the news at lunchtime, the conversation of the men I was with dealt firstly with the embarrassment of the German propagandists through having 'sunk' the ship so many times before, then with the number of men on the ship, then with how it was sunk. When I got home to my lodgings Mr H said the ship was in tow at the time so that it was thought not so many lives were lost – one of the most consoling features of the news.

Ernest van Someren
Today Laurie learnt to read a few words, and Julia crawled her first forward step.

A quiet evening reading. We have some new library books, Linklater's autobiography and a psycho-analytical book called *Man Against Himself*. We fixed up an arc-lamp and had ultra-violet treatment on our toes for our chilblains.

TUESDAY, 18 NOVEMBER

Ernest van Someren
Left off early and went to buy myself a cycling cape, and bought a picture book for Laurie – not for immediate use but to keep and give him later when someone wants to give him a present and ask us to choose it.

Pam Ashford
The Russian winter is setting in, and the news reports German soldiers dying from cold on the battlefield. The Russians won't have mercy, no more than I should have on an invading army here, but all the same one feels one's heart strings plucked. Perhaps Mr Mitchell was in the same mood; for quite suddenly he said, 'I wonder what has happened to Harry Jakob?' and I said, 'And Johanna Brautigam. And

179

Margaret's brothers.' This is a conversation that often occurred in the early days of the war, and has laid unspoken and unthought (at least not much on my side) for perhaps as long as two years, and today there was a ring of pathos in our voices. We are inconsistent creatures, of course, for he goes about wanting every German on earth gassed as vermin, and I am desirous of learning to use a rifle against them.

Edward Stebbing
I am sure that not many people do football pools nowadays, but a man who was on fire-watching with me tonight spent a considerable time filling in his coupon.

THURSDAY, 20 NOVEMBER

Edward Stebbing
At last the Army is doing something. The advance into Libya, if big enough, may be a second front which will have important effects on the situation in Russia. A man's comment: 'I don't think they'll make the mistake of stopping halfway this time. They want to go right on to Tripoli.'

FRIDAY, 21 NOVEMBER

Ernest van Someren
To town by train, took K's watch to be mended again, it is so delicate that it goes wrong every few hours. It can be put right easily, but only by an expert.

At about four I fed the hens and gave Julia some orange juice, then took her for a little walk to see a new bungalow. The place is a study in the use of substitute and synthetic materials, built to last 12–15 years, largely of prefabricated slabs and sections. The roof is low-pitched and unlined, the bathroom is only 5ft 6ins square, but the sitting room is large and there is a refrigerator in the kitchen. There may be a call for a lot of houses some day of whatever materials are available, and one of our local builders is pioneering.

Pam Ashford
The Royal Infirmary collecting box has been unlocked and the contents removed. (We have a box in the office, by the way.) By whom? Nor is it an isolated instance of petty theft, there are others. The subject intrigues the staff more than the war in North Africa.

Edward Stebbing

Referring to the Libyan campaign, a man said, 'I don't know which is the worst to endure, the huzzahs and hosannahs of the advance, or the glib excuses for the retreat.'

SATURDAY, 22 NOVEMBER

Pam Ashford

We know who did it.

SUNDAY, 23 NOVEMBER

Pam Ashford

Feeling against Germany is terrible. Take this. I: 'The carnage now is nothing to what will come when Germany has been defeated in the field. The conquered nations of Europe are going to massacre every German they can lay hands on.' Mrs Stewart: 'That is our trump card.' I: 'Yes, but very shocking. I can see Gt. Britain and America protecting the Germans.' Mrs Stewart: 'An eye for an eye, and a tooth for a tooth, that is my policy.' I: 'My disposition includes mercy.' Mrs Stewart: 'I would have no mercy. If you could see my husband's arms (totally disabled in the last war)! And he is one of the lucky ones. (Wealthy.) He always insisted on our visiting regularly the men he knew at Ralston and Erskine (hospitals for totally disabled men). We were with one of them just a few hours before he died and he said then he wanted to exterminate every German. Bill says they did the most terrible things to the British wounded.' Mrs MacDonald joined in with stories of mutilations inflicted on Russian prisoners of war, the truth of which I don't doubt.

SATURDAY, 29 NOVEMBER

Edward Stebbing

Three posters have attracted my attention today. The first was a Ministry of Health one which says 'Coughs and Sneezes Spread Diseases' and then says 'Use Your Handkerchief'. The next one was issued by the Communist Party and says, as near as I can remember, 'Start an Offensive in the West Now'. The third was a National Savings one, a variation on an old one, 'Lend to Defend *His* Right to be Free.' This shows a picture of a little boy and should appeal to parents.

There is also an advertisement which has appeared in the press frequently: 'Britain's boys are all born fighters, Bovril builds the little blighters.' This, like two of the above mentioned posters, contains a rhyme, which, though not essential, seems to be desirable in a good poster.

Ernest van Someren
In the afternoon put up the climbing frame for Laurie, which is a good solid job. The Chanters came to tea, with their boy Julian, and after tea I took some photos of Julian sitting on his father's knee.

SUNDAY, 30 NOVEMBER

Ernest van Someren
Cleaned my typewriter, which has not been working perfectly smoothly, and made it much worse.

New neighbours came to tea in the afternoon, John Strange and his wife and child Richard, aged 6 months. They are Quakers who have taken the Hodgkin's House. He works in a lamp factory and is a chemist like myself on the borderline of physics, a bit younger than me, married soon after the war started. One of his former colleagues was in love with my sister Tessa before she went to the USA, but has got over it.

Edward Stebbing
The attitude of children to Christmas in wartime is interesting. I listened to two children, one about eight, the other a little younger, talking to their grandfather about it. The latter said that Father Christmas wouldn't be able to bring them much this year as he couldn't go to Germany and get toys there. 'He can go to Russia,' said the older child, 'and America.' Their grandfather then tried to explain why this was not possible, but it took a lot of explaining to two children who really believed in Father Christmas, without disillusioning them, why he couldn't go to America on his reindeer, since they wouldn't accept the fact that if he went on a ship he might be torpedoed.

MONDAY, 1 DECEMBER

Maggie Joy Blunt
Milk ration now reduced to 2 pints per adult a week.

There is to be a debate in parliament on making conscription of women to the Services and industry compulsory.

Ernest van Someren

Went to call on the vicar, to ask his advice about well-informed people in the parish. I am looking for some to form a local 'Brains Trust' for an entertainment. He gave some useful suggestions.

Pam Ashford

Did I mention in the summer that Mr Hutchison has inherited a greengrocer's shop in a tiny Scottish village? Today he had a phone call from the assistant to say that under the points scheme the Food Ministry has dumped 600 tins of meat on him, and he had to have them whether he willed or not.

At the Soroptomist Lunch the table talk could not get away from food; possibly an added stimulus today was the remarkable emergence of steak and kidney pie.

Edward Stebbing

The new BBC announcer, Wilfred Pickles, seems to have taken some people's fancy. When I was home for the weekend two people asked me if I had heard him. Tonight, as soon as he started to read the news, my landlady's husband said, 'Pickles.' Perhaps it's only his name.

TUESDAY, 2 DECEMBER

Pam Ashford

The war in Russia is followed with a kind of interest; the war in North Africa definitely provokes interest. Conscription remains the subject that you can't get away from. Mr Ferguson has taken to writing the Ministry of Mines, as well as the Admiralty, to try and get the F&C on a protected basis, but both say the issue lies entirely with the Ministry of Labour, which is not disposed to put merchants on the same footing as producers.

WEDNESDAY, 3 DECEMBER

Ernest van Someren

After work I went to town with SH, the former colleague who left and is now training as an inspector of welding. He is a Captain now, and with special pay and allowances and living at home he earns about twice what he used to with our firm. He also invited the girl assistant who left our lab recently who has since been his mistress for a while. This was awkward. For one thing he is married and has a son two years younger than her, who works for the same firm as she does.

183

Now the situation is eased as she has fallen in love with another member of the Pacifist Service Unit in Stepney, a man more nearly her own age. Well, SH was treating us both to an evening out, and we had a beer at Liverpool St Station when we met, and then went to a café in Leicester Square for supper, and a little dancing on a very small floor. Crawled rapidly to bed at 1.30.

Pam Ashford
I would love to volunteer for the guns, while knowing perfectly well that I have not the strength for arduous jobs. I contemplate putting my name down on the supplementary register, and at the same time conclude that it is my duty to try and keep the F&C together when the young ones go (if they do). I thrill at the thought of the wonderful adventure it would be to get right out into the world, and shrink from the dirty trick of forsaking domestic responsibilities at home. Next comes the inevitable 'It will be some time before the thirty-nines are conscripted, so there is no hurry'. Agnes has ever been a conveyor of inaccurate information, and gave us this: 'The Govt. are giving every household a pick and mace to drive off the invaders with.'

THURSDAY, 4 DECEMBER

Ernest van Someren
After shaving and dressing, my digestion let me down drastically, and I most reluctantly went back to bed after only one cup of coffee, which I was unable to retain. I slept till 12.30, had a bath and then lunch, and felt nearly normal.

FRIDAY, 5 DECEMBER

Edward Stebbing
The general approval which the press claims for the Government's conscription of women is something which I do not believe exists outside newspapers. In fact most papers have for days been running a campaign, the purpose of which was not to *express* public opinion in favour of female conscription, but to *force* public opinion in that direction, by telling people what they ought to think. The *News Chronicle* today says that the girls concerned have accepted 'the call to arms in a quiet, philosophical manner'; my interpretation of that would be a 'half-hearted' manner. This is shown by the views of half a dozen girls interviewed, which are by no means enthusiastic. I am glad, however, that married women are not to be conscripted. I am sorry, on the other hand, that the military age has been lowered to

18½ and that children of 16 to 18 are to register. Why do the very youngest have to be brought so directly into contact with war? By this decision large numbers of the young and vigorous will be eliminated, there will be a majority of old people, and the young that are left will have been contaminated with the experience of militarism.

The regimentation of youth is one of the worst features of the dictatorships and it was to be hoped, for the sake of the future, that the youth of the professed democracies would have been spared this. What is this paradox which makes it impossible for a democracy to fight a dictatorship without becoming less democratic and more totalitarian?

SUNDAY, 7 DECEMBER

Ernest van Someren
While I was cleaning out the henhouse L washed my bicycle for me, and we finished it together and I oiled it. After supper listened in a bit, and heard of the Japanese attack in the evening news.

Edward Stebbing
Mrs H, in spite of difficulties, has succeeded in making five Christmas puddings, although they contain no candied peel, less suet than usual, and are mixed with stout instead of milk.

The news tonight makes war with Japan inevitable, I think. (The news was of the Japanese attack upon the American fleet at Pearl Harbor.) 'I don't see how America can keep out of it now,' I said to Mr H. 'If she don't come in now, she never will come in,' was his reply.

MONDAY, 8 DECEMBER

Ernest van Someren
Got down in time to hear the 8.00 news about Japanese attacks, and went to work by train as it was very frosty. People commenting at lunchtime said that 'this'll teach the USA that it's a World War' or 'this'll bring them in at last' from 3 or 4 people, and no one seemed shocked at the Japanese aggression. Stayed a little late at work enlarging a photo I took yesterday afternoon of L and J together. I also took one of the Stranges with their baby, which is excellent.

Came home and put L to bed, then listened to Roosevelt's speech to Congress, which was good and short. Later listened to Churchill, who was not as good as usual, sounded exhausted or drunk. He made a bad break speaking of Japanese aggression as 'lasting more than 4 years' when he might have said 8 or 9, and implying that the Japanese are inferior to the Nazis in villainy is also absurd. I think the Japanese are as far ahead of the Germans as the latter are ahead of us in the practice and theory of bullying.

Edward Stebbing

One of my first thoughts on getting up this morning was to wonder whether we had declared war on Japan. (At 8.30 this evening, as I write this, I still don't know the answer.) At lunchtime today the men at my table were quite light-hearted about it. They made remarks about the kind of propaganda films Hollywood would now produce. 'I shudder to think of it,' said one. He also 'shuddered' to think what the cartoons would be like now, 'with all funny little men showing all their teeth'. Another dreaded the new heights of silliness to which the popular songs would probably rise. (Surely he meant to say 'depths . . . sink'.)

My landlady this evening said it would have bad effects for us, as America would not be able to send us any more arms.

At least two papers have been trying, in the last week or two, to belittle Japan's strength and her chances if she should become involved in a war with Britain and America. I only hope they don't have to eat their words too soon.

9.30pm Churchill's speech and the news already indicate that the Japanese attack is no laughing matter, that Japan's strength is not to be despised.

So now the whole world, with negligible exceptions, is at war, and the prospect, which had begun to look a little brighter, now seems darker. One feels that it would be pleasant to be an Eskimo or a member of some other uncivilised community which does not know war.

Pam Ashford

Mr Mitchell and Mr Hutchison agreed that 'this will shorten the war by years'. (In other quarters I have heard 'this will lengthen the war by years'.) Mr Mitchell: 'They will be sending you out to Singapore as a soldier, Tom.' Mr Hutchison: 'That is what I expect. That is where the war is going to have its last phase.' Mr Mitchell: 'Stay on after the war. You could become secretary to a big oil company, and it would be a wonderful opportunity.' Mr Hutchison promised to think about it.

I have recorded today's war comments. Beside them is (1) a discovery of mine that Libby's tinned sausages at 2/6 count 16 points at Cranston's and 24 points at Cooper's, which discovery communicated to the office has roused intense anger at Cooper's frauding the public, alternatively at Cranston's tricking the Food Ministry; (2) The arrival of Miss Crawford's successor, Miss Clark. Everyone thinks she is a nice girl, with the inevitable comment that 'one thing, she cannot be as bad as what went on before'.

The Soroptomists had a business meeting today. What a marvellous soup – lots of milk in it – and the trifle that wound up the meal was like a pre-war dream.

Chapter Seven

NEW YORK SKYSCRAPERS
CRASHING TO THE GROUND

Never a wasted word or a woolly sentence: Churchill inspects the House of Commons Home Guard.

9 December 1941–5 March 1942

10 December The Battleship HMS *Prince of Wales* and the battle cruiser HMS *Repulse* sunk in the South China Sea, followed a week later by heavy losses in the Mediterranean.

19 December Age of conscription in United States lowered to 19, bringing another 2.4 million men into the war.

25 December Hong Kong surrenders to Japanese troops.

10 January 1942 Stalin makes significant counter-attacks against the Germans in Russia, as Japan makes advances in Philippines, Singapore and Malaya.

21 January The British routed by Rommel in North Africa.

26 January The first American soldiers to arrive on British soil set foot in Belfast.

1 February German U-boats employ the new cipher Triton, encoded on a four-rotor machine rather than the three-rotor Enigma code being deciphered at Bletchley Park.

8 February Hitler appoints the architect Albert Speer to run the offices of armament and war production.

9 February Soap rationing begins in Britain.

12 February The German battle cruiser *Scharnhorst* badly damaged in Atlantic conflict as the RAF loses 42 aircraft.

15 February Singapore falls to the Japanese.

19 February Churchill shuffles his war cabinet, bringing in left-winger Sir Stafford Cripps as Lord Privy Seal, and dismissing Lord Beaverbrook.

22 February Arthur 'Bomber' Harris takes over as chief of Bomber Command.

4 March Utility clothing in Britain means shorter hemlines and the end of men's turn-ups and double-breasted suits.

TUESDAY, 9 DECEMBER

Maggie Joy Blunt
The whole world at war . . . It is almost too gigantic a thought for human intelligence. The German campaign in Russia has come to a halt. (Those marvellous Russians!) But German power is not broken. During the winter one supposes they will now turn their attention to us and the Atlantic again. Neighbour Mrs C asks, 'Shall we ever see peace again?'

Pam Ashford
The opening up of the war in the Pacific has had its effect on Glasgow spirits – gravity is mixed with humour. Reports of Mayor La Guardia's directions to the New Yorkers inevitably make us smile in the way that a person who is convalescent from, say, measles, smiles to hear that someone else has got it.

Agnes has harrowing stories of New York skyscrapers crashing to the ground – in imagination. I said, 'After all they are built on steel frames and have deep foundations, they should stand a bit of shaking.' Agnes has seen them 'at the pictures' and regards the entire population of New York as good as dead.

Ernest van Someren
At work today it was generally agreed that Churchill's speech was poor, except by a few enthusiastic admirers of his. People hoped the USA would jump on the Japanese hard, but doubted their readiness to do so and on the whole realised the gravity of the situation for us all more than on Monday.

WEDNESDAY, 10 DECEMBER

Edward Stebbing
I was somewhat staggered when my landlady told me that two of our battleships had been sunk at Singapore. The Japanese have certainly made a good start from their point of view.

Discussing oratory at lunchtime, two or three of the men gave the opinion that Roosevelt is a better orator than Churchill. I think Roosevelt is at least as good as Churchill in this respect, but would not say better – their styles are quite different.

Pam Ashford
The new girl. 5 minutes late the first morning, 15 minutes late the second morning, 30 minutes late the third morning. She is agreeable, however, and I hope for the best.

THURSDAY, 11 DECEMBER

Pam Ashford
The war is lighting up all right now! The losses of the *Prince of Wales* and the *Repulse*, combined with the American naval disaster at Pearl Harbor, the invasion of the Philippines, and what is going on at Malaya is causing gloom. North Africa looks better. The malady that has made the earth sick must run its course, and each new phase means that recovery is a little less far off. The knowledge that the war cannot spread any further now – unless the Martians are to come in – is in itself a relief.

FRIDAY, 12 DECEMBER

Edward Stebbing
It is evident now that the *Prince of Wales* and *Repulse* were not sunk by suicide squads, human torpedoes, or secret weapons, but by a skilful attack by ordinary bombers and torpedo-bombers. It shows how much the Japanese were underrated that the theory of 'human torpedoes' etc. should have been given so much credence in the press. It is good that these theories have been squashed at the start and the true nature of what we are up against revealed.

Pam Ashford
What would be, I should think, the fullest week in the history of the world (always excepting the Seven Days of Creation) produced few notes. You know that the centre of a cyclone is dead calm. Here, at the heart of the Empire that is the subject of this vast plan of aggression, most people's emotions show only the slightest ripples.

I shudder at the terrific German losses in Russia too. However abominable Nazis are, they *are* human beings, and that is the pity of it. But mine is an exceptional angle: Mr Mitchell is gloating over the 85,000 killed near Moscow, and repeats his desire that every German be exterminated.

MONDAY, 15 DECEMBER

Pam Ashford
Agnes continues to explain the war. 'If it were not that it helps the Japs I should be very glad about the American defeat. A puffed-up set, the Americans, this will take them down a peg.'

TUESDAY, 16 DECEMBER

Edward Stebbing

It has been almost funny the way all the countries have been declaring war on each other and the situation has now become so complicated that one cannot comprehend it all at once. Many people have remarked on this. One man said that one needs a table showing with which countries any particular country is at war and which not. Another said, 'The world's gone raving mad. They can do what they like as far as I'm concerned. I've lost all interest.' This is not so much bewilderment as a recognition of the craziness of the world. As far as I am concerned, too, the world is just one big madhouse.

THURSDAY, 18 DECEMBER

Edward Stebbing

I am afraid I shall ignore the official request this Christmas asking people not to travel. I shall be having four days off, so am going home for the holiday.

FRIDAY, 19 DECEMBER

Edward Stebbing

I came across a rare creature this evening: a man who always carries his gas mask (and steel helmet too).

SATURDAY, 20 DECEMBER

Edward Stebbing

Tried to do a little Christmas shopping, but it was hopeless – there were crowds of people everywhere. All I bought was a book for myself, but that was easy, as I knew what I wanted (*For Whom the Bell Tolls* by Ernest Hemingway).

The *Daily Mirror*, I notice, asks for the complete control of Father Christmas, so that we may be spared 'the hypocrisy of his blither about peace and goodwill'. The *Daily Mirror* is often too realistic, sometimes to the point of making itself absurd. The Christmas tradition is one of the oldest and strongest in this country; it will probably never die out. Personally, I think it is a good tradition, which ought to be kept alive, and Christmas is, in many respects, the time of year I like best. For a few days, at least, some people behave a little better to each other than they usually do and there is generally an atmosphere of warmth and friendliness. It may be rather hypocritical in these times, but it is the times which need changing, not Christmas.

Pam Ashford

At one I went straight to the Cosmo to see *The Cat and the Canary* (an entertaining enough thriller) and *Our Russian Allies*. In the course of the film there was clapping four times, twice for Stalin and twice for Timoshenko. The Cosmo is not the kind of place where people clap.

MONDAY, 22 DECEMBER

Maggie Joy Blunt

A long time since I worked as hard as I did last week. Indexing Blue Books at the Fabian Society offices from 10am to 5.30 or 6.30pm, then home and typing out the research work I did last year. Rarely in bed before midnight and sometimes much later and up again at 7am to catch the 8.20 bus. Stayed with June last Friday night, Xmas shopping all Saturday morning. Home to tea and worked until 2am. Finished the report next morning, then rushed off to W – for the night and this morning to have my hair done in London, finish shopping, delivered the opus to the Fabian Society and returned home. Tomorrow I go to Farnborough for Xmas but have an interview with the BBC on Wednesday.

Pam Ashford

There was something about President Roosevelt's speech to Congress on the American Declaration of War against Japan which when broadcast appealed to our Dick (the vibration was terrific and that may have been it), and after 18 months of silence he set about trying to drown the President's voice with outbursts of song. And what is more he has been doing it ever since.

WEDNESDAY, 24 DECEMBER

Ernest van Someren

K and I went out to a party at the 'Studio', I wearing my Hungarian embroidered tunic to show that I felt like a party. We took some scones and mince pies with us. There were about 14 people, mostly young and connected with the WEA, and they had an old copper water-bucket (from Venice, via my mother) on the floor with beer in it.

Home at about midnight, playing carols on my recorder.

Edward Stebbing

Made the journey home in the evening quite easily. The train was almost full, but I managed to find a seat. According to the *News Chronicle*, the official policy of no extra trains seems to have been ignored.

Pam Ashford

In 1938 Mass-Observation had a directive about Christmas Preparations and how much I enjoyed writing that report. In those days, for weeks before the staff were typing labels and typing up parcels until around the 22nd, then we sent to the Post Office for mail bags – eight bags to be stuffed with calendars, cigars, cigarettes and pipes, books, handbags, various novelties. This year at the last moment the calendar printers let us down; the wholesale tobacconist could only supply a limited range and quantity; only a few cakes were available; the warehouses would not let us have the handbags (i.e at wholesale prices) for the trawler owners' wives; and so on. Speaking for myself, the Christmas preparations have been nil.

The firm gave us a box of shortbread for our tea in the morning, and a gift of money. Mr Mitchell has given me a 10/- book token, and I was very glad to be able to give him a slab of chocolate and half lb. of assorted chocolates for Aileen and Alistair (Charlie got them from the Cosmo kiosk). Miss Gibson gave me a bottle of perfume, and I gave her a tea strainer.

My heart is full of secret wishes that I know can never be fulfilled, but to one this day has bought the most unexpected realisation. For the last six Christmas Eves I have longed to buy mistletoe for the office, just to see what would happen. (Miss Hedley used to call the F&C 'death heated up', so you can see perhaps that it is not the gayest of places.) Once I said so to Margaret and she felt like that too, but certainly I could never rise to that level of audacity.

At 9.30 this morning, Mr Ferguson, Managing Director (of all people), came up to me (why me?) with a huge bunch of mistletoe. I thought he was going to kiss me and got a table in between us as quickly as possible, but it was only a present, and I put it in a vase on Mr Mitchell's mantelpiece.

CHRISTMAS DAY

Pam Ashford

I took advantage of the morning off to wash my hair and then typed out a little more diary. Christmas lunch. Chicken, which Mother for weeks has been saying would be unobtainable, but which as far as I can see has been plentiful in the last few days, and pudding. Then an enjoyable three-quarters of an hour with the *Brains Trust*. In Partick I found a good many of the small, general shops open and at a fruit shop bought a tin of Armour's spiced pork.

Edward Stebbing

Got up about half-past nine. Spent the morning at my sister's and read some of *Poverty and Progress*, Rowntree's social survey of York. A relation came round and talked to my father about the war. Regarding the entry of Japan he said, 'I reckon it's put two years on the war.' My father agreed and said, 'Undoubtedly they wiped out practically the whole of the American Pacific fleet. Still, I suppose we shall muddle through and finish.'

Gifts this year were on the small scale. There seemed to be plenty of cigarettes about (I had 30 cigarettes and two ounces of tobacco). Those who could spare coupons used them on small articles, such as ties, socks, and handkerchiefs. The rest consisted chiefly of what are described as 'fancy goods' – bottles of scent, jewellery, etc.

We had our usual Christmas dinner, including roast chicken and Christmas pudding (with threepenny bits in it). Everyone I know around here managed to get a chicken for dinner. 'Aren't we lucky to have all this?' said my sister. 'It's as good as peacetime.' 'If we don't do any worse than this for the rest of the war,' said my father, 'we shan't starve.' Yet according to Rowntree's survey there were many families in peacetime who were living below the minimum nutritional level required for health. How are they faring now?

For supper we had sandwiches of 'Treet', the imported American food, which we all thought very tasty.

Ernest van Someren

Up at about 7.30 and put in new lamps and lampshades over our bedroom washbasin as a present for K. Fetched Laurie out of bed, he had already looked through a stocking-full of small gifts. K brought Julia up after feeding her and Mother joined us in our bed where we all opened parcels together. K got the usual jobs done, and a turkey cooked and stuffed for a punctual lunch. Mother and I listened in first to the Christmas Party at the White House.

After lunch I put on films for Mother. K came down and shared with us the Holiday 1939 (Alpine) film, which we enjoyed twice.

FRIDAY, 26 DECEMBER

Ernest van Someren
To work by train, very cold. Listened to Churchill's Senate address, which I thought the best speech he has made for a long time, although the press reports hardly did it justice.

Pam Ashford
Dick nearly burst himself inside out with enthusiasm when Mr Churchill was broadcasting.

SUNDAY, 28 DECEMBER

Maggie Joy Blunt
Have just finished *Mansfield Park*. Its colouring is a little subdued compared with her other novels. There is a primness about it, a touch of the Old Maid, a foretaste of Victorian prudery which is disappointing. But it is still the inimitable Jane. I gobbled it up. How exact, how perfect is her picture of English home life as it has dominated our society for at least two or three hundred years. The aim of all classes – to lie as Gentlemen of Leisure. That is, to have enough capital to provide a home and servants in which the mistress does no more than supervise, act as her husband's hostess and marry off her daughters, and the master a Country Gentleman looking after his very comfortable estates, liberal, well-bred, upright, with good taste in literature and morals . . . This has been the pattern upon which our disintegrating society has tried to mould itself.

Wishy-washy copies of this way of life may be traced in every suburb and country town. Our democracy preached the right of every man to live his life in his own way and every man has wanted to live that sort of life because nothing more desirable was offered to his imagination. The few who struggled to the top proved that there *was* room for those with talent and cunning. But what we would not admit was that we have not all the same kind of talent and cunning and that if every family was to have its 'residence in the country' with servants then there would be no country, and who would be servants anyway?

Ernest van Someren
Very cold. Made fire, went to meeting by cycle, and got a fresh crop of chilblains. Afterwards went to call on a neighbour about taking part in a 'Brains Trust' which I am organising. Went on a similar call in the afternoon, with the whole family, but the victim was out.

MONDAY, 29 DECEMBER

Edward Stebbing
Looking back on the past year, I must say that it has not been humdrum or uninteresting. War certainly brings movement and excitement into one's life, although at the same time it may make it less happy. The world scene, too, has changed its colours and proportions frequently, and gives one much to conjecture on, though one may not approve of many happenings.

In the last year I have been both more happy and more unhappy at different times than ever before. I have read more and danced more, one a serious pastime, the other frivolous, but both things which give me the greatest pleasure. It has been a full year of experience and has left me individually in a better position mentally and physically (though I may not have thought so all the time) than this time last year. Some would say I have been lucky, but I do not believe in luck.

As a world-citizen, however, I despair more and more of the world situation. The main aim of the nations seems to be to plunge themselves into every possible crime and degradation. It is so tragic, it sometimes seems comic. The prospect for 1942 does not seem brighter, but gloomier if anything. I am reconciled to a long and weary war, but as far as I am concerned the world can carry on in its own sweet way.

NEW YEAR'S DAY, 1942

Ernest van Someren
We did not see the New Year in last night, just talked to Mrs Prime till nearly 11. My chief went to a party and didn't get to work till noon today.

Laurie has invented a method of breaking the deadlock which sometimes occurs when he refuses to do something which we have asked him to do, but can't force him to do (or won't). He says, 'Shut your eyes,' and then starts doing it, making a joke about it. This saves his face, and saves us both from the 20 mins tears and yells which might otherwise ensue.

FRIDAY, 2 JANUARY

Maggie Joy Blunt
New Year. There seems no hope of suitable employment for me anywhere. 'Your application has been receiving our consideration but ...' 'We regret that there are no vacancies on our staff ...'

199

A little batch of these sort of letters has greeted me every night this week on my return from the Fabian Society. The shadow of the ATS looms larger and larger . . .

Edward Stebbing
What a striking contrast to the usual run of news is Switzerland's decision to abolish the death penalty! It is strange how Switzerland always manages to remain neutral. She is probably too insignificant a country to matter in any military sense, but as an example of progress and humanity she puts the rest of the world to shame. She has no Empire, but are her people any the less happy for it?

SUNDAY, 4 JANUARY

Edward Stebbing
This passage from the *People* seems to me highly suspicious of a trumped-up atrocity story: 'Germans killed children and drained their blood for blood transfusion for their own wounded.' It just does not seem likely or feasible, or that it would meet the purpose for which intended. What mentality allows such stories to be printed?

Maggie Joy Blunt
What a tin of plums may do! One in my store had been oozing and I went to consult C as to the wisdom of eating contents or not. The conversation veered to jobs and Mr C advised me strongly to explore the possibilities of the Trading Estate. I did make a half-hearted attempt last week to find the local Labour Exchange, but am now full of enthusiasm. The advantages of finding a job locally cannot be ignored.

THURSDAY, 8 JANUARY

Maggie Joy Blunt
Swiftly putting Mr C's suggestion to the test I have as swiftly had a response. Was interviewed by a very intelligent and helpful girl at the Labour Exchange who sent me to see XYZ – one of the largest factories on the estate, aircraft works and producers of aluminium with large research laboratories, Library and Publicity Department. The publicity department want someone to write up readable articles from their own material for the building trade press and it seems nearly certain that I shall get the job. Had a long interview this morning and feel convinced that the work would not be beyond me. I have said I will start on Monday week at £5 and only await official confirmation.

SATURDAY, 10 JANUARY

Edward Stebbing

Noticed two more health posters, one on precautions to take against influenza, the other on precautions against scabies. The great drawback of both was that they had about five minutes' reading on them.

Maggie Joy Blunt

We have been and are promised to be the best fed nation in Europe. My relations are saying that they can remember in the last war feeling hungry but have not done so yet in this. They have high praise for Lord Woolton. If I had no stores in I could still feed myself adequately. A regular supply of butter, marg, cooking fat, cheese, bacon, sugar and tea arrives each week. As much bread and flour as I need. Custard powder and starchy things like rice, tapioca and so on can be had at intervals liberally without 'points'. The milk ration is helped out by tinned and powdered varieties. There are still plenty of tinned beans, carrots and soups. Potatoes, carrots and some greens at nearly normal prices. Eggs are very scarce. Meat is more difficult than it was, but there is often sausage meat and corned beef as substitutes and makeweights. Fruit is very scarce but I have had several lots of good apples from greengrocer recently and occasionally dried fruit. Cakes and pastries are still obtainable by order or by queuing from most reliable confectioners. I can still – if I go to London often enough – get at least 20 cigarettes a day. The biscuit supply varies but one gets them at intervals. Pubs still do a good trade but beer is not what it was and it is difficult to get occasional bottles for home consumption.

But now, the papers warn us, Japan's attack on American merchant conditions will make a difference and we must expect to 'tighten our belts' and may yet get poorer menus. But I do not think we shall starve.

Ernest van Someren

In the afternoon went to the library, and did a little excavating in the garden to annoy the rats, for whom I have bought a new kind of poison.

In the evening I worked on a comparison of last year's expenses with the three previous years. Expenditure has gone up, but not on food, clothes, or personal things. Only on insurance, taxes, fuel and children, which means that we have cut our standard of living in precise proportion to the rise in the cost of living.

MONDAY, 12 JANUARY

Ernest van Someren
Very hard frost, min 20°, slight stoppage in one of our water pipes.
My mother rang in the afternoon to say that Grandma died this
morning, in her sleep. She caught a cold about a week ago and has
been weak lately. We are rather relived, as she was bored with life
and mentally weakening at 85.

Budgetary Summary

	1938	1939	1940	1941
Expenses				
Rent	60	60	60	60
Rates	27	27	28	28
Insurance	35	37	37	48
Subscriptions	10	10	10	15
Tax (Income)	10	18	18	43
Post and Telephone	12	11	11	12
Periodicals	2	3	4	4
Food (including canteen lunch)	72	127	127	107
Garden, and Hens in 1940–41	4	5	11	16
Household and labour	60	61	63	58
Light and Fuel	20	31	32	32
Doctor and Dentist	4	7	8	21
Personal, Father	48	68	61	56
Mother	30	55	40	44
Son born 1938	44	8	12	17
Daughter born 1941				64
Total	438	528	522	625

	Income		Salary	
(After 5% Pension deducted) from 1940	442	523	533	616
Misc. earnings	14	18	23	24
Total	456	541	556	640

Excess of income over expenditure in four years = 70

Notes:

Two evacuee girls, aged about 10, were billeted on us for 5 months in 1939–40, and the billeting allowance has not been shown, but is credited to food and fuel.

Food: Since 1939 it also includes about 5 p.a. on drinks, alcoholic, a war extravagance.

Doctor and Dentist: Since 1940 we have a maintenance agreement with a doctor for 5 gns p.a. for the family. A course of massage for myself put up this year's figure.

Savings: Mostly go straight into Insurance, which was increased at the birth of each child.

THURSDAY, 15 JANUARY

Ernest van Someren

Went home to lunch, and afterwards with Mother and her house-keeper to Grandma's funeral. The cemetery was misty, frostbound and silent under snow, we sat waiting in the car for a time while the preceding funeral was got over. Then into a small chapel where we met the coffin, and a chilled Anglican priest. He did a shortened form of service, during which the coffin was led off to the crematorium so quietly that my mother never saw it move at all.

We were driven quietly back to my mother's home, where she found a form about disposal which she had mislaid and which I had to send off for her. My brother tactfully wrote that Grandma mentally had been dead for some time, and this was merely a last stage in the process and therefore ought not to be much shock. I stayed to tea with mother and spent some time tidying up and scrapping many of Grandma's papers. We decided to keep the letters mother wrote to Grandma during the last war as useful documents. I found out what I had never quite realised before, that Grandma divorced her first husband for mental cruelty (in California) in 1880. After tea a musician who is living with my mother played us some music on the grand piano which she has brought with her.

FRIDAY, 16 JANUARY

Ernest van Someren

Not a good day at work and got very little done. In the evening made fudge with K, iced a cake for L's birthday. He is four today and had some nice books given him by various people.

SATURDAY, 17 JANUARY

Edward Stebbing

Overheard in a barber's shop: 'I wonder why they (the Germans) always keep this barbarian spirit. You'd think they would lose that in evolution.' 'Well, this is an organised thing. In the last war some of our men did some funny things, and they have in this war, but that was only one or two here and there with the hooligan spirit.' 'It's horrible when you come to think of it, isn't it?' 'It's worse than the Boxer Rising, and that's the worst thing I remember in my life. This is ten thousand times worse.' Then the two men agreed that we should not make the mistake of letting Hitler escape punishment after the war. 'Still, there are not many places he could slope to,' said one, 'only Switzerland and Portugal and Spain.' 'Yes, I daresay old Franco would be glad to have him.' 'It's marvellous how Switzerland always manages to keep out of everything, isn't it?' 'No one ever seems to take any notice of her.'

Ernest van Someren

In the afternoon we arranged for Julia to be taken out by a friend while we had a party for six of L's friends. He invited three more – one of the parents phoned to warn us but the other two arrived quite unannounced. This was a bit of a shock, but we smiled and phoned a message to a neighbour to ask for some more crackers.

Nine children and four parents were duly fed, K made imitation ices with stiff custard between wafers, these were specially enjoyed as a novelty, and the candles on the cake caused the usual fun. Games were a bit less neatly organised than I had hoped because my wife left it largely to me, but no one was hurt and nothing broken.

SUNDAY, 18 JANUARY

Ernest van Someren

In the afternoon we packed a warm drink for Julia in her pram and went skating in a park in Hoddesdon, L came and pottered round on the ice and we pushed the pram on the ice part of the time. It was good ice and not too crowded, I enjoyed it until I scratched my eyeball with a twig when holding a tree on the bank.

TUESDAY, 20 JANUARY

Maggie Joy Blunt

Yesterday was worn to a shred with the nervous strain of 'being new' again. But have no temperamental editor to cope with. The head of the department Mr A is young and scarcely appears, let alone issues impossible orders and watches me with impatience. I work in a pleasant room with an attractive young Irishman called TH and a good natured, pink and white youth called B – our 'commercial artist'. There are two other men I haven't met yet and a swarm of typists in a room of their own. There is lamentably little work being done apparently. We do not have to be punctual in the morning but I don't know how late I dare to be yet. One foot of snow outside my cottage door delayed me half an hour today. We were all allowed home early tonight because of the weather.

There is, however, plenty of work for me to do in the way of reading up and learning about my new subject. I am learning an awful lot about metals and alloys.

Edward Stebbing

To a good many people the rationing of paper for book-publishing does not matter much. But to anyone like myself, who loves books of all kinds, it is of major importance. Without books – and I mean good books – life would be almost intolerable. The *News Chronicle* has done good service in emphasising this grievance. Authors and publishers are unanimous that it would not require much adjustment of the present scheme to make more paper available for books. More paper could be allowed for high-class publications.

English literature, in my opinion, is the best in the world. If it is to continue to be so, fresh talent must not be discouraged. It is part of the culture for which we are fighting.

WEDNESDAY, 21 JANUARY

Ernest van Someren

After supper went for an ultra-violet dose at my doctors, as my chilblains have been very bad lately. At his recommendation I started wearing long pants yesterday, my first since leaving school.

THURSDAY, 22 JANUARY

Ernest van Someren
My married sister Esmee came to tea and stayed the evening. We talked family most of the time, and provisionally arranged for her boys to come and visit us in their next holidays, they have never been here and we haven't seen them for 4 years. She is just going to start work in a factory near Wells, as both the boys are boarders at school now, and her only job recently has been part-time in a British Restaurant.

SATURDAY, 24 JANUARY

Ernest van Someren
In the afternoon a good lecture on Developments in Rheology by our Secretary, and a discussion on definitions and terminology. Afterwards I stopped and chatted with the secretary about some of the things we might do. He has an assistant who is a psycho-rheologist, a very lively woman with an almost unique job, that of evaluating the concept of 'firmness' in substances like cheese.

SUNDAY, 25 JANUARY

Pam Ashford
I wrote to the Organising Secretary of the Women's Parliament asking if I could come, and got an invitation.

I have never been in such a mixed gathering in my life, nor do I remember an occasion when so many strands of my own life were brought together simultaneously. Prominent among those present were Mrs Tebb, Speaker (Headmistress of Glasgow High School for Girls); Isabel Sinclair, the Women's Editor of the *Daily Express* and Dr Lloyd, Mrs Tweeddale (Director of Studies at the University). Besides all this intelligentsia there were numerous factory workers, both refined women on war work and the genuine thing. And all inspired with a single thought, i.e. to get down to clearing up some of the injustices women in work have thrust upon them.

At the afternoon session of the first two hours the Deputy Speaker was in the Chair, Miss Jeanette Jack (teacher). In fact as she walked in the door we singled her out, not for her apparent capabilities but for the rakish hat and sequinned dress, and Miss Tucker exclaimed, 'Who is this bird of paradise?' and we concluded it must be Vivien Leigh, for there was a rumour circulating around us that Vivien Leigh was representing the Stage.

We passed a Bill stating that women don't get a fair deal. We have the power and have had it for twenty years, but we have failed to use it.

(a) Wages. Women employed in industry should be paid the same as men for similar work, whereas now they are regarded as cheap labour.
(b) The working week for women workers should not exceed 54 hours, including overtime.
(c) Women working in factories should be given the same facilities for Trade Union Organisation and the election of their representatives in the factories as are given to men.

It is desirable that a deputation of women from this Parliament go to London to interview the appropriate Ministers and urge that the proposals should become law. This depends on funds, and it is out of the question at present.

Congratulations to the principal speakers, all who took part in the debate, to delegates, and to all who helped during the past week and came today in terrible weather. Men would not have been tough enough to turn out in such numbers. (Loud and long cheering.)

Ernest van Someren
A friend and colleague Martin came and called for me and at 7.30 we went to a British Legion entertainment for the troops in Hoddesdon, where we staged a 'Brains Trust' for 40 mins of the programme. Martin was Question-master and did very well. We had six in the team and as over half the questions had some scientific aspect I did more than my fair share of the answering. K came too, Laurie's headmaster was in the team, and it went off very well. There were plenty of questions and the audience seemed to like our answers, so we may be asked to do it again. It was an anxious time for me as I had selected the team with very little advice from other people. The one weakness was a member who was hardly audible at all.

MONDAY, 26 JANUARY

Pam Ashford
Another feminist meeting today, but oh how different, viz. the Soroptomist Lunch. The Speaker was Dr Laidlaw, second in charge of our Public Health Dept and head of their Tuberculosis Section. His subject was 'The Tuberculosis Rates in Wartime'.

The point is that the incidence in Glasgow has risen 25% under war conditions. The Public Health Dept think the cause is that the younger people are overstraining themselves. It is in the younger adult life that the consumptive tendency establishes itself, and the rise is definitely among the young in heavy industries, not the young in clerical work. These people are doing overtime, on top of which they do home guarding, etc. That would not overstrain them if they went home to bed then, but they don't. They must have their dances and the pictures as usual, and they undermine themselves, and the bacilli get their chance to do their fell work.

TUESDAY, 27 JANUARY

Maggie Joy Blunt
Churchill has made another magnificent speech. Such imagination, sensitivity, vitality . . . he gives us masterpieces of modern oratory. Never a wasted word or a woolly sentence. Unstinted tribute to the Russians. He pleads with diabolical eloquence for a vote of confidence and I am sure he will get it.

THURSDAY, 29 JANUARY

Pam Ashford
The *Barham* has been lost. Another of the ships whose name I knew in my childhood Devonport days. The *Barham* was the only ship damaged at Jutland whose damages did not necessitate her getting straightaway into port near the East Coast. In other words, the only one that could get as far as Devonport under her own steam. And she got there with a terrible lot of her crew dead, dying and injured. She was immediately handed over to my father to repair, and going on board her made him frightfully ill, the phrase I remember was 'like shambles'. Higher powers took the job from him, however. He himself was suffering from pernicious anaemia then, and died very soon after.

Maggie Joy Blunt
On my way to the Canteen today, which lies some way from the main office buildings, I peeped into one of the workshops. Passions of white flames from furnaces lit the whole interior. Lamps in the roof cast lime-coloured light over the scene. Enormous parts were being heated and hammered. Brawny men moved about naked to the waist or with shirt sleeves rolled. The sound of hissing flame and hammers on metal, the pale lights in the high roof, the shadows and the steam . . . artists should paint it, poets should pen it, musicians

translate it. Modern industry, all turned now to making guns. 'Thirty thousand a year!' said Lord Beaverbrook last night. Thirty thousand guns! Forty thousand guns . . . fifty thousand . . .

> 'an jest for 'alf a yard o'mud
> Between two blades o' grass . . .'
> But the ants said, 'We are fighting the battle of peace!'

SATURDAY, 31 JANUARY

Pam Ashford
Today there has been a flag day in aid of Russia, and an empty shop in Renfield Street that gets used on such occasions is decorated with artificial snow, as an advertising medium. But at this time two years ago the same shop was used by the Finnish relief, and if it is not the same snow, it is very much like it.

In August 1938 the afternoon express from Edinburgh to Glasgow crashed at Castlecary with loss of life. On Friday the same train crashed a few miles nearer Glasgow, in fact within the boundary, again with loss of life – 11 dead. In 1938 that was a 'sensation', but in 1942 no one is interested.

SUNDAY, 1 FEBRUARY

Edward Stebbing
The weather is now a main topic of conversation. For the time being the snow is the first thing people talk about.

But talking about after the war my father said, 'There'll have to be a conscripted army for a few years after the war, however it turns out.' Also he said, 'There'll be a good many women doing men's jobs. Employers will take the cheaper labour.'

'Time seems to go more quickly in wartime,' said Mrs A. 'There doesn't seem to be any time,' said her husband. 'Time doesn't mean anything . . . It's just a waste of the years.' 'Everything's disorganised,' said my father. 'Where you used to do a thing automatically and everything seemed to fit in, things are disjointed now.' To me, time goes at a tremendous pace, yet, looking back on it, the war seems to have lasted an eternity. It seems to have blotted out all previous existence.

THURSDAY, 5 FEBRUARY

Ernest van Someren
At lunchtime a Ministry of Information film entertainment was provided in the canteen for the factory girls, it was my idea, and went quite well. Only two films (25 mins), one *The Pilot Is Safe* and one about Empire soldiers and L. Henson talking. The latter was criticised as unsuitable by staff over our lunch. We heard from my sister in Florida, she seems to be learning some sort of 'radiolocation' in her spare time and is very interested.

In the evening we asked Honor P. in to supper and baby-minding, and went round to the Stranges ourselves, they talked about various friends of ours, and about folk-dancing at which they are experts, who were among the English team at Stockholm in 1939.

Edward Stebbing
'I see they won't have Sir Stafford Cripps in the Government,' said Mrs H this morning. 'Well, he refused,' said Mr H, 'because they wouldn't give him a seat in the Cabinet. Quite right, too. It's the same job Beaverbrook had, and he ought to have a Cabinet seat the same as Beaverbrook.' 'Churchill will be losing the faith of the country if he goes on like he is,' said Mrs H. 'It's no good fighting against social changes; they've got to come.' 'These Government changes make hardly any difference,' I said. 'Not a scrap of difference,' agreed Mr H. 'No, he's keeping his old cronies in,' said his wife. 'They'll be having him (Churchill) out of it, if he's not careful . . . There'll be a Labour Government after the war,' he said.

SATURDAY, 7 FEBRUARY

Ernest van Someren
Laurie met me in the morning when I came home from lunch, and went with me to the bookstall where we bought some chocolate, 4 bars. When we got home L gave me one, gave K one, said he would keep one and put one in his 'store'. I firmly explained that I had bought it, except one bar for which he had produced the money, and all except his bar would go in OUR reserve store. Since his birthday he has had a small reserve in a cupboard, to use to bridge over the gap between supplies in shops, and he takes pride in looking after his own sweets, and rations himself quite modestly, and offers us small pieces regularly.

SUNDAY, 8 FEBRUARY

Maggie Joy Blunt
Sir Stafford Cripps has just given an inspiring, stimulating, moving Sunday night Post Script broadcast. He compared our relative comfort and security with the privations and sacrifices now being endured by the Russians and urged us to make more effort in a way that will move everyone in sympathy with Russia and irritate the anti-Russian faction excessively. Am sure there is no lack of willingness among workers to speed up production, and large sections of the Services and middle class civilians are wanting to do more to help the war effort. (Cripps made one ashamed of one's thought for new clothes and curtains and cigarettes and extra food.) But there is a feeling of frustration. We would if we could but we *can't*. *Why* can't we? Why do shop stewards have to organise protest meetings, why should so many women still be idle, why for that matter is there such appalling slackness in my own department? What is this block of resistance, how can we fight it instead of giving in, saying, Oh, it's not my fault!? Must we experience another and another Dunkirk or an invasion to stir us into united action again?

MONDAY, 9 FEBRUARY

Edward Stebbing
The soap rationing came as a surprise to me, as it did to everyone, I think. It is not a great inconvenience, however. What worries me most is the idea of the surfeit of atrocious jokes about it we shall have to put up with from the radio. My landlady said she had got some packets of soap-flakes put by.

The membership of the local Communist party has increased by 50 per cent in the last three months. Membership is now nearly 60.

Pam Ashford
Mrs Petrie started with us this morning. She was an operator at the Central Exchange, left on marriage, returned last year, left at Xmas because the hours interfered with her shopping. She would be in the mid- to end-thirties. She has a husband in work with no immediate prospect of being called up. She looks very nervous and has found our switchboard difficult. Everyone is dreading tomorrow when Mr Ferguson will be in. We all expect her to clear out very soon, and Mr Mitchell said, 'She won't stay a week.' You don't know what a bad employer is until you meet Mr Ferguson.

TUESDAY, 10 FEBRUARY

Edward Stebbing

The feeling is growing that we are having our present reverses in
Libya and the Far East not merely because of inferiority in numbers
and equipment, but also because the enemy are really too clever for
us, or rather that we are too stupid for the enemy. This, of course, is
the last thing that most people will admit.

'We never seem to do anything adequately,' said my landlady. She
told me that a woman had said that her husband in the Army had
told her that there would soon be an uproar over Churchill, as he
was always drunk!

WEDNESDAY, 11 FEBRUARY

Pam Ashford

Modern Youth! Our office specimen, George, 15, is at it again. Till
3 o'clock this afternoon we had not seen him since Friday last. No
telephone message, no medical certificate, no nothing. This
afternoon in he walks as large as life, to explain that he has joined the
Merchant Navy and 'had to make his preparations'. He will go on
the 'Burmah', Henderson line, but does not know when he starts. No
one regrets his decision to leave – work is a practice he persistently
rejects, and there are other weaknesses. He is full of the adventures
ahead, and I myself think he will get on much better at sea than in a
commercial career for which is clearly unsuited, firstly because he
will be following the vocation he wants to follow, and secondly
because in the Merchant Navy they may cure him of work shyness
better than our efforts at the F&C. He thinks nothing of the dangers
run by those who go down to the sea in ships – or war risks either.
And having written all the foregoing I have a soft spot in my heart for
George and shall follow him in my thoughts for a while at least and
wish him the best.

THURSDAY, 12 FEBRUARY

Pam Ashford

The long drawn-out cold spell drags me down and down and down.
I wish I were a hibernating animal and could sleep through the whole
thing. I came home with Miss Whittan. We got talking about girls
marrying Poles, and she thought they would have an awful time
when they get to Poland after the war. Not because of anything the
Germans have done there, but because Polish women have achieved

212

little emancipation. I said, 'Some Poles talk of emigrating to America. Perhaps the Scots lassies would prefer that.' She thinks America will refuse to take in any Polish immigrants after the war. However, it was an impossible subject to discuss – what life is going to be like when this war is over is beyond conjecture. I said, 'What would keep me from marrying a Pole was the possibility of his having a wife in Poland as it is.'

FRIDAY, 13 FEBRUARY

Edward Stebbing
Fancy letting three German warships get through the Channel without sinking one of them! And then to lose 42 planes into the bargain! It is almost unbelievable. 'It's about the worst packet the Admiralty have had to face,' said one of my lunchtime companions, 'and they've had to face some.'

Then one of the men remarked on a wireless statement that some of our troops in Burma had driven the Japs back 'at the point of the bayonet'. He said he felt like throwing something at the receiver every time he heard that phrase. This brings one to the questions of pikes and bows and arrows for the Home Guard, about which everyone is joking now. What further humiliation and ridicule are we to bear? We are making ourselves a laughing stock.

Said my landlady tonight: 'I wonder if we shall win this war. Sometimes I feel doubtful.'

Pam Ashford
A spirit of deep pessimism is about; even that incurable optimist, Mother, says yesterday she felt as if a pall had descended on her, and she was so depressed she did not know what to do. She went over to Mrs Craigie and said, 'I know in my bones something terrible is happening,' and Mrs Craigie said it was in her bones too and she had spent the morning weeping her eyes out.

Mother thinks the news is terrible. Well, it is certainly worse this morning with the Germans forcing the straits of Dover, and a shocking blow to our naval prestige. But in these matters one inevitably learns one's own losses before one learns those of the enemy. My advice to Mother is 'Don't read the papers', and she wishes she had my courage to refrain from doing so.

The way news is reported has burst into conversation just as it did in the early days of the war. There are contrasting views. Some people are extremely angry at the way we give information away to the Germans. For instance, Agnes and Miss Bousie are indignant with a

213

pilot who described over the radio recently planes with four-gunned rear-turrets. Other people (quite often the same people) are extremely angry about the way information is withheld from us.

Rumour is afoot too. The story that the *Warspite* and the *Queen Mary* are gone is everywhere. In regard to the latter, the story is that she was used as a troop carrier for American Forces and was lost with all hands off the West Coast of Ireland. The changes in my life have been so gradual that I do not feel conscious of much change at all, but all round me there are stories of women being conscripted and having their whole lives turned upside down. Hostility to conscription is being replaced more and more by an acquiescence in an unpleasant necessity. The ATS appear to be rising out of the mud. A view commonly expressed by the twenties and twenty-ones is, 'If we stay at home there are no men. In the ATS we will get men.'

SUNDAY, 15 FEBRUARY

Edward Stebbing
Dissatisfaction is now being shown not only with the Government, but also with the Prime Minister. I have often said things against him, but not until the last week or so has a voice been raised against him in public. The *Daily Mirror* says: 'Is it any longer true that we trust the Prime Minister, but do not trust his Government?' The *News Chronicle* says: 'Have we not been hypnotised by Mr Churchill's personality . . . into acquiescence in an inefficient war direction?' By his refusal to listen to the demands of Press and Parliament Churchill has brought their anger on himself, and if he does not soon alter his Government they will put him out of office. Our recent reverses have lowered his own prestige considerably.

MONDAY, 16 FEBRUARY

Pam Ashford
Singapore! That is news indeed! There are recriminations galore! People say Mr Churchill has taken on too much, he is a dictator, etc., but when asked if they want Mr Churchill to go, they hastily reply, 'No, but they want to see about half the cabinet go.' (There is no member who is not included in someone's list of those 'who never would be missed'.) The Jeremiahs are having the day of their lives too. Agnes has already announced the capitulation of Australia as a foregone conclusion, and even the optimists cannot rally themselves to a reply.

At the Soroptomists Miss Dewar said, 'I am thinking that it will be

214

Russia that wins the war. It will be Russia that goes to Berlin to dictate the peace. And what shall we get out of a situation like that?' Mrs Fife, JP, replied smiling, 'If Russia wins the war, I shall be so glad that I shan't mind what she takes.'

Maggie Joy Blunt

Went into Slough after cigarettes during lunch hour today. Since I stopped going to London daily cigarette problem has been acute. Rothmans usually have some for non-registered customers on Wednesdays at midday, but they are vile cigarettes. Sold ten of mine almost at once to the office boy. Yesterday the canteen only had Players Weights. If it weren't for Jules sending me an odd hundred every now and then don't know what I should do.

Paragraphs in the press indicate that soon there will be little but 'utility' clothes for our coupons. Have noticed several women without stockings lately. Don't know how they endure it in this weather but if one hasn't stockings, slacks or coupons what can one do but go without? After all we played games at school all through the winter without stockings and survived.

Which reminds me. School magazines arrived last week. Old Girls are ATS and WRENS and WAAFS, VADs and other Volunteers in alarming array. Others are in the Land Army, the War Office, the Air Ministry, helping in Welfare Centres for evacuees – all kinds of Government work. One is Official Indexer, whatever that may be, another a District Inspector for the Ministry of Health, another is interested in the International Women's Organisations and their plans for reconstruction. And one girl whom I knew quite well (although in Selfridges not long ago we decided not to recognise each other) has been working a longboat on the Worcester Cut with another woman, carrying freight, and is now to train women to do the same kind of work for the Grand Union Canal Co.

Electric torch batteries – no No 8s in the village now. Bought 3 in 3 weeks at Boots recently – they all gave out before I had used them more than twice. TH says it is a racket. Man in village shop says that all batteries are now only half-filled.

TUESDAY, 17 FEBRUARY

Pam Ashford

It is the economic aspect of the Singapore disaster that strikes me deeply today. There are so many. The transition of the oil, rubber and other sinews of war will lengthen the war by so much. The loss of foodstuffs from Australia and South Africa through the decreased

215

control of the seas will reflect itself here. At the Soroptomist lunch one day I was hearing from people who have friends in both Dominions of the terrible losses in oranges, pineapples and other fruits through the impossibility of shipping them. And no more than any one else do I want the privation and poverty that looks as if it will be here for a long time ahead.

WEDNESDAY, 18 FEBRUARY

Pam Ashford
Home to a red letter day in the history of my musical education. With the broadcast of Sibelius' Second Symphony I could say for the first time that I appreciated him. If it has never been said in this diary before, let me say now that musical appreciation did not wake in me until the wireless came, indeed not for several years after that did I stop turning symphony concerts off with hurried gesture and ugly grimace. In 1929 I made the daring experiment of 'listening' to one, and the story of my musical odyssey since then is one that I love telling myself. There was an unforgettable experience in June 1930 when beneath Toscanini's baton in the Eroica Symphony I apprehended Beethoven for the first time!

Ernest van Someren
Visitors came after supper, new neighbours of ours, Noel and Irene Ripley. He is a CO who has been transferred from the FAU to the Friends War Victims Relief Cttee, known as the War-Vcs for short. He and his wife are jointly responsible for running a hostel here for a few families from E. London, mothers with young children mostly. They live with them and have no privacy, so are glad of an evening out.

Yesterday when I came home I went skating for half an hour in Hoddesdon on the usual lake, as there was time before dusk. The ice was a bit rough and no one else was there, so I didn't enjoy it much.

I had an ultra-violet dose on my toes, and listened in to a remarkable programme on democracy in China. It ended with some Chinese music which was allowed to blend with the chiming of Big Ben, with an incongruity which I found rather moving.

FRIDAY, 20 FEBRUARY

Edward Stebbing
The new Cabinet changes seem to be welcomed by the Press, and it is certainly good to see Cripps in the Cabinet, but I do not think the

changes are by any means adequate. Kingsley Wood, Attlee, Greenwood, Anderson, Margesson, Morrison, Bracken and several others all ought to be removed from office. By this slight concession, however, Churchill has probably avoided political defeat.

Pam Ashford
The difficulties in the Far East are food for thought to everyone. The recriminations did not extend beyond Monday, but on that and subsequent days there have been loud demands for Sir Stafford Cripps and satisfaction is felt at his appointment to the War Cabinet. Apprehension and regret on the one hand, and inflexible resolve on the other, would, I suppose, indicate in general terms the nature of these elusive moods. On the station wall opposite us some imbecile has chalked 'Stop the war – Useless to resist further', which is about as far from the current common sentiment as anything could be, but that sort of nonsense has been being chalked up ever since the outbreak of hostilities, and I honestly think that you need to be a Mass-Observer before you notice it at all.

Often I wonder which subject comes first in conversation, the conscription of women or the food situation. I suppose it depends how near you are to being conscripted whether you allow that subject to get ahead of food. Today at any rate food is sweeping forward in great crescendo under the impulse of the release of tinned fruits next Monday, and as shop after shop puts into its windows piles of delicacies of this type. Either the shops themselves don't know or else they don't want to alarm the mouth-watering, wonder gazers, but we are all stuck to know how the scheme works.

SATURDAY, 21 FEBRUARY

Pam Ashford
I met Dorothy Wallace on the bus again. She is in a pretty pickle, for they have stopped making shoes for size 2½, so what is she to do when her present stock wears out? Her news shook me up, for if they have stopped production at her end of the scale, they may have stopped at mine too, vis 6½–7. However, I could always buy boys', they go up to about 10s. Dorothy says Mrs Wallace has had difficulty to buy salt and is more worried about that than anything else.

Edward Stebbing
Went to see Epstein's new sculpture, *Jacob and the Angel*, and was considerably impressed by it and chiefly by the physical strength which must be required to shape such an immense piece of stone. To

make a recognisable shape at all, out of a huge slab of rock, let alone a work of beauty and meaning (which I think it is), is a great achievement worthy of praise.

Ernest van Someren
I did an article about our budget and sold it to *Housewife* for five guineas.

MONDAY, 23 FEBRUARY

Pam Ashford
Often I wonder if the wartime diet has reduced our resistance to cold. The last Mass-Observation report said people were losing weight, but not to a grave extent, and last spring I dropped half a stone. (Was I not glad, for it enabled me to wear my brick colour frock. That was a bargain I bought in September 1938 sales meaning to use in the office the next summer.) However, since October last I have put on 9lbs. That must be due to the replacement by farinaceous foods and root crops of my former main stay of fruit (fresh and tinned) and fresh vegetables, such as tomatoes, combined with the total elimination of fish, which can only be had by those able to stand in queues, and the drastic reduction in eggs.

Today the tinned fruits were put on the market. Massey's had a queue of 15 persons, and Cooper's one of about 50.

TUESDAY, 24 FEBRUARY

Maggie Joy Blunt
Hairdressers in this area are doing well. In Slough it is impossible to book an appointment on a Saturday afternoon for 6 or more weeks. Weekday evening appointments cannot be made much later than 5 o'clock. For anyone who works until 6pm as I do, hair dos are a problem. Fortunately our Mr Bubb in the village was able to do mine last Saturday, but even there one has to book a week or two in advance.

Imagine that this situation is similar in every suburb or town near an industrial centre. Women at work too busy to do their own hair, or cannot get shampoos, and hairdressers staff drastically reduced. Officially, I suppose, hairdressing is a luxury and should be stopped. But I don't think so – a good hairset is a definite and essential aid to morale.

Edward Stebbing

I was glad to read Stalin's statement that the Russians were not fighting the Germans simply because they were Germans, but because they were invaders of their country, and that the Russians did not aim to exterminate the German people, but only the Nazi clique at their head. This is good propaganda and, if Stalin means what he says, good ethics. If we are to have a real peace after the war there must be none of this racial hatred. Some of our newspapers, however, adopting what they call a 'realistic' policy, have scorned the idea that we have no grudge against the German people. Their attitude has been the opposite of Stalin's professed one. Personally, I bear no malice towards the Germans as a race, or towards any other race. To talk of destroying a whole race is ludicrous, and to carry it out would be virtually impossible.

WEDNESDAY, 25 FEBRUARY

Edward Stebbing

Have just seen an official pamphlet, dated 1941, called 'ARP (Air Raid Precautions) at Home'. I am fairly sure that not one in 50 of those who receive it will bother to do more than glance through it. To read this wordy, 28-page booklet would bore anyone to tears.

Maggie Joy Blunt

Allowed morning off last Saturday to attend cousin M's wedding. When I asked for this my boss said it was *most* irregular but grinned broadly when he heard M was in the RAF and had just returned from Russia.

Sat next to cousin-in-law Peggy in Church. She has just been put in charge of a large scabies-clearing depot. Gave me detailed description of the cure while we waited for the bride. 'Our skin man,' Peggy whispered, 'told us that it was caught chiefly from your bedfellow. It just depends who you sleep with.' Glad I've been warned.

Bride in white, bridesmaids in dark green velvet carrying daffodils. Best man was the pilot who shot down the plane over Victoria Station. Snowstorm as we came out of Church. Reception at hotel in Acton, where M had been head of ARP until he joined up. Food, provided at 4 days' notice, remarkably good – chicken and ham sandwiches, trifle, fruit salad and cakes in quantity. Drinks not so good. On Monday B asked cheerfully if I had got tight at the wedding. Impossible for anyone to get tight at that wedding.

Ernest van Someren

In the evening gave K and L some ultra-violet treatment with our arc lamp, which isn't very good but helps a bit for chilblains, from which we are all suffering on account of this very long cold spell. After supper tackled the oboe, Mr Tait has lent me a book of instructions and given me some advice, tried for an hour and learnt some of the fingering but couldn't make a single squeak, the reeds are very tricky things to work.

Pam Ashford

It would have been better if Mother had kept out of Maclean's with the two pink books. They sold her a tin of pineapple and a tin of peas against 20 points in one book, and put her name on a list for the next allocation of peaches and pears against the 20 points in the other book. In the afternoon I located identical tins at Cooper's – beneath that tantalising notice – marked 8 and 3 points respectively. Now Mother is well treated at Macleans – firewood, matches, oranges, jellies, chocolate biscuits and the like, and they often send the parcel round for her – but nevertheless this is the second time there has been something wanky about the points.

THURSDAY, 26 FEBRUARY

Edward Stebbing

I read Sir Stafford Cripps' speech with approval. It sounded as though something might be done to make the sacrifice more uniform for everybody, to make the news more honest, to stamp out profiteering. And I especially liked his deprecation of dog-racing and boxing. Of course, we need recreation, but these so-called sports (also horse-racing) are not really recreation. I cannot feel that those who patronise them get any real pleasure out of them, but only a temporary excitement and an opportunity for gambling. They refresh neither the body nor the spirit and, as Cripps said, are out of accord with the times we live in. Even in peacetime they are in opposition to culture and a sensible way of recreation. Cripps struck me as the first of our leaders, not excluding Churchill, to have a sincere intention to improve things on the home front, to smooth out injustices, to back up the ordinary man. It needed a Socialist to do this.

Maggie Joy Blunt

Reading *The Road to Bordeaux* by Denis Freeman and Douglas Cooper. A fascinating, horrifying account of the collapse of France, seen from the defeated, retreating front line during hot summer weather. Not, perhaps, as good, from the literary point of view, as Cicely Mackworth's *I Came Out of France* which N and I both think one of the best pieces of objective description we have ever read. But absorbing. The trouble is that these vivid pictures of broken France don't register as real at all. Those blazing towns, those starving, wounded refugees choking the roads, those deserted hospitals and lost, fleeing armies read like some Mephistophilian fantasy. It can't have been true. I in England at that time was pulling up forget-me-nots and planting violas and musk and thrift. White butterflies were haunting the purple lilac. I saw the lilac die and the violas bloom. The news was terrible but it seemed to touch the life of ordinary people scarcely at all.

We are an incredible people. What would our reactions be to an invasion such as France suffered? Would our Wonderful Policemen and Town Authorities lose their grip too? Would we pour out of suburb and village leaving our treasured possessions?

But the British are incalculable. Read an article recently in *Saturday Evening Post*, written before America entered the war, in which the writer, who had just returned from Europe, said he had been unable to discover any coherent Allied plan to match that of the Axis Powers. As far as one can judge we still have no plan. And from what one hears of our inadequate defences, muddled armament production, financiers in control, our tottering War Office, our ancient Navy and vanishing Empire one would think that the Germans – highly organised, terrifyingly efficient – could and would have invaded and conquered us by now without much difficulty. Why haven't they? Is ours an enchanted island? Or is there some subtle pact between the Powers on either side to leave us relatively undisturbed so that the war can go on? Not that I think the war can end only with the defeat of the democracies. I am quite sure that the democracies won't lose. Quite sure. Only we seem to be so damnably stupid and inefficient I can't see how we can possibly win.

Miss de G tells me there was an enemy transmitting set in a hollow tree in the Beeches last summer. How exciting.

SATURDAY, 28 FEBRUARY

Pam Ashford

I am so sorry Garvin is leaving the *Observer*. Miss Bousie thinks the Govt has turned him out for being critical. Charlie said tersely, 'The circulation has gone down badly.' Before the war Scrutator (Sidebotham) and Garvin were my guides, sometimes one was ahead, and sometimes the other. Since Mr Sidebotham's death Garvin has been the only leader writer I have read closely and continuously. Charlie does not care so much for the recent *Observers*, and rates the *Sunday Times* far higher. By the way we have the extraordinary number of five as our Sunday papers – *Observer*, *Times*, *Express*, *Chronicle*, *Mail*. Charlie thinks them all so thin that you have to buy more to get the same amount of reading matter.

MONDAY, 2 MARCH

Pam Ashford
I see the reports that morale is low in this country. That is probably so. Today I could not but say to Mr Mitchell, 'This country is in for a bad time,' and he agreed. Apathy is evident enough. I feel that the wartime diet through this exceptionally long and cold period is an element.

The speaker at the Soroptomist Lunch was John S. Clarke on 'Personalities I Have Met'. The first two were dismissed in a sentence apiece, viz. Lord John Sanger, the Circus Proprietor, and Louis de Rougemount who had lived among the cannibals, and was reckoned to be the world's greatest liar. Mr Clarke then passed on to Lenin. Somehow Mr Clarke in 1920 acted as English interpreter for three weeks in Moscow. Lenin could speak English with perfect pronunciation, but it was dead slow, just one word at a time. We saw a signed photograph of Lenin, in which his Mongolian blood was unmistakable. Lenin sought Mr Clarke out to treat his spaniel which would not walk. Mr Clarke found a tuft of hair had grown between two toes, which he cut out in a couple of minutes; thereupon the dog frisked about delighted. For this Lenin thought Mr Clarke one of the most wonderful men on earth. Civil war was raging all over Russia at that time, and Lenin took that calmly, but not so the suffering of his dog.

Another Russian personality was the President of one of the Soviet States who spoke 'the most perfect English Mr Clarke had ever heard'. This man had escaped from Siberia to London and worked as a guard on the London Underground for seven years on about 25/- a week.

TUESDAY, 3 MARCH

Maggie Joy Blunt
Suddenly much milder. Such a relief, as it is to be getting up in daylight and returning home in daylight.

Our department is hectically active just now preparing for

222

propaganda for the Works for Warships week. Slogans and posters everywhere. B's desk looks as though something has hit it. He spent hours last week trying to find out the colours and order of the flags of Nelson's Last Signal. Phoned Selfridges Information Bureau (closed for the duration owing to shortage of staff), the Imperial War Museum, the Admiralty and God knows what else. No help anywhere. Miss de G found it eventually on an Xmas card. We are going to have a tall flat staff with the signal fluttering on one side and little sailors climbing the other, each holding a notice giving the Savings achieved every day. B drew out the model sailor yesterday to unending and useless criticism from everyone who saw it.

WEDNESDAY, 4 MARCH

Maggie Joy Blunt
Skirts are to be 17ins from the ground. Most of mine are already 16ins and one feels awfully cold about the knees. All my summer frocks will have to be altered again. Or shall I just be old fashioned? Will long evening frocks go out? Shall regret that deeply.

No swansdown puffs to be had, says Miss L. She, like me, uses no other kind and we are disturbed.

THURSDAY, 5 MARCH

Pam Ashford
The public seems to be aware that its morale is below standard – I only wish that realisation would set us off in the opposite direction. This morning a wealthy Jew called to see us about coal supplies for his works. He manufactures and fits furniture for ships (including the *Queen Mary*) and before the war went to Germany once a month. He drew an ugly comparison between what he had seen there and the slackness he sees in the shipyards here.

Then Miss Bousie is full of a broad 'German peace offer', which she takes to mean that they regard us as down and out. Agnes: 'The Germans are at the top of their form now.' I: 'At the top of their form! With three millions killed in Russia!' But defeatism is in the air and this diary knows what the community does not, viz. that I feel it too.

Chapter Eight

THE POOLING OF BLOOD

For months they have been unable to find anyone to do it: fire-watching from the roof of the Royal Academy of Music.

6 March–21 June 1942

11 March General Douglas MacArthur gives up the Philippines as a lost cause and moves to Australia to lead the Pacific Command.

19 March Home Secretary Herbert Morrison threatens to ban the *Daily Mirror* for being unpatriotic and critical of the war effort.

21 March Sir Stafford Cripps hints at the prospect of independence for India.

24 March Heavily outnumbered, British defeat Italians in battle for Malta.

29 March Led by Bomber Harris, RAF devastates the German port of Lubeck.

2 April The first British female conscientious objectors face tribunals.

6 April Also in Britain, white bread officially replaced by cheaper off-white bread.

14 April Purchase tax doubles to 66 per cent, resulting in cigarettes at 2s for 20; the standard rate of income tax remains at 50 per cent.

24 April Heavy bombing of Exeter, Bath, Norwich and York in response to RAF damage to Lubeck and Rostock;

25 April Following her 16th birthday, Princess Elizabeth registers for war service.

12 May The Russians break through the German line at Kharkov.

17 May Sir Stafford Cripps supports calls for a second front in western Europe.

31 May Mass bombings over Cologne and Essen.

1 June Following midget submarine raids on Sydney Harbour, Australians fear full-scale Japanese invasion.

6 June Strategic US naval victory over Japanese off Midway Island near Hawaii.

21 June Rommel captures Tobruk and 35,000 prisoners.

FRIDAY, 6 MARCH

Pam Ashford

A conversation between Mother and me. I: 'If I could only do more in this war.' Mother: 'You do your duty which is more than many.' I: 'I do all that lies within my strength, though what I do is so slight. The itch to join the ATS goes right through me, but I just could not do all that drill and marching.' (I was bedridden from June 1925–August 1928, and disabled for several years after that. I did pull up and get back to work, but I can never decide how far it was a genuine physical improvement and how far a victory of mind over matter.)

The prejudice against the ATS is receding rapidly. The cry used to be, 'Anything except the ATS,' now it is, 'The Army is far better than a factory.'

Edward Stebbing

If one can judge by the newspapers (which is very doubtful), our Indian policy is likely to prove disastrous if it doesn't soon alter, for the Indians seem likely to offer more hindrance than help if the Japanese start invading India.

Obviously we should let the Indians govern themselves.

SATURDAY, 7 MARCH

Maggie Joy Blunt

A soldier has dug my two cabbage patches for me. He is stationed in this area and seems to get quite a bit of free time in which he comes to aid the gardener-less folk around here.

Penalties are to be imposed for wasting paper. Housewives urged to use greasy paper for lighting fires, not newspapers. How many will be able to do this? I know I shan't.

Chemist had no Vapex or anything of that nature. No talcum powder. This is difficult to get anywhere now. A store in Slough has a window full of cheap and unnamed product and I bought a packet marked 'Sample' for 1/9d at a hairdressers not long ago. Our chemist was selling jars of his own make of cold cream and liquid shampoo. Got 2d of Nestle's plain chocolate and some chewing gum at the sweet shop.

B remarked that the Press generally was getting very Red. Russia's magnificent resistance has been the best kind of propaganda it could have had here. Everywhere one hears of admiration for the Russians, of a growing interest in their way of life which won't be easily suppressed – only the other day I overheard a woman in the canteen saying fervently what a marvellous country she thought it, properly organised for total war, every woman doing her bit, not like *some* she knew in England. Even staunch conservatives like my stepmother Ella and Aunt Aggie praise Stalin and the Red Army generously.

For supper – mutton stewed with sundry vegetables and one onion; rhubarb and prunes and a mince pie. All very good. (Feel like Pepys.)

SUNDAY, 8 MARCH

Edward Stebbing
Java is as good as lost, and today I see quoted in the *News of the World* this message from the Dominions Office to Australia: 'At the moment the Empire team is batting on a sticky wicket, and the Axis fast bowlers have had some success. Our best bats are still to go in, and the score will, in time, show that we can give, as well as take, punishment.' My God, what a sublimely complacent attitude! What a gorgeous example of the sporting mentality which is running this war as some sort of glorified Test Match! Heaven help us if we don't soon rid ourselves of the kind of people responsible for this sort of thing.

TUESDAY, 10 MARCH

Pam Ashford
I came home feeling as I often do nowadays, sick with myself, for while I deplore other people concentrating on their own private affairs, in what way am I different myself? I yearn to be strong. Physical strength never appealed much to me before. I have grown used to the loss of the recreations in which youth delights – hiking, sport, dancing and nights at the theatre and cinema. Instead I have sought beauty in music and art, truth in philosophy and learning. Never going far along any avenue, always a dabbler, nevertheless in these I have found my nature fulfilling itself. The love of beauty has not been blurred by the war – the effect is rather to the contrary – but I no longer feel that is enough. To be a member of a community is, of course, another essential to self-fulfilment and before the war coal exporting gratified me there, but nowadays I feel less and less that I am playing a significant role in society. But I am not fit for anything but sedentary work, and long hours only make me ill. So I just have to go on being sick with myself.

WEDNESDAY, 11 MARCH

Maggie Joy Blunt
Made such a noise coughing at the office this afternoon PA sent me home. Have no cold and don't feel at all ill, just exhausted – unable to sleep or smoke. Cough began last week and won't be put off by any mixture or lozenge.

Stayed Monday night with June. June saw a film recently in which Churchill and Stalin appeared. For Churchill – a few polite claps. For Stalin – a storm of applause.

Menu outside a Piccadilly restaurant quoted pheasant at 25/- or 27/- a helping. Bought a swansdown puff (with handkerchief, without coupon) for 3/11 (a fairly reasonable price), black cream mascara which I never use, and cuticle remover. Noticed several taxis with their tyres painted white – this is probably old news, but I had not noticed it before. As I crossed Victoria Station black-out time was being announced through the loudspeakers with the times of trains and a request that passengers pull down carriage blinds.

THURSDAY, 12 MARCH

Maggie Joy Blunt
In bed all day. Fanny in this morning as usual. She comes every Monday and Thursday morning to clean the cottage and on Wednesday for a short while to do the fires and wash up. As I have not seen her since January we gossip most of the time. She does not like the idea of eating standard bread. I tell her she should be glad to have bread of any kind in quantity.

Pam Ashford
During the past two weeks I have mentioned tinned rhubarb to Mother several times, but she has rejected the idea.

Edward Stebbing
My landlady told me about some members of a local women's club who went to see what sort of meals their children were getting at school. The headmaster tried to prevent them from going in (suggested getting a letter of authority, which would have given him warning), but the women more or less forced their way in and saw the food the children were having. The meal consisted of a little soup with one undercooked potato, which most of the children did not eat, followed by no more than a spoonful of some milk pudding, an obviously inadequate meal. The headmaster then complained that

there were no proper facilities for providing meals. The leader of the women said that was what they wanted to rectify. The point is that the mothers would not feel disposed to go out to war work (and volunteers had been asked for in this district) if they knew that their children were not receiving adequate meals at school.

Ernest van Someren
In the evening Mr Holmes came to see us, our former neighbour who now lives and works near Sandringham. He told us that people there resent the Royal shooting parties which go on about once a week, in particular the use of troops as beaters. On one occasion when the shooting-party wandered across the factory premises they were greeted with rude shouts, and remarks such as 'If you want some shooting, why not go to Malaya?' Of course it is convenient to have a lot of pheasants about, for poaching.

FRIDAY, 13 MARCH

Maggie Joy Blunt
So exasperated with cough I got up and cycled to Dr B's morning surgery. Could do nothing but cough at him for first 5 minutes or so. He has sent me back with special syringe, lotion, lozenges and orders to stay at home, keep warm and relax for 3 or 4 days. Called at butchers – they are short of beef this week but are sending me loin. Don't know what my cats live on but they all look fairly well nourished.

Pam Ashford
The Cosmo had *Destry Rides Again* with Marlene Deitrich and James Stewart. It finished at 2.50, so I got to the Academy at 3. Miss Currie, a member of the class, gave us a song recital. Mr Mackie played us the eight gramophone discs he would want on a desert island (a series called *Desert Island Discs* is at present running on the Forces Programme on Thursday evenings).

Edward Stebbing
The loss of 13 Allied ships in the battle for Java is another great blow to our sea power. But the mood of the *Sunday Pictorial* seems to me the wrong mood altogether; its nauseating heroics leave me cold. There is no room for this sickening sob-stuff. What is needed now is a more purposeful mood, a cool and calculating, rational outlook. We cannot see clearly through this smoke-screen of emotion. It will not matter much if we are to get fewer newspapers if this is the stuff

they are going to befog us with. The cold, scientific planning of our enemies is more than a match for our deathless heroism and skill in withdrawal.

Ernest van Someren
Cycled to work, haircut in the lunch-hour, was offered a weekly called *Soviet War News* by the barber. We were going to have a film-show at work, but at a preview we decided that the film sent us this week was too technical for the girls, so we skipped it.

SATURDAY, 14 MARCH

Maggie Joy Blunt
A mild and lovely day. Slough Warships Week begins. Should be attending an opening with local Red Cross detachment, or working overtime at the office, or having my hair done. The problem of which of these most important now solved. I can do none.

Pam Ashford
A quiet day. Did some more German Correspondence Course. I enjoy it. In enrolling for that course I reasoned, 'When we have won the war, we shall want to write to our German customers again,' but sometimes a dreadful feeling comes over me: 'If we lost the war, then you would bless your knowledge.'

SUNDAY, 15 MARCH

Maggie Joy Blunt
Military activity in the Beeches again. Soldiers with lorries camping in clearing outside cottage – have never known them do this before. Last year they parked lorries there, set up AA guns, picnicked at midday and once set the heather on fire but never stayed the night. They fetch water from Lady S's kitchen.

Not all landlords are raking in huge profits. Have just gone through accounts for the house I share with my brother. It is in a London suburb. We get £85 per annum rent. During the last 12 months we have had to pay out £22. 10s. 4d Property Tax, nearly £90 for decorations, repairs and maintenance, £2. 10s Insurance premium, £6. 9s. 6d War Damage Contribution and we begin this year with £32. 7s. 6d Property Tax and an unpaid builder's account. As I have no time at all now to attend to these matters personally and brother is in Suez am having to hand management over to agent. I know this agent fairly well and believe he is reliable but he will claim his commission.

MONDAY, 16 MARCH

Maggie Joy Blunt
Cough has gone. I can smoke again.

WEDNESDAY, 18 MARCH

Maggie Joy Blunt
Meals: Breakfast – tea, cereal and black treacle. Black treacle is the only thing that makes my inside function properly. I take a teaspoonful every morning with cereal or porridge. A 2lb tin lasts me several months so long as I use it for nothing else, but it requires ingenuity to keep the supply going. At the office – cocoa at 11am (made with powdered milk). Lunch in Slough, Williamsons – where I overheard a woman discussing the Woolworth fire. The Manager, she said, suspects sabotage – fried haddock, chips, roll and butter, prune tart and coffee. Tea and biscuits at 4pm. Supper at home – pot-au-feu soup, raw vegetable salad (cabbage and grated carrot mainly) with peanuts and cheese, wholemeal bread and margarine, and stewed apples (bottled last summer in preserving tablet solution).

BL picked me up at H Corner this morning. She is not well, complaining of earache. M de G is away with a sore throat. Miss B has been away nearly a fortnight. N on phone this evening says she has had a bad sore throat for ten days and is getting nerves about it. Minor illnesses seem general.

Lift from stranger this evening. A rattly old car, 'but it goes' as he said. We discussed petrol restrictions and viewed the future when all cars but those on essential service will be off the roads. We agreed that our use of petrol has been monstrously extravagant. We discussed also shoe repair difficulties, shortage of rubber and the care we shall need to preserve bicycle tyres. The war, we sighed, seemed to be going on indefinitely – when and where will it end?

MONDAY, 23 MARCH

Maggie Joy Blunt
Jules phones. Says his part in this war will have been to provide me with cigarettes. Tells me that L is now working in a cigarette factory and will be able to send me 100 a week.

WEDNESDAY, 25 MARCH

Maggie Joy Blunt
A mild, misty, heavenly day. Sun pours into our office and is almost too strong. Meg and I decide to lunch in Windsor – by the river if possible. In experimental mood we enter a riverside hotel, are ushered into a dim, draped, red and gold dining room, where, in company with young Etonians, ladies with bright hair, officer ATS, Brass Hats, dowagers and pekes, we eat potato soup, fish cake and sauce, chicken hash topped with poached egg, mashed potatoes and greens, and stewed figs for 6/- each. At our canteen we can get the same quality and a larger quantity of soup, meat, vegetables, sweet, roll and butter, cheese, tea or coffee, for under 2/-. But we enjoyed ourselves. We were paying for the head waiter's white tie, the cunning hessian drapery and red silk lampshades, the rent and the salaries and all the other exorbitant expense of a select riverside hotel in the shadow of Windsor Castle. We sat on the riverside wall afterwards, reluctant to return to work. Swans waggled their beaks at us. Over the dreaming Thames a mist lay like golden gauze – one felt that when it lifted the long delaying spring would make a spectacular entrance.

THURSDAY, 26 MARCH

Edward Stebbing
Bus-conductor's remark this morning: 'The Jews are the ones who are making money out of this war. A Jew's war, that's what it is.' It is rare to hear anti-Semitic views nowadays.

Ernest van Someren
Julia's first birthday, Laurie remembered it almost as soon as he woke up. But on account of his cold the tea is postponed. He was kept home from school.

I went to work by train, on to town to the Patent Office library, then to Trafalgar Square. There I changed my plans and decided to go to a lunch-hour concert, so bought some sandwiches and ate them on the steps of the National Gallery. There was an interesting crowd to watch, and a dull speech from a sort of model battleship advertising Warship Week. There was also a Coach and Four, with costumed driver, standing by the pavement by the ship, which I thought very poor publicity, suggesting an old-fashioned and slow navy. I much enjoyed Irene Scharrer playing Chopin and for once felt really conscious of the existence and continuity of this nation, as demonstrated by these lunch-hour concerts. The War Artists Exhibition was more interesting than I expected, but I didn't have time to look at it much. Went to another library, and then to call on a consulting engineer at Pinner. I stopped and had tea with him and talked about oboes, and he found that the one I had been lent was slightly defective, which partly accounts for my difficulty in getting any sound out of it.

SATURDAY, 28 MARCH

Edward Stebbing
The Anderson shelter which has stood at the bottom of my landlady's garden and which was used a few times at the time of the blitz has now been taken out by my landlord to make more garden space.

MONDAY, 30 MARCH

Pam Ashford
Soroptomist Lunch. All around the table expressions of loathing for the Japs went up. 'The yellow peril', in contrast to which the Chinese were praised for their culture, philosophy and other magnificent qualities. Without in any way disputing that point, I did say to Dr Knight, 'Surely the phrase "The Yellow Peril" was originally directed against the Chinese?' She thought so too.

Talk turned on marrying coloured races. Extreme loathing was expressed again. I do think that the future of humanity lies in 'the pooling of blood'. But to marry a black man is to me horrible too.

WEDNESDAY, 1 APRIL

Pam Ashford
Sir William Beveridge is reported in the papers as saying that a scheme has been worked out at 3/- a week to insure the individual against economic insecurity in various forms – sickness, unemployment, blindness, old age, widowhood. All these cases would get £2 a week.

Edward Stebbing
Although our promise of self-government to India is very belated, I think the Indians would be very foolish not to take the opportunity of accepting the proposals. It may be that they do not trust us to keep our promise, but this is hardly conceivable, as no government which makes such a promise could survive if it did not keep it. The consequences will be very serious if the Indians reject our plan.

Ernest van Someren

Laurie finished his term today, and brought home quite a good report. Put out some new rat poison in the evening.

THURSDAY, 2 APRIL

Ernest van Someren

Cycled again, film show in the lunch-hour of films by the Gas Association. Found one hen dead this morning, as she had managed to get at some of the rat poison I suppose, most depressing as she was laying well, that leaves only three. In the evening dug a good hole and buried the hen. K was very overtired and depressed, but a friend has found us a part-time help who will come for two mornings a week, beginning tomorrow.

SATURDAY, 4 APRIL

Ernest van Someren

Up a little later than usual, found L downstairs and already dressed, excited at the prospects of the Zoo and visitors. We went off by bus at 10.45, met my sister E with her boys Nigel and Richard at noon, at Camden Town. Into the Zoo, with lunch-basket and cine-camera. It's rather thinly populated now, but there was quite enough for three total beginners to see and enjoy. Laurie was particularly impressed by the monkeys, and by the automatic postcard-selling machines. All three boys loved the tunnel under the road, in which they shouted merrily. E missing the flowers, most of which are cleared out for the vegetable growing. We had our lot of sandwiches, lemonade for the boys, milk for L and later my sister and I visited the bar while the boys climbed the stone lion outside.

SUNDAY, 5 APRIL

Pam Ashford

Holy smoke! The Points Scheme is to cover breakfast cereals now. I have 10 boxes of Weetabix, two of Ryevita, and one of cornflakes.

MONDAY, 6 APRIL

Pam Ashford

Glasgow always has its Spring Holiday on Easter Monday. All the work shown at the Exhibition of British Art Today, as arranged by the Contemporary Art Society, is very good, though there is something about the general effect that strikes me as dull. The picture that delighted me most after that was 'Rock Garden, Cookham Dene' by Stanley Spencer.

The room that faces where the bomb fell and which must have had a shake-up is open now and I went in. That is the stuffed bird section, and some of the stuffed animals are there now. There is a notice that owing to enemy action some of the birds are not looking so well as they used to.

Ernest van Someren
We all got up a little later, to make up for having lost 2 hours' sleep on Saturday night by going to bed late as well as altering the clocks. By the way, the three boys (aged 9, 6, 4) got up first on Sunday and made tea and bought it up to their parents on a tray, at about 7am. We did not ask them to do it again, though it was quite well done.

WEDNESDAY, 8 APRIL

Pam Ashford
At 8.45 I observed large consignments of tinned fruit being put on Massey's shelves. I asked for pears, though knowing it was a registered-customers-only shop. They have changed this rule, however, and I got the pears. I feel elated.

FRIDAY, 10 APRIL

Edward Stebbing
The apparent ease with which the Japanese airmen sink our warships has become an alarming matter. The news of the sinking of the *Hermes* is all the more grievous when, as in tonight's radio bulletin, it is immediately followed by an account of how some of our bombers attacked a German ship and 'probably damaged it with near misses'.

SATURDAY, 11 APRIL

Edward Stebbing
The failure of Sir Stafford Cripps' mission to India, which has for some days dominated all other news, is a great disappointment. Especially must it be so for the *News Chronicle*, which printed a headline the day before saying, 'Congress Accepts British Proposals'.

Talking about after the war, a man said it depended on which way the country turned whether there would be an economic slump. If, as was quite probable he thought, it turned Socialist, money would be found for necessary construction. If it remained under Capitalist control, there would be a waiting period while the capitalists decided which were the most profitable interests in which to invest their money. He and another man agreed that this country would never turn Fascist.

Pam Ashford
India. A shocking business. Mother says she understands the Indian attitude perfectly. 'They mean the British to put the Japs out, and then when the British are exhausted from the fight with the Japs, the Indians mean to put the British out.'

I got a second 16 point tin of pears at Massey's this morning.

WEDNESDAY, 15 APRIL

Pam Ashford
This is the time of year when one's observing is apt to turn from the 'masses' to 'nature'. This evening one could say not as a scientific observation , but with joy in the heart, 'the trees are opening'. In fact, the horse-chestnuts are well away and the lime trees are very pretty with tiny scraps of pale green bespangled from slender boughs. The crocuses are now lying flat on the ground and the first daffodils are unfurling their petals. Spring is late this year, but not one whit less beautiful.

This morning at Peacock's I got a box containing six portions of Velveta Cheese at 6d. I have not bought any more tinned fruit. All the week both Ferguson and Massey's have had blackberries (both wild and cultivated) at 12 points, and Ferguson's had pineapple cubes at 16 points on Monday. I slithered around a lot over the pineapple proposition, but decided to wait. The story is that last Friday a Glasgow newspaper said 'dried apricots' were to come on the market during the week commencing the 20th. The rumour has been radiating in all directions for several days. Whenever you go you hear it. Mother says the English Society Whist Drive yesterday was quite unsettled by it.

Edward Stebbing
The most staggering part of the new Budget is, of course, the big increase on tobacco and after that, probably the increase on entertainment tax. The latter was the main cause of comment at lunchtime today. My own expenditure on tobacco is so small that even another 7½d an ounce would not make it prohibitive, but 2/- seems such an excessive price for an ounce of tobacco that, all the

same, I may feel compelled to give up smoking and spend what I save in this way on entertainments, which are much more important to me. Even so, it will mean having to be content with inferior seats at the theatre.

Ernest van Someren
I went off to a big meeting at the Institution of Civil Engineers on statistical methods in Quality Control. The hall was full of a very mixed audience, and I was deeply impressed with its opulent ugliness, and the appalling ceiling paintings. The speeches were good, and varied, and I stayed till a bit after five. Then I had to go and leave the oboe at a shop to be mended, buy some coffee, and meet my mother at six for supper. We had it at Bertorellis, but eating in a restaurant isn't the pleasure it was before the war. Then we went to the Scala for a show of new Russian films. They were very slow in getting going and I saw four shorts, and only a little of the main film of the evening, which looked like being a good straight drama, *The New Teacher*.

SATURDAY, 18 APRIL

Pam Ashford
One day this week Agnes was lamenting the impossibility of getting dates. I had seen them recently, I said, and would watch. There they were again this morning. Seeing Agnes ahead of me in Hope Street I ran after her and said she should go back to Peacock's, but she had not her points with her. An immense queue outside a fruiterer under the Bridge yesterday – they had raisins. Several people report grocers without rice.

If all the psychologists in the Kingdom had been given the job of devising a way of keeping the women folk from worrying about the war, they could never have devised anything that would do so more effectively than Lord Woolton and his points.

Ernest van Someren
Our sixth wedding anniversary. Laurie who had been told it was coming gave us each a present at breakfast, both things he had found in the house and wrapped up for us, Kay a napkin ring and for me a torch battery.

K made us a special dinner to celebrate, with a written menu, and the aid of two tins and a bottle of white wine from Luxembourg.

SUNDAY, 19 APRIL

Edward Stebbing

Two of the men on fire-watching duty with me said they thought they were doing more for the war effort by continuing to smoke than they would be by not smoking and putting the money thus saved into war savings, because the man who does the latter gets his money back with interest, while the smoker gives his money back to the Government in tax without any chance of getting it back.

Pam Ashford

The Women's Parliament held a Brains Trust today at the Cosmo. Mr Frank Waters (of the *Express*) was the question-master, and inevitably he began his introduction with 'This is a unique occasion'. Then he quoted La Rochefaucauld who said, 'The intellect of the greater part of women serves greater to strengthen their folly than their reason.' (Loud laughter.) Then the Brains Trust was introduced. Dr Wattie, Medical Officer for Child Welfare, Glasgow. Mrs Kerr, shop steward. Miss Jack, Secy. of the Scottish Non-Graduate Teachers Association. Mrs Hunter, Civil Defence Worker, Greenock. Dr Lloyd, formerly of the Technical, now Women Power Officer for Glasgow. Mr MacLaren, shop steward in Howden's.

Question: Would the Brains Trust approve of women being appointed to the higher posts in the diplomatic and consular services, and why?
Miss Jack: At the Round Table Conference at the Peace we should *see to it*, not merely approve, that the women of the countries concerned should have a share in the making of the terms of the peace. As they have borne the brunt of the war, so they should have the brunt of the peace. We should support Lady Astor's efforts.
Dr Lloyd: I should say women are so much better suited than men that the marvel is that any man has ever taken on such difficult work. Women are the peacemakers. They spend their lives settling trouble, start with cradle-rocking, then their own men's troubles. What do women talk about? Trouble. Girls talk of young men. Older women talk of other people's men. Old women talk of their operations. They could carry on, on an international scale, what they are doing all the time.

Question: Is it essential that women should look to their looks in wartime or is it merely the advertising slogan of beauty specialists and hairdressers?

240

Miss Jack: Making the best of oneself means 'dressing to suit the part'. There should be a welfare supervisor in every factory to advise girls who don't realise that they should be dressed in a workmanlike manner.

Women at all times and of all ages should make the best of themselves. It has a beneficial psychological effect. It gives one confidence. It is a great help in getting a point over to an audience. And in getting a point over to schoolchildren. Why not in wartime? I have, however, no use for the woman who spends a long time making herself look nice for her boyfriend, but is a slattern when in the house.

Dr Wattie: There is another aspect of long hair. Some girls don't brush or wash their hair for weeks on end. Typhus is carried by the body louse and possibly by the head louse. We are addressing another campaign to the women of the country on keeping their heads clean. We would like the shingle. We are not likely to get so far as that, but we are hoping for the liberty cut.

Question: Is it true that women are worse gossips than men?

Mrs Kerr: Men gossip as much as women but they do so more in a matter of fact way. Men gossip in pubs. Where women are not to be seen.

Dr Lloyd: Women more, men worse. A woman only talks about troubles, and very often she settles them.

Miss Jack: I consider that women are greater gossips than men, and I admire them for it. Men take up the attitude, 'It has happened and nothing can be done about it.' Women, however, talk about it and something comes of it. Women are genuinely interested in affairs of people around them. Owing to heredity, environment, social circumstances, men are interested in bigger things. Women are now coming out of their homes. We have not had the opportunities of meeting in pubs and learning how men live and their problems. Women have not had the opportunity of mixing with people outside their own little circle, and that is why we become gossips in it. We will get on to gossiping about something worth while.

WEDNESDAY, 22 APRIL

Pam Ashford
DRIED PEACHES! A tin of Heinz oxtail soup lured me into Peacocks this morning and there was a box of dried peaches (not visible from the door). I doubted my eyes so much that I had to ask the assistant what was in the box. Mrs Muir went around at 12.30 and they were gone then.

Ernest van Someren
Received a cheque for 5 guineas from *Housewife* for an article which appears tomorrow on A Wartime Budget.

SUNDAY, 26 APRIL

Pam Ashford
Mother woke me up this morning with the dramatic words, 'There is news today.' Naturally I was startled. 'Exeter bombed.' Mother comes from Exeter. We sincerely hope no harm has come to the Cathedral. What made me sit up, however, was the one o'clock news which mentioned Bath. Mr Ferguson and Mr Hutchison went to London on Thursday to see the Admiralty and we were uncertain if they would have to go on to the Admiralty Contracts Dept at Bath. Charlie is very satisfied with the performance of the RAF over Germany.

The Women's Parliament.

Schoolchildren. The child is almost the greatest sufferer of the war – short school hours, uncontrolled leisure and freedom. His development is stunted and his reactions anti-social. His physical and social standards must not be lowered by the war. If so we shall lose the war in the next generation whatever the Forces do.

Full-time education has been restarted in Glasgow. Yes, but prior to the war that meant a total of six hours a day. Now four hours is accepted as normal. In the winter 3 hours was accepted.

Adolescents. The raising of the school age was postponed. We must see that they are trained between 14 and 16. Leisure must be guided and made pleasant and useful. Up to 14 they belong to the Ministry of Education; after 16 to the Ministry of Labour. Between 14 and 16 they are nobody's bairns and are a danger to themselves and the community as a whole. We hear of young criminals, but there are none. There are spoilt boys and girls, spoilt by their educational system or the lack of it.

Ernest van Someren
Another fine but cool day. Julia has a new trick: if you throw a cushion on the floor she crawls up to it and lays her head down on it for a few seconds, looking at us for approval. Laurie discovered this, and suggested that I should photograph it, which I did this morning. I tried to get him with his head on the same cushion, but Julia tried to push him off so I had to give him a separate one. Then I made a

bonfire and started tomatoes, I also had to replace some broken glass with Windolite.

TUESDAY, 28 APRIL

Pam Ashford
Mrs Stewart, our neighbour, has been in bed for a week. Seeing her today, I enquired. She said it was a mystery illness and named several others (all near relatives) who also had it. She had a terrible pain in the stomach. The doctor blamed it on the new bread. White flour is passed through a filter. Wholemeal flour is too coarse for the white flour filters and has to be used as it is. Some bakers have put filters on for wholemeal flour, however, and 'if you knew the foreign matter that has been removed . . .' She considers she had a particularly big share of foreign matter.

WEDNESDAY, 29 APRIL

Pam Ashford
The news of the attack on York has shaken Mother and me. The BBC says the Minster was not struck. We were at the Minster in 1935, 1937 and 1939 so that it is pretty fresh in our minds.

Bath, Exeter, Norwich, York – the four Cathedral towns in order. Can it be the Cathedrals they seek to destroy? If either York or Exeter were destroyed it would be like a knife going through my soul. Those I have known and loved. The paper reports that a girls' high school was struck at York. There is a school of that type within a stone's throw of the Minster. The papers also say historical buildings were struck at York. The blind asylum is an historical enough building, just beside the girls' school. Can it be? And probably we shan't know until the war is over.

THURSDAY, 30 APRIL

Edward Stebbing
To my landlady and her husband one of the most significant facts about the recent German air-raids on Bath, Exeter, York and Norwich is that they are all cathedral towns. I said I didn't think they picked those towns just because they had cathedrals; there would not be much point in it. But Mrs H said, 'We set store by our historical buildings.' Yet I wonder whether we really do set great store by them, or whether we only think we do because we have been told we do so often. After all, it is our dwelling-houses and places of work we care

about most; I doubt whether any but a very few are terribly upset if a church is destroyed. Only a minority go to church and only a slightly larger minority have any feeling for the beauty or antiquity of a church. There are only a few exceptions, like Canterbury Cathedral, St Paul's or Westminster Abbey, for which there is any sort of general regard.

SATURDAY, 2 MAY

Ernest van Someren
A fine day, Julia climbed the stairs for the first time, 17 of them, twice in the morning and again at bedtime. Of course with one of us in attendance to prevent a slip back. Kay has a horrible cold, so in the afternoon she rested and I took the children out for a slight walk, and mended a playpen. She meant to go and see our Hilda in hospital, where she is getting over a miscarriage involving twins.

SUNDAY, 3 MAY

Ernest van Someren
While K rested I took the children for a walk down by the river, at one boathouse I counted 14 cars and 8 motor cycles, and there was a queue waiting for boats, there were also a few boys bathing. We looked for tadpoles in side streams, but couldn't find any, so we went out and got some from another stream after tea, and put them in a small cement tank in the garden, which I have given Laurie.

MONDAY, 4 MAY

Pam Ashford
The Soroptomists met for lunch today, the guest speaker being Miss Macallister of Jordanhill Training College, Lecturer in Speech Training. It goes without saying that as a speaker she was good. She described various experiences with University graduates and young men and women with higher leaving certificates, who could write all right, but were lost when they had to speak. In some cases it was the quality of speech that was bad (slovenly English) but in that group, it was the inability to express themselves that mostly mattered. Her talk also included a clinic belonging to the Hospital for Sick Children with speech defects. Cleft palates seem to be common there. The hospital operates on the mouth and gets it right, but the child continues to speak in a 'cleft palate' manner. There are very few instances in which the defect has not penetrated to the subconscious

244

mind, and the psychological approach is not less important than the elocutionary one – more important often. Stuttering is entirely due to psychological causes, she said. The talk was appreciated.

Edward Stebbing
Occasionally a newspaper prints something worth printing and today the *News Chronicle* excels itself and prints two pieces I am glad to read. One is another exposure of the furniture racket, one of the worst examples of profiteering in this war. The other is an editorial attack on methods used at Army Battle Schools, where attempts are made to instil 'synthetic hatred' into the minds of soldiers. Not much need be said about this. It is so obviously a characteristic of Nazism that one can hardly credit it happening in this country. Deliberately to try to breed hatred among men and nations, as if there were not enough already, is contrary to our supposed war aims and to all civilised ideas, and it would make the establishment of a real peace after the war more difficult.

Ernest van Someren
Fairly busy at work. In the evening made a round of visits to neighbours, including a wounded soldier who sometimes comes to WEA classes, a boy of 21 who had his leg run over by a train soon after he joined the army. He has work now, but is ill at home with trouble in his stump.

FRIDAY, 8 MAY

Ernest van Someren
The spectrograph arrived today, and I had the most interesting job of unpacking and inspecting it, it's a different one from the type I have formerly used, and costs about £500 without its accessories. It can't be used till I have a stand made for it, and for the last few days I have been doing some unusual experimenting on a very old piece of French apparatus which I hope to adapt to make sparks for my new job.

SUNDAY, 10 MAY

Edward Stebbing
I recently remarked that the fear of being given tit for tat is the strongest deterrent against any country using gas in war, and I think Churchill said the best thing he could have said in his speech tonight (when he warned Germany clearly that she would be the victim of large-scale gas warfare if she used it first), to prevent it being used.

All the same, how horrible it is that this threat should have to be given and still more so if we should have to carry it out.

Ernest van Someren
A fair and cool day. In the morning did some odd jobs about the house, including cementing up some mouseholes. There was a rat hunt with a ferret yesterday, and we think we heard a rat under the floor last night. After lunch we went by bus to Hertford and then out to Woodhall Park, with Julia in the rucsac.

In the evening I did some writing and Mother did some sorting of letters she wrote to her Mother during the last war. She sat up till after midnight alone and heard a rat.

TUESDAY, 12 MAY

Ernest van Someren
In the evening the biology lecture was at our house again, the lecturer came to supper with us and we talked about music. I borrowed a microscope from our doctor and he demonstrated the circulation of the blood on a freshly killed frog he brought with him, rather to the distress of three members of the class who preferred not to see such things. One frog behaved very badly and jumped off the stage of the microscope although technically dead.

SATURDAY, 16 MAY

Ernest van Someren
Yesterday Julia climbed the stairs by herself for the first time. She did it under supervision a week ago, but K was surprised to be unable to find her downstairs, and found her on the top landing pulling newspaper from under the carpet.

The rat is still with us. He went upstairs this morning, and later ate some poisoned cheese.

SUNDAY, 17 MAY

Edward Stebbing
There is no doubt good reason for confidence at the present time, but the newspapers, as usual, are somewhat overdoing it, going wild with prophecy and explanations of strategy, the only basis for which is in the imagination of the writer. Seeing the headline, 'Hitler will be defeated by 1942,' my landlady said, 'I do wish they'd stop prophesying.'

MONDAY, 18 MAY

Pam Ashford
On Thursday Miss Gibson's little budgie Goodie died. Goodie would never take much interest in the black market budgie seed she gave it, and utterly refused to eat crumbs and other suggestions. Miss Gibson says starvation is the cause. Then on Friday Margaret's budgie died. They fed him on packets of seed now being sold in shops and they killed him.

Cranston's have 'budgie seed' at 6d a quarter lb. I asked them what was the composition and they did not know. I said, 'I would not risk my bird with anything I did not know the composition of,' and they said, they were 'selling a lot'.

Ernest van Someren
Laurie happened to go downstairs first, and got a scare from hearing the rat running across the darkened kitchen, at which I was much annoyed. I went down and found the rat in a drawer of the dresser, but it rushed out and took safe cover before I was able to get a slosh at it.

In the evening I nailed a strip of wood under the dresser to barricade the drawers against rats and mice, both of which have been know to run up the leg and get into the paper-bag drawer for a feast. I went out to a PPU meeting, we had a discussion on education and class segregation, which was quite interesting. Afterwards, we borrowed the cat from next door and kept him in our house all night. Laurie woke up once saying he heard the rat, but this may have been a dream.

WEDNESDAY, 20 MAY

Pam Ashford
My pet hobby horse is feminism – equal work for equal pay, family allowances, married women working if they want to, etc. – and my mind sometimes wonders, when these subjects arise, how far one can use the war situation legitimately and how far one is exploiting the nation's trials.

Mother has got our little mite of a bird on to mashed potato which he is eating voraciously. For years we fed the sparrows on potato which they were daft about, but Dick never took to it before. Miss Fuller also saw Mother today and said she enjoys Dick's singing. (The outburst that began when USA entered the war continued.) The losses Miss Gibson and Margaret suffered last week have given Miss

Bousie a turn. Her Jackie (budgie) is still dining off the hoards of imported seed laid in. I have begged her again and again to get him accustomed to alternatives while there is still time. She is afraid to strike out with vegetables.

TUESDAY, 26 MAY

Pam Ashford
When speaking to Mr Lawson this afternoon I said I should be wanting a winter coat in August and he said I should buy now. He has just returned from England and his suppliers are losing their girls in the hundreds. By August there will be scarcely any labour left in the clothing industry. All this about utility clothing is talk. By next winter buying an article of clothing will involve intensive searching of the retailers.

THURSDAY, 28 MAY

Pam Ashford
The Glasgow papers have a photo of York Guildhall burning. On the way to York Station after my last visit three years ago I stood on the spot from which the picture was taken, looking across the river at that beautiful piece of medieval England and saying, '*Au revoir*, I will return.' Little did I suppose that I should ever see a photo of the Guildhall from that angle – with the flames belching from its windows.

FRIDAY, 29 MAY

Pam Ashford
Nursery schools are part of the war effort now.

For some time I have seen a small notice on a wall in Sauchiehall Street headed 'Conference on Nursery Schools' and I visited today.

Miss A. Pirie, of the Glasgow Education Dept., principal speaker, then gave the address and said that there have been nursery schools for 20 years, but the war has brought the opportunity of development.

What makes a child happy? Having something to do. He is a vortex of energy. He is made to be creative. We must see that what he creates is something worthwhile and that his activity is not misdirected into destructiveness.

The pattern of behaviour is formed in the first five years; it is then that the child is turned into a gangster or into a boy scout leader.

Love is an essential part of a child's make-up. Miss Pirie described mothers who think they are maternal whereas they are possessive. What we call love is something savouring of wisdom. The child also needs fresh air and sunshine. Why do we stress the play side? In play a child feels that he counts for something. If that outlet is denied neurosis may develop.

We were then asked to turn our chairs so as to face the model nursery. I found myself in the middle of the front row! To my surprise 18 children came in. The highlight was a wee mite of about 4½ in a waterproof apron who spent twenty minutes or so bathing an enamel baby in a bowl.

MONDAY, 1 JUNE

Edward Stebbing
Much talk today about Saturday night's terrific RAF raid by over 1000 bombers on Cologne. Why was Cologne chosen? Why was the raid concentrated into one and a half hours? were two of the most interesting questions.

TUESDAY, 2 JUNE

Edward Stebbing
Raids by over 1000 aircraft are very awe-inspiring and exciting, but on examining them rationally they lose something of their glamour. One man, after another had told him of the second mass raid, said, 'Isn't it disgusting?' 'Do you know how many were killed in the first one? . . . twenty thousand,' said the other. 'I know war is war, but they shouldn't glorify twenty thousand killed'.

The *News Chronicle* today says justice must be done 'in no gloating spirit', but 'gloating' is exactly what the papers are doing, with their detailed descriptions and eulogies of praise for those who planned and executed the raid. It is difficult to know what attitude to take, as a civilised person, towards air-raids which are nothing less than massacre, but which, on the other hand, may shorten the war. And raids on industrial targets which are thickly populated, must inevitably involve great loss of life. This 'we-must-be-cruel-to-be-kind' point of view sounds like hypocrisy, yet it is the only point of view which can reconcile wanting to win the war and not wanting to hate our enemies. Yet what cries of horror and rage would go up if the Germans made a series of similar raids on our big cities! If one accepts war one must accept air-raids; if one accepts air-raids one must accept them on any scale; if one accepts them on any scale

249

one must accept death on any scale. I repeat: what, as a civilised person, is one to think? I, personally, do not want to accept war, but neither do I want to accept the rule of Nazism – so I am caught between two stools.

Pam Ashford
At 1pm the BBC says in emotional tones that we had made a second raid on Germany, 1000 planes strong. I want everything that helps to give the United Nations victory, but I can find little rejoicing in this large scale destruction. My German friends did not approve Hitler though they kept their mouths shut when at home, and I am sure they were not unique. There is also enforced labour in the Ruhr drawn from the enslaved nations. The people who have lost their lives in Cologne and Essen are not necessarily worse than those who survived. What a pity you cannot label the bombs in advance, viz. 'This is for an SS man', 'this is for a Jew baiter', etc. What one wants to get at are the people who plan those dreadful barbarities being perpetrated on the Czechs, the Yugo-Slavs, the Poles, etc.

Ernest van Someren
Fine and hot. A neighbour dropped in and I got him to help me spray the apple tree (which is infected with insects) and I also sprayed roses and pinks, used my stirrup pump with great success, as it's like a big tree.

An alert at about 3.00 which woke L, of course, and he rocked the bed and woke Julia. I went and reassured him, and they didn't make any disturbance. I was relieved that it was not a reprisal raid around here. These mass raids may be effective, but they won't win the war.

WEDNESDAY, 3 JUNE

Pam Ashford
Lieut. Pat Craigie came to say goodbye. He is leaving for 'foreign parts'. Maybe India, maybe Africa. The conversation was mostly monosyllabic, and did not last long. According to his mother he broke down completely at the last moment (I should be astonished if his mother did not too). Miss Craigie however says, 'What is the sense of crying about it?' Mrs Craigie will not hear from him for three months and has requested all her friends to refrain from asking after him because she cannot bear it. When she hears she will say. She has used up all her coupons in fitting him out in new clothes from top to toe. Who would not feel the parting?

Ernest van Someren

Fine and hot. In the afternoon we received a parcel from my sister in the USA of some tinned meats and dried fruit, and a few sweets. All very welcome. We had supper in the garden and one of my colleagues called for me, and we cycled to a WEA lecture. This was the first of a course on Psychology. There were 23 students, all women but two. The lecturer was young and clear, a girl from a psychological clinic.

Had to go out afterwards to remind a couple of people about fire-watching, they slacked off round here, and the Council tried to appoint a paid organiser to rearrange things. For months they have been unable to find anyone to do it at the official pay for the job, and now I am trying to reorganise it in this road.

THURSDAY, 4 JUNE

Edward Stebbing

In a letter my sister expresses what is perhaps a widespread opinion on the mass-bombing of Germany. She says, 'What dreadful raids we have made on Germany. I hope they are not in a position to retaliate in the same way. I wish aeroplanes had never been invented.'

Ernest van Someren

Breakfast in garden again. It was so hot that when Laurie went down the slide in the recreation ground he said it burnt his bottom.

FRIDAY, 5 JUNE

Pam Ashford

Miss Smith, who works in a YMCA canteen on Saturday nights, says, 'When the war is over no one is going to look at a sausage again.' High tea there is all the time sausage and mash. If a soldier says he simply cannot eat sausages, they say, 'We will prepare a rissole specially for you.' This is done by skinning the sausage and frying the inside.

At 12.15pm Mr Ferguson came into the office and said to me, 'Is this your brother been presented to the King and Queen?' There it was in the *Herald*. Imagine the Ministry of Aircraft Production keeping that a secret. Mother and I of course wanted to know all about it when we saw Charlie, and he said, 'They were just an ordinary man and woman, no different from any other business callers.'

Ernest van Someren

Breakfast out again. Julia climbed over the threshold of the french window for the first time. She says a few words now, pitty and biccy and woof-woof (for any quadruped) and Laurie is very fond of her, says he wants to marry her when he grows up.

SATURDAY, 6 JUNE

Ernest van Someren

Went round to neighbours with a pool in their garden in the afternoon, Julia enjoyed watching children bathing, Laurie ran around in the shallow water but didn't want to go right in. I went in once. Kay is rather tired, and is starting her seasonal hay fever, so I cooked the supper, a bacon omelette.

SUNDAY, 7 JUNE

Ernest van Someren

Fair and not too hot, spent the morning doing garden jobs and cleaning Kay's cycle, with Laurie of course. In the afternoon a Dr H motored over and fetched us all in his car, took us to a village the other side of Berkhamsted where our cousin Faith lives in a delightful bungalow. All went well except that Julia was sick in the car, mostly on Kay of course.

TUESDAY, 9 JUNE

Pam Ashford

Charlie has five photographs of himself with the King and Queen. Three beautifully mounted ones and a print of another all from one paper, and an ordinary press photograph from another. None of the photographs were published. It was he who received the King and Queen at a 'factory in Lanarkshire!' and spent 30 minutes taking them around. The conversation dealt with aircraft production and he has not repeated any to us. He liked them, particularly the Queen.

WEDNESDAY, 10 JUNE

Ernest van Someren

Had to wear gloves cycling to work. Fairly busy, but not anything specially interesting. In the evening the Hodgkins called, they are going to N. Ireland tomorrow, to open a hostel for the Friends War Relief Service. It is so cold that there was a touch of frost in some gardens, and people have lost outdoor tomato plants, and in some cases potato, quite heavily.

THURSDAY, 11 JUNE

Pam Ashford

There are large American contingents here. (It is said that the King and Queen visited American ships down the Clyde – there are lots of things they are said to have done.) In the office it was also said that there were many Canadians coming here. I know that at 2 (something to do with the public house hours) Canadian boys are rolling about drunk most days under the bridge, but the position does not seem to me different than at any other times in the last two years. There is little doubt that many British soldiers – after a long and arduous training – are going overseas, or expecting to go soon. Mrs Muir sums up with the words 'there is something going to happen this summer', and there is general agreement therewith.

SATURDAY, 13 JUNE

Edward Stebbing

My opinion of the Anglo–Russian treaty may strike a note of disillusionment in the midst of so much eulogy, but I think it is the only honest view to take. Admittedly the treaty expresses good intentions, but mankind has never lacked good intentions, but has almost always lacked the ability to put them into practice. During the last 20 years treaties have meant next to nothing, and the League of Nations has been a tragic failure. There seems to be no promise, at the present time, of any high ideals being realised and it is absurd to pretend, as the newspapers are doing, that the mere signing of the pact is a guarantee of peace and prosperity after the war.

A man said yesterday that in the photograph of the signing of the treaty Churchill's expression was as though to say, 'Sour grapes – but I've got to eat them.' It is certainly difficult to imagine Churchill collaborating with Russia in peacetime economic and political measures. I shall be very much surprised if, as a result of this treaty, the world becomes happy, peaceful and prosperous for everyone; it would be naïve to expect that it should.

Pam Ashford

A week ago Charlie stripped our hall of its pictures and today they are exhibited on the screen in the Cosmo hall under the title of 'Pictures by 5 famous Scottish artists and one infamous non-Scottish artist'. The latter is Adolf Hitler, and is a print of two of his works (on one sheet) cut from an American magazine and framed. The film at the Cosmo was *Love on the Dole*.

Ernest van Someren
In the afternoon K had a rest, and went to sleep, I took the children for a walk to the library and shopping, bought L an ice, which I consider a foolish indulgence as ices are very poor now, they even contain wholemeal flour.

TUESDAY, 16 JUNE

Edward Stebbing
There has been so much talk about a second front just lately and so many speeches by public figures saying that there is going to be one this year that, though I think there ought to be one, I'm beginning to feel it's all a bluff. For it seems silly to go on telling the enemy what we are going to do and where and when. I don't think our leaders are quite as stupid as that. Probably we are not strong enough to invade the Continent this year, so the next best thing is to try to make the enemy think we are. If we were really going to open a second front, surely it would be kept as a surprise.

THURSDAY, 18 JUNE

Maggie Joy Blunt
Wish I had more control over this diary. I think of things during the day, overhear conversations, make observations, memorise incidents, jot down notes, forget everything and lose the notes. A week goes by and I have done no work on the diary. I make frantic notes in a small book kept for the purpose. Another week goes by. I have prepared, eaten and cleared away a meal, darned some stockings, watered the lettuces, answered two phone calls, written a letter and listened to the 9pm news, and I have nothing to do until it is time to black-out at 11pm.

Bought Du Maurier cigarettes today. The only brand I really like but can rarely get.

I find myself taking a detached, intellectual interest in the war. Am distressed that we have had to evacuate Rezegh and Adem. I praise and thank heaven for Russia. Wonder at intervals what is really happening in the Pacific, Australia, Mexico, China, South Africa. The news is perplexing and disturbing but the war seems to be affecting my personal life only indirectly. Food and clothes restrictions. Transport difficulties (the last bus leaves Slough at 9.20pm which means that if one wants to attend any function in the evening beyond easy walking distance of home one must leave it in the middle, or cycle, or undertake a 3–4 mile tramp back). Small, irritating matters. The odd thing is that one accepts them, on the whole, cheerfully. We do things gradually in Britain. For instance, there was tremendous and gloomy speculation when the petrol cut was first instituted. 'What *shall* we do without a car?' An appalling privation . . . But in six months' time we shall be doing without our car, just as we are doing without bananas, grapefruit, butter, jam, stockings. When the idea of shortages is thrown at us we are shocked. Our imaginations paint a drab and pinched existence. But the shortage occurs, commodities are controlled or rationed or disappear altogether, and gradually we discover that we are doing with less or without. And life continues to be, in the main, agreeable and interesting.

There is an air of uncertainty about our department, as though we were waiting for it to crumple up at any moment. The Government, so I have heard, is opposing post-war development work. If that is true it is a very silly and short-sighted policy, but possibly they find too many able-bodied men and women taking refuge in jobs under that title. I fall between Publicity and Development. Little to do in the way of present publicity, but plenty to do in the way of research and preparation of publicity matter for post-war purposes. Only one doesn't know what post-war conditions will be, or what our management's post-war policy is (not at all sure that they know themselves). We are an important war production firm – have eminence, in fact, through the war – our materials, plant, labour and research laboratories are good and improving daily. But we are quite definitely a Vested Interest, a privately owned capitalist concern, with an energetic managing director who was known to have had strong pro-Nazi leanings before the war (yet in 1938, through his close business contacts with Germany, was so sure of this war, he had extensive and first-class shelters built throughout the Slough works and set our ARP going). One doesn't know what will happen or what our position will be. One can only suppose that our management will do their utmost to safeguard their own interests, keeping a wary eye on political movements, and supporting the system that now supports them. Meanwhile their employees in publicity (or Technical Publications as we now call it) view with high disfavour the methods of British Big Business and discuss the Socialist movement with more fervour than knowledge.

Pam Ashford
The firm is trying to get recognised under the Essential Works Order and it is said that 48 hours per week are obligatory. But 39 hours wear me out badly and are near my maximum. I could never take on night work as well. You can be sure I don't want my employers to know that I am not strong and my lips have always been tightly sealed on the subject of the very bad illness to which sometimes I alluded in this diary. As a precaution I saw Mr Hutchison, the company secretary, and gave him formal notice that I would go on with the same hours as I have, no matter what the Essential Work Orders said. My tears flow easily, and I think he was more anxious to avoid getting wet than anything else.

Ernest van Someren
In the evening made some fire-watching visits, then supper, and a little gardening, and listening in. Left my bicycle outside a house on the other side of the road, and forgot it until I was going to work the next morning, fortunately it was still there. I was deeply shocked and relieved, have had six cycles stolen in 25 years, and thrice there was contributory negligence on my part.

SATURDAY, 20 JUNE

Ernest van Someren
Off across Hitchin to call on Helen Herklots, whom I haven't seen for about 13 years. She now has four children. I stayed to tea and met three of them, but missed her husband Rev. H.G.H., who was away on business, he is Youth Secretary for the Commission on International Fellowship and Social Responsibility of the Churches. In spite of its name, he does good work.

SUNDAY, 21 JUNE

Maggie Joy Blunt
10am Red Cross canteen in the village. Local policeman came in for a cold Horlicks. Four ducks were stolen from a house near his last night. People, he says, are helping themselves liberally to small items – his neighbour's chickens, washing, etc. One woman had joint taken from oven while helping another to hang out her washing.

Chapter Nine

DOUGHNUTS THE SIZE OF TEA PLATES

Americans are peculiar: GIs entertained in an outdoor extravaganza.

24 June–24 September 1942

2 July Churchill wins a vote of censure in the House of Commons by 476 votes to 25 with 30 abstentions.

7 July Allied arctic convoy destroyed in the Barents Sea, with 23 merchant ships and 100,000 tons of cargo lost.

11 July FBI arrests 158 German nationals in USA accused of endangering national security.

22 July Members of the Jewish ghetto in Warsaw are rounded up and deported to Treblinka.

26 July Sweets and chocolate join the ration in Britain.

7 August US Marines land at Japanese outpost at Guadalcanal and Tulagi in the Solomon Islands and endure heavy casualties.

9 August Gandhi arrested following riots for Indian independence.

12 August Churchill and Stalin hold four days of talks at the Kremlin, during which Churchill promises a Second Front 'as quickly as possible'; just over a month later a convoy of 27 Allied ships reach Russian waters.

20 August Canadian infantry defeated at Dieppe.

31 August Utility furniture introduced in Britain; an upholstered armchair costs £3.12s.

10 September More than 1,000,000 incendiaries are dropped on Dusseldorf.

15 September The US aircraft carrier *Wasp* is sunk in the battle for Guadalcanal.

23 September Plans for an atomic bomb announced in Washington DC.

WEDNESDAY, 24 JUNE

Pam Ashford
Tobruk is a matter for dissatisfaction. There is a general feeling that there is something wrong with our Forces. I said, 'Most of our men were civilians till recently and they don't appear equal to the intensive German training over a long period.' Mrs Muir thought it was our generals who were not equal to the German generals, they get out-manoeuvred every time. Or it may be that we give Russia so much equipment that we get short ourselves. Reading the evening newspaper I sat up. 'De Gaulle in Glasgow.' The paper reported that he had inspected the Glasgow University ATC, Senior Training Corps, ATS and other sections. I could kick myself. I was sitting upstairs on the bus returning to town at 2 and wondered what on earth the University Forces were being inspected for. De Gaulle within my line of vision and I never knew!

I got seedless raisins at Massey's this morning.

THURSDAY, 25 JUNE

Pam Ashford
I saw Miss Whittan. The mate whose leg was maimed at Dunkirk is to have the MBE for that and other service. His ticket to Buckingham Palace admits two and his mother feels too old to travel. His brother does not want to go. He has asked Miss Whittan. It is no doubt both a pleasure and an honour, but more of the conversation between us went on how to get dressed for Buckingham Palace on the clothes ration.

We are doing very badly in Libya and Egypt. Mr Mitchell is prophesying the replacing of Mr Churchill by Sir Stafford Cripps within a month.

Ernest van Someren
Relaxed a bit at work and made six glass saltspoons, with gold leaf on the handles, and put them in a furnace to anneal at night. I shall give some for a wedding present. In the evening we asked the Primes to mind the kids, while we all three went to a concert, a Speech Day concert at Haileybury and the Imperial Service College (recently amalgamated) 3 miles away. It was a lovely evening and a very good concert, with a large audience, some in evening dress to mark the occasion, which looked a bit absurd in the bright sunlight. A Mozart piano concerto for two pianos was the star event, the music master and his wife featuring in it. We stopped for a beer at a pub on the

way back, and a man gave a spaniel a drink out of his pint glass, then drank the last half himself (the dog couldn't reach it) to my wife's horror. Stayed up fire-watching till 2am.

FRIDAY, 26 JUNE

Pam Ashford
The wireless had a play on about what Gt. Britain would be like in German hands and I had the feeling that it would not be suitable for Mother. She said that we had sent 1000 planes to Germany last night. The subject was mentioned in the office, but caused far less interest than the continuing dearth of elastic.

SATURDAY, 27 JUNE

Ernest van Someren
In the afternoon we went on the river here with the Chanters, five grownups and three children in a punt, which we paddled. We had a picnic in a hayfield which had been mown, but no bathe. The kids enjoyed it very much, Laurie had an extra paddle in the canoe and nobody fell in. Julia has begun to walk this week, just a few steps at a time, with no special encouragement such as having her hand held. She says about 5 words, and overworks PITTY which may mean flowers, or birds, or just admiration, or trees.

MONDAY, 29 JUNE

Pam Ashford
You would not know there is a war on. Here in Glasgow there are long queues for the limited accommodation on the Arran steamer and Dorothy Wallace said a reporter was going along the line saying to individuals, 'Is your journey really necessary?' which annoyed them for as they said, 'Reporters go about the world and see things, so they don't need holidays.'

Mother and I are going away on Saturday to Berwick, and I know it is only the annual fortnight of fresh air, relaxation and agreeable exercise that keeps me from collapsing altogether beneath the unpleasant features of Glasgow.

Smallpox has broken out in Glasgow. 19 cases, 4 deaths. This is announced today, and the authorities are vaccinating children right away and are giving free vaccination to anyone who will get done. Glasgow had a very serious epidemic in 1920 that raged for the whole summer, and it had a disturbing enough effect then without having a war thrown in.

TUESDAY, 30 JUNE

Edward Stebbing
I am amazed that Churchill and Roosevelt can declare that 'the overall outlook is more favourable now than it was last year'. In spite of this, Churchill will have to face a pretty critical House of Commons in the debate on Libya. Someone had even had the nerve to move a vote of censure. One would have thought there was no limit to the disaster into which the present Government could lead us without losing the confidence of the House. Even now there is only a remote chance of the censure motion being carried – Churchill's personality is still too strong. Still, we are getting on – one disaster more and we might get a new Government. But it is astonishing that Parliament can be so hypnotised by one man that the Government of which he is the leader can survive defeat after defeat.

WEDNESDAY, 1 JULY

Pam Ashford
The sales in the Glasgow gown shops are in full swing. According to the press the Board of Trade does not approve of sales. The shops advertise that in accordance with the Board of Trade's wishes they are not having sales, but they are clearing some unessential lines.

Ernest van Someren
Cooler. A new male assistant, a young graduate, started work in our labs today as an analyst. He is a dull chap from the Midlands called Bishop.

THURSDAY, 2 JULY

Ernest van Someren
People in general seem disturbed over the direction of the war, the men I lunch with are rather cynical about our continued reverses, and say that something ought to be done. I even hear suggestions that the people responsible for the mysterious incident to tanks on June 13, and the surrender at Tobruk, would be more wisely treated by the Russian method of liquidation.

Nothing special in the evening, just a little light gardening.

FRIDAY, 3 JULY

Maggie Joy Blunt
Week's holiday began last Saturday at midday. Spent weekend and Monday at home. Weather perfect. On Tuesday met Ella for lunch in London and took her to see *Sky High*.

West End shops not what they were. Window displays still good but stocks low. Brushes of all kinds difficult to get but managed to find a stiff one for the dustpan. Also an electric boiling ring, mending silk, face and talcum powder and a lipstick refill. Tried to buy lace – still unrationed.

On Thursday Sadler's Wells ballet in afternoon. *Comus*, *Les Patineurs* and *Hamlet*. Delightful. Both the ballet and *Sky High* beautifully dressed – no stinting of quantity or quality of material. How do stage managements get round the Board of Trade?

The fall of Tobruk depressed us all greatly. We began to wonder whether Churchill had gone to the USA to be out of the way, and then whether all our fine pledges to Russia were given because the anti-Red government faction hopes or expects Germany to defeat the Soviets ultimately, but thought it politic to pacify our people with this alliance in the meantime.

Edward Stebbing
Tomorrow I start a week's holiday. I have been very busy at work just lately, especially for the last ten days while another member of our staff has been on holiday, so a break will be very welcome. This year I am splitting my holiday and shall be having another week in September. Normally I would be entitled to three weeks, but everyone is being cut down to two-thirds of their normal entitlement this year.

Ernest van Someren
Indigestion as usual, am having a series of mornings of it (6–7am) probably as a result of bad war news.

SATURDAY, 4 JULY

Edward Stebbing
Spent the day in London. I just strolled round in the morning, had lunch in a milk-bar, and in the afternoon went to see Somerset Maugham's play, *Rain*, at the St Martin's Theatre. A small audience, but a very interesting and well-acted play. Afterwards I would have gone to the Albert Hall to hear the Promenade concert, but there

would not have been time to catch the last train home, so I had to give it a miss.

Pam Ashford
We are staying at Askew Crescent just beside Tweedmouth Station, which is at the opposite end of the railway bridge across the Tweed from Berwick Station.

Ernest van Someren
Went to the dentist again, and was fitted with a gold back to a front tooth, a long and intricate but not painful business. I felt depressed because I thought I had lost a pound note, but it afterwards turned up at home.

MONDAY, 6 JULY

Pam Ashford
This morning we went to Berwick and looked at some of the shops. There was a grocer's shop with Bird's blancmange powder that they sold to us without a query. They also had a dozen or more jars of Heinz's piccalilli and pickled walnuts. Mother and I had different ideas there, but on talking it over later she saw how glad Charlie would be if we took some pickled walnuts back to him. Going into the Co-Op for morning rolls we were astonished to see 2d trifles and bought two (sponge, raspberry jelly, custard and synthetic cream).

TUESDAY, 7 JULY

Pam Ashford
It is quite true that there are cakes for sale here on all days and at all hours. There are, however, practically no biscuits, and what there are are all water biscuits and unsweetened. The stocks carried by the Berwick shops are much lighter than in pre-war days and one naturally does not expect to be away from coupons, points and registrations, but there is little beyond this to suggest there is a war on.

Mrs Lamb has a son called Godfrey in Ayr. He owns a bakehouse and makes pies and potato scones which he sells to the bakers shops there. He has spoken on the dense crowds at Ayr and money flowing. 'You can sell anything at Ayr.' He is 34 and bakers are reserved. He says, 'When they come for me to join the Army I'm ready, but in the meantime I am making all the money I can.'

Ernest van Someren

Up soon after 5, and caught the 7.25 to town, then the 8.55 from Paddington to Cardiff. A dull journey, I read Pearl Buck's *Dragon Seed*, a very good novel. Lunch in Cardiff, which I have never seen before, and then to the University to see a man who has a spectrograph with some special electrical circuits. He gave me the information I wanted, in a friendly way.

4.50 train to the North. This train wasn't so full, and I had a compartment to myself most of the way, and practised the recorder a bit.

WEDNESDAY, 8 JULY

Edward Stebbing

Went to London with my sister and brother-in-law. We did a little shopping in the morning and in the afternoon went to Kew Gardens, a very pleasant refuge from war worries. We had a very good tea there; lobster mayonnaise salad, tea and cakes, at a reasonable price. We left there about 6.30 and took the rest of the evening travelling home, including an hour's wait for a train.

Pam Ashford

When I was here 8 years ago I wondered why Berwick has not developed into a popular resort, and the only answer I could hit on was that the Town Council had never spent a farthing (so far as I could see) on propaganda. But happiness is a bird that eludes you if you pursue it with a net, and if you don't trouble about it at all, it is quite likely to make itself your own without the asking, at least that's so in Berwick when the sun is shining and sky is blue.

THURSDAY, 9 JULY

Pam Ashford

Commandos (shall we say?) were practising at the Bathing Pool Cove. There they were out in boats and rubber dinghies canoeing, invading a defended coastline, and when it was tea-time the party crossed a gravel path leading home, scaling a cliff with a rope. It was a realistic invasion exercise with a fair amount of shooting. The thousands of men here look happy, I must say. Some are in their teens, but many are in their thirties and forties, with bald pates and grey hair. I remember Lieut. Craigie saying once that the recruits were either boys or mature men. Those in between were taken long ago.

FRIDAY, 10 JULY

Pam Ashford
The newspaper reports that there is some mysterious work to be pressed forward requiring building and civil engineering. I think we are going to put up immense coastal defences. The fear that is never far from my mind and which begins to gnaw at the slightest provocation is invasion, not blitzing. I have just read a newspaper which says that at no point in the war was invasion so remote as now. I don't believe soothing statements like that, though at the moment an invasion could not happen with Russia taking up so much German energy.

SATURDAY, 11 JULY

Ernest van Someren
In the afternoon we all went by bus to Waltham Cross to tea with the Pilchers, one of my colleagues in the lab. Their girl is 6 weeks younger than ours, larger and slightly more nimble, but with fewer teeth, words or good looks.

Litzi Deutsch came to visit us, a refugee from Vienna aged about 17 who was commended to us by an old friend in Southampton, who is shortly to become her employer. I escorted her to the police station to report, cycling to Hoddesdon and leaving our cycles out of sight while she did her business.

SUNDAY, 12 JULY

Edward Stebbing
In nearly all the homes I have been in this last week there has been a great deal of jam-making and fruit-bottling; the crop of gooseberries and currants has been good, and now that it has rained there will be at least a few raspberries. These things will doubtless be scarcer than ever this winter, so everyone who has any fruit is preserving it somehow or other.

MONDAY, 13 JULY

Pam Ashford
This morning we called on the drapers from whom Mother bought a frock last week – by appointment – as we wished to try it on before completing the alterations. This is the largest and I should say the best drapers here yet their prices are far below Glasgow's. I bought a

266

yard of broad elastic at 1s/2d a yard. Mother was aghast at the price, but I purchased just the same, for it is simply impossible to get it in Glasgow. I shall cut it down the middle and turn one yard into two yards. I also got a pale blue satin blouse at 25s/6d. The highest price I ever paid before the war was 14s/6d, but I think the quality of this blouse is better. I have a 39in bust which limits my choice.

Ernest van Someren
LD spent the day in town, and came back soon after. Then, she goes to Cambridge tomorrow for a few days' holiday in a Hostel there, also arranged by my friend in Southampton. She is a cheerful, plump, talkative and friendly girl. She has a brother in the Poineer Corps here, but her parents are out of touch with her, possibly in Jugo-Slavia. I hope her guardian in this country finds it possible to arrange a good Jewish marriage for the girl.

WEDNESDAY, 15 JULY

Edward Stebbing
Picture Post today has an article on the increasing popularity of serious music (I noted my own greater interest in it only the other day). There must be some reason for this increase in the number of lovers of good music, but what it is is not apparent to me, unless it is that the better class of music is more inspiring and heartening in these troubled times.

Ernest van Someren
In the evening we went round to the neighbouring Home for girls on probation about our temporary help, Barbara B, who was refused by the A.T.S. and accepted by the Land Army. Her Probation Officer finds she has been stealing things, small things from our house, and recently a pound note. She accounted for this by saying that an RAF officer and his wife were staying with us, and each tipped her 10/-. When her room was searched they also found some soapflakes in a paper bag, and a small silver purse, both recognisably ours. We were asked if we would charge her, but we refused as she has already been in a Borstal institution for two years, and it doesn't seem to have done her much good. We had a talk with the matron about her, and then a very brief talk with Barbara when we said we couldn't employ her any more and would not have her charged with theft. She wept a bit. She is a twisted nature, owing to an unhappy home life and it has made her an awful liar, but I don't think she is incurable.

THURSDAY, 16 JULY

Pam Ashford
Our mornings are always the same. Into Berwick, then to the shop that sells ginger cake; on to the golf course to gaze over the sea and to watch the soldiers exercising. They do different things each day. One day it was bayoneting, another day tommy guns. Today they are lying about in rows with rifles directed towards single soldiers who are pacing up and down as moving targets. The walls of Berwick were built by one of the Edwards and the ramparts by Queen Elizabeth. Mixed up with all these fortifications you find rows of wooden and corrugated huts, trenches, pits, etc. – what a jumble of warfare, ancient and modern.

Ernest van Someren
A rainy day, was very busy at work on the spark apparatus. In the evening thought of going to the movies, but was deterred by a queue from seeing *How Green Is My Valley* and went to a WEA class where Mrs Cole was talking about changes in our political system. She neatly described Churchill as a great 18th-century politician, who unfortunately thinks of this war in an 18th-century way.

FRIDAY, 17 JULY

Ernest van Someren
Busy again, today two possible candidates for jobs came to be interviewed, and I helped them as usual. One thing I ask, to try to find a girl with a visual memory, is (if she rides a cycle) can you draw a bicycle, just diagram, not details. Four total failures and three poor attempts have convinced me that girls don't look at bicycles at all observantly, and tests on my friends confirm this.

SATURDAY, 18 JULY

Ernest van Someren
A stormy morning. In the middle of the night a policeman made some noise in the house, he was upstairs on the landing and com-plained that our light was visible, and our door was open. The Yale lock had failed and the door blew open, also K forgot a small light in the upstairs hall. I showed the policeman out shyly as I was quite naked, and he flashed his light in through the glass door as I went upstairs to confirm this.

MONDAY, 20 JULY

Pam Ashford
Before the train home, Mrs Lamb was telling us about the stealing on the railway nowadays. Recently when her husband opened a wagon that had a consignment of footwear he found thieves had been ripping the cartons open to get pairs that would fit, unsuitable pairs being flung in all directions. He called a policeman. This week he had two cases that had contained whisky and all 24 bottles were gone. Stockings too – thieves had been taking not one pair, but dozens. The thieving appals him and he says the women are much the worst.

Ernest van Someren
Busy day at work. In the evening went to a Peace Group and WEA joint meeting, which should have been a discussion on Education. I was voted into the chair, and to my disgust the old local headmaster who was visiting us talked about the prospects of the war instead, from a slightly pacifist point of view. I cut in after 15 mins' misery and left the chair, which someone else took. This threw him off his stride and we had a general discussion on Education, over which we all disagreed with him, and said so with all the aggressiveness which our manners and our position as his hosts would allow. He took it very well.

WEDNESDAY, 22 JULY

Edward Stebbing
A man said he knew a girl who was taken out of munitions and put in the Land Army. She was sent to an Earl's estate, and her job there was to look after the Earl's orchids!

The BBC's new policy on dance music – to exclude 'slushy' sentiment and to substitute more 'virile' songs – is not going to be liked by those who listen to dance music. The BBC has taken no account of what songs are the most popular in making their decision; if they had, they would have found that the songs they call 'sugary' are the very songs which are most popular. I am quite willing to admit that the words of some of these songs are painful and that 'anaemic performances by male singers' are to be deplored, but, on the other hand, some of the most virile and robust songs are also absolutely senseless. It is deplorable that, because somebody at the BBC doesn't like a certain kind of music and thinks nobody else should, we should be deprived of hearing some of the best songs. I only hope that the public and the dance-band leaders won't let the BBC get away with it.

Ernest van Someren
After work I went to the dentist and had a very painful stopping put in, and my gold one finished off, and paid a large bill (4 guineas for the half-year).

THURSDAY, 23 JULY

Pam Ashford
The points period ends on Saturday and we have three books to complete. I gave mother two and said to her to see what she could do at Miss Maclean's and they gave her a tin of American meat, a large tin of salmon, a small tin of sardines and tin of Beefex. That used 24. I think it was a good choice. I took the third book into town and asked Peacock's for dried apples, but they had none, and I got half a pound of dates and 1 lb prunes. I think I shall use the remaining eight on Weetabix. I have Weetabix for breakfast, and by a marvellous stroke of luck had just built my store up to 10 large boxes when the points scheme swept Weetabix in. 3 of the 10 are left.

Ernest van Someren
At work we had notice of our change of hours, which has been long impending, we are to work 5½ hours more per week, from 8.45 to 5.45 with 1 hr for lunch, only till 12.15 on Saturdays. It might have been worse, and we are to get a second week of summer holiday all round. Also, some junior staff will get overtime pay for the longer hours.

FRIDAY, 24 JULY

Pam Ashford
Evidence is coming forward of the reflections on the Essential Works Order. There is George, the office boy. So overjoyed was he to learn that 'he could not be sacked' that he stopped working entirely, and lay back in his chair and did nothing: he has been late each morning and taken two hours and more for lunch. Scolding the boy has never had any effect on him. He just smiles back. Miss Bousie keeps on saying that she wishes his father would take George to a doctor as it is clear that his mind is affected. Other people think he is 'cute'. The fact that he likes the classical composers and has dark blue eyes has endeared him to me so much that I never know what to do about his many failings.

SATURDAY, 25 JULY

Pam Ashford
Various bodies have done well in providing entertainment for those heeding the advice and not travelling for their holidays. The Parks Dept. has had bands, orchestras and entertainers going about. Extensive publicity has been given to the facilities for tennis, putting and boating. The *Daily Express* has put on seven nights of good music, and one of the evening papers has put on free variety shows, moving from one suburb to another.

The Corporation has devised two carnivals, with a circus.

At 1pm I had sandwiches in the office (sandwiches nowadays are made of bread and margarine with nothing in the middle).

SUNDAY, 26 JULY

Maggie Joy Blunt
Grave anxiety over Russia. Clamour for a Second Front increases. Heard a good story about the British Army in training. Someone found an important section of it practising withdrawal for hours (or was it days?) All we are good at.

Filled in fuel form. Harvey has promised to alter wiring in cottage for power and immersion heater so that in the winter I shall not be entirely dependent on coal and paraffin oil for heating and cooking. But the Electric Company must not know. System in this area fully loaded – not even an extra light being allowed.

Office. PA has recommended me for the August bonus. Firm is making so much money it does not know what to do with it.

MONDAY, 27 JULY

Pam Ashford
Sweets rationing starts today. We are giving all our coupons to the Cosmo which has kept us going in chocolates for three years.

TUESDAY, 28 JULY

Ernest van Someren
K is 33 today, there was a posy at the table for her at breakfast, and I gave her a pair of grey gloves. L sent her a picture-postcard. I took K to a pub and stood her a drink for her birthday, then we saw 'Rebecca', a very competent film which we all enjoyed.

WEDNESDAY, 29 JULY

Edward Stebbing

The news from Russia is black indeed. The stubborn Russian resistance seems to be of no avail against the German onslaught. And still our policy seems to be one, from a military point of view, of almost complete inertia.

Have just finished reading *Out of the Night*, by Jan Valtin. This book is a detailed – so detailed that it can hardly be anything but authentic – account of the activities of an agent of the Comintern from 1918 to 1938. It throws a glaring light on Communist methods, which are shown to be as unscrupulous and brutal as the methods of the Nazis.

The chief aim of the Communists is to gain power and, once this has been gained, to retain it by every means of treachery and oppression at their disposal. In these days of Russian resistance to German aggression we are inclined to forget that Stalin is as much a dictator as Hitler, that the Russian masses labour under as great a tyranny as the German people. Any system of government which depends on a secret police and acts of terrorism for its existence is a bad system, and Russia is ruled by such a system. I am not easily swayed, but *Out of the Night* is as impartial an account of Communist activities as it could be from the pen of a former ardent revolutionist, and the fact that he does not try to idealise every Communist idea or everything that is done in Russia gives greater conviction to his words. And these words have greatly disillusioned me about Russia and Communism.

Pam Ashford

This morning I saw Kiaora Orange (very rare) in Peacock's and bought a bottle.

THURSDAY, 30 JULY

Ernest van Someren

We set a mouse-trap in our bedroom.

FRIDAY, 31 JULY

Ernest van Someren

Mouse was caught in the night. Laurie pottered with me in the workshop of the hotel, where I made a little paddle-wheel for the stream, and he stacked coal briquettes.

Went for a walk along the canal tow-path, with Julia in the rucsac, finally having a picnic on the back of the Dee. We found a soldier asleep near us, and gave him some tea when he woke up.

SATURDAY, 1 AUGUST

Edward Stebbing
Went to the Promenade concert at the Albert Hall. How uplifting is the mighty surge of sound from a full symphony orchestra, what a tonic to a war-weary spirit. I feel sure this must be the reason for the ever-increasing popularity of orchestral music. Modern dance music can excite; it can never inspire or satisfy in the way that great classical music can.

Ernest van Someren
Pottered round in the morning, and went to the village to get some beer. In the afternoon was shown a fine wasp-nest in the yard behind the hotel. I found a large knife on the road and gave it to Laurie.

In the evening we heard much talk about air-raid damage in Liverpool.

WEDNESDAY, 5 AUGUST

Ernest van Someren
After lunch we went with our tea for a ride in a Barge on the canal. Coming back Laurie was travel-sick but I saw it coming and he had his head over the side. I gassed the wasp-nest with cyanide in a flower-pot, at bedtime.

THURSDAY, 6 AUGUST

Pam Ashford
There has been plenty of talk about Germany cracking up internally, but sometimes you think that the British Empire has its weakness too. The news from India is disturbing. Mr Mitchell: 'We should get out. We have no business there.' Miss Bousie: 'Gandhi is absolutely right.' On the other hand, Mother: 'He is bent on causing civil war in India. The evil wretch.'

Mrs Muir knows about the thieving on the railway and that women are the principal offenders. She has a shopkeeper friend who deals in lingerie and stockings, and every package that reaches her, without exception, has been pilfered. 'It is most foolish for manufacturers to put their labels on, as it invites theft.' What happens is that the railway women take lingerie, go down to the ladies' room, change into the new clothes, and put their own down the WC. Apart from theft, the need arises for a plumber to clear the drains. It is from the plumbers that the railway company has got to know what happens.

Edward Stebbing

Used my first four sweet coupons, half a month's ration. Not having been able to buy many sweets for a long time, I have lost much of the desire I used to have for them, and it is strange to be allowed more than one really wants. But the sweet eating habit is not so easily got rid of, and it is one which has always given me more pleasure than the smoking habit, so I think I shall give up smoking temporarily and buy sweets instead, which will also be less expensive.

FRIDAY, 7 AUGUST

Maggie Joy Blunt

Second Front *Now*! was scrawled in white paint across the road at H. Corner a few days ago but has now been removed. Even people who take relatively little interest in the political aspect of this war are getting worried. But however dumb a Britisher may appear and however little he understands the implications of a struggle, if his honour is involved, there comes a point when he wants to help the losing side. When the news was given in an evening paper this week that Parliament had gone into Secret Session PA said, 'Wonder what that means. Russia making a separate peace with Germany? If I were being cut to pieces like that and no active help was being given where it could be given, I'd feel like making a separate peace.'

Many people say, 'But we are sending heaps of material.' And 'We are not ready.' Why are we not ready? Authorities should have foreseen this Second Front possibility last year, surely, and begun preparations at once. We should have at least some plans made, men trained and material collected for launching an attack on the Continent *now*. Material to Russia is not enough.

One loses heart and faith in the people who are in control. As Vernon Bartlett says, 'Why is not Mr Churchill, rather than his critics, standing on the plinth of the Nelson column shouting for a Second Front and demanding greater efforts from every man and woman in the country?' The desire to make that effort is there. The people would respond instantly to the right word from Churchill. We have the feeling, strongly, that Powers That Be wish to see Russian might crippled before they will move a finger to help. They do not want Russia to have any say in the peace terms. Capitalist interests are still vastly strong, and the propertied bourgeois, although a minority, have still an enormous influence on the conduct of our affairs and are terrified of the idea of Socialism.

Socialism is inevitable. Any intelligent individual needs but an elementary knowledge of history to see that it is something which has been developing through centuries and cannot be stopped. It will reach fruition in its own time, like all growing things, though it may take centuries more yet of blood and toil and tears and sweat.

War time restrictions increase. Minor irritations are endless. Crowded trains; queues for buses, for shops, for food, for public conveniences; shortages of this, that and the other; the war being given as an excuse for every kind of inefficiency; approaching winter fuel difficulties; one's leisure hours limited by transport problem.

The India revelations this week were a great shock. Every newspaper except the *News Chronicle* is screaming about the Traitor Gandhi. They think now that they can get him and the Congress gang out of the way. But we do not know the whole Indian story, and do not understand their psychology or the extent of our problems in India. Gandhi's approach to the problem does appear to be impracticable – possibly because he is a man far in advance of his time.

SATURDAY, 8 AUGUST

Maggie Joy Blunt
A fine Scotch mist all day and very low cloud. Soon after 6pm the sirens went here and 10 minutes or so later, as I was cutting thyme in the garden, a plane swooped over the trees. It was such an unfamiliar shape I looked for its markings – it was quite low enough – but mist curled round and swallowed it. Then came the sound of rapid machine gun fire. He circled round and went down the Beeches, peppering them. Guns went into action slowly, one could still hear the plane, but presently the sound died away, the guns ceased and the All Clear went. A Jerry right over my cottage and I saw it! I began to feel excited again about the war. Action on my doorstep. A voice over the telephone wire: 'Can you be at the Point in 20 minutes?' I saw myself there in immaculate uniform within 15 and being a miracle of calm, collected efficiency. That will never happen.

Ernest van Someren
Home again. We got up a bit later than normal for home, nearly as late as on holiday, and had breakfast in the garden, annoyed by

wasps. After lunch I did some work on altering the henhouse for our 4 new pullets.

Cycled to Hertford to go to meeting, with K. Cross, and as I sat there the full shame of the morning's news about the arrest of the Indian leaders gradually soaked in to me, and I realised that this proves that we are not really fighting for Freedom in any absolute sense, but only the right to run the World our way instead of having it run the Nazi way. From the point of view of most people in the world, including coloured ones, we merely represent the lesser of two evils.

SUNDAY, 9 AUGUST

Pam Ashford
Mother and I are overjoyed that Gandhi has been arrested. Glasgow has been feeling pleased that the smallpox situation has been improving. Yesterday a patient at Robroyston who would have been dismissed in three or four days' time, escaped from the hospital and was loose in the city for three hours. Now the authorities are appealing for everyone who could possibly have been in contact with him to get vaccinated.

Fire watching is to be compulsory for women.

Edward Stebbing
Gandhi's protests of his love for the British may be genuine – probably are – but one can't help thinking them hypocritical, for Gandhi must know that he has chosen the worst possible time, for us, to start a civil disobedience campaign. My landlady is dead against Gandhi, says he is a Nazi agent, in league with the Axis. Whatever he is, it is difficult to see what the Indian Government could have done except arrest Gandhi and the other Congress leaders. But this has not prevented rioting and already people have been killed. The *News Chronicle* rightly describes the sequence of events as 'tragic'.

Maggie Joy Blunt
Critic voices the opinions and feelings of a large section of the population in this week's *New Statesman*. As the *Observer* military correspondent, whom he quotes, says, we are faced with a political issue as profound as Munich and the Declaration of War. We are not united in our aims and ideas. We never have been. And it is this division among us which I am sure Hitler is exploiting to the full and relies on.

276

Critic's frequent reference to our nation's secret or unconscious fear of change is noteworthy.

Perhaps by the time we reach the end of this war, if we ever do, we shall realise that our problems are psychological, not economic. Perhaps we shall then listen to the real preachers of morality in our time such as Professor John Macmurray and Dr Graham Howe who are telling us, now, that the causes of war are within every individual. We all have our fears. Fear of change, of opposition and criticism, of loss of social position, of poverty, illness, darkness and death. But fear cannot be overcome by any attempt to destroy or uproot it, nor can our idea of evil. We have to learn the nature of fear and evil and how to accept these and similar forces which we at present try to destroy, ignore or escape.

Neighbour Mrs C has just told me that the Jerry over here yesterday machine-gunned the local fete and dropped bombs on the trading estate. Two people killed.

Am reading *I Had a Row with a German*. An absorbing, illuminating account of the activities of the RAF, although this sort of sentence makes my heart turn over and sink: 'my last chance would be gone to send some loathsome murderer to his end'. Exactly what in the minds of the RAF exempts them from being 'loathsome murderers' too? I suppose they see themselves as St George and the Germans as the Dragon.

MONDAY, 10 AUGUST

Maggie Joy Blunt
Gandhi and Congress leaders arrested. The *Star* splashes an account of Gandhi's luxury prison quarters in the Aga Khan's Palace at Poona – Empire and American raisins; a special British type of soap; rooms furnished by the most expensive London firms; the bed in the Royal boudoir large enough to sleep 18 and where a millionaire Mohammaden slept with all his 12 wives at once; sheets of silk; gardens cooled by fountains . . .

'Well,' said Meg, 'we *shall* win the war with all that on the front page.'

Meg voices the opinion of the majority – considers Gandhi a twerp and better out of the way. I don't think it is as simple as that. Gandhi is a man in advance of his time. Nor can I believe that the obstructions are made all by our Government. India is a vast country with a complicated history. There must be other reasons for our refusal to give India her freedom now, besides those relating to our Imperial interests which the Communists shout about. Time may reveal. All the same this present development is another gift to Goebbels.

The Nazi plane which paid us a visit on Saturday was seen by nearly every other person 'just above my house'. One of our typists was at the fete which he machine-gunned. No one was hurt but a row of deck chairs was shattered. Reports of bombs that fell vary in number from 9 to 2. Damage to some lorries parked by railway line. Two policemen killed.

Pam Ashford
Fire-watching: Miss Bousie, who is far beyond 45, and no one could think otherwise, is kicking up a din about the whole thing. She 'will *not* go on the roof'.

Ernest van Someren
To work by cycle, arrived a little late for the new times (1 hr longer per day) and found I was expected now to sign a book every time I arrive late. My chief was later himself. Had an attack of diarrhoea, so stopped on the way home at my doctor and was advised to fast for it. Had no supper except barley-water, and a lazy evening reading.

THURSDAY, 13 AUGUST

Ernest van Someren
Still not well, so stayed in bed. Julia came up after her breakfast and played on the bed for an hour pleasantly. I read the paper and a book and wrote diary. There were a lot of wasps about. Dr D. came and saw me again. I semi-fasted, had a quiet evening.

SATURDAY, 15 AUGUST

Pam Ashford
The tomatoes have gone right off our market. The eating cherries are off the market too, but there are large quantities of what are called 'bottling' or 'preserving' cherries, which could do nicely for tarts I should think.

If only we had someone to stand in queues for us at fruit shops. When I was going to work at 9 I saw (unripe) plums being delivered at several fruit shops – these are our first plums. Norman McCombe at 4 had blackcurrants, redcurrants (everyone has this), raspberries, gooseberries – and a queue 'as long as for an execution' as the Glasgow phrase goes.

Ernest van Someren

A lazy evening at home. Yesterday K had a parcel from my sister Tessa, a jar of honey and two used cotton frocks, some dried banana and orange preparations, maple sugar and old silk stockings as packing. We are all pleased.

SUNDAY, 16 AUGUST

Edward Stebbing

Poster seen at the top of an escalator in a London underground station says: 'Must you travel?' This seems a feeble way of trying to get people not to travel. The poster is simply a meek appeal; it does nothing to persuade the traveller that his journey isn't necessary after all. As it is, everyone's immediate answer to the appeal is 'Yes, I must', for each feels that his or her journey *is* necessary, and the traveller goes on his way with a clear conscience.

MONDAY, 17 AUGUST

Pam Ashford

This morning Mr Mitchell came to work saying that thousands of people saw Mr Churchill in Glasgow last Tuesday, and he had gone to the Gareloch (where the seaplanes are kept). He had flown to Moscow to talk over the Second Front with Stalin. For weeks past (not days) people have been saying, 'Where is Mr Churchill?' I have said, 'Perhaps he is on holiday and keeping it quiet. Mr Chamberlain got enough abuse for having a few days fishing in the summer of 1939.' I told Mother at lunchtime but knew nothing myself officially till she told me on reaching home at 6.30 that the wireless had his visit to Moscow. She was full of it. I am sick of people demanding 'A second front'. Mother and I agree on one thing, the people who are shouting for a second front would change their tune quickly enough if the government said that they were to be put into the British Expediency Force. All in good time. The second front *will* come, but not yet. We shall have to go on being a nation of goalkeepers a little longer.

One of the London papers yesterday – the *Times* or the *Observer* – said, 'As from the 25th, biscuits will be on the points. Not that it will make much difference to householders who in any case have not seen a biscuit for months.' Good gracious me, is that what things are like in London! We have always been able to get as many plain biscuits as we like. A fortnight ago 1lb of shortbread biscuits at Cooper's, two months ago a pound of Macaroons at Massey's. Mother got a pound of Macaroons at Ross's about a month ago.

TUESDAY, 18 AUGUST

Ernest van Someren

To work, had news of a rise of £25 a year, and of a small overtime bonus increase of 15/- a month. This was a surprise to me, it is calculated on a curious scale, a man earning about £5 a week gets 15/- a week extra, which is quite reasonable. In the afternoon 6 baskets of raspberries came for us, by rail, rather squashy.

WEDNESDAY, 19 AUGUST

Pam Ashford

The raid on Dieppe! Great news! And also the interesting report on Mr Churchill's visit to Cairo. What satisfaction there is everywhere. We had seemed to stand alone so long.

Maggie Joy Blunt

The news of Churchill's visits to Moscow and Cairo has heartened us but tonight's account of our latest commando raid brings a familiar depression. We have lost, apparently, many men and planes and much material. If this is the start of a big attack it would not seem to matter so much, but these nibbles at the French coast – what do we gain by them?

Still without domestic help. Have reduced living to its simplest. Except at weekends all meals and ablutions in the kitchen (the bath and sink being in the kitchen and no other taps in the cottage). Sitting room and kitchen I clean on Monday evenings, the upstairs rooms on Tuesdays, and daily mop, dust and wash up (when there is time) and fling bed together before I leave in the morning. There is, however, washing, ironing, mending and gardening to be done periodically. What time for letters, reading, writing or social activities? Soon we are to be in the office at 8.30 every morning. Someone said today the war would go on for another 6 years.

Yet this seems to be the sum of my grievances and while I grumble young Russia waits in agony for our Second Front. Here in England we are divided, despondent and without faith, ruled by old men, governed by money. The old fears, the old distrust are deeply rooted. 'A noble fight! (But let Russia bleed – we do not want a strong Russian ally when WE make the peace.)' They do not see in that bruised but valiant country their children's salvation. They do not know that in Russia the word goes round: 'Every nation in Europe who has trusted England has been let down . . .'

Ernest van Someren
My 39th birthday, K gave me a knitted sweater, which she had ordered made for me in very good wool. Laurie gave me a small tin of paint he had mixed in the workshop as a surprise for me. It was a surprise, but I was able to think of a use for it. My mother gave me a belt and some razor blades. At breakfast when we bowed for a silent grace before starting, Julia bowed too, for the first time.

THURSDAY, 20 AUGUST

Pam Ashford
Last evening closed (for me) with the war commentary on the convoy to Malta. What a tale it was and coming on top of the two other good war items made yesterday a day of note.

Peacocks window this morning was a sight to behold. There were dishes of every known dried fruit (Mother corrects me, not dried pears); there were piles of individual steamed puddings (sultanas, ginger and college); there were several boxes of tomatoes inside.

The wireless reported that Lord Woolton had been saying that for some weeks dried fruit would be rare but it would come on again. Astonishing in view of the plentitude here. He is also introducing a fish scheme. The fishmongers here have lots of fish, but not attractive fish like plaice or sole. They have lumps of 'fish flesh' that might be a whale cut up in 1lb bits.

FRIDAY, 21 AUGUST

Pam Ashford
Woolworth's have face powder today and have been besieged.

SATURDAY, 22 AUGUST

Ernest van Someren
In the afternoon, I took Julia out with me on a house to house hunt for our lost pullet, which K missed this morning when she fed the hens. I spent a long time in the garden of their nursing-home, which runs behind our garden, viewing their hens and chickens with the matron. No sign of hen.

SUNDAY, 23 AUGUST

Pam Ashford

There is an RAF exhibition at the Art Galleries, certainly the most overcrowded exhibition I've been to yet.

The walls were covered with large photographs and some of these I liked, e.g. the WAAF's photograph of nine airmen with VCs and a description of their feats, and photographs of the RAF in Russia. But more numerous were the screens that bored me stiff. These were headed 'Middle East', 'Bomber Command', 'Training Command', 'Servicing', 'Coastal Command', 'Fighting Command' and pictures of carnage done by us.

There were models of German planes, and of British planes – the British ones were large and beautifully made, the Jerries smaller. There was a screen covered with pictures of different types of British aircraft, with a board of buttons in front, and when the appropriate button was pressed the corresponding aircraft would light up. But it was not working.

Ernest van Someren

Had a wasp sting on Friday, and my hand is swelling. At home when I was feeding the hens I looked behind the henhouse and found the missing pullet, still alive but wedged.

MONDAY, 24 AUGUST

Ernest van Someren

In the evening came home early for massage, had tea and went to Dr W at Watton for manipulation. He was very annoyed because of an emergency call to an old man with a weak heart who had just collapsed, said the old chap could only keep alive if he stayed in bed, but wouldn't, so he wished he would get on and die instead of keeping alive and needing attention. This seemed to me reasonable, and W put in more time than usual on trying to twist and untwist me, in the hope that the patient would die at once.

TUESDAY, 25 AUGUST

Ernest van Someren

Have gained a bit of weight, over 1lb last week. Towards the end of the afternoon we had an alert, but the siren in our building failed to sound, and I didn't get to the shelters, nor did the juniors in my lab. Our works ARP organisation has got a bit slack. Afterwards heard a bomb had been dropped before the warning a couple of miles from home, further out of town. Had a busy evening with diary, and poisoning wasps.

WEDNESDAY, 26 AUGUST

Edward Stebbing
I hope they won't make too much fuss over the death of the Duke of Kent. It may be a sad event for his family, but to other people it is of little interest. I am no more moved by his death than by the death of a complete stranger.

Ernest van Someren
The wasps are satisfactorily executed.

SUNDAY, 30 AUGUST

Edward Stebbing
There have been so many events in the last week or two – Churchill's visit to the Middle East and Moscow, the Dieppe raid, the entry of Brazil into the war, the American success in the Solomon Islands, the Japanese withdrawals in China – all of them of considerable importance, so that the general picture of the war is rather confusing and difficult to keep in clear perspective. The picture, however, seems definitely brighter, for all the events I have mentioned have been in our favour.

There is one other part of this ever-changing picture, though, which is perhaps dominant and attracts most attention, and that is Russia's terrific struggle with the main enemy of the Allies, Germany. The ability of the Russians to withstand the massive German onslaughts and to launch powerful counter-attacks excites the admiration of all. The battle for Stalingrad, especially, is being watched with suspense, for on this depends whether the picture remains bright or again becomes dark. The fate of this battle is perhaps the fate of the whole German campaign in Russia, the fate of the campaigns in the Middle and Far East.

MONDAY, 31 AUGUST

Ernest van Someren
Holmes [old friend] left early the next morn, before we were up, to start a long journey. We packed some lunch for him, which he forgot.

TUESDAY, 1 SEPTEMBER

Ernest van Someren
Laurie had a slight row with K, who spoke to him so severely that he said, 'If you talk to me like that I won't speak to you again till 1944.'

THURSDAY, 3 SEPTEMBER

Edward Stebbing
The war is three years old today. I must say that three years ago I never thought the war would last as long as it has done. Now – the end still seems a long way off.

To mark the third anniversary today has been a National Day of Prayer – why, I can never understand. It seems to me just a waste of time, as well as rank hypocrisy. For God does not seem to me to come into this war at all. This war, whatever label is attached to it, is a violation of all Christian ideas. It is an insult to God to ask him for his support.

FRIDAY, 4 SEPTEMBER

Pam Ashford
At 12.30 I went up to the Ministry of Labour Appointments Committees (as a graduate I don't need to go to the Labour Exchange) and asked for an interview. The American Forces are all over the place. There are sailors galore, and like the Canadians, the American sailors get drunk. No. 19 Hope Street is a public house and at 2pm there were two American sailors just put out, who had had enough but were still able to stand, and a girl of about 17 rolling. She had one arm around the sailor's neck, and if it had not been for that she would have been on the pavement. There was the bartender trying to persuade her to take her handbag which she left behind and she just would not. So in the end he returned to the public house with it. Of course, it is possible she was not used to drink and got tight on very little. I doubt if the soldier knew what to do with her.

SATURDAY, 5 SEPTEMBER

Ernest van Someren
In the afternoon we went to a concert given locally by the Polish Army Choir, who sang extremely well. We took both children, and sat in front, and the kids were very good till nearly the end. We gave them a longer interval than the rest of the audience had. Then we had

tea and I mended the greenhouses of which L had broken a pane of glass yesterday by throwing something wildly.

TUESDAY, 8 SEPTEMBER

Ernest van Someren
One of my colleagues, Mance, came round after work to try out the borrowed projector with me, but I burnt the lamp out by a mistaken connection, so could do nothing. Later the producers of the 'Brains Trust' came to try over records with me, to time some to accompany silent films, but we couldn't do this either. I was rather depressed. After some lengthy telephone calls we went out and had a drink of beer.

WEDNESDAY, 9 SEPTEMBER

Ernest van Someren
Fixed up the projector and left Mance to operate it, went off to sup at a café with our question-master and 5 of the 'Brains Trust' team. The supper wasn't quite a success, as we didn't have enough general conversation. A local doctor, a local ex-lecturer and philosopher, a retired missionary (lady) who was one of the first Girton girls, the assistant education officer (an ex-Everest explorer) and Margaret Cole were the team. We went on stage after a preliminary film (of birds) and answered questions for nearly an hour. Then there was a BBC speaker to announce discussion groups, and two films borrowed from the BC Gas Association. To finish with there was a 3 minute film of my own, on Broxbourne Sunday, in colour, which we showed once forward and once backward, so that people left amused.

THURSDAY, 10 SEPTEMBER

Pam Ashford
Agnes is always on about the increase in prostitution, and I am not saying she is wrong. All I can say is that my mentality is such that I just don't see things she sees. I can certainly see that the Americans have not taken long to get girl friends for themselves, and that the money they flash about has something to do with it, but so far as I can give judgement it is on pictures and restaurants and dancing that the money goes. The British troops (and allied troops too) don't get drunk often – it is the Canadians and the sailors and munitions workers. People explain the Canadian drunkenness to me by saying that they have more money than the British troops. I explain the

Canadian drunkenness to people by saying 'what an unfriendly atmosphere there is in Glasgow. These men have nowhere to go but the pub. How I wish it were possible for me to entertain them.'

I got a letter advising me that my name has been put on the Supplementary Register and that I could call for an interview any day between 9 and 12 or 2 and 4. I went at 2 today. I said straight out, 'I want to tell you why I want a transfer. I think I have a very poor salary.' The administrator looked at the form and said, 'You have.' Then I went on, 'I have repeatedly asked for a rise and when we came under the EWO I wrote to the M of L and asked for information about the fair wages clause. I was asked to visit Mr Abbott of the Industrial Relations Dept. who explained the legal position to me. Acting on his advice I pointed out to the Company that my salary was below the fair wage and if they could not come up I should have to get in touch with the NSO. The Managing Director then said to me that if the NSO ordered an increase he would take my work away and then get rid of me on the grounds that he had no work to give me. I have thought things over and think that the most suitable answer is to find another job.' The interviewer thought so too. She advised me to get out of the Forth & Clyde as quickly as I could. 'I hate you being with that horrid man' (what an English expression!) Of course I assured her that I only came into contact with Mr Ferguson when I wanted money, and that my life with Mr Mitchell was a very happy one. She suggested that I should advertise.

FRIDAY, 11 SEPTEMBER

Ernest van Someren
We got a very good press report of our show on Wednesday, and made about £6 for the blind.

SATURDAY, 12 SEPTEMBER

Pam Ashford
During the week I chanced to read that *Murder in the Cathedral* was to be performed at the Glasgow Cathedral on Saturday afternoon, and from the Minister's introductory remarks I was to learn that 'it was an historic occasion. The first time such a thing had happened since the Middle Ages.'

The play had been condensed for the Pilgrim Players. We had first the return of Thomas a Beckett and his temptation by four tempters. Then came the Christmas Sermon, preached from the pulpit. This was tremendously real and moving. Then came the murder and speeches of justification from the perpetrators. That brought the play to an end. The Minister of the Cathedral put up a prayer then and the audience broke up. It was an experience I shall not lightly forget.

SUNDAY, 13 SEPTEMBER

Edward Stebbing

Went to one of the *Daily Express* Centres of Public Opinion, held in Chelmsford, and spent a very enjoyable afternoon. The two platform speakers were Beverley Baxter MP and Tom Driberg MP. Before they spoke there was some community singing, finishing up with 'Land of Hope and Glory'. Driberg, a recently elected Independent candidate, spoke first and said that he was sorry to hear 'Land of Hope and Glory' being sung, because he objected to the words 'Wider still and wider shall thy bounds be set', which were too imperialistic for his liking. Then he dealt with India and said he was dismayed at Churchill's statement, criticised the 'strong-arm' policy, and suggested that China, Russia and USA should be called upon to give their help and advice. Then he went on to the controversial subject of whether we are fighting the whole German people, or only the Nazis. In this matter he declared he was an anti-Vansittarite (which I was very glad to hear) and that the idea of all Germans being irredeemably wicked and of waiting to exterminate them was as bad as Dr Goebbels' racial ideas. For the idea that the Germans were a very special race on their own and had evil in their blood was simply Nazism inverted – the super-race theory in reverse. Also it was bad political warfare, as the Germans could use it against us in their propaganda. Driberg finished by saying that the leaflets we dropped over Germany should be made public.

Driberg's speech was in every way more rational than Baxter's, whose speech was blandly hypocritical and cleverly abusive towards Driberg. I agreed with almost everything that Driberg said and disagreed with nearly all that Baxter said.

There were 12 speakers from the audience altogether, and such a meeting as this, no doubt, does not give a truly representative picture of public opinion, but it certainly gives people an opportunity to air their views and as an example of democratic free speech is really quite remarkable.

Just before the end I happened to glance at the community song-sheet and read the last four lines of the National Anthem, which so struck me that I must write them down here. I had never read them before and I am sure few people know them:

May peace her power extend
Foe be transformed to friend,
And Britain's rights depend
On war no more.

Ernest van Someren
An old friend of Kay's, Ethel Eaves, turned up for lunch and stayed for supper, and we had a lot of talk. She is a secretary in the Drama Dept of the BBC and herself a dramatic woman, who frequently falls in love with men who are usually technically ineligible, but rarely inaccessible or unresponsive.

MONDAY, 14 SEPTEMBER

Pam Ashford
This morning I went through the *Herald* advertisements at 8.30 (Charlie's paper) and cut out one for a Secretary. And then I stood with that snippet of paper (2 lines of tiny print) in the sitting room when the draught lifted it out of my fingers and though Mother and I have been crawling about the sitting room floor ever since we cannot find it.

At 2 I handed in an advertisement to the Herald, reading 'Secretary (39) seeks employment. 20 years experience, M.A., commercial diploma, shorthand, typewriting.' Price 2/-.

TUESDAY, 15 SEPTEMBER

Pam Ashford
Mother went to a whist drive with Mrs Saddleton. Mrs S. simply cannot get over the contrast between fruit and vegetables there and here. In Kent at present they are 'overrun' with tomatoes. There simply is not the transport to take them off the growers' hands. Tomatoes are on sale at far below the maximum price, but even so there is a limit to what Kentish throats will swallow.

They have peaches at Sittingbourne at 6d each. Melons too. I have not seen a melon since 1939. And the plums. In Glasgow we are well pleased at the abundance on our market. It is true that thousands are rotten when they reach us, but the shopkeepers go over their stocks and cast the bad ones aside (on business not ethical grounds probably). The Saddletons fresh from Kent are aghast at the appearance of the plums we are mopping up enthusiastically. But I have not seen an onion since the capitulation of France.

The advertisement was in today's *Herald*. I dropped in to the

Herald office at lunchtime but should have been much surprised if there had been any replies so soon. On the opposite side of the road is Cranston's and they had a window full of doughnuts. I bought one for 4½d and had half for tea. These doughnuts were the size of tea plates with a small hole out of the middle and 1½in thick. The one purchased caused a sensation both at the office and at home.

WEDNESDAY, 16 SEPTEMBER

Pam Ashford

I have had three replies. Two from solicitors, and one from a Wishaw firm building engines. I shall visit the solicitors; but I shan't rush into law for the M of L does not regard solicitors' staff as essential labour. Wishaw is too far away for me. Lilian lives there. I said to her, 'Would you like a job in an engine works in Wishaw?' and her eyes glistened. I gave her the letter.

Then at teatime Charlie said that the Ministry of Fuel and Power want applications.

Ernest van Someren

Left work early for massage. At home found a parcel from Tessa containing a birthday present of socks, fruit (dried), tinned olives, chocolate and a bit of 'Dutch' cheese. Duty of 2/6 was not excessive. We are very fond of olives.

FRIDAY, 18 SEPTEMBER

Pam Ashford

Cochran Stout & Dunlop. This is a really big firm of solicitors, four partners and two entire floors. The partner I saw was a young man of about 35. One look at me was enough. He said, 'The post would not suit you. It is for a junior shorthand typist.' I said, 'Mr Cochran in answering my advertisement knew what my qualifications were.' I had ten minutes' pleasant talk with this gentleman who did seem anxious to know about me, even though there was nowhere there to offer.

There is all this talk of women power, and I have no doubt that where work is unskilled or requires only slender training there are jobs galore, but for better types of work I do not think that the position is greatly improved.

SATURDAY, 19 SEPTEMBER

Ernest van Someren
K went to town with Laurie, for a treat. She had managed some shopping, lunch with my Mother, and a new theatre show which L had enjoyed very much, although he is only 4½. He is of course used to home films. The Mickey and Pluto film was his chief delight – and of course the escalators, which he was allowed to use plentifully.

TUESDAY, 22 SEPTEMBER

Ernest van Someren
In the evening Falconer came to supper, and I went afterwards to the first lecture of his new course on Heredity and Eugenics. A good lecturer, but a very small class. After went to the White bear with some of the class, and found myself receiving a lecture on high-speed welding from a man whom I had never met before.

WEDNESDAY, 23 SEPTEMBER

Pam Ashford
The Ministry of Fuel and Power, 7 West George Street, has offered me a job and I have accepted it.

I went around at 1 o'clock and met Mr Howell, who is Chief Executive officer. Lord Trapain is head of the show. I shall be secretary to Mr Ballantine, who is another principal. His appointment was mentioned in the papers recently and he was head of the LMS in Scotland and has been called out of retirement for this job. I shall also work for Mr Reid, who is General Manager of the Fife Coal Co. and is their Production Manager. I shall have 65/- less my insurance and if I pass an R.S.A. speed examination that is held periodically I shall get 8/- more. Mr Howell said it was at 100w.p.m. This part of the Ministry is concerned with mining. I certainly shall be in the cream of the coal mining industry in Scotland.

THURSDAY, 24 SEPTEMBER

Edward Stebbing
Paid my first visit to a British restaurant and had a very good lunch; stuffed lamb, potatoes and cabbage, date roll and custard, and a cup of tea, at the very modest price of 11d. Thinking of the food situation as a whole, I think, I have thought for a long while, that Lord Woolton is one of the ablest Ministers in the present Government.

Went to see *Gone with the Wind* in the evening. Boosted perhaps more than any other film, it is certainly an extraordinarily fine film and I did not begrudge the 4/- I paid for a seat, though in principle I fail to see why such excessive prices should be charged for a programme only a little longer than a normal programme.

Pam Ashford

Last evening my feelings were of pleasure and excitement. I did not sleep till 1.30 and woke many times thereafter.

My notice was all over by 9.20. I said to Mr Ferguson – pleasantly and politely, 'I want to give you my notice, Mr Ferguson. Here is the form. I am going to the Ministry of Fuel and Power.' He said, 'That is where Mr Ballantine is.' I said, 'Yes, I am to be his secretary.' Mr Ferguson said, 'God help you! He was the most hated man on the railway. He is a slave driver. I pity you.' I said, 'The Ministry of Fuel and Power would like me to start on 1st October.' He said, 'That is impossible. We have to get someone else in first.' I said, 'There is space on the form for you and you may say that here.' He said, 'I will let you go when I see fit.' I said, 'The Ministry of Labour would like the form back quickly. The Order gives three days for its completion.' He said, 'Don't talk to me as if I were a school child.' So I went away.

Mr Mitchell arrived at 9.30. He was so upset he could not read the incoming mail and I had to read everything and tell him what was there. What an amount of time was lost to me today for again and again I was standing beside him patting his hand and saying, 'Of course, I am not going to leave you with things incomplete. I like you far too much to leave you in a mess.' However, in the course of the morning for some reason (I might guess the reason but the guess might be wrong) he swung around and spent an hour telling me what an appalling man Mr Ballantine is.

In the depths of Mr Mitchell's despair I said to him, 'If the F&C offered me better money it is possible I might change my mind.' Actually I don't think it would change my mind, for I had thought the thing over from that angle before, and ten minutes later I said to Mr Mitchell, 'I dislike Mr Ferguson so much that I could never be happy in this firm. I am so happy with you. That is the rub.' I came home to lunch depressed and when I sat down at the table the tears rolled over my lids, but I certainly did not want Mother to think there was a hitch and I wiped them away.

Chapter Ten

A GENUINE VICTORY

The sort of thing which makes me see red: the royals try a stirrup pump at Windsor.

25 September–31 December 1942

14 October Germans resume extensive assault on Stalingrad.

23 October Montgomery begins El Alamein offensive.

26 October Milk allowance in Britain reduced to 2½ pints per week, but pregnant women allowed more.

31 October Canterbury hit in Luftwaffe reprisal for RAF attack on Milan.

2 November Rommel begins retreat at El Alamein as Montgomery becomes a hero.

10 November Churchill tells a Mansion House audience, 'This is not the end. It is not even the beginning of the end. But it is, perhaps, the end of the beginning.'

20 November The Red Army launches its comeback at Stalingrad.

27 November French ships scuttled at Toulon Harbour to avoid German capture.

1 December The Liberal economist William Beveridge outlines plans for a Welfare State.

6 December Mass Allied air attacks on Holland and France.

13 December Shark U-boat code cracked at Bletchley Park.

17 December Foreign Secretary Anthony Eden reads a joint Allied declaration condemning Nazi extermination of Jews and promising retribution.

25 December Red Army encircles Germans in Stalingrad, but faces starvation in Leningrad; Vera Lynn's 'The White Cliffs of Dover' becomes an unforgettable hit.

FRIDAY, 25 SEPTEMBER

Edward Stebbing

More than once in this journal I have felt compelled to mention the gradual whittling away of democracy in this country. A piece of recent news which is deeply disturbing is the report of a Conservative sub-committee on the education of youth and the control of young people's leisure. This Conservative report, which advocates compulsory leisure-time training for boys and girls aged 14–18, is unquestionably Fascist in essence. The conscription of youth is one of the foundations of the German Nazi regime, and if the report becomes Government policy it would mean the end of democracy here, too. That the youth organisations would be used to instil into young people Conservative propaganda, and Conservative propaganda only, goes without saying. The thin end of the wedge has already been driven in by the system of youth registration and the 'voluntary' enrolment – with a little gentle persuasion – in some youth organisations. How easy now to change over to a compulsory system!

Ernest van Someren

Mother came to spend the weekend with us, as she has a long weekend off work. She brought news of Tessa, who has been offered a post as secretary-companion to Gracie Fields, whom she has met recently in Saratoga Springs NY.

MONDAY, 28 SEPTEMBER

Edward Stebbing

The meeting at the Albert Hall, convened by the Archbishop of Canterbury to define the part the Church must play in the post-war world, was very interesting and not a little encouraging. For some time now I have felt that the Church was a lifeless thing and, as such, not worth bothering about. It's a religion which seems out of touch with the society in which it exists. But if, as seems likely from recent utterances by the Archbishop, the Church is going to lead all those who want progressive Christian society, I am prepared to follow it. It is a new social morality in everyday life which is needed more than anything else in world affairs.

WEDNESDAY, 30 SEPTEMBER

Pam Ashford

I hope that never again shall I be called on to go through a day like today. Mr Mitchell arrived in a condition of despair and anxiety to an extreme degree such as I have never encountered before. I am writing this on Sunday and oddly enough I cannot remember much of what he did say – it was so much confused. He said last Friday he was in Mr Ferguson's room and saw my form there and said to Mr Ferguson, 'Miss Ashford is perfectly right to leave,' where Mr Ferguson said, 'How so?' Mr Mitchell said, 'The organisation of the place has driven her out.' Mr Ferguson said, 'It is Miss Smith's job to organise the place. She shall hear what you say.' Mr Mitchell said, 'It has nothing to do with Miss Smith,' but Mr Ferguson insisted on buzzing for her and when she went in, he said, 'Mr Mitchell says the way you organise the place has driven Miss Ashford away.' Mr Mitchell said, 'It has nothing to do with Miss Smith. It is you, Mr Ferguson, who drives our women out. They won't put up with your bullying and shouting. You have had five telephone operators in 12 months. There is an ugly spirit among the women in this place.' Miss Smith said to Mr Ferguson, 'What Mr Mitchell says is true.' It subdued Mr Ferguson a bit and he said, 'I am not like that, David?' and Mr Mitchell said, 'You are. The girls here are not happy and you are the cause.'

I came back from lunch in a state that was not very far from collapse.

THURSDAY, 1 OCTOBER

Maggie Joy Blunt

Day off on Monday to shop in Town. It poured and I had no umbrella. Resorted to taxis. Searching for winter coat, Weatherall's no. 1 (top of Bond Street) – no stock at all. Weatherall's no. 2 (Regent Street) – coat advertised in *Vogue* in window. In *Vogue* it looked smashing and just what I wanted. Actually frightful – a sort of gabardine with trashy lining. Tried on a navy, belted, fairly good, fashionable cut, said to be 'pure wool' but badly finished with a ghastly Red Cross-red lining (all their coats now seem to be lined with this material). It needed pressing and looked shoddy. Price 15 guineas. Jaegers, Regent Street – stock extremely limited and nothing under 19 guineas. A very indifferent assistant, did not want to show me anything. Said that they were not allowed to keep back garments if one had not enough coupons. Wanted to use strong language but went instead to Nicholls further down Regent Street. There the assistant was most helpful. A choice of several good coats but I fell for the first one I tried on – a very soft, real camel hair, great, belted, of classic cut and perfect fit. 13 guineas. A most serviceable all-the-year-round coat which I can wear over coat and skirt if necessary, and should wear well (it will have to). Lack 8 coupons but they are keeping the coat until the 12th. Hats 3–4 guineas. Decide to make do with one bought 2 winters ago at Dickens & Jones for 1 guinea and still has an 'air' for special occasions, go without to work or wear a scarf if cold. Shops generally: stocks very low and much absolute rubbish being sold at high prices. Saw *Bambi* after lunch – a typically enchanting Walt Disney film.

American soldiers to be seen everywhere. Spent Sunday night with June. Kassim reports that there is much ill feeling in British ranks at Americans' better pay and conditions. Tommies not openly hostile but are resentful. (B.L says Americans in Wycombe are not very popular. She finds the 'typical' American to be 5ft nothing with a leathery skin and not her fancy at all.) Kassim says that the trouble with the British private is that he does not know *how* to complain. Grumbles enough but when an officer appears is dumb. Is it due to the pressure of class distinction, inadequate education, or inherent, characteristic British shyness?

Gone With the Wind being shown in Slough this fortnight. One hears it being discussed in every bus and queue. Attempted to see it myself with B.L on Tuesday but did a spectacular faint half way through and had to be taken home.

Pam Ashford

I slept long and heavily and woke up feeling fine. Then at 8 the post was dropped in through the letter box and there was my release. Joy filled me. Mother and Charlie were jubilant. Then I went into Mr Ferguson. 'I have my release, Mr Ferguson.' He growled, 'That means nothing. You will not be allowed to go till I have a substitute.' I said, 'But it is a clear release.' He said, 'You stay away and I will have you prosecuted.'

Edward Stebbing

Heard some men talking about Hitler's latest speech, which I had not read. One of them thought it 'very much to the point' and 'one of the most brilliant speeches of the war'. Another appreciated his remarks about Churchill and said, 'You can't expect to wear funny hats and not be laughed at by the enemy.' The first man said that most of

Hitler's speeches had been fulfilled, whereas we had had 'three years of speeches and nothing for them'. The general opinion seemed to be that most of Hitler's statements were fully justified, and one man wondered why the papers had been allowed to publish it.

When I got home I read the speech and told my landlady I thought there was much truth in it. She agreed. It was a very confident speech and some of the remarks struck me as rather witty. It was much more matter-of-fact and coherent than usual, in fact quite different from Hitler's usual speeches. But it was not all truth and did not show any lessening in Hitler's ruthless and malevolent outlook.

In the same paper I read a statement by Churchill on the Dieppe raid, which was thus robbed of much of its success and Hitler's speech was given added emphasis. I also noted that the life of the present Parliament is to be prolonged by another year, a fact which I view with much disappointment. If ever a Parliament needed invigorating, this one did. It is like a very old man, gradually decaying into complete helplessness and uselessness, but refusing to die a natural death.

MONDAY, 5 OCTOBER

Pam Ashford
At the F&C it is customary for a departing member to give a tea party and Monday is a desirable day for Mr Ferguson is at Granton then.

However, I have been too utterly limp to do anything about making arrangements. Mother on Friday afternoons stands in Currie's queue to get something for Sunday's tea and on Friday last bought a big 1/3 cake. Absolutely plain inside, but prettily decorated with a sticky substance sprinkled with coconut. I said yesterday afternoon, 'Can I have the cake?' and got it. Then at lunch time I went to six bakers. Fullers and Cadaro, sold out. Cranstone, queue for scones only. Gordon, London buns only – I bought six. Peacock's, Paris buns only – I bought four. Reid's the last shop to visit, had a big selection of buns and I got 10 mixed. Everyone kept on saying what a magnificent spread it was. It was the best I could do, and in all the circumstances I did not feel ashamed.

What I want now is the courage to go forward to where I am going. What it is to have a divided will. What it is to have all the powerful instincts in operation simultaneously and all pulling in different directions.

WEDNESDAY, 7 OCTOBER

Pam Ashford

I slept on and on until 11. Then I phoned to say I was sick. Nervous exhaustion would be a more precise clinical description of course. Oh how worn I have been today. I just lay in bed doing nothing until 4.30 and now I am sitting in the armchair at the fire at 7, still nine-tenths asleep. I'm not going in tomorrow.

Mrs Saddleton has met Mother and says on the journey from Kent to Glasgow she slept with her head on the back of the carriage and got vermin in her hair.

Edward Stebbing

Today a speaker on the radio said, 'Hitler's speeches should no more be taken seriously than his little black moustache.' What an amazing, and at the same time idiotic, statement for a radio commentator to make! The pronouncements of the supreme leader of our chief enemy – not to be taken seriously?

FRIDAY, 9 OCTOBER

Pam Ashford

My fortieth birthday today. Generally I am prone to look back over the years and try and remember previous birthdays, but one after the other has been so uneventful that no recollection whatever remains. Today is going to be an exception if I am spared a long enough life to continue that process of looking back. I went in. In a way I was afraid to – and so was Mother. Suppose it were one of Mr Mitchell's difficult days and I got knocked out again. But it was not. He has been pleasantness itself, and thinks I am right in going. We are sorry to part but sentiment has not loomed large. I say when the war is over I am going to be looking for a job and he is full of plans for 'when the war is over'. Always the urge is on him to 'get away from this place. To start for himself, etc.' So we shall be coming together again. But something intuitive tells me that will never be.

There is to be an office presentation tomorrow. I had been wondering on that point and had decided to ask for a watch, but apparently a statement that mine had absolutely gone dead a month ago produced a response and they have been searching warehouses, but there is not a watch to be had. Mr Mitchell thinks Miss Bousie on behalf of the ladies has got a dressing case with difficulty.

300

SATURDAY, 10 OCTOBER

Pam Ashford

I began work straight off at 9 and 9.30 Mr Ferguson called me into his room and gave me the staff presentation, a beautiful brush, comb, clothes brush and mirror in a case. It was all very formal and insincere. However, I went around to everyone's desk thanking each individual and found friendship there. Then I typed out Mr Mitchell's testimonial viz.:

> Miss Pam Ashford, M.A. of Glasgow University, has been my right hand since she first became associated with the Forth & Clyde Coal Co. Ltd, Glasgow. Her duties have been those of Foreign Correspondent (French and German) as well as Secretary. Correspondence with clientele at home and abroad has been out of the usual commercial correspondence but Miss Ashford has reacted to each variety of circumstances and her work has been most satisfactory.
>
> She has a 'legal' mind and on many an occasion has caught me up on a point. Her enthusiasm is overflowing. Any studies that she thought would widen her knowledge have been taken up very seriously and she has secured first place in examinations. Any business gentleman who has Miss Ashford as his secretary will soon appreciate his good fortune.
>
> I am extremely sorry that Miss Ashford and I should part after 7½ years together, and it is only because of changed conditions in the Export Trade occasioned by the present war that she is leaving to take up a better appointment.
>
> My sincere wishes follow Miss Ashford in her new appointment and in all her future activities.
>
> Signed D.C. Mitchell, Export Manager.

There was no grief. In fact I was so calm when I left that I crossed to the seedshop and bought Dick 2lbs of charlock, for I shall not be near that shop again, and I had a talk with the salesman and told him about how much Dick liked the experiment with the charlock. There was a bowl on the counter with a card 'Tonic canary mixture – dandelion, Scotch thistle, charlock, lettuce and hemp'.

SUNDAY, 11 OCTOBER

Edward Stebbing

Mankind's goodness and desire for progress, and mankind's stupidity and capacity for evil, are both brought out in this week's news. First, there is the attack which is to be made on tuberculosis in this country. The methods to be used: mass radiography of supposedly healthy, as well as suspect, people and maintenance allowances for the dependents of those undergoing treatment, are a great step forward in the fight against tuberculosis, which has increased enormously since the outbreak of war. This is one of the best pieces of news I have read for some time. On the other hand there is this ridiculous fuss about tying the hands of prisoners-of-war. Bombs may be dropped on each other's cities, every kind of weapon used to kill each other's men in the fighting line, ships sunk and the people on them drowned, but prisoners may not have their hands tied! The governments concerned rail at each other like children – 'You tie the hands of our men and we'll tie the hands of yours.' 'You do that and we'll tie up three times the number we did at first.' The British Government admits that five prisoners captured in the raid on Sark had their hands tied, but the fact that four of them were shot in trying to escape doesn't seem to worry anybody.

Maggie Joy Blunt

India has died out of the news. Present popular topic is the chaining of British prisoners and our Government's reprisals. A barbaric, infantile, lunatic action on the part of Germany which can only do more harm than good. The *Observer*'s leader on the subject very good – it would have been much better politics on the part of our Government if they had refused to retaliate on the same lines.

Usual sort of day at office today. A Bristol Hercules engine is on show in the Canteen. We supply all the aluminium alloys for this engine and the R.R.Merlin, besides making many aircraft parts, e.g. prop blades. Know nothing about engines.

The question of women's equality with men cropped up. I maintain that women are not equal, or inferior, but *different*. Watch young children together. June's little boy is at a school in Cornwall, and all the boys are keenly interested in aeroplanes and engines – June's son (7 years) knows every plane by sight. 'That's a Whitley,' he tells his mother who hasn't the least idea herself. On the other hand the little girls show no interest at all in aeroplanes and engines or any of the things that enthral little boys.

It is true that we have been given a vote and are accepted as independent individuals. It is true that we can work for the same exams and do as well and sometimes better in them than men. It is true that we have proved our ability in many spheres once governed only by men. But we find that in achieving this 'equality' we do so at a sacrifice of much of our private happiness and fulfilment. We have come out of the kitchen and away from the cradle to find that we are still women and masses of us are drawn year by year by instincts stronger than reason back again. Yet for many of us it isn't enough. We want to compete with men – and when we find ourselves on a level with men, doing men's work, the difference remains. We are in a state of perplexed growth and experiment. We are aware of our difference but haven't yet discovered how to define it or in the least how to use it outside our familiar domestic enclosure.

Walked home through the Beeches in the October dusk. Sunset split the clouds with a bar of light above the Common. Home. Garden dim and the cottage cold. Cats and kittens raced to meet me.

Ernest van Someren

Got involved in dirty jobs which took me the whole morning, sawing wood, and clearing out the woodpile in the coalshed. There was a rats' nest under the wood, and I got a neighbour to help me kill eight or more babies, who were then transferred to the bonfire to make sure. The parents probably escaped, but I found a tunnel of theirs and filled the entry with cement.

After supper I played with Laurie's Meccano.

TUESDAY, 13 OCTOBER

Edward Stebbing

Churchill's speech at Edinburgh was, to me, almost boring. Apart from a few interesting remarks on Hitler's speech, it was the same old stuff all over again. I am getting a little tired of his rhetoric and metaphorical allusions, with never a really solid and encouraging fact, except in some minor field, to hang on to. Always Churchill speaks of the growing power of the Allies, never fully grown, of the offensive that is to come, of German atrocities that will one day be atoned for, of the 'ring of doom' that is closing in on Hitler (though from where he doesn't say), of the dark days we must pass through, and invariably finishing up with a reference to the light that is broadening and brightening and coming nearer, but never shines fully on us. If he can quote a piece of poetry, all the better.

SATURDAY, 17 OCTOBER

Pam Ashford

The first week has been very arduous. I am in charge of the office, with four ladies under me. Mr Ballantine is very nice up till now. He seems a tired old man, with a bad memory, who I think I shall have to look after, though it will be a different process from that in Mr Mitchell's case.

Central heating in Glasgow is forbidden before 1 November, except under permit and hundreds of applications for permits have poured in. I get overtime at 1/10 an hour. Three hours this week.

On Tuesday Mr Mitchell 'phoned to ask about some things he should have known for himself, and said that my replacement Miss Macintosh was slow but intelligent, and they got on well. She had, however, fainted that afternoon (her heart is bad – and she had gone home).

Maggie Joy Blunt

Bought today at Paddington bookstall, a periodical I have not seen before called *Seven* published by Newport Publications, 1/- quarterly. A magazine 'of People's Writing' – of the people, for the people, by the people. I sense the C.P behind its production – or some very Left organisation. It is clever, quite interesting.

SUNDAY, 18 OCTOBER

Maggie Joy Blunt

We are an astonishing, incalculable race. Eric Linklater writes: 'We do not know our capabilities and our power. A year or two ago our pilots and navigators and airgunners were the people we rubbed shoulders with in the streets. We took no particular notice of them then. They were clerks and mechanics, they were sheep farmers, they sold second-hand motor cars and life insurance and radio sets, they were agents and managers and bus conductors, they were even the products of those public schools which have been the object of so much unkind criticism – they were the ordinary people of our country. But in these ordinary people was a virtue, a strength, a mystery that we did not recognise . . .'

An ordinary young man left our office in April to train for the RAF. An amusing, sociable, obliging young man, with no apparent desire to work in any shape or form. A weak chin, a flabby handshake and a childish temper. Effete, undisciplined. But he wanted to be a pilot, he wanted to be 'at the controls'. They said,

'He'll never stick at training, he'll be kicked out in three weeks.' But we heard this week that he is flying. What is beneath that flippant, amiable surface? We do not know and neither does he. He is the type that has surprised and frustrated the German High Command who thought they did . . .

Ernest van Someren
In the afternoon we took the children on our bicycles up to the Roman Road and picked some sloes, then had tea at a cottage where we bought some apples, and tentatively booked a fowl for Christmas eating. In the evening a WEA friend came in on business, stayed to sup and talked at great length. He was one of the early Mass-Observers, who failed to make the effort to keep the habit up, for years he was busy with a rather unsuccessful courtship, now over.

FRIDAY, 23 OCTOBER

Ernest van Someren
Killed a hen, our oldest one who hasn't been laying for some time, before going to work. The butcher said he was too busy to clean it for us, so K had to pluck and clean it for the first time, with the aid of a magazine article of instructions.

SATURDAY, 24 OCTOBER

Pam Ashford
When I joined the Ministry of Fuel and Power last week practically the first thing I heard was that they were to move to Edinburgh. I took no point of view till last Wednesday when Mr Howell, the Chief Executive Officer, told me so officially. I said, 'I gave up a permanent post to come here. Surely it is up to the Civil Service to do something for me.' He said when the time came he would ask the Ministry of Labour to get me an equivalent appointment in another Govt. Dept.

It will be a very strange thing if my work for the Ministry is to be so short-lived after the tremendous mental conflict I went through in deciding to come! I don't think there is anything to do but to wait and see.

SUNDAY, 25 OCTOBER

Maggie Joy Blunt
Wednesday at the RIBA all day and saw the Technicolor film of the prefabricated house which Mr J has brought back from America.

305

Intensely interesting. All parts of these houses of timber or wall boarding fabricated and cut out to standard measurements in factory, transported to specially prepared site and erected within a few hours. Are being built in California for Emergency Defence Housing.

Ernest van Someren
For lunch we had the old hen, who was a bit tough but tasty.

TUESDAY, 27 OCTOBER

Edward Stebbing
The forthcoming report by Sir William Beveridge on social insurance is receiving a good deal of attention in the Press. The report that one of its proposals is a minimum of £2 a week for every home after the war does not sound very promising however. £2 a week is inadequate to keep a family, even if it is only husband and wife, at a reasonable level of existence.

WEDNESDAY, 28 OCTOBER

Ernest van Someren
At breakfast there was some remark of ours about the war, and Laurie said, 'This silly old war, if there's another when I grow up I'll go over and kill the Germans myself, with a dagger.'

SUNDAY, 1 NOVEMBER

Edward Stebbing
Saw a silly picture in the *Sunday Pictorial*, the sort of thing which makes me see red. It was a photo of the King and his two daughters 'practising' with a stirrup-pump. Part of the caption says: 'The King – just like you – has made a careful study of fighting incendiary bombs and insistent on regular practice by his family.' What sheer humbug! 'Just like you,' it says with oily flattery, knowing full well that the majority of people know little or nothing about fighting incendiary bombs. And if the King has made a careful study of the subject he should know better than to pump without his foot on the stirrup (as he is doing in the picture) and better than to have two people holding the hose, instead of one to hold the hose and one to fetch another bucket of water to be ready to use when the first is empty.

WEDNESDAY, 4 NOVEMBER

Maggie Joy Blunt
Miss L gave us each an orange today, the first I have had in months. As she is under 18 she gets plenty.

A supply of Coty rouge available in Slough. All typists in our department invest and are immensely excited.

THURSDAY, 5 NOVEMBER

Maggie Joy Blunt
Took an Intelligence Test this afternoon, voluntarily (when asked if I would, found it difficult to refuse). It was a paper set by the Institute of Industrial Psychology for clerical staff, and all our typists have taken it. Was in a panic about it – have had no clerical experience and thought it rather unfair, but PA was very soothing. He told me that several long established Executives have taken it and with appalling results.

The Beveridge Report has appealed widely. At lunch today a man from the Rate Fixing Dept. was saying that it will be the plank on which the next election will be fought – MPs will have to declare openly whether they support it or Vested Interests.

Edward Stebbing
This morning my landlady said, 'Rommel's been routed.' Looking at the paper, I said, 'They've destroyed a lot of tanks.' Mrs H: 'Yes, it's a proper rout.' 'I hope they keep it up,' I said.

At lunchtime comment on the Egyptian success was as follows: 'Good news, isn't it?' 'You wait a bit.' 'It sounds different this time though – they've blasted their way through.' 'There's nothing to crow about yet, but they've smashed a stalemate, which is something in these times.' 'They're not out of Egypt yet.' 'They might not get 'em out of Egypt even now.'

Thus, although the news was accepted with caution, it was felt that this time it really was something to get excited about.

The news had a different ring about it. This time it was no half-and-half affair, but a genuine victory. It promises to be the first really big victory on land that we have had.

SATURDAY, 7 NOVEMBER

Edward Stebbing
The newspapers are in ecstasies. There are more maps than ever, showing arrows pointing in all directions, arrows inside arrows, arrows straight and arrows coiled and curving like snakes, and various other wonderful symbols. It is a military map-maker's paradise. As Mr H said, 'You'd think the war was over from the *Daily Express* headline.'

SUNDAY, 8 NOVEMBER

Maggie Joy Blunt
Weekend with step-mother Ella. Her neighbours have relatives in Guernsey. News reaches them in this form – 'Mother Hubbard very evident.' 'A brasserie would be welcome.' 'Gerald is in your room and likes it very much.'

MONDAY, 9 NOVEMBER

Ernest van Someren
Was very busy at work, am trying to get some results on a line which has been thoroughly worked out in Germany and dropped as impossible, and in the USA has been side-stepped by a neat device using a material we can't get here. Shall be very surprised if we get any success at all, ever, but it would be a good thing if we managed it. In the evening I went to a meeting of the local Peace Group.

TUESDAY, 10 NOVEMBER

Ernest van Someren
In the evening went to the Heredity class, we had a good talk on the mechanism of inheritance, illustrated by budgerigars. The lecturer had brought a dozen or so stuffed ones with him to show the colour variations.

WEDNESDAY, 11 NOVEMBER

Edward Stebbing
Bought a poppy this morning, but begrudged giving sixpence for the scrap of cloth and wire you get for a poppy now. A man I know refused to buy one, saying he refused to buy all flags,

etc., on principle. As for keeping the two minutes' silence, I was busy at the time and forgot all about it.

Hearing the statement on the 6 o'clock that the church bells will be rung next Sunday to celebrate the victory in Egypt, my landlady said: 'That's daft. They should wait till it's all over.'

THURSDAY, 12 NOVEMBER

Ernest van Someren
I think the war may end in 1943 or 44 instead of 45 or 46 after this propitious beginning to the Second Front. I have always regarded the Mediterranean as the centre of the world, and so quite expect it to become the focus of the war.

FRIDAY, 13 NOVEMBER

Ernest van Someren
Julia showed sign of a new progress today. After I had gone to work she went up to K and made a kissing noise, then walked off to the front door carrying my bag, pretending to go to work. She has spontaneously begun to try to say thank you instead of Ta, but only says Backoo.

SATURDAY, 14 NOVEMBER

Ernest van Someren
Went on to town by train after work, met K on the train. On to the Royal Photographic Society, where some technical photographs of mine are in an exhibition of photography applied to Science, my first showing in London. After only a few minutes on to the Albert Hall for a concert. It was about one-third full, a programme of Delius, Handel, Bartok and Brahms, oddly mixed, the Brahms Fourth Symphony was the chief attraction for us. Saw nobody we know, but recognised the conductor of the Polish Army Choir in the audience.

We went on to a central London cinema and saw *Fantasia* and part of a good French film. We much enjoyed the beginning of *Fantasia*, but agreed that the Pastoral Symphony scenes were poor and sloppy.

MONDAY, 16 NOVEMBER

Edward Stebbing
I liked Sir Stafford Cripps' weekend speech on post-war policy. It gave no definite proposals, but it showed a clear realisation of what

was wanted and a sane attitude towards post-war problems. I was glad that he wanted no vindictive approach to Germany after the war, as when he said that a policy of splitting Germany up into small states would only give rise to a movement for national unity in Germany, and that the problem of Germany cannot be dealt with separately from the problem of Europe as a whole. At present, I think Cripps is the most capable and progressive man to lead us after the war.

TUESDAY, 17 NOVEMBER

Edward Stebbing
Herbert Morrison, however, is one I would prefer to see out of politics, although he is a member of the same party as Cripps. Power has gone to his head, and I regard him as a traitor to the Socialist movement. Five other men with whom I conversed at lunchtime today had more or less the same opinion. Some comments they made on him were: 'Bumptious twerp,' 'Hypocrite,' 'I always switch off the radio when he's on,' 'I switched off and reached for the health salts,' 'I don't like his face – he looks like a prig.'

THURSDAY, 19 NOVEMBER

Ernest van Someren
In the evening I went to a meeting at the Council House called to elect a local Youth Advisory Cttee to the County Youth Cttee. About 39 organisations were represented and we failed deplorably to agree, so elected a Sub-Cttee to carry on and try and elect a larger committee. Rather silly.

FRIDAY, 20 NOVEMBER

Ernest van Someren
A neighbour called and left us a Homeopathic tract, and a report on the analysis of some other neighbour's urine. The latter was probably an oversight.

WEDNESDAY, 25 NOVEMBER

Ernest van Someren
In the morning read in the train going to work, and did not happen to be with anyone I know, so missed my station and had to travel back three stations, got to work 35 mins late. Was very annoyed. Our neighbour Helen Strange rang up earlier, she has two friends as

lodgers, the wife is in bed with pleurisy developing into pneumonia, and the husband with influenza, so she is very busy.

SATURDAY, 28 NOVEMBER

Ernest van Someren
Had a morning off, my first for some months, and went to town with Laurie. We went to the Royal Photographic Society house, saw the Scientific Photography exhibition, and browsed a bit in the library, as Laurie had asked me to find him a picture of a volcano.

Thence we walked off to the Chessington Circus at the Scala Theatre – the real reason for our visit to town. The matinee was at 1.30 and we got there in good time. We had stalls in the centre, not high enough to see the Ring as a circle at all, but good seats. About one-third of the audience was under 14. Laurie was keenly thrilled, especially by the clowns and seal, a fine performer. The acrobats and fun with water tickled him too, and the elephants were a bit impressive. Horses and the Corps of Chessington Charmers left him cold, and as usual there was a good deal of horse-show, nothing especially fine or novel to a circus fan like me.

MONDAY, 30 NOVEMBER

Edward Stebbing
Two men said what they thought of Churchill's speech. 'The main idea,' said one, 'seemed to be to stop us thinking we're getting on too well.' The other said, 'Evidently he expects the collapse of Italy.'

My landlady said the milk shortage was to be expected because of the number of cattle which had been destroyed because of foot-and-mouth disease.

WEDNESDAY, 2 DECEMBER

Maggie Joy Blunt
Meg returned from her month's mumps last week. H is now away with bad bronchial catarrh. Roger is groaning and coughing and talks of staying away. Self sneezed all Monday afternoon.

W.E.A classes are in abeyance. The Replanning Britain ones have been postponed on account of lecturer's illness. Last week went to a class for Scotch Folk Dancing and enjoyed it immensely. But I doubt if I'll be able to continue. Missed the class last night and there is so much to learn that one should attend every class without fail. May play table tennis with Meg instead.

BL cycled over with two American officers from Wycombe one Sunday 3 weeks ago. They bought cane sugar, canned beer, boiled sweets, chewing gun, pop-corn, cigarettes. We walked them through the Beeches to our 'lakes' on the edge of the Common but they were not impressed. Then we brought them back to the cottage for tea. They remarked on our English afternoon tea custom which is unknown in the States. They paid a tribute to the women of England – said that if American women had had to put up with half as much as we have they would have made a terrific fuss. We played silly games and they appeared to enjoy themselves but under it all was a feeling – what? Sort of 'we are strangers and resented'. I don't know how they are received in Wycombe but British provincial people can be abominably hostile to any 'foreign' element. I proposed this tea party weeks ago which made BL want to give one herself but her mother said 'I'm not having any Americans in my house!' She was, however, persuaded in the end. After the one who came had gone she remarked, 'He is rather fascinating, isn't he?'

Edward Stebbing
The Beveridge report merited all the fuss that has been made about it, after all. It is something to look forward to after the war, if it is achieved, something worth fighting for. It is one of the most encouraging signs so far that the world after the war will perhaps be a little happier to live in. Hitherto there has been hardly anything to give one to suppose that the post-war world will be any better than the pre-war world. The Beveridge plan is a step forward, both practical and idealistic, and the enthusiasm with which it has been greeted in many quarters is also a welcome sign. Some of this enthusiasm may be feigned, and there is bound to be some opposition from the reactionary forces. However, a man said to me today, and I agree, 'I wouldn't mind betting the bulk of it is adopted within two years after the war.'

THURSDAY, 3 DECEMBER

Maggie Joy Blunt
Home early tonight on account of fog. General reaction to Beveridge Report appears to be favourable. Roger – who reads nothing but the *Telegraph* and steers clear of all 'politics' – considers the proposals good. Mr O muttered something about 'only the old Insurance racket'.

Tonight ate cheese sliced thinly and cooked in margarine with tomatoes and milk, followed by raw cabbage, celery and apple salad and a pudding made from stale scone and some vile ABC jam sponge cake soaked in prune juice, mixed with plenty of home made plum jam and steamed. The plum jam is beginning to go mouldy. June says that she has heard of many people's home made jam doing this this year. Possibly due to its being beet, not cane sugar.

N's doctor friend – a woman GP in a London suburb – is grossly overworked and was recently called up 12 nights in succession. How does she keep going? Mr G's secretary is away now with a 'strained heart'.

MONDAY, 7 DECEMBER

Edward Stebbing
Heard the first carol-singers tonight, but they seem quite incongruous and it took me some little time to realise what was going on. They seem to belong to a separate part of our existence, or some previous incarnation that I had almost forgotten.

Ernest van Someren
In the evening went to a Peace Group meeting, a discussion on the use of compulsion or coercion. The group contains one anarchist, so the controversy was keen. There were seven men and one woman present, the latter dozed off part of the time and let her husband do most of the talking. The subject ranged from the punishment of children to the Beveridge Report. I am pleased to see that the Beveridge Report very much resembles the Social Security plan put forward by the Fabian Society.

WEDNESDAY, 9 DECEMBER

Edward Stebbing
Mrs H said she went into a shop to buy some black-out material, but it was 10/11d a yard, so she didn't even look at it. 'It's all a racket,' said her husband. In spite of price controls, profiteering is still rampant in many commodities.

SATURDAY, 12 DECEMBER

Edward Stebbing
The London theatres, I should think, are doing more business now than they have ever done. Almost every available theatre is being used for some kind of theatrical production and almost all of them are playing to capacity, especially at weekends, when the West End is

thronged with people in search of entertainment. People are probably not so particular about the quality of the entertainment they get now and many members of the Forces, perhaps with only a few hours' leave, are glad to get in where they can, which is why many inferior shows, which would not run more than a few weeks in peacetime, are now running for months. This (Saturday) afternoon I tried four theatres, with little hope of getting a seat and with less success. Two of them had no seats left at all, one had a £2/10/- box left, and the other had a few at 12/6d. In the end I got in for 10/6d at a play I did not really want to see. This was *Murder Without Crime* at the Comedy Theatre.

WEDNESDAY, 16 DECEMBER

Maggie Joy Blunt
H let forth on the Beveridge Report this morning. As I thought he would, he tore it to shreds and sees in it only a weapon which interested parties will seize to keep the people quiet. But Meg's father – who is no socialist – said much the same thing: that it will be used as a means to check the spread of socialism. Yet it is the first attempt Authority has made to encourage *practical* proposals for improving social conditions. Hasn't it its value as a stepping stone to better things?

Ernest van Someren
Have heard the Beveridge Report discussed a bit at the lunch table, and I lent a copy of it to one of our accountants, who was critical of certain financial details as quoted. In the evening friends came in to see us, John and Helen Strange and Bill and Olive Bright, the latter are newly married WEA members. We talked about children and astrology and mountains and houses and semi-superstitious cults. They are all pleasant people and stayed later than they intended.

SATURDAY, 19 DECEMBER

Ernest van Someren
I went and had my sight tested by the local optician, a friend of mine. It was tested 7 years ago and I was told I ought to wear glasses, but the errors were slight and after breaking the glasses twice I gave it up. Now the errors are slightly worse, and the close work I have to do by artificial light makes glasses advisable.

WEDNESDAY, 23 DECEMBER

Ernest van Someren

I made some chocolate fudge, K plucked and cleaned a duck. On Sunday evening I had been to see a French neighbour, and bartered a bottle of white wine for one of his ducks, he keeps quite a lot of poultry for his boarding house. We had a long search earlier in the evening through Laurie's papers for a letter which came in the post and which he had pinched before we even opened it. To our great annoyance we didn't find it.

CHRISTMAS DAY

Edward Stebbing

Christmas is always a time of good things to eat and drink, so here are the meals we had today. Breakfast: egg and bacon (instead of the usual boiled ham); dinner: roast duck with vegetables, Christmas pudding; tea: trifle, iced cake, mince pies etc; supper: cold tongue and pickles.

Gifts were fewer this year. Mine consisted of two handkerchiefs, a few cigars (by smoking which I broke an abstinence of four or five months), and 15/- in money. Things scarce or missing this year were drinks (except soft drinks), nuts, figs and dates, Stilton and Gorgonzola cheese, and fruit; but sweets, as far as I remember, were more plentiful than last year.

We spent the day quietly until teatime, when we went to a family party at my sister's mother-in-law's house. There were eight of us altogether. After tea we played various games and tricks and did the 'Hokey Cokey', all of which caused much amusement, until about twelve o'clock.

The news of Darlan's assassination came as a surprise, but everybody to whom I spoke thought it was no loss to us.

Ernest van Someren

L got up early and looked at the things in his stocking (a large one borrowed from me) then turned his light out again, and let us rest till about 8am, when we got him and Julia up into our bed and let Julia dig out an apple and some chocolate from another stocking. K had a cup of tea in bed, and Mother had her breakfast in bed while we had ours. Then we took the parcels into Mother's room and opened them all together. The kids had mostly soft toys and books, and chocolate, also some cash. Laurie managed to find the letter from Tony which he had pinched. I had some shaving things, a book and some music and a book token, Mother gave us a bottle of port which she had won in a raffle. For dinner we had roast duck, Christmas pudding or raspberry jelly (home bottled berries) and afterwards some good Madeira.

SATURDAY, 26 DECEMBER

Ernest van Someren
In the afternoon we went to tea at the Stranges, had an uproariously noisy party as far as the three children went. Their baby Richard impressed me by climbing onto the window-ledge and walking round it (a big bow window) and trying to draw the curtains. Another quiet evening at home, enlivened by a little three-handed bridge.

TUESDAY, 29 DECEMBER

Ernest van Someren
Laurie is enjoying his Christmas books and we are still sharing the fudge I made last week. He has a Russian book which starts off as a fairy-tale but has an aeroplane too, an admirable way of making the best of both worlds. He also likes a white knitted elephant he calls Arthur, after one of the Babar book elephants. He is also pleased with a pocket torch and some pencils.

Kay made me a little cabinet in which to display one of the 'sake' cups in our collection, a black-velvet lined box with a glass front which looks very nice on the mantelpiece by the lamp. We shall change the lacquer cup often.

THURSDAY, 31 DECEMBER

Edward Stebbing
The past year, like the year before, is one I can look back on with satisfaction from a personal point of view. I have enjoyed both work and leisure hours, have been in as good health as is to be expected, put £25 in the Savings Bank, increased my knowledge and widened my tastes.

From an impersonal point of view, the first nine months of 1942 were perhaps the most depressing of the war, but in the last three months the position has improved beyond belief. On the home front some restrictions have proved irksome, but I think we are better off than most other countries at war and that we could put up with much more inconvenience before we could be said to know what real hardship is. (There are individual exceptions, of course.)

1943 promises well.

Chapter Eleven

A VICARIOUS THRILL IN BOMBING BERLIN

We got talking about girls marrying Poles: Polish airmen and local girls at the Tower Ballroom, Blackpool.

1 January–2 April 1943

2 January Japanese overrun by American troops at Buna, Papua New Guinea.

11 January The Red Army launches an offensive against German forces around Leningrad, while the Battle for Stalingrad reaches its conclusion.

14 January Churchill and Roosevelt meet in Casablanca, while Stalin is too occupied at home.

16 January The RAF returns to raid Berlin after a 14-month interval.

21 January Jewish freedom fighters stage an armed revolt in Warsaw.

23 January Montgomery drives Axis troops from Tripoli.

31 January The first Germans surrender at Stalingrad.

4 February Guadalcanal is in American hands, but there are an estimated 6300 US casualties and 24,000 Japanese.

10 February Gandhi commences his three-week hunger strike to protest against his imprisonment.

20 February Rommel victorious in the Battle for Kasserine Pass, Tunisia.

3 March Panic and suffocation at Bethnal Green tube station, London, as a fall on the steps during an air-raid warning causes 178 fatalities.

5 March The Battle of the Ruhr begins as RAF bombs German industrial heartland; bombing of Berlin intensifies.

22 March German long-range rocket plan revealed when a conversation between two captured German generals in London is bugged.

NEW YEAR'S DAY, 1943

Edward Stebbing

It is good that we are to have a Ministry of Town and Country Planning, but why on earth do they choose Mr W.S. Morrison, of all people, to be the head of it? For a job that requires foresight, boldness, expert knowledge, and creative ideas, they have chosen one of the most insignificant, least imaginative, least informed, and least revolutionary of men! Let us hope the new Ministry will soon be placed under the control of someone more suitable.

WEDNESDAY, 6 JANUARY

Edward Stebbing

Saw Noel Coward's much-boosted film (said to be the greatest British film ever made), *In Which We Serve*. It is indeed a fine film, realistic yet restrained, free from the blatant propaganda which spoils so many films of this type, extremely well-acted, technically brilliant. But I do not think it is the greatest British film. Although the story is good, it is not really a great and moving one.

SUNDAY, 10 JANUARY

Ernest van Someren

K's old friend Ethel E. came to lunch with her new betrothed, Aubrey Danvers Walker, they both work for the BBC. He is a very friendly sort of chap and L took to him and rather monopolised him, Julia liked him too. In the afternoon he went out for a little walk with us, just to air the children. It was a horrid foggy day and the train on which he came from town took 110 mins to come 17 miles. They stayed to tea, then started off for another dose of LNER. K and I had a quiet evening, with some recorder practice.

SATURDAY, 16 JANUARY

Ernest van Someren

Laurie's 5th birthday, but he had to stay in bed. I got up for breakfast, but felt very bad and went to bed too, L moved into the same room. Dr D came in the morning and saw us both and said it was something like a cold. As L's gone to the ear he prescribed medicine, but rest would be enough for me. We both had some lunch, later Julia woke from her rest and had hers on my bed. Laurie took sulphanilamide, with great difficulty, and promptly developed a feverish reaction and went to sleep while I was practising the recorder a few feet away. We all had tea together, but L fasted, in spite of the sight of some chocolate-iced shortbread which K had baked, and garnished with 5 candles in his honour.

SUNDAY, 17 JANUARY

Edward Stebbing
The calm has been broken unpleasantly by the return of the German bombers over London. The air-raid siren went for the first time in months in this district (extreme North London). 'That's because we raided Berlin,' said Mr H. 'I thought they'd be over,' said his wife. However, no bombs fell near. The guns fired almost continuously, sounding like distant thunder. Some of us stood at the back door looking out, but there was nothing to see. Mr H said he liked to see what was going on rather than sit in doors wondering what was happening and imagining all sorts of things.

MONDAY, 18 JANUARY

Edward Stebbing
Sending reporters with the bombers which raided Berlin struck me as a refinement of horror, a kind of ghoulish gloating. Do we have to turn something which ought to be distasteful to normal people into a sensational newspaper story with all its lurid details, so that newspaper readers may be able to enjoy a vicarious thrill in bombing Berlin? It is a perversion of what is anyway inhuman.

There was a good deal of talk today about last night's raid. 'We're going to have that game again – Berlin, London; Berlin, London,' said one man. 'And what good does it do?'

THURSDAY, 21 JANUARY

Edward Stebbing
There has been some unfavourable comment on the air-raid warning system after the two recent raids. In the night raid on Sunday and the daylight raid on Monday, the guns started firing immediately the 'All clear' went. It is reported that the warning had not gone when a bomb fell on a London school, killing many children.

There is some speculation, too, about where Churchill is, since Attlee gave the war review in the House of Commons. North Africa has been mentioned as a likely place. 'If he doesn't get a picture of himself wearing a fez in the papers,' joked one man, 'he's missed the chance of a lifetime.'

THURSDAY, 28 JANUARY

Edward Stebbing
For the first time since the war began, we are getting used to good news. For about four months we have had a continuous run of favourable news, from Russia, from North Africa, from the Far East, and the tone of German and Italian news has been such as to give us increased hope. The capture of Tripoli seemed to follow in the natural course of events, rather than as a climax to a period of suspense and uncertainty. We are in danger of falling into complacency again.

A new word has come into our language, or at least it has only just come into fashionable usage. The word is 'global'. Newspaper commentators now talk wisely about 'the whole global conception of war' and 'a global offensive', though what such phrases mean heaven only knows.

SUNDAY, 31 JANUARY

Edward Stebbing
The daylight raids on Berlin yesterday were a piece of daring which appeals to one's sense of humour as well. The thought of Goerring and Goebbels being forced to run for cover as they were about to make their speeches (whether that was actually the case or not) is a comic one, which reinforces the present public mood of confidence. The fact that the speeches of the German leaders were lacking in their usual arrogance was another encouraging point.

MONDAY, 1 FEBRUARY

Edward Stebbing
German attempts to represent their defeat at Stalingrad as something heroic are being belittled by various commentators, but there is no doubt that if we had been in the same position we should have tried to do exactly the same thing.

Listening to some records of Kreisler this evening, I wonder again at the strange kink in human nature which makes men able to create such beautiful music and at the same time wage the most bestial war.

WEDNESDAY, 3 FEBRUARY

Pam Ashford

I am now an American civil servant and not a British one. Sooner or later and probably at a quite inappropriate point I will work in the story of the three diary-less months and the route traversed from the Ministry of Fuel and Power to my new job at the United States War Shipping Administration. Twice a month the American Embassy in London sends me a cheque in dollars drawn on the Treasury of the US Govt. at Washington. I am now at the United States War Shipping Administration in Hope Street.

I don't get told much in my new job. At first I thought my new boss Captain Macgowan did not intend to give away secrets till he knew me, but there are many indications that he trusts me – I have a key to the safe where all the private papers are put away. A reserved disposition is a big element, coupled, I think, with a belief that I should be upset if I knew 'all about' submarine attacks and the like.

The captains of American vessels have instructions to look us up on arriving and most of them like being in an American atmosphere so much that they come back again and again. *They* talk freely enough and I am getting to know heaps about life and sea and what seamen are like on shore.

It is a novel environment for me. A woman's woman, an ardent feminist, a patron of cultural clubs with cups of tea and little cakes (not too plentiful nowadays) me, to suddenly be plunged into a super-masculine world. I must say that viewing them at close quarters, men are getting much better than I thought them before – by men meaning American captains.

I am not worked hard. At first I thought that was because we had just opened and that in time things would begin to hum. But now I think they never will hum. At first I used to think too that it was strange that Captain Macgowan should want the topmost level of secretary at the topmost salary when a sixteen year old straight from college could do the work equally well. But now I think perhaps he wants someone to guide him (as well as the captains) in everyday matters – they are lamentably ignorant, and he certainly wants me to act as hostess. Also, no one has had the foggiest idea how a letter should be written, far less how to dictate one. I make up all the letters for him. Nothing can persuade Captain Macgowan that 'Yours Faithfully' is the customary termination to a business letter. He says it sounds like a love-letter: 'Who else would you want to be faithful to except your sweetheart?' I put 'Yours truly' now, though I have pointed out that that is nineteenth century. Captain Macgowan would rather be nineteenth century, he says, than write and tell a ship's agent that he was faithful to him.

Captain Macgowan and I are teaching one another about our respective countries. There is so much he does not know – our money for instance. However, today's big lesson was on early closing, the Captain having discovered that the shops were closed yesterday (our early closing day) and being perplexed to know what holiday it could be.

THURSDAY, 4 FEBRUARY

Pam Ashford
Now to give the essential links between the previous instalments and this new one.

I was at Buchanan Street for nine weeks. Mr Ballantyne, ex-Chief of the LMS in Scotland, had a steady stream of meetings with 'key men' and I used to be called in to take a report of their proceedings. Meeting big men in the industry has taught me what very little fry I used to deal with. It is better to say no more.

When the administration offices were removed to Edinburgh I was sent to the office of the Assistant Regional Coal Officer for Glasgow to fill a vacancy as second grade typist, the previous holder wishing to leave on account of a baby coming.

Then the Ministry of Labour phoned and asked me to call and they gave me a green card for the Ministry of War Transport, St Enoch Square. It was all fixed up there and then for me to start the following day, as Secretary to the Port Representative of the United States War Shipping Administration, Captain Macgowan.

Captain Macgowan had been in this country only about a week, having flown the Atlantic. We spent nine days together at St Enoch Hotel, I sitting in the Duty Officers' Room. That was another field of experience – all too brief, but not so brief that I did not make friends with the staff of the 'our sponsoring department', Ministry of War Transport. On 31st December Captain Macgowan and I moved into our premises at 93 Hope Street. We have two rooms with a marvellous view up Gordon Street.

Edward Stebbing
'I think the Government are initiating these debates on post-war reconstruction to take Parliament's mind off present times,' said a man at work today. 'Yes, a smoke-screen,' said another. These are two youngish men of the sort that likes to make an impression by saying cynical and pessimistic things. The cynicism of one seems to

324

stem from disillusionment, while the other's seems to come from a desire to emulate him, without necessarily expressing his real private opinion. They merely try to outdo each other in making witty and, as a rule, destructive remarks.

FRIDAY, 5 FEBRUARY

Pam Ashford
Captain Macgowan thinks this has been a very busy day. In the telephone calls they refer to boats by letters and numbers so that not much would get conveyed to anyone who happened to overhear them. We have a priority number and get our trunk calls right through. Most days there are several exchanges between us and the American Embassy in London. Captain Macgowan does almost all of the work. Perhaps he would delegate something if he believed more in me.

SATURDAY, 6 FEBRUARY

Pam Ashford
After work I went straight up to the Cosmo. That sounds ordinary to you, but it is less ordinary to me. My last appearance there was when *Fantasia* was being shown in September. They were showing a German film today, called *Regina* – not bad. I came home to do the usual washing of dirty linen and then settled down to read the German Grammar Book. Imagine a working day with so little in it that I am not tired out when the evening comes.

I cannot say how elated I feel. Can I start to read again? Do you know that last time I read a novel through in the normal manner was in the summer of 1935 when I read *The Good Companions*. I have taken the *Oxford Book of Modern Verse* into the office. Can it be that I shall read that? If so, my method of helping the war effort will be OK by me.

SUNDAY, 7 FEBRUARY

Edward Stebbing
Sir Stafford Cripps' weekend speech was a timely one and reaffirms my confidence in him. We must not be deprived of a better life after the war though lack of resistance of the activities of anti-progressive forces.

MONDAY, 8 FEBRUARY

Pam Ashford

The tinned fruit season opened today.

Here am I having not only the easiest time in my life, but an easier time than I should have believed could possibly fall to anyone on earth. But with it all, there is a certain amount of loneliness to contend with. There have been days when I have sat alone all the day with never a word by 'phone or otherwise with anyone.

It is not, however, so much that kind of loneliness that I mean; what I mean is that I meet so few Scots and the one or two who do come in almost always comment on the extremely American atmosphere and I have to put in some gay little remarks, where what I want to say is, 'Is Scotland still on the map?'

What I also mean by loneliness is that I am cut off from my own sex, not completely but very nearly. There is an office on the same floor as us – they are agents for the US Salvage Corporation of New York and act as surveyors for damage done to US boats. They have a girl called Helen Magaw, 18, bright and likeable, who often comes in with messages and how glad I am to see her; they also have a cashier, Miss Alexander, about 55, to whom I say good morning, but I don't think any friendship will develop on that side. That is the beginning and the end.

TUESDAY, 9 FEBRUARY

Pam Ashford

America is to go on a points system for tinned foods. Over there you are supposed to declare what you have in the house already. About 'biscuits', I have had instructions from both Mr Treckman (Long Island) and Mr Moore (Texas) on the differences in our respective terminologies, and the wording I am adopting is the following:

Here	*There*
Unsweetened biscuits	crackers
Sweetened biscuits	cakes
Cakes	bakers' oats
Scones	biscuits

The Captain got a box of tea-balls off a ship. The Americans don't make tea in a pot as we do. Tea balls are tiny paper bags each containing about a teaspoon of tea. If you have ten people to tea, you have ten cups of hot water and ten teaballs. People put the teaball in and when the tea is the colour they like, they put it in the saucer. If they want another cup of tea, they fill up again with water and put the tea ball back in the water – the Captain's mother gets four cups out of a teaball.

THURSDAY, 11 FEBRUARY

Pam Ashford
A ship arrives here. The captain comes ashore in civvies, glad to be on land; up to see us, in a mood that is much like yours or mine when we descend on Scarborough or Torquay for the summer vacation, except that with them the pleasure is of an external type, after the hazards of the crossing and the uncertainties of the immediate future temporarily withdrawn. They like talking to someone – Capt. Macgowan that is to say, not me – who understands and is permitted to listen, and the story of the trip comes out; they also like being in an American atmosphere and the next thing is that they are coming in to see us, without any excuse at all, but just because they were passing, and down they settle in our premises, beaming satisfaction. Captain Macgowan, who I know is horribly lonely, really likes having them here, though when we happen to be alone he expresses regret for the way these 'boys' have interfered with his work. American absence of 'side' is a constant revelation to me.

FRIDAY, 12 FEBRUARY

Pam Ashford
These Americans have their stock phrases. With Mr Moore it is, 'This weather ain't no good for nothing. It ain't fit for human consumption.' Mr Treckman said, several times because he found it a good joke, 'What are they trying to keep Hitler out of this country for? Let him come and let all the German army come. Put them in hotel bedrooms with no heating on. They would get pneumonia and die. Why get up an Army to kill them off when we could get rid of them so much more easily by giving them the British Isles.' 'Give it to the Indians' was a phrase Mr Treckman often used, and finding Mr Moore using it too, I pressed for an explanation. The American Continent, of course, belonged to the Indians, and if you feel disgusted with your environment you say, 'Give it back to the Indians.'

SATURDAY, 13 FEBRUARY

Pam Ashford
I broke the journey home at lunchtime at the Art Galleries so as to visit the Utility Furniture Exhibition of the Board of Trade. Utility furniture is all right if you *have* to buy, but it is not likely to excite anyone to *want* to buy. If you are going to have wood that is neither polished nor painted, then you want a wood with a nice grain, whereas some of the pieces shown looked as if they had been made out of disused oranges boxes. There was a lack of comfort too – an awful lot of chairs with wooden seats, and the armchairs though upholstered did not look as if they had much in the way of springs. The pieces were all small in accordance with English standards and would look lost in the large rooms which are general in Scotland.

SUNDAY, 14 FEBRUARY

Edward Stebbing
'They keep on talking about the war going on into 1944,' said my landlady rather regretfully. 'I think it will, myself,' said her husband.

The *Sunday Pictorial*'s latest 'campaign' is for the BBC for 'brighter Forces programmes'. Personally, I think the BBC does a very good job in trying to cater for all tastes. There are bad programmes, of course, but on the whole the programmes have improved considerably. The *Sunday Pictorial* is very much mistaken if it thinks the BBC ought to be like itself – cheap, glaring, superficial.

THURSDAY, 18 FEBRUARY

Pam Ashford
Coming to work two men (middle-aged) behind me on the tram were talking about what one called the 'American advance westward', meaning, of course, the reverse the Americans had in Tunisia yesterday. One said, 'We know about the US Army – all talk and chewing gum.' The other said, 'They are green – don't know the way to fight.' The first said, 'They will need to learn. But they *will* learn.'

The drinking that goes on is appalling. I could name half a dozen officers who come up here regularly, and are not only known to get intoxicated, but talk about their intoxication openly. Captain Macgowan only drinks ginger beer, for which I am very glad, and he says, 'These fellows get up to be first mate, or whatever it is, but they never get any further, they stick at the one job, because no one is going to make them captains if they might go drunk at any minute.'

There are also 'women'. I cannot get orientated on that subject. There must be scores of 'beautiful blondes' (the usual description) hanging around hotels trying to catch American captains. It seems to me that they are mostly after a free meal, but they all drink like fish. Again and again, I've heard some officer around here afterwards exclaim with both wonder and admiration that they did not know 'how she could get so much down'. These women can obviously out-drink their hosts any night.

Believe me I am learning a lot about 'men' in this place – that's drink and women disposed of, but the language that some people use is shocking. In America they use 'Jesus Christ' as a swearword.

FRIDAY, 19 FEBRUARY

Edward Stebbing
Some talk at lunchtime today about the debate on the Beveridge Report. One man said they ought to have shelved the whole thing until after the war, as we could not afford it now. We ought to wait until we are prosperous. Also, he said, the Report presupposed a long era of peace, whereas, he thought, we were in for a long period of war, perhaps for the next one hundred or two hundred years(!). Another man disagreed entirely – he thought the Beveridge proposals were a necessity. (The first man is only about 30, the second is over 50. One might have expected their views to be the reverse.)

Pam Ashford
Meeting of the Glasgow Association of University Women.
The first course (the 'meat' course although there was no 'meat' in it) consisted of all manner of root and green vegetables chopped up, baked in big pie dish, beneath dried egg top, and accompanied by a baked potato (cooked in fat like chops). What a dog's breakfast – using the expression literally for once. With extreme tactlessness as I handed around the plates, I gasped, 'What is it?' However, everyone as she took her first bite exclaimed, 'How nice!' Then all those hackneyed remarks cropped up, 'How we talk about food nowadays.' 'What a difference from before the war.' Mrs Bagsich said, 'I thought the stock subject in Scotland used to be money. However, why should not one talk about food? I love food.' Everyone else said that she did too.

SUNDAY, 21 FEBRUARY

Edward Stebbing

The Ministry of Health's Press advertisement, 'Ten Plain Facts about Venereal Disease', is a useful first stop in its campaign against VD. A lot more is needed yet. These plain facts must be followed up by more detailed facts and by arguments as well as facts. The propaganda must be long-term and persistent, because the prejudices and ignorance to be overcome are deep-rooted and not easily broken through. People must be gradually and persuasively re-educated. Fact No 7 in the advert seems bad psychology to me, with its rather disapproving talk about 'free-and-easy sex behaviour' and 'clean living is the only way to escape infection'. This merely serves to antagonise the people who it most directly concerns, by making them feel socially undesirable, morally culpable. Whatever their morals, however, diseased persons must be sympathetically treated. The Ministry of Health would do far better to recognise the weakness of human nature than to make the puritanical remark that 'abstinence is not harmful', which is very much open to dispute.

Ernest van Someren

Laurie got up at 4, having made a mistake in reading the clock when he woke in the night. He had permission to get up and dress at 7.45. Unfortunately he fell downstairs in the dark and woke us all with screams. I got up and undressed him and took him into my bed where he slept till 8. I took both children out for a walk, went to the Braithwaites and returned a magic lantern we had borrowed, and they gave us 4 apples for the children. The Holmes boys came to ask us to tea, but we didn't go as Julia was feeling crabby.

WEDNESDAY, 24 FEBRUARY

Edward Stebbing

The problem of clothes is becoming almost acute for me. I am going to work with darns in the knees of my trousers, which I have never done before. I am almost ashamed to be seen in them. I am badly in need of pyjamas and socks, but cannot buy them until the next 20 coupons come into use, which fortunately will not be long now. I shall have to reprieve an old suit which I had not intended to wear any more, but at least there are no holes in it.

Ernest van Someren

Our canteen has bought a lot of bulbs in bowls, and we now have daffodils on our table at lunch. Until about 1940 they used to manage a fairly regular supply of flowers on the lunch tables, but these have been too expensive for the last year or two. For the Directors' monthly lunch they manage carnations in winter, and other flowers in the season.

SATURDAY, 27 FEBRUARY

Edward Stebbing

My landlady has no patience with Gandhi. 'I hope he does die,' she said. 'He's been bought by German money.' Her idea about Indians and all coloured foreigners is that 'They're nice to your face, but the minute your back's turned they'll have a knife in you.' And again, 'You can't treat them like white people.' In my view, our very mistake lies in trying to treat them like ourselves. Their totally different habits, beliefs and traditions demand totally different treatment. As it is, we don't understand them and they don't understand us, except in individual cases – not as whole communities.

Notice seen in a restaurant: 'Is your roll really necessary?'

SUNDAY, 28 FEBRUARY

Ernest van Someren

We got up late. Laurie had been given the clock so that he could get up earlier, but we forgot to give him his clothes as well, so he politely waited.

A friend called Joe D, who often comes, came and stayed for tea, had to see me about WEA matters. He was going on to see another man for a lesson in conjuring. This expert told him he would give Joe an hour's coaching in sleight of hand if he would afterwards listen to half an hour of religious instruction. The chap is an evangelical, evidently of the irrational kind.

MONDAY, 1 MARCH

Pam Ashford

The Women at War Work Exhibition. During the morning the staff sits and knits, 'bored to tears'; in the afternoon they are dazed with overwork. They have 7000 visitors a week; the other Saturday (I rather suspect it was the day of my own visit) they had 4000. The M of L would have liked fewer people because they could then have got hold of people who are genuinely interested and pressed information home. With such large numbers they have their hands full in chasing small boys away from exhibits marked 'Do Not Touch'. The airplane propellers exhibited whiz around when a switch is operated. The switch is carefully hidden out of sight of the public. One day they took a party of distinguished visitors around and my colleague Miss Berry went over to the place where the switch is hidden and set the propellers in motion; thereafter turning them off. They had hardly turned their backs on the propellers than they were in motion again, this time set off by two small boys who had watched Miss Berry and the switch.

Ernest van Someren
Cycled to work. John Strange has been away for the weekend, he didn't get back till after work today, and found that there had been a burglar in the house, who stole some clothes and a watch and a ring and things and damaged stuff belonging to the owner of the house, to John, and to his sub-tenant Armitage.

TUESDAY, 2 MARCH

Pam Ashford
Today's big thing was a telephone message from the American Embassy to visit a Glasgow address and deliver a confidential message, and when I telephoned back to tell Capt. Devlin what had happened, he thought I had done wonderfully well. Capt. Devlin trusts me far more than Capt. Macgowan does. Capt. Macgowan, though he is opening out, is very reserved and will never be anything else: it's his nature. I should like to see him with a group of friends, but it is dreadfully hard to get a person with a temperament like that into the swim of events. I said to him today, 'You don't get enough pleasure.' He said, 'I get my pleasure at the Anchorage going about the boats.' However, he has got a 'date' for March 12th. When he was having dinner last night two men sat at his table. These two belong to a group that have dinner at Ferrari's periodically, and they invited the Captain to the next dinner, viz. 12th March. They are bound together with a common hatred for women, and while the Captain said he could not go as far as that, he can eat his dinner without having a lot of women hanging around him. I said, 'I'm glad to hear it. There are far too many harpies in Glasgow. I have met them again and again in city offices – girls who think themselves respectable, but if they think a man has any money on him, they don't rest content till they have skinned him.' The Captain said he

332

was safe, having no money. I said, 'I am thankful for that, but all the same you don't know what these people are like. By the time they have finished with Mr Treckman he won't have a brass farthing.' The Captain said that Mr Treckman was happy with his girl friends, and why should we try and stop him being happy. What an amusing situation! They are trying to save me from American men, and here I am trying to save them from British women.

WEDNESDAY, 3 MARCH

Maggie Joy Blunt
Sometimes the gaps in this diary grow so big the only thing to do is to jump them.

N and her cousin came for Christmas, and we spent it lazily and pleasantly. I roasted a rabbit and some pork, managed to get some mince pies from the village at the last moment and had made an 'austerity' (*Listener* recipe) Xmas pudding.

January: Played table tennis some evenings with Meg at the Social Centre. We have been doing this for an hour after work once or twice a week since before Xmas. I tried to get a bat early in December but was told that they were being issued now only to clubs by special permit.

In the house I manage much better that I thought I should. The chief thing is not to worry about dust in corners. As an article in a recent *Housewife* explains, many people are discovering that the 'woman' can be done without and that the kitchen floor does not look dirty if it is never scrubbed.

February: We began to discuss one morning the scandalous prices now asked and paid for drinks. Cherry brandy 2/9 a glass. Nearly all the stuff is black market. Publicans cannot get legitimate stock, demand is great and people pay what is asked. On Boxing Night one round cost one man 15/-. Some men spend as much as £10 in one evening.

It is astonishing what one will pay put if one has the cash. I must spend over £40 a year on cigarettes. A neighbour of mine spends £80.

We also discussed the exorbitant amount Government officials are allowed for expenses alone e.g. £1000 per annum in addition to salary. New Minister for Town and Country Planning is to receive £5000. What a start for Post War Planning.

Meg bought a Hovis the other day and hugging it to her said, 'If only I had half a pound of butter I'd sit down and eat this now!' She and Roger hope to get married in June. Have not yet found a house or flat but are slowly collecting things for their home. They attend auctions and pick up second hand household ware when they can. Furniture is the major difficulty. Meg wants everything to be ultra modern, Roger favours old oak and copper. Both varieties almost impossible to obtain and prices appalling. At an auction recently a small, plain oak table which might have cost about £4 before the war went for £27. Meg is violently opposed to the Utility furniture – I think she is influenced by highbrow critics in architectural and art press.

Left light on in bedroom one morning and was not back until after 10pm. Soldiers reported light showing after dark to Warden who fetched local police who had to borrow a neighbour's ladder and climb in window. Have been charged and will receive summons in due course. Policeman very nice about it – he had to charge a Chief Constable's wife not long ago.

Have been meeting more Americans. I like them, but I can't say that I find them very easy to get on with. But it seems to me the unselfconsciousness of children. There is a naivety about them, their confidence doesn't strike one as the confidence of mature adults. I look at them, listen to them. Am amused by them, find them likeable, kind, generous, but they are a different people, they have different roots, their whole structure and outline is different. But so far I have only met officers. There is something about the officer class which is trying in all nations.

Food situation still excellent. Have steak and kidney for the weekend. Mrs T has sent me three more fresh eggs. Have been eating raw vegetable salads, curried vegetables, bacon, and tonight some fresh spinach from the garden. Milk plentiful – junkets, custards and cocoa all possible this week.

Edward Stebbing
The district hopes to raise £120,000 in 'Wings for Victory' week. There are about six dances and three whist drives to be held in aid of it. Personally, I never bother much with these tank, warship and aeroplane weeks. I don't see the point of them. Having these campaigns will make no difference to the number of tanks, etc., produced, and they will be paid for anyway. They are merely ways of decreasing the spending power of the public, which may be a good thing, but in themselves contribute little or nothing towards victory and are mainly a waste of time.

THURSDAY, 4 MARCH

Pam Ashford

The Americans had a fish called 'sheepshead'. Mr Moore saw sheepshead on the menu at lunch and ordered it expecting fish, and he got half a sheep's head.

There is a phrase, 'nigger rich', which means possessing very little. If a nigger has a few dollars, he thinks he is rich. I saw a negro in naval officer's uniform today, which surprised me. Both the captain and Mr Moore were upset by my using the word 'nigger'. I said, 'Of course I know coloured people don't much like the word, goodness knows why.' In America it must apply much more than it does here. Mr Moore said, 'The word is negro. When you say nigger you are imitating America.' I tried to get at what it is that is so offensive about 'nigger', but only got them more determined to have the word banished from the premises.

FRIDAY, 5 MARCH

Edward Stebbing

The catastrophe at a London tube shelter during an air-raid two nights ago, when 178 people suffocated in an accident at the entrance to the shelter, was a major topic of conversation today. I don't think anybody believes that, as the official statement says, 'there was no sign of panic'. There must have been panic. In a situation where panic would be expected it is stupid of the authorities to say there was none, when the accounts of some of the survivors make it clear that there was panic. One man said it was directly comparable to the first statement about the fire on the *Normandie* in New York, when it was said straight away, before any enquiry, that there was no evidence of sabotage. Again, there is the usual official reticence about where the incident occurred, one of the first things people want to know. I have already heard that it was Bethnal Green. This is the sort of occurrence which, if the facts are not given as soon as possible, will be grossly distorted by all kinds of rumours.

I noticed a slight alteration in the Press advertisement about venereal disease. In the final paragraph dealing with the first symptoms of syphilis and gonorrhoea, we are now told where the symptoms appear, a point hitherto omitted. I see by today's paper also that Church leaders are much concerned over the increase in sexual immorality. This is a very controversial subject, but I will say that it is not necessarily immoral to *have* VD; the method by which a person contracts it may or may not be immoral. Certainly the Church

335

is right to condemn the spread of sexual immorality, but immorality is increasing in almost all other aspects of life. It is an immoral world we live in and war, the greatest immorality of all, is one of the main causes in the spread of VD.

SATURDAY, 6 MARCH

Edward Stebbing
There was a huge crowd round the Lancaster bomber in Trafalgar Square this afternoon. This seems to be one of the main propaganda showpieces in London's 'Wings for Victory' week. One or two remarks I heard in the crowd were: 'It isn't really very well done. It doesn't look as big as it really is,' 'Isn't it a lovely one!'

As I walked towards Piccadilly tube station I noticed one of those magazine stands that come out after dark; a light is fixed so that it shines on the lurid covers of pornographic books. Then as I entered the tube station there was a policeman controlling the people, so that there should be no more accidents such as happened the other day, and suddenly I felt completely disgusted with our civilisation, in which people call bombers 'lovely', gangsters and heroes, vendors of pornography come out at night, and policemen have to prevent people from suffocating themselves in their panic. With the image of the play I had seen still in my mind, I thought how petrified our civilisation is, not free, natural or happy, but cold and hard and cruel, like a stone, like a frozen corpse.

Ernest van Someren
In the afternoon did garden jobs, with Julia watching, while K and Laurie went to the movies to see *Bambi*. In the evening I went out with the Stranges to see *Bambi*, and a lively film about trapping animals for a zoo.

SUNDAY, 7 MARCH

Pam Ashford
The other day at the Sorotomist Club Mrs Muir was blazing about the H. of Commons standing out of respect for the Jews who were being massacred in Europe. She thought the world was well rid of the Jews. Is not that dreadful?

MONDAY, 8 MARCH

Pam Ashford
Soroptomist Day and in aid of our coastal battery we raffled the
contents of a parcel of food received from one of the American Clubs.
Eight prizes, sum raised was 9/6. Prizes were a bar of chocolate, a tin
of Ovaltine, cough sweets, tea, grated cheese (in a packet), soup
powder and other things.

TUESDAY, 9 MARCH

Edward Stebbing
The speech made yesterday by Henry Wallace, Vice-President of the
USA, was one of the most significant in recent months. It brushes
aside all pretence and gets down to hard facts. It crystallises the
prospects for the post-war situation. When this war between
'democracy' and Fascism is over, then, if we are not careful, the
conflict between capitalism and communism will lead to another war.
This, I think, should be the overriding consideration in our post-war
conduct (providing, of course, that we do win the military war).

WEDNESDAY, 10 MARCH

Edward Stebbing
Went to a dance in aid of 'Wings for Victory' week. The chairman of
the local British Legion branch made a speech and said, among other
things, that 'Hitler has as much chance of winning this war as a
celluloid cat has of getting through hell chased by an asbestos dog'.

THURSDAY, 11 MARCH

Ernest van Someren
In the evening went to the movies with K, saw *Mrs Miniver*, which
struck us as a very competent propaganda film. There were two
obvious mistakes, one about the stopping of a church service when
war was declared, the other a matter of times and distances. We
walked home with the Stranges, who were there too.

FRIDAY, 12 MARCH

Pam Ashford
Last Sunday the Capt. lost his car. When he went out to the kerb
where he had left it, it was gone. However, the US army had left a

note to say they had taken it. They have put another one in the garage now. He saw it last evening – a regular army vehicle, camouflaged, with a large star on the roof so that the United Nations pilots won't bomb it by mistake.

WEDNESDAY, 17 MARCH

Pam Ashford
During January Capt. Macgowan repeatedly said unpleasant things about our climate. He has since developed an attitude of calm and silent resignation. He goes about what he calls the 'waterfront', i.e. the docks, and gets wet feet with painful consequences. He has had cramp and rheumatism and won't do anything about them. He has had a bad cough this week, which frightened Capt. Devlin when he has heard him over the telephone. There is no standing up to the battalions of germs the Captain is filling the atmosphere with.

TUESDAY, 23 MARCH

Pam Ashford
A Dig for Victory Exhibition opened this afternoon and will close on Sunday. It is comparatively small but nicely got up, consisting mostly of diagrams illustrating ways of growing potatoes, tomatoes, turnips, parsnips, peas, beans, beetroot and fruit, and ways of destroying insects. There was a fine table of fruit bottled by members of the WRI and the lady in charge explained the process to me. She has a friend who did 70 bottles of fruit last summer for herself, husband and two sons. There was a magnificent bottle containing about 24 peaches. There were also marvellous looking raspberries and lots of ways of carrying vegetables over to the winter. How I grow sick of never-ending starch – bread, bread, bread.

Ernest van Someren
Cycled, had a particularly busy day, and mentally made an important new step in an invention which I started in 1934, which I haven't worked out yet.

WEDNESDAY, 24 MARCH

Edward Stebbing
Churchill's speech tonight was about the most satisfying one he has given, though not completely so. It had at once a steadying and a heartening effect. He was right in making no promises, for we do not

338

want promises, but at the same time he gave us something optimistic about 'after the war'. He showed that the Government has been thinking about post-war problems and intends to tackle them with some degree of imagination and boldness. Hitherto, it has been the lack of official explanation and reassurance about post-war policy which has caused much of the misgiving and dissatisfaction of recent months. Churchill's speech should act as something of a sedative. I was not, however, satisfied with his remarks about election prospects and one could make other criticisms about what he omitted to mention, but one can't expect everything and what he did say was very encouraging. My landlady said afterwards, 'That's to buck us up, that is.'

Pam Ashford
My remarks about the Dig for Victory Exhibition persuaded Mother to go along this afternoon so as to watch the cookery demonstration. She saw both the D for V. and the Battle for Fuel Exhibitions, and then entered the Fuel Theatre under the belief that that was where the demonstration for cooking vegetables was to be held. She was soon to find out that the gathering was a Brains Trust on the Battle for Fuel. I gather that eight ladies on the platform had questions put to them by a question master. 'Why should you not wash under running water?' for instance. The answer is that coal is required to pump water.

Ernest van Someren
In the evening to the movies to see *Thunder Rock*, a remarkably good film, by producers of whom I had not heard before. There were a couple of small technical defects, and photographically the good camera work was marred by poor developing of the print, but on the whole it was unusually good, and a very small audience.

THURSDAY 25 MARCH

Pam Ashford
Not only is it 22 months since we had a visitation, but it is 22 months since we had an alert (excluding an accidental sounding of the siren one cold December midnight last year). I was in a doze at 12.20 when the siren sounded. Yes, there was gun fire a long way off, the noise coming nearer and nearer, rising from a pianissimo to something pretty good in the way of a crescendo. Over our head I could hear the

upheaval in the Fullers. I think they were throwing their valuables into attaché cases. And what a deal of running about on the stairs. Three times enemy planes passed over the house.

I had just got into a nice sleepy condition again when the all clear woke me up completely.

Today a Captain came in dressed like a cowboy and with all the mannerisms of one. In America, outside of New England, it must be the recognised practice to throw on the floor cigarette and cigar ash (and the Americans go through vast quantities of cigars).

SATURDAY, 27 MARCH

Pam Ashford
The tremendously nice captain who is dressed like a cowboy came in again. He has a red shirt with black stripes, a hat with a big brim, a leather belt and a cigar. These Americans cannot wear waistcoats much at home for nearly always their waistcoats are many shades cleaner than the rest of their suits. Whether they wear them here for warmth or to imitate the British, I don't know. There are some queer sartorial styles come in here. There was a man this week with khaki trousers, navy flannel, a tweed coat, navy blue knitted hat, and a cigar. He was chief steward. I said to the captain, 'That man was very shabby.' The captain said (what I thought but would not have said), 'Shabby! It was the dirt I noticed. Imagine having your meals provided for by anyone as dirty as that.' As I have said, Americans have no side about them.

Edward Stebbing
The Ministry of Health have adopted an imaginative and determined policy of issuing a new Press advert on venereal disease every Friday. Yesterday's offering, in the form of a letter to a doctor and the latter's reply, struck a human note, which is very desirable. I hope this technique will be continued and improved. There is still much ground to cover.

MONDAY, 29 MARCH

Edward Stebbing
Tucked away in an inconspicuous corner of the paper today were three lines saying that over 1000 tons of oranges, condemned as unfit for human consumption, had been dumped on Tees-side. How did such a scandalous occurrence come about? Why was such a large quantity of a valuable food allowed to go to waste?

Pam Ashford

Mr Johnson set out to tell me the 13 original states and broke down at 12. On looking them up in a little Oxford pamphlet I bought recently I find that he missed four states out, and 12 were arrived at by including three names that should not have been put in.

Today the Soroptomists gave their annual treat to a party of disabled men from Erskine Hospital. I have always been rather afraid of this engagement for I am too sensitive not to shudder at unpleasant sights, but at the same time there is no question of not doing one's best to make the treat as big a success as possible. I was given a seat near the top table between two boys in blue. My two partners were both men with paralysed right hands. First one and then the other pointed out to me what I took to be the most unusual members of the party. One man was only 16½ years of age. He has lost one leg, had his foot amputated from the other, and he had lost all the fingers on both hands. He was in the Merchant Navy and these injuries arose from a voyage to Russia. One man said, 'When we go anywhere, the photographers take his picture; perhaps you have seen about him in the papers.' I replied, 'I have, though it is a strange coincidence. Last summer, when I put away my summer clothes, I wrapped them in sheets of newspaper, and when searching for a pair of stockings last week happened to see a headline about a Russian convoy – under the date September 1942.' Now I read everything I can about Russian convoys and I read the story of a Glasgow boy who had been brought back after terrible experiences.

Ernest van Someren

I had a cup of coffee after supper and at 8.00 went out with John Strange and was picked up by Dr Thompson to go to a 'Brains Trust' at Wormleybury, a convalescent hospital in the home of the Treasurer of the Zoological Society. There were only four of us as Mrs Holmes was ill. Dr Fairchild came too. Joe Daish was the questionmaster, and managed to establish an informal atmosphere in which supplementary questions could be put in by the audience, of about 40 soldiers and 4 staff. We invited the owner of the house to help answer one biological question, about which he knew hardly anything, and we had a cup of tea with him afterwards.

TUESDAY, 30 MARCH

Pam Ashford

If I liked to accept invitations from my 'visiting' captains I could go out a lot. I find it strange – 40, obese, old-fashioned (in clothes as well as ideas!) and with no sex appeal. On their side, loneliness is the motive, and I am afraid that I bring the invitations on myself by my emotional nature leading people to think I care more for them than I do, and by being, I think (even though quiet and with little talk), nevertheless less dour than the Scots.

Capt. Z went back to the States recently, after about two months in Glasgow. On his last day he wrote a lot of 'goodbye' letters in our office, and how the captain and I laughed at the addresses (I had the job of posting them). His Bristol girl, his Liverpool girl, and three Glasgow girls. He took Capt. Macgowan out to dinner three times and each time he brought 'the' girlfriend – three different girls.

THURSDAY, 1 APRIL

Pam Ashford
It was Mother's birthday two days ago and I have not yet got her a present. It is no end of a job buying presents. Where to get it? How to get into the shop that has it?

In my eyes, some Americans completely fail to perceive there is a war on in this country. They repeatedly assert, 'In America we make it a point of giving guests the best of everything, and now we are here, the British ought to give us the best of everything. We ought to have bigger food rations and more clothing coupons than the inhabitants. It is the least you could offer in the way of hospitality.'

FRIDAY, 2 APRIL

Pam Ashford
I got Mother's present, a cream coloured oil silk apron with oil silk border. 2 coupons, 6/11. There were other sales being made of this not altogether essential garment. I got it at Reid & Tod's, who specialise in umbrellas, and I feel sure it is oil silk that would have gone into umbrellas had steel frames been available. There is an oft-heard story that there are no umbrellas for sale.

Americans are free. This afternoon Johnsen called me 'Tootsie'. Imagine such a thing!

Chapter Twelve

A PROSTITUTE SAID HULLO

Each feels that his or her journey *is* necessary: travel posters meet with resistance.

6 April–24 July 1943

7 April Hitler and Mussolini meet in Salzburg to discuss their African defeats and plan next phase of attack.

12 April In the British budget, Chancellor Sir Kingsley Wood announces a 100 per cent increase in purchase tax on all luxury goods.

20 April Churchill announces that the ringing of church bells, once designated a signal of invasion, can recommence.

26 April Fierce fighting in the Warsaw ghetto as Jews are either shot or transported to concentration camps.

29 April It is announced that more people were killed on the roads in Britain than in the UK armed services in the first two years of the war – 147,500 compared to 145,000.

30 April Fighting intensifies in the North Atlantic.

7 May The Allies capture Tunis, and soon take control over North Africa.

8 May Part-time war work becomes compulsory for British women aged 18–45.

16 May 19 'Dambuster' Lancasters set off for the Ruhr with their bouncing bombs.

24 May U-Boats withdraw from the North Atlantic.

25 May Churchill and Roosevelt conclude their talks in Washington with an agreed date on the invasion of Europe next year.

1 June It is announced that the number of illegitimate births per year in Britain has increased from 32,000 before the war to 53,000 last year.

17 June The RAF bombs Naples and intensifies bombing of the Ruhr.

9 July Germans thwarted on their assault on Kursk by Soviet tank forces.

10 July 150,000 British and American troops land in Sicily in Operation Husky.

16 July Education secretary R.A. Butler announces major reforms to the British secondary school system, including a raise in the school leaving age to 15.

22 July General Patton advances through Sicily to take Palermo.

25 July Mussolini is sacked by the Italian King and then arrested.

TUESDAY, 6 APRIL

Edward Stebbing

According to the *News Chronicle* anti-Semitism is on the increase, and from various incidents which have been reported recently it would appear to be true, but I have not noticed any evidence of it in this district or among people with whom I have come into contact.

This evening my landlady, her daughter and I spent a long time talking about the sweets which have gradually been vanishing from the shops since before the war. It made our mouths water to think about chocolate drops, liquorice sticks, slab toffee, coconut squares, peppermint bulls-eyes, coconut ice, sugared almonds, etc. Shall we ever be able to get them in any quantity again?

WEDNESDAY, 7 APRIL

Pam Ashford

Annan's have an exhibition described as Fifty Fine Prints, for one week only. I went in at 5.30. There was one by Van Dyck, several Millais, 4 watercolours and about 4 etchings by Whistler. (One of the Whistlers is reproduced in the Outline of Art.) Wm. Strang had two; one, subject Mrs D'Oyly Carte, signed 'To Oscar from WS', the Oscar being Oscar Wilde. There was a Goya – that was priced at £3.3s, so I reckon his stock is low at the moment, though it was not an attractive subject – bull fighting. The top figure was a Rembrandt at £600, 'Jan . . . something'. It had something tear-drawing about it (though none were spilled). I often shed tears over music though never over art. The effect of art so far as I am concerned is to elate and fill with joy. One Durer was £21, another £120.

Did you ever hear of a Limey? That is American for an Englishman.

Ernest van Someren

To work by train, and spent part of the morning talking about pacifism, but did a little work. Went on before lunch by train to town with K and Julia, who started off with a small folding pram and rucsac. We went to a restaurant near Kings Cross for lunch, Julia's first meal in one, we had rabbit pie and she ate some, finally we gave her a large bone to knaw and she took it in both hands remarking 'By Goggy'.

We went by bus to Bloomsbury County Court where I came before a Tribunal as a Conscientious Objector. Mine was the first case after lunch, and took about 25 mins, I took no witness but had a letter from James Fraser, an ex-moderator of the Presbyterian Assembly. They questioned me patiently and at length on my not quite logical position, and on the statement (filed with my diary for Apr. 1941) which I made when I first registered. I said as little as possible, they did not elicit the fact that I am a member of the Society of Friends or of any other organisation at all. They decided that I was eligible for non-combatant service only with the Forces, and as my firm will probably secure my deferment regularly this would make no difference except that I cannot be requested to join the Home Guard.

WEDNESDAY, 14 APRIL

Pam Ashford
The diary has been broken during the last ten days. Mother has not been well. Whether it is a chill (as she thinks) or something wrong with the food (as I suspect) she has not been fit. I notice that the milk in the office goes bad within twelve hours which could not happen to fresh milk in April, and read a passage in the paper that Glasgow now gets milk from Northern Ireland that is three days on the way.

SATURDAY, 17 APRIL

Ernest van Someren
I had the day off and took Laurie to town on the 9.22. We bought sandwiches, and a present for K and a book for each of us, and went to eat our lunch on the edge of the lake in St James Park, where we fed ducks. The early spring made the place extraordinarily lovely, and the lack of railings improves it further. We went on to a Royal Photographic Society Lecture on the development of Cinematography in the Army. This was very tedious, especially for L, but he looked at a book and drew pictures, and thought it was worthwhile for the sake of the films at the end, of Army instructional films about booby-traps, car ignition, and unexploded bombs. Then we went to tea at a serve-yourself Lyons, where he was delighted at the conveyor belt for our trays, and at the good chocolate to drink.

MONDAY, 19 APRIL

Pam Ashford
I like the American friendliness and absence of side but I am beginning to think that in some respects their standards are lower than ours. They regard our austerity as something that is absolutely wrong in itself, and as a legitimate subject of outwitting and evasion.

I used to be alarmed at the number of new socks the Captain brought into the office.

The Soroptomist speaker was Professor Small. The theme was 'Refrigeration'.

WEDNESDAY, 21 APRIL

Maggie Joy Blunt

Not only left light on in bedroom in February, but again about 4 weeks later and the whole performance of policeman climbing in after dark while I was out to turn out light was repeated. Excused myself from attending Court for first summons and was fined 3/-. On the second occasion was charged with breaking black-out regulations *and* wasting fuel. When these summonses arrived all the men at the office set on me saying that second fine was likely to be very heavy.

I attended the Court as bidden on this last Monday morning, quaking. (PA's parting shot on Saturday – 'It'll be £50 or 21 days at least. You take the 21 days and I'll arrange for your salary to be continued here. See you in a month's time.' Les offered to plead for me (for £10.10) that I was mentally defective. Mr M when he heard it was a second offence exclaimed 'a hardened criminal!' and J said, 'She has a complex about light switches, she just cannot turn them out.') I was expecting to have to pay out £5 (at least £3 for the second black-out offence and £2 for the fuel charge). I pleaded guilty, accepted the policeman's evidence and explained in a small voice that I worked from 8.30 to 6 every day, was alone in the cottage, had no domestic help and had to get myself up and off in the morning by 8 o'clock, had not been well and was that week losing sleep because of troublesome cough and that therefore in the early morning rush it was easy to forget the light. The Bench went into a huddle and then I heard the Chairman say, '£1 for each charge.' £2 in all! Which I paid promptly. Everyone at the office as astonished as myself and think me very fortunate. But Heaven help me if I do it *again*.

Cough was troublesome in March. Kept me awake a lot and the office bullied me into seeing local GP. Was thoroughly examined and tested and had one X-ray taken. Doctor found no cause for anxiety at all and cough has since cleared up almost entirely, but there is some doubt about X-ray and am to have another after Easter. Personally I think it was due largely to vile wartime tobacco in cigarettes (am cutting down smokes), general end-of-winter debility and certain private, psychological tangles which aggravated it.

It is now close on midnight. I have eaten, and done the washing up. Must now clean shoes, do my washing and have a bath – Sunday tomorrow. All morning in bed if I want to, heavenly thought.

Pam Ashford
The Captain said, 'You should have seen the girl I was engaged to. She went to cocktail parties night after night. She flew everywhere by airplane. She was in the Secret Service.' I said, 'Good gracious, tracking down spies!' He said, 'Yes, she used to go to naval and army balls and dance with the officers and find out which ones were giving away secrets. Then she worked as a waitress so as to hear what was being said at the tables. Then she would go and live in a wigwam alone in the wilds for a rest.' I said, 'If she ever comes to Glasgow, I should like to book her as a speaker for a Soroptomist lunch.'

THURSDAY, 22 APRIL

Edward Stebbing
An alleged milk shortage has caused a spot of bother at work. All milk for morning and afternoon tea has been stopped, no tea is served to non-resident staff with the midday lunch. All the non-resident staff are grumbling about it, and nobody seems to believe there really is a shortage. One of the typists told me that the milkman takes away 20 gallons a day because a certain person in authority won't sign for it. We have been making our morning and afternoon tea with dried milk, but it doesn't taste very nice.

FRIDAY, 23 APRIL

Edward Stebbing
Referring to a remark by a radio commentator last night that 'there is no sign of war-weariness', my landlady said, 'Everyone I meet is war-weary, fed-up to the hilt with it.' The commentator probably meant that there has been no great lowering of spirits, but all the same, the way the war drags on and on is becoming more and more monotonous.

SUNDAY, 25 APRIL

Edward Stebbing
No hot cross buns or Easter eggs this year, but I don't think anyone misses them much.

After tea I went to have a look at a crater left by a landmine, which fell in a field during the air-raid. I did not expect to see such an enormous pit. It was about 20 or 30 feet deep and about 30 yards across, big enough to hold a couple of houses. The earth inside had been churned up, great clods of earth had been flung all around the crater, branches had snapped off trees, and the general impression was as though there had been an earthquake. Several people stood looking at it – it has become one of the local sights, and it is really quite an experience to see it. One is conscious of the awful force which the mine must have had. It was indeed a blessing that it fell in open fields, and not among buildings. My Aunt N said that it was the biggest one that has fallen in England; a specialist had been to see the crater and said so.

MONDAY, 26 APRIL

Pam Ashford
I went into the Art Galleries where there is an Exhibition called 'Soviet Youth at War'. It consisted of literature for sale and screens bearing photographs (very largely of young persons who have been awarded decorations) and Russian posters. Their propaganda is of an 'horrific' character. That is natural enough, but to me, at least, it was sad to find a girl guerrilla of 14 represented as a heroine for having killed four Germans. She is, of course, but if she is sensitive, what a scar on her mind. One translation read 'Blood for blood, death for death'. The Christian attitude can only be directed to the extermination of Nazism, but who would have believed that civilisation could have regressed to pre-Christian standards of 'An eye for an eye, and a tooth for a tooth'. What kind of world is the post-war world going to be?

TUESDAY, 27 APRIL

Pam Ashford
A woman called Bubbles rises above the horizon. She is an ATS who is on 10 days' leave now, and 'phoned the Captain this afternoon to take her out to dinner this evening. The Captain got quite chatty about her and I said, 'Some of these ATS are very lonely. I should dearly love to meet her.'

WEDNESDAY, 28 APRIL

Maggie Joy Blunt
BL said today that the Americans in Wycombe were fairly well liked but that residents' first enthusiasm had worn thin. The Officers were

at first deluged with invitations and were able to select, but now were glad of any invitation.

They are tightening up on saluting regulations – an officer must stop any man that has saluted him.

Roger has made me an excellent cigarette lighter from parts of an old one of his and an old lipstick container of mine.

Edward Stebbing
Some men were talking at lunchtime about the American troops in this country, and all agreed that they were untidy, slack, spoke a different language, were altogether different from us. This seems a pretty widespread opinion.

Pam Ashford
I can't make head nor tail of this Bubbles affair. He must have arranged to meet her tonight, for in the afternoon she 'phoned to say she was not feeling well. So he just said, 'Phone again when you are better.' Then he said to me, 'I know the idea. She wanted me to go out to her house to see her. But I am having nothing to do with people who are sick. People have no right to be sick.'

FRIDAY, 30 APRIL

Maggie Joy Blunt
Yesterday in London all day. Saw 'The English Town' exhibition at St Martins School of Art, Charing X Road, the RIBA exhibition 'Rebuilding Britain' and War Artists at the National Gallery. The Rebuilding Britain exhibition is excellent. Our architects could not have a better advertisement of their talents and potentialities.

MONDAY, 3 MAY

Pam Ashford
The Captain did not mention Bubbles on Saturday. He had work to do and just missed the date. He said, 'I cannot be bothered with women. Work comes first. Women won't have that. You have to spend all your time running after them.' It was a difficult point to answer. I could only look. Then he went on, 'Look at yourself. You don't get any pleasure from running after men. I am the same. I don't get any pleasure from running after women.' I said, 'So far as men go I treat them as things to fight with.' (There is a big feminist rally on 16 May and it takes up a lot of my thinking.) Realising this was tactless I went on, 'Not that there are not men that I have been

awfully fond of. I adored Mr Mitchell. There were others too.' I nearly said 'Max', but thought that too long a story, and went on, 'But it would bore me stiff to go out with anyone at night. The men I have been awfully fond of have all been men I have been working with.' Then, thinking I was plunging down into a still worse abyss, I got back to Bubbles quickly and asked her Christian name, but it turns out that the Captain had never thought of asking her that.

TUESDAY, 4 MAY

Ernest van Someren
Cycled to work. Soon after breakfast Julia fell from the back doorstep and broke two teeth slightly. The dentist said the teeth were pushed out of place, but he could not yet size up the damage. After tea I mixed some cement.

WEDNESDAY, 5 MAY

Edward Stebbing
In spite of the recent further increase in the milk ration, we are still not allowed any milk for morning or afternoon tea, nor a cup of tea at lunchtime. This is just ridiculous official perversity. Yet when the Public Health Committee came down yesterday they had the best of everything. This is the sort of thing which makes me feel like joining the Communist Party.

Some people now get too much milk. One married man, with two children, said: 'We have to stop the milkman leaving it, or the milk bottles pile up in the hall like a row of skittles.'

Today the *News Chronicle* prints a brilliant cartoon, showing the Beveridge Report as Sleeping Beauty, vested interests as the witch, and seven members of the Cabinet as the Seven Dwarfs, weak and timid, with the caption 'No Prince Charming'. In spite of Churchill's recent broadcast, the plans for post-war reconstruction leave much to be desired.

THURSDAY, 6 MAY

Edward Stebbing
Getting unhappy in my work. We are having more and more work piled on to us, expected to do it in the same length of time, lack of co-operation and consideration from some of the medical and nursing staff becoming more marked. The meals we get at lunchtime are gradually getting worse and worse, chiefly due to bad cooking.

Sometimes accumulated circumstances make me feel as though my nerves will snap, but they never do and this seems to make the strain more acute. I feel the need of some emotional outlet.

Maggie Joy Blunt
Second X-ray taken yesterday afternoon. Shall hear verdict from Doctor I think tomorrow. An unpleasant presentiment has pursued me about this since Tuesday. Am sure I am coughing more from sheer nerves.

Ernest van Someren
Cycled, did a lot of reading and abstracting work and came across a discovery in a German periodical which I promptly tried on our apparatus and found it will save us a good deal of trouble. It is a simple stunt with an old gramophone needle.

FRIDAY, 7 MAY

Pam Ashford
The Americans have a thing called Mother's Day. People send their mothers flowers, candy and telegrams. I heard about it from the Captain before and have seen advertisements in the various cable companies' offices. The Captain was typing three cables when I got in this morning. Being an American, he read them out to me, nice friendly greetings. One for his mother, one for someone else, and one for Mrs Devlin. I said, 'If that is not disgraceful. Imagine Captain Devlin getting you to send off a personal telegram like that.' However, it turns out that it was from Captain Macgowan himself. In the States, no one would think it odd to send a friendly telegram to a colleague's wife. They were nice messages I must say.

SATURDAY, 8 MAY

Edward Stebbing
Went to the barber's. The barber said that the Germans cut off the ears and take out the eyes of some British prisoners.

SUNDAY, 9 MAY

Pam Ashford
From various quarters information reaches one of people suffering from contaminated food. The Fuller household, the Forrest household and Mrs Baird have all been in the same state as Mother

and I were. Now I have got a second dose of the same trouble. I might as well say that the symptom is diarrhoea of a clearly abnormal character; not painful, but going on for eight to ten days wears one out. I blame milk. My second dose came on about eight hours or so after taking a few sips of tea with Glasgow Dairy Milk in it.

MONDAY, 10 MAY

Edward Stebbing
For lunch at the hospital today we had fish and chips (we get this twice a week) followed by a pudding which consisted mainly of damp bread. Witty remarks absolutely sizzled across the table.

FRIDAY, 14 MAY

Edward Stebbing
Saw four posters about venereal disease on official notice boards. One showed a silhouette of a man walking past the signs marked with the months of the year and with the words 'Delay is dangerous' and 'Free advice is available'. Another showed the silhouette of a woman walking along some parallel lines towards a clinic entrance, with the words 'Treatment must be continued'. The third showed the figure of a bride in a wedding dress, captioned with the words 'Here comes the bride' and at the bottom words to the effect that the man who infects his wife commits a monstrous crime against her and against any child that may be born. The fourth poster was just a list of the nearest treatment and advice centres. My main criticism of these posters is that they were not large enough to attract much attention.

Ernest van Someren
Was called up because of an alert at 2.00am and stood out in the street for a bit with the neighbour who was fire-watching, staring at what proved to be a distant thunderstorm. Then I sat upstairs at a window watching the lightning until about 3.00 when the all-clear was sounded. It was a good storm in East Anglia, and must have disconcerted airmen rather since the lightning was largely horizontal, odd stuff to find beneath you.

SATURDAY, 15 MAY

Pam Ashford

For several weeks past a German–American captain has been visiting us every day – in fact, several times a day on many days, and we have grown very fond of him. He came to say goodbye to us this morning, and I felt that the nicest captain we have ever had had gone.

He was in the German Navy in the last war and emigrated afterwards. Now he is absolutely American in his outlook. He is so kind. One day he sent up four rolls (say, 4d each) made of white flour as a present for us.

Edward Stebbing

My Saturday morning off. I thought about spending the day in the country, but bus services being what they are I decided against it and went up to London instead. I tried to obtain seats at three theatres without success, and at the fourth could only get seats for the matinee. Between lunch and theatre I sat in Leicester Square gardens and finished reading the poems of Oscar Wilde. Then I went to the theatre, where *Let's Face It* was showing. It was feeble even for an English musical revue, which is saying something. When I came out, a prostitute said 'Hullo' to me near Piccadilly, but I ignored her. Even had she been young and good-looking, which she wasn't, I would not have risked it – I have no desire to contract VD.

Ernest van Someren

Woke early with diarrhoea, which K soon had too, and we got up both feeling mouldy. John went to work but I stayed home and lay down part of the morning, remaining active when K wanted to lie down too. John came home to lunch, which only he and Laurie ate. He is feeling a bit off too, and Laurie developed milder symptoms later. Richard had one messy go in the night and is now all right. We conclude it was something we all ate, probably boiled bacon.

SUNDAY, 16 MAY

Pam Ashford

This afternoon there was held at the Commons the inaugural meeting of the Women for Westminster Movement. The aim of the movement is to encourage energetic and able women to present themselves as candidates for election to local Councils and to Parliament, to assist in securing their adoption and election and to help those who feel they need advice and education.

At present a woman has got to be better than the men to get an opportunity. Confidence is wanted to overcome inhibitions that have prevented women from taking a full share in public life.

It has also been said that politics is a dirty game and no decent person will go into it. If that is so, it is time decent people got in. It is up to electors to put this right. Women should make democracy a respected form of Government. Democracy has been represented as a Cinderella with two ugly sisters (Nazism and Fascism) pointing at her in ridicule.

Ernest van Someren
K much better today, I'm well enough to eat breakfast. More alerts in the night. Stayed home all morning, Carola Pickering who used to live next door visited us with Jane her daughter. She had a glass of sherry in the garden (orange juice for us) and then came indoors and saw films of our holiday in her orchard in 1940 and some pictures of Laurie and of her children. We were very glad to see her again. In the afternoons we went by bus to tea at Miss Beck's who lives 3 miles away and farms soft fruit etc. I was still too unsound to eat, but enjoyed the occasion, the children enjoyed her garden and lots of rabbits.

TUESDAY, 18 MAY

Edward Stebbing
Comments (all made by men) on the RAF raid on Germany's two biggest dams: 'Wasn't it a fiendish trick, though!' 'Why haven't they done it before?' 'Do you think Germany will pack up now?' 'I can't see it.' 'Considering the size of Germany, it's just a pinprick. Because they fill a newspaper with it, it doesn't make it any more than that.' There was also some discussion as to whether there were any similar dams in this country.

I am in two minds about it. It was certainly a brilliant military exploit, skilfully carried out, and may do considerable damage to Germany's war industry, thus helping to shorten the war. But I can't help thinking of the people who will be flooded out of their homes or drowned.

WEDNESDAY, 19 MAY

Ernest van Someren
More alerts in the night, not too noisy. We have been so long enjoying quiet nights that this recurrence is very annoying. On these

356

clear nights I feel the Germans can usually be relied on to hit something more important than us, as we are outside the industrial area, but on cloudy nights they might make a bad mistake some time.

FRIDAY, 21 MAY

Pam Ashford
A dearth of biscuits is descending on Glasgow. Glasgow, where so many biscuits are made, Glasgow that did have biscuits when the people in the South revelled in their onions and fruit. Is our own lamb to be taken from us?

Ernest van Someren
Mother's 66th birthday. We sent her a cheque for three guineas as I had found a cheque for that sum dated 1939 in an old pocket and she couldn't remember what it was for. She put it with some other cash towards buying a large gay turquoise ring, nearly as big as a wrist-watch.

SUNDAY, 23 MAY

Edward Stebbing
Saw another poster about VD.

Another poster which attracted my attention was one advertising Volunteer Agricultural Camps, where one can go for a holiday and help on the land at the same time. The details looked so inviting (half fares paid, good meals, work paid for, evenings free, entertainment facilities etc.), that I decided to write for full particulars, as it would be a complete change for me to work on a farm and lead an open-air life.

TUESDAY, 25 MAY

Ernest van Someren
K went out to a meeting of the Gramophone Club at which records of incidental music to Shakespeare plays were interspersed with selected readings from the plays, read out by six anonymous voices behind a screen, one of them being Kay.

I went to the local church Mans Group, as also did John Strange, the speaker was John Hadham, formerly known to me as James Parkes. He gave a good provocative talk, on the necessity for a Christian new world order if any change for the better is to be started here. James came home with John and me afterwards for a cup of coffee and further talk; he finds his triple functions as author, politician and parish priest rather exacting but exhilarating. He also got married last year, I am very curious about his wife.

THURSDAY, 27 MAY

Ernest van Someren
In the evening did the final laying of the lino on the scullery floor, which has now been cemented throughout and was touched up this evening. I had to cut bits off for doors, drains and bulges in the wall, and we laid newspaper under it, so the job took most of the evening but is very satisfactory now it is done.

FRIDAY, 28 MAY

Edward Stebbing
I am not now so keen on going to an agricultural camp for my holiday. A girl I know who went to one last year said they had to sleep on the floor beneath a leaky roof and there wasn't much to do in the evening. Also, in the local paper today there is news of a complaint about lack of sanitary arrangements in a nearby camp. I have also received particulars of the camps for which I wrote and find that, instead of 26 camps to choose from, as advertised on the poster, there are only 11. Only the bare facts of what is expected of you and what you must take with you are given. There is no information about food, sleeping accommodation, or recreation facilities. So on the whole I feel less and less inclined to go.

SUNDAY, 30 MAY

Edward Stebbing
(At home for the weekend.) My sister's recently acquired table-shelter looks quite well in the living room. It is comfortable, too, and B says she feels safe in it. It apparently satisfies the urge to get under the table in an air-raid and at the same time gives genuine protection. As one can have one's meals off it, it serves a double purpose.

TUESDAY, 1 JUNE

Pam Ashford
An exhibition called 'The Spirit of France' was opened at Kelvingrove Art Galleries this afternoon. Charlie gets tickets for the opening ceremonies of all these exhibitions and Mother made use of the opportunity to attend.

Mother feels that every French person who could possibly be got to the Art Galleries was got; the atmosphere was entirely French; it was not sufficient for a Frenchman, recognising another Frenchman, to bow, *à l'anglais* but there had to be an immense display of expression, and as most of the French people were constantly recognising other French people, the atmosphere became highly charged with emotion.

When the exhibition was declared open and the gathering about to break up, someone spontaneously began to sing the Marseillaise and the audience took it up. The effect was moving, for every one of those French people was singing the words from his or her heart, and Mother says in sweet sounding voices. Men stood at attention. This was the incident which Mother feels will last longest in her memory.

Heinz's soup has been allocated to this area after quite 12 months without it. Many shops have it though they restrict to one tin. I am getting in a stock while I may. But what do you think I got at Massey's? Celery hearts. This time last year I built up a stock of celery hearts, broad beans and French beans. Mother kept on saying I was overdoing it, but I persisted. Then these things went right off the market. Mother has opened a tin each Sunday. The French beans were used up in about January; then about 2 months ago the celery hearts were ended, then the broad beans. Two tins of celery hearts!

THURSDAY, 3 JUNE

Maggie Joy Blunt
There was no cause for anxiety. The spots on the lung which suggested tubercular infection were 'inactive'. Doctor said that cough had probably been due, as I thought, to too much smoking and that I should make 15 cigarettes a day my absolute maximum. I did for a short while.

Now another bad gap in the diary which must be jumped. This week at the office all is bustle and hustle for our Wings for Victory Week which begins on Saturday.

At home the biggest problems are domestic. Food ample for my requirements, but claims of housework, garden, catering, washing and mending are exacting. And I only manage to maintain the minimum of order and cleanliness – just managing to keep the cottage above the slum border line. A week or two ago saw a notice in the paper of a woman who had been fined £2 3s for absenteeism. Her defence was that the long factory hours left her no time to shop or feed herself properly so that she had become ill. If that is true I deeply sympathise and think the judgement rather hard.

Pam Ashford
Captain Macgowan said, 'They are bringing the German prisoners to Glasgow.' Our local papers made this announcement about a week ago, and they camouflaged the port of disembarkation in such a way that everyone knew what was intended. He went on, 'They are going to turn the people out of their houses in your part of Glasgow and house the Germans there until the ships are ready to take them overseas.' This was said seriously. I could not quite tell what the appropriate answer should be. I just said, 'I should love to see the German prisoners when the ships arrive. Could you not give me an indication?' He said no. I said, 'It may be safe to bring Germans here, but if they landed them in the South of England I expect they would have been lynched.' He said, 'Don't the people like the Germans there?' I said, 'Look how terribly they have suffered. Look at Torquay with all those little children killed.' He did not know about this. I went on, 'In Glasgow we have had little experience of war, so that I daresay the Germans are safe here.' He said (gasping), '*You* have little experience of war. Why, I have been starving ever since I came here!'

FRIDAY, 4 JUNE

Pam Ashford
This is Glasgow's Wings for Victory Week and after work I invested £18 in War Savings Certificates at the City Bakeries. Their biscuit counter has been turned into a place for receiving money. They wear fancy dresses that I recognise as belonging to a pre-war campaign they had to sell some Dutch biscuits. The Dutch hats are not, however, included in the Wings for Victory outfits.

SATURDAY, 5 JUNE

Edward Stebbing
Woman in bus, to another woman, 'It's hard to hate everyone because they're German. I know I can't, anyway.'

SUNDAY, 6 JUNE

Pam Ashford
There is a book drive. The tram notices said the books were for salvage, and I am too fond of my books to like the idea of seeing them reduced to pulp. However, other appeals have stated that the books collected are for division between blitzed libraries and the

Forces and only useless stuff will be pulped down. The drive lasts a fortnight and Glasgow's aim is 2 million books, or 200,000 a day. At Charing Cross and at the corner of Dumbart Road and Church Street (and I daresay in other places) are indicators to show the progress. During the first half of the week the books received were 180,000; during the second half the numbers soared up into the 230,000s. Charlie has given away a lot and this evening I have gone through our cupboards.

Ernest van Someren

Laurie had a cross fit at teatime and refused to eat anything, but relaxed over a tomato. In the evening we had some friends in, Dorothy and Douglas Lea and Kathleen Cross. We made savoury snacks and drank our last bottle of Luxembourg Moselle, a delicious wine. We sat and talked, and looked through the collection of Sake cups again.

MONDAY, 7 JUNE

Pam Ashford

The speaker at the Soroptomist Lunch was Rev Macanna on the Jewish Problem today and tomorrow.

He said that some of the publicity given to the Jewish Problem was ill-advised. The 'Let my people go' type could be harmful. This was a private meeting, from which nothing would be reported, and he could speak freely.

The problem of Jewry today is largely one of Hitler's creation. There are other aspects, the economic and the political, and there is the age-old problem of anti-Semitism. At the present moment these varying issues have been fused together, so that we have to think clearly when we speak of the problem of Jewry lest we fail to separate it from these other problems.

The first fact to be realised is that Jewry has been liquidated throughout Europe. This began with German Jews being insulted, and then their businesses were taken from them. As successive countries were occupied so this process spread. Today Jewry is entirely liquidated in the old Reich, but not entirely in the extended Reich. The question arises: after the war shall we put the Jews back in their businesses? No. Those businesses have been handed over to other people to carry on, and if there were an attempt to drive out the present owners of them, anti-Semitism in its most acute form would be raised throughout Europe. Mr Churchill said (I think it was a private meeting), 'It would not be our wish to see the Jews restored to

361

their former businesses. To do so we would have to put a British army into every country in Europe so as to counter effectively the anti-Semitism roused. We have not got those armies.' There are other possibilities. Poland, Hungary, Romania and Bulgaria are just on the threshold of industrial revolution. There are signs that if the Allied Governments will find the capital to finance the industrialisation of those areas, the Jews could be fitted in there, not in their old occupations – they are gone for ever – but in industrial positions.

The second fact to be realised is the re-education of Germany. It is not the case that the training of German youth in Nazi thought was begun with Hitler in 1933, the process had begun in 1924, and there are already several generations of German youth brought up in that philosophy. However, for the security of mankind, this re-education of Germany must be done.

It has been said that the Government – the British Government and the Allied Governments – are not doing enough to get Jewish refugees out of Europe. Take Palestine first. We promised to make visas available – we published the figure 29,000, but actually 33,000 was the figure, for Jews who could take advantage of them. But those visas have not been taken up because the Germans won't let them go.

It can be said that any Jew who gets to a neutral country will be able to get on from there to somewhere else and if he is going to be useful to the war effort transit will be available for him.

We must remember that the Jews are not the only people in Europe who are suffering. That must be said in order that we can keep the perspective right. What we can say is that they have been singled out for extermination. There are the atrocity stories. Not all are true. Some are propaganda, but Mr Macanna has evidence of deeds too horrible to be spoken of.

Some time ago the paper gave out the information that the German prisoners from North Africa would be landed at a port in the West of Scotland, and today they report their arrival yesterday. I heard something from a shipping man whose car bearing a high priority number on the front shoots past all sorts of barriers unchallenged. Visiting King George V Dock yesterday, he accidentally on purpose drove his car up to a shipload of prisoners and tried to board. Thus he got for himself an excellent view. Then he saw crowds already landed in pens behind chicken wire. He commented on their youth and small stature. They were taken somewhere to be deloused.

Shocked I said, 'The Germans, whatever their faults, are not lousy.' He then said that the Germans were bathed and as their clothes had to go to a steam laundry they were put into British uniforms for the meantime. During the day from our windows we have seen a steady succession of small parties of British troops marching up Hope Street and entering the Central Station by the main entrance (not an unusual sight at any time). My informant insisted that these were Germans on the way to prison camps. I said, 'They would not march the Germans through the streets like that. They would escape.' He said, 'They don't want to escape. They are better off here. Besides, if anyone did try to escape the British would put a bullet through him.' He seemed to regard the German behaviour as satisfactory. I said, 'When the Luftwaffe was attacking this country in strength and large numbers of German airmen were being shot down, some of them were most unpleasant. One German who was wounded was treated by a British nurse and when she had done what she could do, he spat in her face.' My informant said, 'They were winning then. They know better now.'

Ernest van Someren
In the evening I went to the movies by myself, saw an intelligent film *Shadow of a Doubt* and part of a good documentary about the coastal balloon barrage. In the newsreel of the Churchill speech to Congress someone raised a clap for the Windsor family. To my surprise, Churchill didn't get much of a clap that night.

TUESDAY, 8 JUNE

Ernest van Someren
In the evening K went to the movies and I stayed home. Two neighbours dropped in to ask different things, from how to avoid Entertainment duty at a concert to how to set a home-made sundial.

THURSDAY, 10 JUNE

Ernest van Someren
Had an odd job at work yesterday and today. The smell of one of our products is causing complaints at an important shipyard in Northern Ireland. What could I do about it? I had to devise a way of collecting the odorous products, and managed to improvise the apparatus and carry out rapid rough tests to prove that the smelly material was not more abundant than it used to be, but merely smelt worse.

TUESDAY, 15 JUNE

Maggie Joy Blunt
This last Whit weekend I spent at Hove with Julia.

The Brighton shore is mined and guarded with barbed wire, many of the huge hotels along the front have been taken over for the Services, and 'The Lanes' where the fashionable strolled on summer evenings after dinner have gone to sea-dried seed. The appearance of the front is very depressing but holiday crowds (90% of which seem to be Jews) still promenade when the sun shines, the doors of the Norfolk Hotel, The Metropole, The Queens, the Old Ship and a host of others still swing open to visitors. The antique shops in The Lanes appear well stocked and thriving. All the best food, says J, goes to the hotels.

The front has not suffered much from bomb damage, only those parts of the town near the station, the viaduct and the gasworks. Many shops thereabouts are boarded up or to let and many houses empty. When raids are bad the population begins to leave.

On the whole I think the war has improved Brighton. The glare and publicity to attract the cheap holiday trade has subsided. Now the Georgian era can be seen – faded but enchanting.

WEDNESDAY, 16 JUNE

Maggie Joy Blunt
Our Wings for Victory Target was £15,000. On Friday it had reached £7,000. Today the total was announced as something over £15,400. Was told that the management would not allow our total to be less than the target at any cost.

Sally who works in wages and was responsible for the Savings receipts said that one man last year brought in £150 in £1 notes – she told him to bring it the next year in £10 notes, and he did. She expected it to be a lot over the target. Last week and the week before she was desperately overworked and looked all-in. Some nights she dreamt about the money.

Edward Stebbing
A man's comment on the King's visit to North Africa: 'When they said on the wireless, "The following important announcement has been made from Buckingham Palace," I thought the Second Front had started. When they said the King was in North Africa it was rather an anti-climax.'

THURSDAY, 17 JUNE

Edward Stebbing

The Labour Party Conference this week has shown to what dismal depths that party has degenerated. Its deliberations have been utterly futile and negative and make one wonder what claim it can possibly have to represent the working classes of this country. Today's main resolution was, to me, the most disappointing of all, when a majority of more than two to one rejected a motion deploring a policy of revenge towards Germany after the war.

Pam Ashford

Divorce is a subject on which American and British ideas are as far apart as the poles. He said to me, 'I would marry anyone; it would not matter if she was a widow or a divorcee.' That's a slur on widows, but was not meant as such. He went on, 'Her past would not interest me. The only thing that would matter is that she behaved herself while she was with me.' I said then, 'If you could marry anyone at all, would you marry a Negress?' That was a shake up, for the Captain can't stand Negroes. He seems to think they are animals. He said, 'America is a free country and if anyone wanted to marry a Negress he could, but I should not want to.' On one occasion the Captain summed up the Blacks in the simple phrase, 'They all look dirty to me.'

FRIDAY, 18 JUNE

Edward Stebbing

Have now definitely decided not to go to a volunteer agricultural camp for my holiday. I noticed in the paper that the organiser of the camps has resigned for some unspecified reason, and this clinched the matter. Instead I have arranged to stay for one week with an aunt in Dorking.

SATURDAY, 19 JUNE

Maggie Joy Blunt

Meg and Roger married this morning. Ceremony at Paddington Register Office and reception at Grosvenor House. Meg radiant in powder blue and navy accessories. Frock was from Galleries Lafayette. Hat had veiling bunched at the back and flowers. She carried orchids and pink roses. She went away in Cumbrian tweed jacket and a grey skirt just made for her. They have gone to Salcombe for a week.

Marriage is not very easy for the young these days. Housing shortage acute. Furniture scarce and expensive, much domestic ware quite unobtainable, and crockery and cutlery very limited. Coupons required for furnishing fabrics and linen besides the bride's trousseau. Short holidays and many husbands of course in the Armed Forces. Roger wanted to join the RAF but has a very slight defect in his hearing – it does not inconvenience him at all in civilian life, but the RAF turned him down because of it. He has quite a good job now in our firm – was recently put in charge of the Press Shop at our new works . . . but Meg is keeping her full time post in the Production dept. because they need the money. It is a wonder, really, that so many people do get married with all these difficulties facing them. There is little incentive. I'm afraid I should live-in-sin, but the majority of Englishwomen seem to prefer the security and social standing which a wedding ring bestows. (There was some difficulty in obtaining Meg's ring too. Roger wanted it to be 14 or whatever carat it is that wedding rings should be and only a very small percentage of these are now produced.)

Reception was at 11 o'clock. They served quite an enticing variety of sandwiches and savoury snacks with the drinks (gin and lime, martini and whisky). Her mother was horrified at the Grosvenor House scandal a short while ago when they were fined heavily for buying too much fish and was afraid it might hinder the arrangements, but there was no hitch in the proceedings at all.

The frame of my glasses snapped on Thursday and as I was in town this morning I took them along to my optician's. The woman in the shop told me that repairs will take quite a fortnight. Cases are now made of cardboard – she told me to hang on to my leather one like grim death.

Ernest van Someren
Our summer holiday. We took the 9.20 train to London, after breakfast at the usual time and clearing up the house a little. Our next door neighbour will feed the hens and another will water the tomatoes. We cycled from L-pool St to Euston in 20 mins, with Laurie and Julia rather uncomfortably perched behind us and our bulging rucksacks, the rest of the luggage was there already. At Euston we scrambled for seats in a through train to Llandudno, got them, and had a warm and rather crowded journey. We carried with us our 11s, lunch and tea, with half a bottle of white wine to cheer K and me and fruit juice for the children, also tomatoes and eggs. From 4 on there was the North coast of Wales in sight, and we arrived a bit late soon after 5.00. We were met by K's parents with a car, her cycle

was punctured so they went in the car and I cycled to our digs.

Here we were crowded into one room with a double bed, single bed for L, and cot for Julia, running water to the basin, and very little gangway. Elspeth with her four children David, Susanne, Paul and Mark had two rooms next to ours. We shared a sitting and dining room about 12 x 24 ft downstairs, which, with ten less aspidistras, would have been quite roomy.

SUNDAY, 20 JUNE

Ernest van Someren
Strolled out before breakfast with the kids, as they woke too early as usual. It was windy and rather cold. We explored the beach with the children in the morning, the tide was coming in, it goes out nearly a mile opposite the house, which is 50 yds from the seashore.

MONDAY, 21 JUNE

Pam Ashford
A past diary entry contained a reference to 'mixed sleeping', and many times I have wondered how far I am old-fashioned. An interesting comment on this turned up at the Soroptomist Lunch. Dr Stevenson said she would travel to the London Conference by the day train as it was so difficult to get a sleeper and talk turned to sleepers. She had two lady friends who were given bunks in a compartment with two men. They complained to the railway company who persuaded two men who had a first class sleeper containing two bunks to make an exchange. In this case the railway company had shown them the way the passenger list was drawn up, and that it had not been possible to avoid putting them in with men. There was comment upon the point. Soroptomists clearly did not like mixed sleeping on trains, but would accept the unavoidable. Miss Crichton (who went to London often when travelling was easier) said, 'It means you must lie down fully clothed.' Personally it never occurred to me to do anything else with a third class sleeper.

Ernest van Someren
Still windy, so we put up the tent after breakfast in a hollow of the sandhills, in sight of the house. This took a long time as we had to level the site a little, but the children were very pleased to have a sheltered playroom of their own outside.

WEDNESDAY, 23 JUNE

Pam Ashford
We have received a letter from Auntie Nellie. Last week in the middle of the night a bomb fell on their terrace at North End, Portsmouth, and seriously damaged the 12 houses comprising it. The alert did not go until after the bomb had fallen.

THURSDAY, 24 JUNE

Edward Stebbing
Took the day off, as I worked Whit Monday and had a day owing to me. In the afternoon I went to see Shaw's play, *Heartbreak House*, with Edith Evans, John Laurie and Deborah Kerr, at the Cambridge Theatre. In the evening I went to the Promenade Concert. I am afraid I nearly went to sleep during Vaughan Williams' new symphony – it was so hot and the music was so quiet. Stravinsky's fantastic *Firebird Suite* and John Ireland's stirring *Epic March* were the two items which appealed to me most.

Pam Ashford
There were tomato and cherry queues today. It is quite impossible to take them on. However, at 9.30 this morning I got a trifle at the City Bakeries. It was lovely for tea. Thick cream on top, the cake soaked in fruit juice (tasted real, probably ersatz) and the cream would inevitably be ersatz too, but it tasted good. It was a greater treat for Mother who has not had a trifle for several years. At the Soroptomists we have trifles that have been left over from weddings. A friend who goes to the restaurants says they never get trifles. Odd as it may sound, Captain Devlin who lives in London hotels was almost in tears over trifles there. They give him trifles day after day until he nearly screams when he sees the plate approaching him.

TUESDAY, 29 JUNE

Pam Ashford
Summer really has come! Saturday, Sunday, Monday and today, all cloudless, all hot. Today you would think you were in Italy, i.e. Italy before the war.

With many Americans there is a peculiar inability to understand that there are subjects that should not be made the subject of humour. The other day I said that it was tragic that Canada had had so little share in the glory of the war; her men had been tied up here and that in many cases they would probably think of this country chiefly as being the place where they learned to get drunk. Then up spoke Mr Johnsen, saying, 'And the Poles will remember this country chiefly as the place where they learned to make love' – this being a tremendous joke. I said, 'I am aware that there have been quite a few marriages between Poles and Scotswomen, but nobody could say that the Poles taken en masse are amorous. It is their sadness that strikes us. Some of the Polish women I meet at the University have grief written in every line of their faces.' Then up spoke Captain Magowan, saying, 'Bring them down here. We will make love to them. That will cheer them up.'

Maggie Joy Blunt
Our film *Forgings in Hiduminium Aluminium Alloys* is now making its debut. We saw it last week. I didn't have anything to do with it so I can say freely that it is really an excellent technical film. It has had one or two special showings and has been very favourably received.

Blitz First Aid lectures and a Prisoners of War Fete held last Saturday at which I helped at the coconut shies. No real coconuts, only wooden dummies. Anyone who knocked one off received 3d or another turn.

Day was fine and many people attended. Flowery frocks and summer hats. A long entertainment on the lawns by school children, dancing classes, Women's Guilds and so on. The usual stalls and side shows, which I had no chance of seeing. Lemon, grapefruit and orange drinks. An Auction – silk shawl that went for £10, a necklace for £27, lemons and peaches for 20/- or 30/- each, a live rabbit for 10/-. Goods included champagne, port, dolls, a patchwork quilt made by an old lady of 82, Maltese lace, a tea cosy and a statuette for which no one would give a bid, not even for Prisoners of War.

WEDNESDAY, 30 JUNE

Ernest van Someren
Fine and hot. Tim and Elspeth went out for the day. In the morning I went on the sands with the children, and Kay followed me after a little shopping, I took some movies, and some of us paddled. The children aren't awfully keen on paddling and rather prefer playing with sand on the whole. Only Susanne is keen on paddling with an occasional immersion. After lunch we had rests, for the older three this means a sedentary game such as dominoes in the sitting room, just to give them a rest from continuous movement. I took Laurie, David and Susanne for a walk over through Llandudno up the

gardens in the Happy Valley, to a rock cave, and down across the townward face of the Gt. Orme. They stopped a little to hear an open-air concert party, but it didn't really amuse them much except as a novelty. Kay looked after the three younger ones. Julia was sick after her rest.

THURSDAY, 1 JULY

Pam Ashford
Getting my men's rations enables me to get things I might not have got otherwise; I discovered this afternoon that Massey's had received a consignment of squashes and got a bottle each of grapefruit and of lemon. From Brechins with whom I registered for meat, I can get pork sausages. The men always have the same thing, viz. mince from which they make what they call 'Hamburger', a patty (of meat). This week one of their meat books would not have been used, and with it I got a tin of corn beef for ourselves. I could have had a pork chop for Charlie, but in this heatwave Mother thought it unsafe to keep a pork chop in the house for the two days till Saturday.

FRIDAY, 2 JULY

Ernest van Someren
Earlier we had some discussion with the landlady over the accounts, in which our tea and milk consumption was much exaggerated, but we finally paid under protest. But for her poor cooking and grumbling nature it was a splendid holiday. Stayed up late cutting sandwiches for the journey.

MONDAY, 5 JULY

Edward Stebbing
Listened to J.B. Priestley's third talk on his new radio series. It is good to hear him back on the air again. Tonight's talk – on what our post-war conduct should be – was a tonic of sane thinking.

Pam Ashford
The Captain says he has a new girl, 22, Katharine by name, who he has not seen yet, but Captain H 'who he has known for years' is going to hand her over when he returns to sea. 'He can still keep Bubbles on because she is at a distance and they need not meet.' He seemed well pleased at inheriting girls from visiting Captains on their return to sea. I said, 'Why don't you go out and win someone for

yourself?' He says he has not got the gift of scrapping acquaintances. He has to be introduced first. This is indeed a new side of life to me. I don't know how far it is American, how far seafaring, how far simply that I have switched over from a feminine environment to an exclusively male one. I feel rather like a big sister to these Americans.

SATURDAY, 10 JULY

Pam Ashford
The invasion of Italy starts! How did the public react? With a complete absence of demonstration. Speaking for our household, we listen every day to the 8 o'clock news, Mother in the kitchen, Charlie in the dining room and me in the bedroom. Certainly we all listen intently, but little comment is made, and none at all arose from the invasion of Italy. I cannot but contrast the situation with the excitement over the invasion of Norway three years ago. I heard no comment on the bus or in any of the shops. I did hear plenty on the difficulty of getting tomatoes.

Edward Stebbing
At last the news we have been waiting for – the invasion of Sicily. It is great news, but lack of any details and its not complete unexpectedness rob it of some of its excitement. At any rate it has come at the right time, when the Germans have just started another offensive in Russia.

In the evening I went with a friend to the Promenade Concert at the Albert Hall. It was a lively programme and a very large audience – we could only get seats in the gallery. A new work by Benjamin Britten received a great ovation.

Afterwards we went to a restaurant near Leicester Square and had some supper, which was alleged to be steak and chips, but we were very dubious about what kind of steak it was. We had grave suspicions that it was horse-meat.

SUNDAY, 11 JULY

Ernest van Someren
In the afternoon went out with K and the children on our cycles and explored Nazeing, one of the nearest villages which we have never seen completely. We found a very out-of-the-way church, of 12th century status, and a golf course converted to flax-growing. In another part we saw a Youth Hostel called Smalldrinks and called in. We found only a 5 year old boy whose name I guessed in two shots as Niels. There was Danish travel literature lying about the hall.

TUESDAY, 13 JULY

Ernest van Someren
In the evening had a big tea at home and set out for the circus with Laurie, by train to Hertford, but they quietly divided the train at the next station and we were let out at a halt called Mardocks, which isn't near anywhere. It was a lovely evening and we walked along a pleasant road until a bus arrived half an hour later and took us to Hertford, where we went to the circus, arriving very late. Laurie saw enough to be very pleased. He liked the clowns and acrobats best and so did I.

TUESDAY, 20 JULY

Pam Ashford
For 7 months I have had it drummed into my ears that here people don't know what good times are. 'Good times' seem to involve overeating and overdrinking, and I rather think a lot of sex, and strike me as vulgar.

It came as an agreeable surprise to learn that there is another side to the Americans. The Captain had cut out from a Glasgow newspaper a paragraph saying that the State of Maine was repealing the laws forbidding bowling on Sundays. Apparently in New England Sunday is observed. Sports are forbidden and it is only 5 years since cinemas could under any circumstances be opened on the Sunday. Then came a gem from the Captain, 'It is as bad in Maine as it is here.'

WEDNESDAY, 21 JULY

Edward Stebbing
The apparent fall from grace of Henry Wallace, USA Vice President, is disturbing news, for he has seemed to be a man of great worth. Was he too radical for certain influential parties in American politics? There has been an alarming increase in isolationist, capitalist, and conservative views in America just lately.

SATURDAY, 24 JULY

Pam Ashford
Yesterday afternoon the temperature soared, and if today has not been the hottest day of the year, it felt like it. Such sunshine deserves the best. After work I went up to Killermont Street bus station and

got the 1.15 bus to Muddockbank, there again to drink deep of beauty and magic. I had brought with me some rolls and jellied veal from Craig's. The flies hovered around, but after 10 minutes found I was not a sweaty customer and disillusioned, retired. Refreshed, I felt I would do some exploration and followed a beaten track leading north. There were foxgloves abounding, some rhododendrons not yet faded and bracken to caress the hand in passing; and there was wildlife too. Whatever the national emergency may be, I am glad the rabbits have weathered the early phase when their demise was demanded and enforced. Again and again as I trod that grassy path a rabbit would show itself in the bracken.

Chapter Thirteen

A PRETENCE OF KEEPING CHRISTMAS

Full of indignation at Gracie Fields: a Forces' Sweetheart but a terrible story.

26 July 1943–19 February 1944

31 July Much of Hamburg is destroyed after five days of heavy RAF bombing.

20 August In Quebec, Britain and the US agree to cooperate on secrets and deployment of the atomic bomb; the Second Front against Germany in France, codenamed Operation Overlord, is also agreed.

23 August The Red Army recaptures Kharkov.

3 September Montgomery lands allied forces on the Straits of Messina, Italy, followed by landing at Salerno.

6 September Speaking at Harvard, Churchill announces his hopes for a common UK–US citizenship.

22 September *Tirpitz*, Germany's biggest battleship, is badly damaged in the Arctic Ocean.

26 September Britain hit by a wave of illegal pay disputes in munitions factories and mines.

30 September The Red Army prepares for assault on Kiev.

1 October Allied tanks move into Naples and the Free French troops take Corsica.

19 October Allied foreign ministers meet at the Kremlin to discuss a post-war Europe.

25 October Almost 4000 repatriated prisoners of war land at Leith from Germany.

6 November The Russians recapture Kiev.

9 November The United Nations Relief and Rehabilitation Administration (UNRRA) enlists 44 nations in Washington, DC; Charles de Gaulle becomes President of the Free French.

19 November The Battle of Berlin begins, led by 440 Lancaster bombers.

20 November Fascist Leader Sir Oswald Mosley released from Holloway jail on health grounds after three-year imprisonment.

25 November Churchill, Roosevelt and Chiang Kai-shek meet in Cairo to discuss strategy against Japan.

4 December Tito elected General Secretary of the National Liberation Party in Yugoslavia.

16 December Churchill falls ill with pneumonia in the Middle East.

24 December Dwight Eisenhower appointed commander of Allied Expeditionary Force in charge of the invasion of France.

26 December The German battle cruiser *Scharnhorst* sunk off Norway.

6 January 1944 The Red Army enters Poland.

18 January The first 600 young 'Bevin Boys' start work in British mines.

21 January The battle for Anzio begins on Italian coast, with strong German resistance.

31 January Southern England hit by new 'Little Blitz'.

4 February US forces victorious over Japanese in Marshall Islands.

9 February British blanket-bombing policy is questioned by the Bishop of Chichester in the House of Lords.

14 February The monastery at Monte Cassino is destroyed by Allies.

MONDAY, 26 JULY

Pam Ashford

The fall of Mussolini! That's great news.

Mother's comment on Mussolini – recorded specially for Mass-Observation with hopes of it being printed one day. 'The world is well rid of him. Good for that man if he had never been born.'

Edward Stebbing

Mussolini's resignation came as a big surprise, but a pleasant one. What was more surprising was the apparent total collapse of the Fascist system. I do not think Italy will hold out much longer, although the new government will have to make a pretence of carrying on the war for the sake of prestige. The new government, however, is not one which I should like to see remaining in power, as it is still mainly a reactionary one, and a very makeshift one at that, with few, if any, really competent men in it. Nevertheless, the event must be a severe blow to Germany and opens up favourable prospects for us.

FRIDAY, 30 JULY

Pam Ashford

Last August the Listeners' Research Bureau wrote that they were preparing for a series called 'Answering You', in which questions on America would be broadcast from London and the answers given by persons in America; members of the LRB were asked to collect questions to form a nucleus. During the week Mother received a postcard from the BBC to say that her question would be answered tonight. We listened in between 10 and 10.30, and sure enough, Mother's name was broadcast from New York. A proud moment, though she is not remotely interested in the question – 'What are the origins of the "Star Spangled Banner", "Yankee Doodle" and "God Bless My Country"? When did "The Star Spangled Banner" become the National anthem?' A Mr Deans Taylor answered. '"The Star Spangled Banner" is an English tune. The words are by John Stafford Smith. It arose out of the conflict between America and Great Britain in the Napoleonic wars. The poet was a prisoner on a British warship off Maryland and after an anxious night when dawn came he saw that the American flag was still flying and wrote his poem in a moment of inspiration. It did not officially become the American national anthem till March 1931, when Congress made it so under President Hoover.'

SATURDAY, 31 JULY

Ernest van Someren
Very hot. Julia woke crabby and was put to bed again before 11. We made tomato jam with lemons in it sent by my sister in California from Gracie Fields' garden.

WEDNESDAY, 4 AUGUST

Pam Ashford
The Captain said to me this morning in startled tones, 'Do you know how much a policeman gets paid?' Reflecting, I said between £6 and £7. He said £6 2/6d. He could not believe policemen could receive so little. Out of respect for British prestige I said, 'Of course they get their footwear free and the Corporation pays their rent.'

MONDAY, 9 AUGUST

Ernest van Someren
I climbed a ladder on to the roof of the works so as to get some photographs of welders at work on new steelwork. On some of these fine nights we hear squadrons of bombers buzzing off at dusk or later, and sometimes at night I wake to hear them coming back, and feel ashamed to think that they have been earning for us the sort of reputation the Germans earned when they started city-bombing three years ago.

FRIDAY, 13 AUGUST

Edward Stebbing
The local 'Holidays at Home' programme is not likely to keep anyone at home for the holidays. Do the authorities really think that a few Punch-and-Judy shows, a miserable little fun-fair, a brass band, a garden fete, and the like will keep anyone from going away?

Ernest van Someren
The problem about the smell of one of our products has cropped up again making trouble in two places, and I have been asked to think of something to do about it, so I drafted a programme of experiments and promptly got them typed in the hope that someone else would be allotted to carry them out.

SATURDAY, 14 AUGUST

Edward Stebbing
Arrived in Dorking about 5.30pm. After tea I had a look around the town . . . saw a new VD poster in a public lavatory. It depicted a small boy standing in a cone of light. 'Tomorrow's citizen' was the heading; in smaller letters, 'Do not let him be handicapped by venereal disease passed on by his parents. Make sure you're fit to be parents of the citizens of tomorrow.'

Ernest van Someren
Spent part of the morning on the steel problem. We got an industrial doctor to come out and sniff at work in progress, with no very helpful results. He didn't think it was a problem for the medical worker. Our big Victoria plums are ripe and delicious this year.

THURSDAY, 19 AUGUST

Ernest van Someren
My fortieth birthday, a fine hot day and I decided to go to work by train instead of cycling, so as not to get so hot on the way home. Kay gave me a book and some cakes for my 11s in a tin, Laurie gave me a little packet of sweets and on behalf of Julia I received a safety-razor blade.

At work K rang me up soon after ten, very upset, to say that Tessa, my sister in Hollywood, had been found shot in bed, in her own room. An evening paper reporter had been to see K and told her. There was also a para in the *Mail* but not in the other morning papers. I decided to go and see Mother, and after a fruitless search around the office for a *Mail* rang up the paper and got the news-editor to read me the story as he received it. He said he had also rung up Gracie Fields the previous evening, who told him that Tessa had flirted with the gardener, and had been dismissed on that account, this he had published. I rang up Mother's office and found out from a colleague that she had not seen the news, so left a message that I was coming to see her at lunchtime. I didn't do much work, but left at about 11 and went to town by trolleybus and tube.

I met Mother in the office, and broke the news to her. By that time most of her colleagues had seen the *Mail* story. Mother was rather shattered, but wanted to go to her old paper, the *Daily Express*, and find out more. There we saw what was on the tapes, and the *Mail* and *Star* stories, and Mother was so full of indignation at Gracie Fields' libellous statement about Tessa that she concentrated on that

380

instead of on her loss. Actually, the gardener-murderer, Guy, had previously been in love with the other resident secretary, and transferred his affection to Tessa, who is usually fascinating to Italians. Tessa didn't like him much, and told us that she had resigned from her job on account of a misunderstanding with Gracie about Guy. Then Tessa went to Canada and stayed with relations in July and immigrated formally into the USA, a thing she has been trying to arrange to do for two years. Well, we went to the Associated Press and Mother gave an interview, giving a very different picture of Tessa from that provided by Gracie F., but of course she couldn't get it published for certain. We had a miserable little lunch at a café, where Mother met an old acquaintance who stopped for a chat. He and I then went back to the office for a talk with another old colleague. It was very hot and I did some necessary shopping and met Mother at 3.15 and took her home by taxi and train from Liverpool St.

At home we had tea in the garden with the children and got Mother to rest a bit before a fresh outbreak of telephoning to people which lasted most of the evening. After tea I took the children to a bathing pool in a neighbour's garden for a paddle. In the evening we skipped the concert for which we had tickets, and had a number of phone calls, including one from my brother Tony, whom I had notified by wire at noon. Mother stayed with us.

FRIDAY, 20 AUGUST

Ernest van Someren

Cycled to work, hot weather again and I was very busy, largely with some tests in the factory by an oven at about 90F. Dull weather in the evening and a good deal of telephoning to do. Mother got from her office an account of an interview with W.P. Lipscomb, an English author who had employed Tessa before and who was possibly going to employ her again, in which he described a meeting with Tessa and Guy in which Guy violently broke a radio in a flash of temper, and told how Guy got a car and a long ladder and entered Tessa's window at night, shot her twice through the head, wounded himself slightly, and is now in hospital getting better. Lipscomb also sent Mother a sympathetic cable on Wednesday, but it didn't reach her until last night. He offered to arrange the funeral and we replied by cable asking him to do so. Our relatives in Washington couldn't conveniently do so. They also cabled to Mother, as did a cousin in Canada. Tony rang up to say that he hoped to fly tomorrow to another island where Gracie F was performing for ENSA and interview her severely. We got a little gramophone music in between phone calls and all felt exhausted.

SATURDAY, 21 AUGUST

Ernest van Someren
I had the morning off but had to arrange an exhibition at the Council House in connection with an afternoon WEA meeting on Post War Housing. Another WEA member and Laurie came to help. We got it fixed and came home by noon, Kay was very busy cooking. On Wednesday morning I killed a hen before going to work and this she got the butcher to dress, but it was an old hen and she found it difficult to make her edible. We tried some for lunch.

In the afternoon Kay went to Hertford to give a blood donation at the hospital. She came with the children to fetch me home, and after they went to bed I went country-dancing for a little at the Stranges', till dusk on their lawn.

THURSDAY, 26 AUGUST

Edward Stebbing
Illness cut my holiday short, and I have not been able to make any notes until today. As the last ten days have been spent in the local hospital (and I may spend many more days in the hospital where I work, to which I am going tomorrow), I can give only a few brief comments on the outstanding pieces of news. Probably the dominant news has been the advance of the Russians, especially the capture of Kharkov. The heavy raid on Berlin was also big news, but the surprising thing was that everybody seemed to know it was coming, including the Germans, as the loss of 58 of our planes proves. The appointment of Himmler as Minister of the Interior in Germany seems to show that Hitler is getting worried about internal affairs. To sum up, the war news has been thoroughly satisfactory for us in all respects.

FRIDAY, 27 AUGUST

Ernest van Someren
In the evening Mother came to visit us again. She is still suffering from indignation as much as from shock at Tessa's death, and is now wondering about what will happen at the murderer's trial, and whether she ought to be represented. She has decided to send a letter to the attorney in charge. In the evening K helped me pick some apples from our tree.

SATURDAY, 28 AUGUST

Pam Ashford
The Beveridge Report. Sir William spoke on his plan to an audience at Edinburgh and Elsie and Mrs Mackay (Soroptomist) went. Elsie says he was a poor speaker and most conceited. I said to her, 'It is strange, the Americans dislike our ideas on social welfare. They think if a man died without making provision for his wife and children, it is fit and right that they should starve.' To my surprise Elsie came out all enthusiastic for the American idea. Mrs Mackay had explained to her how wrong the Beveridge Plan was. The burden of paying for the insurance will ruin any amount of British businesses and the workers won't be a halfpennyworth better in the end, in fact most of them will be much worse off. I expressed the view that few workmen get three quarters of their wages during sickness (Mrs Mackay had told Elsie that that was universal throughout British industry, but I indicated dissent).

WEDNESDAY, 1 SEPTEMBER

Pam Ashford
Today is the fourth anniversary of the invasion of Poland. That Friday is impressed on my mind indelibly, and merely to think of it again brings back the powerful emotions of that day, the fear, the determination and I am afraid the head that swam too much for comfort (a usual accompaniment of intense reeling with me). Yes, the fear and the determination still live, even though they are now viewed in the distance as from a high place, securely founded. The outbreak of war on the 3rd Sept. moved me much less. It therefore seems strange to me to find Mother reacting differently. She does not remember anything particularly about the 1st, and then produced this gem, 'Let me see, it was the invasion of Poland that started the war, was it not?' Oh yes, she remembers the 3rd of Sept. and she thought the war would be over within a few weeks. I had said then that I thought it would last a decade. Well, we are two-fifths through a decade now! At the moment, I think a decade may be too long, but I don't see the war ending very quickly. It is so obvious that when Germany cracks, all the occupied nations will wish to make a holocaust of Germany. How far the British–American alliance will wish to control that situation, or could so do, exceeds my vision, but the disorder in Europe will take us a long time to clear up. After which the Pacific will have to be cleared of the Japs, and I think all the signs are there of a long and slow war.

THURSDAY, 2 SEPTEMBER

Edward Stebbing
Black-out episode: I was just taking the black-out down before getting into bed and kept the light on to take part of it down. No sooner had I done so than there was a knock at the door and a lady warden told my landlord about a light showing. I had not noticed that there was a piece of cardboard missing from the small top window, which showed the light when I took the curtain down. But, as Mr H said, 'She must have been waiting on the doorstep.'

Pam Ashford
Week away and my place was taken by Helen; she comes in and out of our place to an increasing extent. As she does not appear to get enquiries for the Army we presume she is still under age, but she looks 20. Helen's youth certainly caused a sensation. Now there have been only the two times when men have annoyed me, though there have been invitations of a harmless character. I thought this was marvellous, at 40 and obese, but Helen's experiences were non-stop. It must have got around the American ships that there was a good-looking young lady there alone much of the time. Throughout the week the ISWSA has been much annoyed by seamen coming in to see Helen. In her innocence Helen explained to a variety of callers what her usual job was, and there has been a succession of men going in there wanting her to make dates. The Captain says that the way for me to handle them is to say that Helen has been transferred to London. Helen negotiates her unwanted callers against a crowded general office background, her phrase being 'they will find plenty of their type of girl down in the street'.

FRIDAY, 3 SEPTEMBER

Pam Ashford
Today is a National Day of Prayer. A National Day of Prayer, or anything like it, must be unknown in America. I should have liked to have gone to a Church service, but thinking my stars inauspicious, said to Captain Macgowan instead, 'It does not matter to me. I don't mind working, but you will find that work stops right throughout Glasgow, and it would be considered very bad form if you disturbed anyone by telephoning.' He said, 'This is an American office!' I said, 'Oh I know you will be going on with your work, but really you must respect the feelings of the people with whom you deal. Many of them will be at Church and not available.' He pointed to a public house

within sight into which a large number of Glasgow business men were at that moment entering, and said, 'There they are, getting fortified for the service! They will be drinking to the health of the boys in the Forces, so can we. (There are two bottles of whiskey in the safe.) I will invite Helen in.' I said, 'Helen had a brother in the Middle East. She might not understand.' He said, 'She will understand.' I said, 'I know she has never tasted whisky.' He said, 'Nor have you.'

Edward Stebbing

I did not remember that this was the fourth anniversary of the outbreak of war until this evening, when Mr H remarked about it being a national day of prayer, which he thought was 'all a farce'. Except that it is not funny enough to be a farce; just plain silly.

Good news about the invasion of Italy, but I heard very little comment about it today.

SATURDAY, 4 SEPTEMBER

Pam Ashford

I had decided to go to the Art Galleries this afternoon, which was as well in such weather. An Exhibition called 'The Present discovers the Past' ends today and another Exhibition called 'New Uses for Glass' ends tomorrow.

SUNDAY, 5 SEPTEMBER

Pam Ashford

At a whist drive on Tuesday Mother met one of her cronies, a widow of about 55, now working at a draper's shop in Argyle Street. The war has put employment into her hands that she would not have had otherwise. She loves her work. She says that the customers are so nice to deal with, again and again thanking her for the trouble she has taken. That confirms a sentiment I have expressed before – that the middle-aged women behind the counters serve you better than the youngsters. If one were asked to pick out youngsters who are indifferent to the customer you would have a formidable task; it would be easier to pick out youngsters who regard customers as 'persons'.

WEDNESDAY, 8 SEPTEMBER

Pam Ashford

I got home in time for the news which, from the announcer's spontaneous introduction as 'the best of the war', clearly was going to be something good. Italy surrenders unconditionally. How exciting. When the National Anthem came on Mother and I both stood to attention, I with bowed head. Then with shining eyes and bated breath we listened to the remainder of the news. The withdrawal of the Germans from the entire Donetz Basin and the Congress of the TUC, with the repetition of Gen. Eisenhower's statement following up. Mother's comment was, I thought, strange. 'It is not the Italians we need fear. It is the Japs. I have just been reading about them in the World Digest.'

I went right out for my evening walk then; my energy must get worked off, and there was the odd chance that I might see someone who did not know. In Cleveden Gardens a man was trimming a hedge and asked me the time. Thinking that anyone who had heard the news would surely know the time, I said, 'About 6.40. Do you know that Italy has surrendered?' He did not. He said we would not make the same mistake as we made in 1918. There would be no mercy this time. The Germans were a military nation and had to be wiped out.

Edward Stebbing

Although I thought Italy would give in fairly soon, I did not expect it just yet. But Mr A had been expecting it all day – he takes the *Daily Mail*, which prophesied big news from Italy 'any second', whereas the *News Chronicle* had no mention of it. Of course, it was very cheering news. S said, 'A landing in the West now will help things on a bit . . . I think it will come before the end of this month.' My father said, 'Germany will crack up suddenly, like she did in the last war.' A factory-worker said that when they heard the news some of them danced round the shop and the women wouldn't do any work. 'It's silly to think the war's over,' said S.

Ernest van Someren

In the evening we saw our holiday films again. Just before nine we tuned in and had a hint of what was coming, then heard the news of the Italian surrender at nine, which cheered us all up a bit, and we had a glass of sherry each.

THURSDAY, 9 SEPTEMBER

Pam Ashford
There are a number of subjects that never ceased being aired. The abdication of Edward VIII is one. Nothing can shake Capt. Macowan's belief that 'he is a splendid fellow and she is a very nice girl'. This always leads on to derogatory remarks about our present King and Queen. He says, 'He does what Churchill tells him. He does not rule. He is just like Churchill's dog. Churchill says "Lie down dog" and down he lies, or "Get up dog" and up he gets.'

SATURDAY, 11 SEPTEMBER

Ernest van Someren
In the afternoon took L on the back of my bike down to Cheshunt to a Victory Garden Show in the grounds of a school. There was an entertainer for the children whom L appreciated, flower and vegetable shows, sports which were rather dull if you didn't know the competitors, and all sorts of stalls to raise money for the Red Cross. A fine warm afternoon after a thunderstorm last night and a good crowd. We came home to tea in the garden and then went country dancing at the Stranges', taking the children to watch. We are trying to get a small group to carry on with dancing in the winter, but have not yet found a room to do it in.

MONDAY, 13 SEPTEMBER

Ernest van Someren
On the way home bought mushrooms at 3/- lb, the cheapest I have seen this year. They like this weather precisely.

WEDNESDAY, 15 SEPTEMBER

Pam Ashford
In the evening, I went to the 'Make Do and Mend Exhibition', a Board of Trade venture held at the Domestic Science College.

When I entered at 7 the place was practically empty. I was recommended by Miss Renfrew to attend a demonstration in paper patterns in one of the classrooms. The idea is to turn cast-off clothes into serviceable garments. A lady's costume was exhibited made out of a man's suit. This is not recommended beyond a 36in bust, as owing to the respective bumps coming in different parts, a good deal has to be cut away at the sides. There was a blouse made out of a shirt, cami-knickers out of an old petticoat; baby's vest out of father's singlet. We were advised to avoid navy blue as a difficult colour to combine with others.

The Soroptomists have been asked to steward the exhibition in the evenings and Miss Renfrew and Miss Whitton were on tonight. Miss Renfrew said confidentially that what the stewards were really there for was to see that the exhibits did not get pilfered.

THURSDAY, 16 SEPTEMBER

Pam Ashford
The more I meet Americans the more do I perceive that the relationship between the sexes is different in the two countries. If it were that women could make friends with men more readily, I might think that emancipation had gone further there than here; but what I see rather is that American men regard women as toys, to be played with for a few years, and then at an incredibly young age, 23 or 24 it seems to me – to be relegated to the attic with the lumber.

FRIDAY, 17 SEPTEMBER

Pam Ashford
Captain Macgowan is an old friend of the captain of a ship at present in port, and is getting many presents of food.

This afternoon he brought up a block of ice cream, marked 1 quart. He cut it in four slices, one for the life attendant, one for himself, one for Helen and one for me. Ice cream does not suit me, but I ate this immense helping. Helen who was called in to our office cut hers in half, the other piece for Miss Roberts, who was then fetched in. As you can imagine, the comments of the British consumers were of the number of years since ice cream had been last tasted. I enjoyed the slice, and felt no ill effects in the afternoon, but at time of writing, 8.30, feel very sick.

SATURDAY, 18 SEPTEMBER

Pam Ashford
After work I went to the Make Do and Mend exhibition again. I watched the Singer's demonstration. A lady put in a beautiful darn on a torn tablecloth, taking no more than a couple of minutes. I have tried this before with equipment bought (at a much lower price than today's 4/6) at the Kelvin Hall pre-war exhibitions. My conviction only grows stronger that dexterity and practice are the secrets of

388

success, and that while demonstrators may acquire them, the house-wife does not get sufficient torn table cloths to do so.

TUESDAY, 21 SEPTEMBER

Pam Ashford
Back to the Make Do and Mend exhibition in the evening.

Two dresses shown were designed to allow a hostess to cook the dinner for a party and then to receive the guests in evening dress. This was achieved by wearing a pink lace slip beneath a kitchen apron for the first operation and then when the front door bell rang transferring from the apron to a garment of pink lace, which looked like an apron skirt, but actually fitted the other way round with the rear covered with a fullness and a large bow on the abdomen.

Enjoying every moment of my four visits (not bad for a seven days' show) and seeing many possibilities of saving money and coupons, nevertheless I came away with no resolves to 'go and do likewise'. There are the twin dragons, 'too tired' and 'no time'.

WEDNESDAY, 22 SEPTEMBER

Ernest van Someren
On the way to town I bought a dynamo lighting set for my bicycle, old stock at a small shop, for 24/-. They assured me it was made in London but on careful examination it is stamped in French 'Importe d'Allemande'.

THURSDAY, 23 SEPTEMBER

Pam Ashford
I believe I mentioned having set out to slim. 10lbs have gone since July 24. It has been done by cutting out potatoes and bread. Ryevita (points!), Weetabix (points!) and oatcakes (no points, hurrah) are a substitute for bread. I go through lettuces galore and have been lucky in getting as many tomatoes as I need. Apples are plentiful at present.

In 1932 I put myself on a strict slimming diet with great success, but then I drew on a wide variety of fruit. Then I should have thought my present slimming diet monotonous to a point of desperation, but now the only desperation I feel is when I remember that as winter progresses lettuces, tomatoes and apples will disappear. Of course, Brussels sprouts will come but the thought of making them one's staple food chills me.

Edward Stebbing

The new Government changes favour the Tory party and do not offer much prospect of social reform. Mr H said, 'I thought they'd have brought in another Labour man' (as Chancellor of the Exchequer). While keeping up the farce of a political truce, Churchill makes certain of keeping any progressive elements out of the Government.

Another disappointing piece of news was the resolution passed by the British Medical Association opposing a State medical service. I appreciate the view that medical science should not be made a political issue, but all the same reform is badly needed in this field. The panel system is often unsatisfactory, so is the out-patient system at hospitals, and there is much to be said for health centres possessing up-to-date methods of diagnosis and treatment, which everybody could go to. Last year the BMA was in favour of this idea, but apparently the thought of losing some of their fat fees has caused them to do a hasty about-turn, or else some reactionary influences have been at work.

Ernest van Someren

Busy at work with odd jobs, including an hour or so glass blowing to salvage damaged measuring equipment. Spent part of the morning X-raying about 50 yards of double tape to find breaks in the wire which my assistant was drawing into the tube of tape yesterday afternoon.

In the evening played 3-handed bridge with Mother again, as it is her last night here of the fortnight her housekeeper is on holiday. It has done her good to be here with us, and she is worrying less about my sister's reputation. A recent letter from relations in Washington has been a bit upsetting, and the friend who cabled us the first direct news of the murder has not yet followed it up by letter, although an account of the funeral has reached us from friends in Pasadena. Mother has got over her cold well, and I have warded off the cold which I nearly started last Friday.

TUESDAY, 28 SEPTEMBER

Ernest van Someren

In the evening the Stranges and their Uncle Harold came in for a chat. The Uncle is a Boer War victim, who has been sitting in a wheeled chair ever since. He has a hobby of making dolls' furniture (it pays well now). We talked about children and people. John and I talked shop a bit. We drank a bottle of cider, being short of milk for coffee.

SATURDAY, 2 OCTOBER

Pam Ashford

In the early days of the war I wrote much about the bus shortage. We did not know we were born then! About six weeks ago one of our two bus services was withdrawn; the intervals between the buses running are long, the crowds dreadful. Now on our route the buses are to stop at the fare stages only, half a mile apart.

SUNDAY, 3 OCTOBER

Edward Stebbing

The military situation continues to be satisfactorily handled, but the handling of the home front leaves very much indeed to be desired. What a sorry show, for instance, came of the Minister of Health's plan for farm-workers' cottages! What a flop the Ministry of Town and Country Planning has been! How completely has nothing been done about the Beveridge Report! There are many other examples. All this has caused a lot of dissatisfaction just below the surface of everyday life, which only requires some small incident, such as has occurred in some of the coalfields and not in itself justifying a strike, to bring the discontent to a head. The attitude of the Government seems to be that because the military situation is well in hand they are safely entrenched and need not bother about domestic difficulties. If they continue to look like this they are heading for a fall.

TUESDAY, 5 OCTOBER

Ernest van Someren

After early supper, cycled to the other end of Hoddesdon to the first meeting of a WEA course on 'The Future of Europe'. The tutor missed his train and was late, but was very good when he arrived, a doctor, N. Elias. Only 13 people. Stopped in a pub on the way home with a friend who invited an intemperate old Dutchman to join the class. This he promised to do.

WEDNESDAY, 13 OCTOBER

Ernest van Someren

Did some aluminium casting in the afternoon, fixing up a gas furnace temporarily in our lab. This annoyed some of the women working there who expected the fumes to give them a headache. In the evening went to a psychology lecture, a neighbour came in and talked to Kay. Laurie has been extra rude today.

THURSDAY, 14 OCTOBER

Ernest van Someren
I reminded Laurie about his extra rudeness when I got him up in the morning, and he dressed quicker than usual and went down and laid breakfast by himself, which I think is better than a formal apology. K went out in the afternoon to visit Honor Prime, who used to live with us and is now visiting a few miles away with her baby Lalage. She found her considerably changed from the literary to the maternal woman, and the child is lovely.

TUESDAY, 19 OCTOBER

Ernest van Someren
I had a snack at a snack bar and went to a EFDS members party. John and Helen Strange turned up later as my hosts, it was a special night for American square dances, with some American and Canadian soldiers to call the dances. This was grand fun, rather strenuous, as I hadn't done much dancing for a long time. I danced mostly with strangers, ranging from a lady with grey hair and dark glasses to a six stone blonde from the US who chewed gum. We purposely missed the proper train home and caught the 10.45, which is a slow and dark journey.

WEDNESDAY, 20 OCTOBER

Edward Stebbing
For the third or fourth successive night the air-raid warning sounded last night and our nerves were again kept on edge by the continuous thunder of the barrage. I asked a man today if he thought these small raids were preliminary tests of our defences before sending over heavier forces. He said no, he didn't think the Germans had sufficient aircraft to make big raids.

Ernest van Someren
Killed our senior hen before going to work, we bartered her to a neighbour for six pounds of onions, she was a tough old bird but made a lot of broth.
In the morning our friend Kate turned up to see us, she brought honey and other food as a present, we gave her flowers and

vegetables to take home. She stayed to tea and supper and talked about the BBC where she works. We had a little zabaglione for supper as a luxury, having some red wine open.

SUNDAY, 24 OCTOBER

Edward Stebbing
Heard Noel Coward's postscript tonight and disliked it intensely. His smug hypocrisy, his sneering manner, his misrepresentations, his sentimentality, nauseated me. He accused those who want to adopt a reasonable attitude towards the Germans after the war of being 'sentimentalists' and then went on to be sickeningly sentimental about wounded British soldiers. His type of emotionalism, in fact, is the sort that obscures the truth, hinders cool-headed thinking, and breeds war. He also accused the 'sentimentalists' 'not,' as he put it, 'of forgetting the dead, but of forgetting the living'. This was just one of his misrepresentations, for those of us who, whilst recognising their misdeeds, are tolerantly disposed to the Germans, are usually those who are tolerantly disposed to all peoples, particularly living ones, and wish to see better standards of living for everyone, whereas cynics of Noel Coward's calibre are the least likely to do anything to improve the lot of the lower classes. My feeling about him was clinched later in the evening when somebody in a variety show sang his latest song, 'Don't let's be beastly to the Germans'. How clever it is, yet how stupid! How persuasive, yet how false!

FRIDAY, 29 OCTOBER

Edward Stebbing
A man at work said that Churchill, in an unguarded moment in his speech about the rebuilding of the House of Commons, revealed that he thought the war might be over by this time next year, when he said that we might be looking for jobs rather than men. I noticed that too, and certainly think that another year will see the end of the war. The German retreat in Russia is no longer planned or orderly.

Ernest van Someren
In the evening I read my diary for October 1933 and the letters I wrote to K and had from her that summer and winter. I went to Copenhagen in 1933 to work, lived in rooms in the centre of the city and enjoyed life with photography, concerts, café evenings, studying Danish and so on. I had known K for less than a year when I left, and during our correspondence and separation we were finding out how

much we were in love. My work there was interesting, in October I heard Dr Bosch of IG lecture in Copenhagen on recent developments in photography, which was very interesting. Another impression which lasted was from the film *Ekstase* which I saw in the original version and found most moving. It's odd to compare my life then and now. I lived independently in rooms getting my own breakfast and dining at a Pension fairly regularly. Often I had a late supper at a café and went to bed towards midnight. I had few friends, but some interesting acquaintances. I wrote K long letters about once a week about all sorts of events, people and ideas and books.

SATURDAY, 30 OCTOBER

Ernest van Someren

In the afternoon we all went out with the pram, and in Hoddesdon I bought a very old sewing-machine (about 1863) and carried it home in the pram. Kay and Julia went by bus. Laurie and I were both delighted with it, it still has all the accessories and the book of instructions. If it won't work I hope to make it into something else. After tea the Perhams came and saw some films of the children together, and of our pre-war Alpine holiday. After supper I examined the machine in great detail, and the Brights came and bought our old carpet for 2 pounds which paid for the machine. They have found a house at last and are moving into it next week. They have a little furniture but no floor-coverings whatever. They have been made rather uncomfortable in rooms, sharing a kitchen with an old grouchy.

TUESDAY, 9 NOVEMBER

Edward Stebbing

I think Churchill has overdone it this time; he has misjudged the mood of the people. In his speech today he once again reminds us that the worst part of the battle is yet to come, that we must redouble our efforts, that now is not the time to rejoice, etc etc. This may be true, but it seems to me that his approach should have been, 'The enemy is beginning to falter now. One more big effort and it will soon be over.' As it is, he asks for the effort, but fails to give the incentive.

SATURDAY, 20 NOVEMBER

Maggie Joy Blunt

We had great difficulty in obtaining permission to make 16 mm copies of our Forgings film but sanction came eventually from the Ministry of Supply and we have now about half a dozen copies which are going the rounds of various aircraft firms and training centres. A film on Castings is now being made. Incidentally we make the Halifax undercarriage. It is the largest magnesium casting in the world and we are awfully proud of it.

On the domestic front food, for me, continues to be plentiful and nourishing. With the one good meal at the Canteen in the middle of the day and a light breakfast, my rations last easily. But I don't get much variety. For weeks now the butcher has been sending me mutton every Saturday. When I had a visitor recently I got some sausage meat. I usually cook my bacon with the meat at the weekend.

Ella came for a week in August, supervised the sweeping of chimneys and helped me give the cottage a really good spring clean. The cottage gets vacuumed and dusted the weekends I am here and has to go dirty for the rest of the time. I simplify the work as much as possible e.g. leave breakfast cup, saucer and porridge plate in soak all day and just rinse them through and leave to drain at night, do no cooking during the week and so on.

The long evenings have begun. The kitchen black-out I leave up all the week (and the cottage *beams* on a Saturday morning when I take it down before going to work because it knows that the kitchen will have the whole day of whatever sunshine there is and that there will be a fire in the range!)

There always seems a lot more to do in the evening during the winter and I wish it were the other way round in a way because of getting home in the black-out when nights are dark and cold and wet. The London Symphony Orchestra was performing on Wednesday for war factory workers only. I should have been one of them but for somebody's error – ENSA sent 2000 vouchers which were allotted to the various factories including ours, but the hall holds only 1000 people and at the last moment all our vouchers were recalled.

Enemy raids last month were frequent and short. At one period the sirens went every night (I did not always hear them).

Meg and Roger still in furnished rooms. The owner of the house has taken an irrational dislike to Meg and they have been searching frantically for other accommodation for weeks. The housing shortage is really scandalous.

Ernest van Someren
Came home by train, and I gave Laurie an ultra-violet treatment for his chilblains, which are very bad now. Kay gave him a talk recently about sex, he has been curious about our differences and has always been told as much as he seemed to want to know. He has now got as far as how a man gets his sex organ into a woman, and realises that he will have to develop considerably before he needs to learn more.

MONDAY, 22 NOVEMBER

Edward Stebbing
Some men were talking about the release of Sir Oswald Mosley. One said that Morrison must have some good reason for releasing him, probably that he is very ill and they do not want him to die in Holloway Prison ('the first Fascist martyr') and that it is silly to start protesting before the facts are known. This is a sensible point of view, and I retract what I said two days ago until Morrison has given his explanation.

WEDNESDAY, 24 NOVEMBER

Edward Stebbing
Morrison's explanation seems pretty reasonable. If Mosley is in a state of health dangerous to life, it would be merely vindictive to keep him imprisoned just for the sake of it. If he had been a Communist, cries of 'persecution' would have gone up from the Left sections of the Press. Mosley is now harmless, anyway, and as he is to be kept under strict surveillance he is not likely to cause much trouble.

FRIDAY, 26 NOVEMBER

Ernest van Someren
Hayes asked one or two people in the works what they think of Mosley's release, they all think it a bad thing. It seems to me that the symbolic value of the act rather than its political one is so important, and so resented.

THURSDAY, 2 DECEMBER

Ernest van Someren
Had a WEA cttee mtg here in the evening, while Kay went to carpentry class and finished a scooter she has made for L. This took

us till 9.30 and people chatted a bit afterwards. By the way, earlier in the week we had two lemons sent on from Kay's parents, who got them from her brother in Italy. We had one between us in hot lemonade with rum in it at bedtime.

MONDAY, 6 DECEMBER

Ernest van Someren
Went to the doctor for U-V treatment of chilblains on the way to work, then was given a lift to work by our managing director, whose car I hailed. We talked about illnesses, in the factory there were 140 girls away ill on Friday, about 25%.

TUESDAY, 7 DECEMBER

Edward Stebbing
After going up to London one day last week to see a play (the comedy *Love for Love*, with Yvonne Arnaud and John Gielgud), I came home with a fearful cough and a sore throat and since then I have been laid up with flu. This is the second time I have been ill while on holiday this year, though my holiday finished two days ago and I have not yet returned to work. I managed to travel back to my digs yesterday, but I don't think it did me any good. It is even difficult to buy any decent throat tablets now.

As far as Christmas is concerned this year, I shall not bother much about it. I may send a few cards. There is nothing in the shops worth buying – nothing but rubbish at absurd prices. There is very little poultry to be had, and without this I don't think one can make a pretence of keeping Christmas.

WEDNESDAY, 8 DECEMBER

Edward Stebbing
Sensible people are beginning to realise that the idea of 'trying the war criminals' is nonsense. As a speaker in a debate in the House of Lords said, we should be shooting Germans for years after the war. I simply cannot understand why some people want to follow up this savage war with a further series of bloody deeds.

SATURDAY, 11 DECEMBER

Edward Stebbing
Managed to find some digs within reasonable distance from my new job [a three-month secondment to North Middlesex Hospital]. After some haggling I fixed it for 35/- a week. Even this I can barely afford. The last week or so has increased my financial burden tremendously. First I had to begin paying Income Tax, and I expect another assessment. Then I became liable for superannuation, including about three months' arrears. Now I have to change my lodgings on increased terms and it will mean double the amount of fares I used to pay and I shall also have to pay a reservation fee for my room in my old digs, to which I shall be going back. Even when I get my increment, which is due, I shall not be able to do more than make ends meet.

MONDAY, 13 DECEMBER

Ernest van Someren
The murderer of my sister (on Aug 19) starts his trial today in California, and Mother has been worried by reporters for a picture.

WEDNESDAY, 22 DECEMBER

Ernest van Someren
In the evening K iced a cake and I made fudge. We had some almonds from K's brother in Italy, made them into almond paste, there was also icing sugar. The BBC did a moving *Marching On* programme on starvation in Europe which made us feel exceptionally fortunate, and perhaps deservedly so.

CHRISTMAS DAY

Ernest van Someren
On Friday evening we made net stockings for the children and put small things in them, an emergency ration of toffee and a biscuit and some raisins, small picture-books, chocolate etc. We told Laurie not to put his light on before seven, and not to disturb us before 7.45, but we heard talk before 5 and K went in and found them excitedly examining the gifts while they ate some sweets. She turned their light out, but talk went on and at 6.30 we moved Julia into the bathroom in her cot, and dozed a bit more ourselves. After breakfast we had a parcel-opening for the children, Mother, Mrs Hopkins, Kay and

myself in the dining-room. There were several dolls and soft toys, a shower of books and painting-books, and some odd special gifts. Notable for Julia was a painted tin of salt and six small plastic cups, one of her favourite games is spooning salt out of one thing into another and this just suited her. I made her a miniature iron at the factory, with a twisted cord to show it's an electric iron like Mummy has. Laurie had a scooter from Kay (homemade) and a box of bricks from me, well-made wooden bricks made by an amateur carpenter. They had jointly a gramophone record from a BBC friend of a news bulletin and a little music recorded slowly so that it plays back at double speed, and the man's voice sounds like a woman yapping. By slowing it down by hand one can recover normal speech for a while.

We had a turkey for lunch, tender but a trifle high, cider to drink, milk jelly and mince pies afterwards. Julia fasted but Laurie ate well. In the afternoon we went for a good walk to woods and a local park, saw very few people out.

We received about 25 Christmas cards, and sent out about 35, small photographs of four sprays of lilies of the valley with a greeting in white lettering, all on a black background, my own photography of course.

Kay received a brooch from Mother, and an extension loudspeaker for the kitchen from me, we jointly had a set of records of a Borodin symphony from Mother. Each of us had money to buy our own presents from various relatives, amounting to about 54/- for Kay and 17/6 for me. Kay is also going to give me a book of my own choice when we next go shopping in London, which will probably be on January 29th when I have a Saturday morning off.

The nearest thing to a Christmas outing for us was a visit to the cinema on Tuesday evening to see *Heaven Can Wait*.

MONDAY, 27 DECEMBER

Ernest van Someren
L took his scooter out, and didn't manage it very well. In the afternoon I did some pruning in the garden, Mother and Mrs Hopkin went home before tea. After tea we played swinging the children. They especially like being swung between us and thrown onto the sofa, especially just after tea.

WEDNESDAY, 29 DECEMBER

Edward Stebbing
Once again I have had to neglect my diary because of illness, pleurisy this time. Since about August I have had a run of ill-health such as I

399

have not had for several years. I wonder how much of it is directly attributable to the war – quite a lot, I should imagine. For some time the health authorities have been trying to make out that the health of the nation is better than it was pre-war. I simply do not believe this. Figures of deaths from certain causes do not prove it, neither do figures of the incidence of certain diseases. There is a whole mass of data on the everyday health of people to take into account: how many people carry on working though not feeling really well, how many have odd days off for minor ailments more than they used to, etc. This would probably reveal a much lower level of health. In any case, tuberculosis and syphilis are definitely on the increase, and the former can be regarded as a rough pointer to the general state of health. When somebody went to get a prescription made up for me, the chemist said that prescriptions were taking longer to make up as there were so many people ill and requiring medicine.

I spent Christmas in bed, instead of going home as planned. However, I had quite a pleasant time. I had about the same number of cards as usual, but fewer presents, though including an unexpected one from my landlady. We had a good Christmas dinner – roast chicken and vegetables, Christmas pudding and mince pies. We also had a Christmas cake for tea, but without icing. All other luxuries were missing.

The most exciting news of the period has been the sinking of the *Scharnhorst*.

SATURDAY, 1 JANUARY 1944

Edward Stebbing
The doctor said I could go home for the weekend, so I went. Having received no wages for two weeks and having paid out nearly all I had, I had to draw £1 from my Post Office savings to pay for my train fare, an unprecedented occurrence. When I got home my father wormed it out of me that I was hard-up, and he more or less forced £5 on me. This may sound funny, but I really was very reluctant to accept it, because it was the first time I had had to borrow money and I hate doing it.

MONDAY, 3 JANUARY

Edward Stebbing
I brought my landlady a lemon, one of about 20 which my father had sent him from my cousin in the RAF in North Africa. Lemons are a fabulous fruit now and oh, to see (and eat) a banana again!

TUESDAY, 4 JANUARY

Maggie Joy Blunt

Many people have been away with colds or flu. There has been a general distribution in all departments to whoever cares to take them of Halibut liver oil capsules. Some departments have been having them twice a day.

Had a cold over Xmas. N with a bad cold too so that we sat and wheezed at each other over the fire most of the time. But we had plenty to eat and plenty of rest which was what we both needed. From all accounts everyone had quantities to eat over Xmas. I heard of one girl who had turkey for middle day dinner on Xmas Day and goose in the evening, chicken the following middle day and duck in the evening. I also had a rabbit which I stuffed and roasted and some pork from my butcher. Also I was able to get some mincemeat from my grocer and made a large mincepie – it was the first time I had ever made pastry, and it was an enormous success.

Beyond displaying my Xmas cards in the sitting room I did nothing to decorate the house. I had meant to cut some holly and evergreen, but there is a limit when one is overtired.

An excitement of magnitude occurred on this front about a fortnight before Xmas. I came home from the office one evening as usual about 6.30 to find the cottage in chaos. Someone had prized open the kitchen window, removing the black-out, opened every cupboard, drawer and box in the place, turned most of the contents on to the floors and walked off with my fur coat, electric iron, two clocks, miscellaneous pieces of jewellery (nearly every necklace he could find, most of them quite valueless, and an old rosary which has been in our family as a curio for years – we were none of us Catholics – but no ear-rings of which I have a great number) and various other odds and ends. I rushed to the neighbours, telephoned the police, took the next morning off (a Saturday and snowing, the only snow we have yet had here) and was a heroine for at least 24 hours.

Of course none of the articles or the thief have been traced, although the police suspect a man of 60 who has done several similar jobs in this neighbourhood. He was evidently looking for money and jewellery. All my private papers had been gone through and scattered, but I never keep cash in the house. Nor have I any very good jewellery. He left footmarks in the flower bed beneath the kitchen window but no fingerprints. Apparently he never does. A cunning old devil. They say he has an appalling police record. He goes about as a jobbing gardener asking for work, then watches the surrounding houses. Several people have said to me, 'But if the police know him why don't they go and arrest him?' which in England you cannot do without evidence. They never seem able to get the evidence.

I had to go away that same weekend, but the local policeman (who, what with burglars and climbing in to turn off my bedroom light, will be getting to know what the inside of my cottage looks like) promised to watch the place for me. I must admit that for a week I quaked when I returned each night, but the qualms soon wore off and I come back now as intrepid as ever – though possibly greeting the cats a shade more enthusiastically than formerly.

The most serious items are the fur coat and electric iron. I am covered by an All-In Policy but not for the wartime increase in values. The iron, for instance, cost me 15/- in 1939. Now, if you can get such a thing, they are about 30/-. My coat was a good dyed squirrel, bought in 1936 and had just been cleaned and remodelled (£10.10 had gone on that). The furrier told me it would sell like that today for £150. It cost me originally £40. The Insurance company are sending someone to see the house this week – but what I am to show him beyond a cracked window pane and a practically empty jewel box I don't quite know.

Ernest van Someren
Kay and Julia have both been a bit upset in the digestion and bowels for a day or two, but not badly enough to fast and stay in bed. Today Kay was better and took Laurie to town for day's shopping, leaving Julia with the Stranges. Julia doesn't mind at all. They bought necessary clothes, and went to a show of short comic films and news which Laurie enjoyed uproariously. They got home at tea-time, and after tea K went to fetch Julia. When I got home Laurie was sitting soberly at the table enjoying a miniature stamp-album and a new purchase of 500 stamp hinges.

FRIDAY, 7 JANUARY

Edward Stebbing
Bought the shirt – price 12/6d.

Two women on the bus were talking about salvage. One said, 'They tell you to put your bones out, but nobody comes and collects them.' This is quite a common complaint about salvage. My landlady has been complaining that the dustman hasn't been for a fortnight. People do not want their homes cluttered up with rubbish.

Ernest van Someren
After supper went to the Psychology lecture, the last of the course,

402

when we had a very lively discussion on the place of punishment in the education of children. The lecturer maintained that it was only a short cut policy to cover our own ignorance or lack of time, never a constructive factor.

SATURDAY, 15 JANUARY

Maggie Joy Blunt
I felt like death all the week but was afraid I might just be pretending to so that I could stay at home for a change and enjoy the cottage. But Doctor B eased my conscience on Thursday and has told me to stay at home until I have seen him again next week and is giving me sun-ray treatment and pills.

I have been told and had it confirmed, and am now suffering it myself, that this year's brand of flu leaves one completely without energy and very depressed. I have little interest in food (just eat because I know I must), cannot sleep at night, don't want to smoke (I have not touched a cigarette for over a week which is for me incredible) and my temperature remains below normal, sometimes nearly as low as 96. I don't want to do anything but lie around and read and listen-in (and get very bored with that) and sleep when I can. I used to be the sort of person that very seldom had even a bad cold during the winter, but general war conditions have obviously been weakening my resistance.

The more I hear and read of conditions in Occupied Europe the more appalled I become by our own standard of living which by comparison is luxurious. It just shows what a pool of wealth we have had to draw on and makes one wonder how much longer it will last. I think that people in my circumstances still have no business to be ill as I am now. I think that I have been trying to do too much, have not been getting enough sleep and have been lazy about my diet – the vitamins one needs are to be had with a certain amount of forethought and trouble. There is no blitz in this neighbourhood and my job is not an urgent, exhausting one calling for much energy and long hours of overtime. Yet what life is it to come home at night, eat, go to bed early in order to be up in time in the morning without strain and over the weekend do little else but chores?

SUNDAY, 16 JANUARY

Ernest van Someren
Laurie is six years old today. He is well and active, can read to himself simple books, but prefers to be read to as he is apt to guess words

403

rather than spell them out. My reading was as good at four, they say. His writing is laborious and unformed. He can use a typewriter fairly safely, but forgets what he is spelling and has to be helped continuously to get anything written. His arithmetic is good, can multiply in his head two digit numbers by a single digit, or add up the bill in the restaurant. He cannot balance on a scooter or cycle, but can manage his body neatly on a small trapeze. He is polite to people he likes and ignores others. I gave him a periscope which I made for him, Kay gave him an Orlando book, we were given a black kitten by neighbours and collected it in the morning. It is about 8 weeks old, house-trained and playful.

In the afternoon five boys and a girl, all school friends of his, came to tea with us and we played games first, they preferred romping about, so we let the games be rather casual.

MONDAY, 17 JANUARY

Maggie Joy Blunt
Am deeply touched by the great loving kindness there is in the world. Neighbours have been so good to me with no other reason than sheer good neighbourliness for being so. I asked Mrs G yesterday if she knew of a strong man who could come in to fill the coal scuttles for me. She wanted to do it herself but I would not hear of it. This morning a little old lady who lives nearby with her sister and with whom I have but the barest nodding acquaintance came trotting in and insisted upon doing the sitting room fire and filling the kitchen scuttles with coal and coke. She had heard from Mrs G that I was ill and was so concerned. 'We,' she said referring to herself and sister, 'can look after each other when we are ill but when you are all alone . . .' In vain did I try to explain that I was not desperately ill and had I needed nursing my stepmother would have been with me. She has brought me some of their Bramley Seedlings and is coming again tomorrow to do the fires and will bring a custard for my lunch. She will not take any milk – they have, she says, plenty of dried milk. It makes one feel awfully humble and ashamed.

Air-raid warden came round this evening to test gas mask. Have not had mine out for nearly two years. It was very dusty but apparently in good condition. He thinks that perhaps the authorities fear gas attack when our invasion does begin. And it does seem now that we are going to invade Europe . . .

THURSDAY, 20 JANUARY

Ernest van Someren

Went off by train to town to try to buy some lenses and a tilting tripod top. This involved a tour of photographic shops, new and second hand, from Gamages westward down to near the National Gallery and back to the Patent Office. I went into a large number of shops and three scientific instrument makers depots for some other apparatus. I also had a good look around in Gamages, which runs a sort of second hand odd and end department which fascinates me. I saw a thing which I had often heard of, diamond-selling on the pavement in Hatton Garden. The stone in question was being examined through a magnifying glass, so I can only assume it was a diamond from the name of the street. I had lunch in a very Victorian pub in Holborn, the Princess Louise.

In the evening K went out to carpentry, I did some typing impeded by the kitten, who is now trying to get on to the keyboard as he considers the typewriter a great entertainment.

FRIDAY, 21 JANUARY

Maggie Joy Blunt

I keep telling everyone I feel better so I suppose I do but I said to myself quite solemnly this morning, 'I don't know whether I am ill or not because I have forgotten what it feels like to be well.' There is no bone where my spine should be – just an ache. What I want more than food or sleep is sunshine and fresh air. The air of Slough is bad. I am sure that thousands and thousands of people are suffering from this same lack of sunshine. When I go back to work I shall ask the clinic doctor if I can have sun-ray treatment there – the apparatus is provided and employees may have treatment free.

At 6pm went to keep my appointment for a blood test, but the Doctor was not there and his secretary who does this minor operation for him is now ill so I had to trail home again feeling cold and exhausted. Coal crisis has occurred. Have used all my small stock of coal except about two scuttles of slack and a tin bath of small pieces which I sorted this morning. Am doing without kitchen fire and trying to burn anthracite in sitting room grate but it is not a success.

Edward Stebbing

About a quarter to nine the air-raid warning wailed. My landlady said, 'I thought that's what would happen. They always come over when they've been bombing Berlin like that. I wish they'd stop doing it.' Then the gunfire started, the heaviest London has heard for a long time.

SATURDAY, 22 JANUARY

Ernest van Someren
In the afternoon K went off to give her blood at the local hospital, her third or fourth time in this war. Faith van S arrived from Muswell Hill, her mother died two weeks ago and her father has been very ill. She went to see him in a convalescent home this morning, and when she said she was very sorry he had been disturbed by the air-raid, and she hoped it hadn't worried him, he answered, 'No, I rather enjoyed it, I put my ear trumpet in so as not to miss anything.' He is a pious old chap, aged 82, who has been bitten by a crocodile and run over by a bus in the course of an adventurous life.

SUNDAY, 23 JANUARY

Ernest van Someren
We managed to ignore the children till about 8.30 and had a late breakfast. Faith stayed in bed for that. I went to meeting later, found it difficult to concentrate. In the afternoon Julia and K rested, Faith, Laurie and I went for a good walk, 2½ hours, trying to find digs for her dog Judy. Judy is a black spaniel, not popular in our household, whom Faith has had to trail about London lately, and she wants to leave her in kennels for a few weeks. We finally found a messy place where they might take her for one week.

MONDAY, 24 JANUARY

Edward Stebbing
The most cheering news tonight was that restrictions on turn-ups to men's trousers, double-breasted jackets, etc., are to be removed. I should think all men are jubilant at this news. As one man said, it was a useless restriction, as the majority of men either refrained from buying suits or else got round the restriction somehow. And I expect many members of the Government disliked it as much as anybody, which may be one of the reasons for the removal of the ban.

THURSDAY, 27 JANUARY

Edward Stebbing
There was much anti-Jewish talk at the lunch table today. Of ten people, including myself, six were definitely anti-Jewish, three expressed no opinion, and one was not definitely pro- but not anti-Jewish. One man mentioned that the only shops with radio valves were Jewish shops, which had bought up the stocks. 'The only way to stop that,' said another, 'is to put a brick through their window and every time they put a new one in to smash it again.' I was surprised to hear such talk; it was reminiscent of the German pogroms.

SATURDAY, 29 JANUARY

Ernest van Someren
K and I went to town by train, and first went shopping in bookshops in Charing Cross Rd. I bought the TVA [Tennessee Valley Authority] book by Huxley, Kay could not find the US novel she wanted. We had 11s in a Hamburger bar and bought typewriter paper and a tie for me. We went to the EMG shops and bought a record, we might have bought more but hadn't a chance to hear any as their listening accommodation had a queue. K bought 2 pairs of stockings, on my coupons as she is short now. Then we met our friend Kate and had lunch at the Barcelona in Beak St, quite a good meal but not cheap, Kate treated us to it. We gave her some new laid eggs. Then we thought of going to a movie, and wandered about for some time, but couldn't find a suitable film at a reasonable price (6/- is too much, we think). We went to the Royal Academy and much enjoyed the Yugoslav exhibition, the sculpture by Mestrovic especially pleased me. We also saw the show *Colour in Everyday Life* which is fairly good, a bit thin K said since colourful things aren't made so much now.

MONDAY, 31 JANUARY

Ernest van Someren
Very busy at work, took a Benzedrine with my 11s. Have to finish the tests started on Friday, and a refrigerator came (on loan from Lyons) whose installation I supervised.

WEDNESDAY, 2 FEBRUARY

Ernest van Someren
Interviewed a candidate for a job, a Jewish–German refugee girl of 19, whom we would have offered a job but that one of our directors has a phobia about employing foreigners. After work called on Laurie's schoolmaster, and on my chief's secretary who is home ill, I took her some eggs. In the evening wrote up diary and did some parcels. Kay's sister in Yorkshire sent us Terrys chocolate and cocoa, as that is our favourite brand, and we have sent her dried fruit and some toffee, the former is particularly scarce up there.

TUESDAY, 8 FEBRUARY

Edward Stebbing
Some opinions expressed during lunchtime conversation: 'Hitler will shoot himself, the other leaders will escape . . . Himmler, Ribbentrop, and the rest should be tortured . . . Remember Rotterdam and Warsaw . . . It doesn't matter what territory we capture as long as we kill Germans . . . The Italian campaign is doing good because we are killing Germans and making them draw on their reserves . . .'

MONDAY, 14 FEBRUARY

Edward Stebbing
One of the women where I work always takes a vitamin tablet at lunchtime to make up for the present deficiencies in diet.

FRIDAY, 18 FEBRUARY

Ernest van Someren
A noisy night, with an air-raid where the raiders apparently travelled to town by the Lea Valley. We brought both the children into our bed, and Faith joined us there too, while a noisy raid went on. The nearest bomb was about a mile away, a small one, but after the raid I was roused by the noise of a fire, and apparently of small ammunition exploding.

SATURDAY, 19 FEBRUARY

Edward Stebbing

I have not been through many really bad air-raids, but last night's was the worst that I have experienced. I was woken up in the middle of the night by explosions and then followed over an hour of terrifying tumult. I thought the gunfire would bring the house down; it was one continuous bedlam of noise and the whole house shuddered with it. Even more frightening than the demented drumming of the guns was the buzzing of the enemy bombers low overhead; they seemed to be circling over our house, and any minute I expected a bomb to come crashing down, but only occasionally did I hear the thud of one some distance far away. Round the edges of the black-out curtains I could see brilliant flashes of light. I did not get up, partly because I was too lazy, partly because I was too scared, and partly because it was too cold.

Ernest van Someren

After tea did a house-mending job, putting up coat hooks. George Hesken (Flying Officer RAF, a gynaecologist and surgeon by profession) came for the weekend. Faith lives with him in a flat in Exeter when they can, with a view to matrimony when he gets a divorce. This is kept a secret from part of her (and our) family and makes life very complicated for her. In Exeter they are regarded by their neighbours as an ideal happily married couple. George went into the RAF in 1940, was out for part of 1942 and 43, and then was called back in. But from the Service point of view it's his legal wife who counts. He is also involved in a bankruptcy, so all is not well.

Chapter Fourteen

ON THE TIPTOE OF EXCITEMENT

When our invasion does begin: Churchill at the ready in May 1944.

1 March–22 July 1944

4 March US air forces join the bombing of Berlin.

19 March German forces occupy Hungary and reinforce their position in Rumania.

24 March Orde Wingate dies in a plane crash as his Chindits continue their assault on Burma.

25 March Allies call off their attempt to penetrate the Gustav Line at Cassino.

31 March 545 aircrew of bomber command die in disastrous raid on Nuremberg.

6 April Japan's march into India from Burma is halted at Imphal, 40 miles inside the border.

8 April The Red Army advances into Rumania.

29 April In the countdown to the Operation Overlord invasion of Europe, more than 600 Americans are killed by German torpedoes in the Channel.

2 May The crossword compiler for the *Daily Telegraph* is accused of giving away two of the beaches for the D-Day landings in the answers 'Utah' and 'Omaha'.

9 May The Red Army invades Sevastapol in a bid to liberate the Crimea.

18 May Cassino finally falls as the Allies advance to Rome.

31 May French invasion targets are bombed, destroying bridges and railway lines.

4 June American forces enter Rome.

6 June D-Day, the greatest seaborne invasion in history; the British naval bombardment begins in the early morning at Normandy, followed by British and US troop landings along the coast.

10 June The Normandy beach-heads of Gold, Omaha, Utah, Juno and Sword link up; Russia attacks Finland.

13 June Germany's secret weapon, the V1 flying bomb or pilotless robot plane, causes large-scale destruction in London and south-east England and mass evacuation.

14 June General de Gaulle returns to liberated France.

22 June About 1.2 million Soviet troops launch assault on German forces occupying Byelorussia and advance on the capital Minsk.

27 June American forces capture Cherbourg.

8 July Allied forces launch heavy aerial bombing on Caen, but troops face much resistance from Panzers within the city.

20 July Hitler survives bomb assassination attempt in eastern Prussia.

WEDNESDAY, 1 MARCH

Maggie Joy Blunt
Began to feel normal again last week. Spent 4 days at Hove at the beginning of February – sea air, rest, sunshine and food helped enormously. Returned to work full of vigour but found that I still tired easily, so for another week or more came home and went straight to bed every evening. Had sun-ray treatment at Clinic up to last week when Nurse went sick and am taking 3 halibut liver oil pills a day.

Air-raids last week were noisy but there were no incidents. Gun fire is terrific. My cottage shakes like a jelly and I wonder when the ceilings will collapse. I lay in bed one night watching the flares. Various relatives and friends in districts near London tell of damage and fires. Some complain of 'nerves' from which they have not suffered before, others say they find these short, sharp raids easier to endure than the old blitz. N, at Swiss Cottage, who is suffering from colds and sinus trouble and much the same debility that I had, says that she feels much more likely to die of illness than under a bomb.

SUNDAY, 5 MARCH

Maggie Joy Blunt
Received full amount from Insurance for burglary, and to my astonishment 18 coupons from Board of Trade for fur coat. The fur coat I have been lucky enough to replace with a kitten musquash which my London tailor and furrier happened to have in stock. He let me have it without coupons – did not enquire too closely why but assumed it to be secondhand, cleaned and remodelled. It is quite a success and many people say they like it better than my old one although I am not passionately fond of musquash. Cost me £60, which some folk think much too expensive but most of the amount was covered by Insurance money and tailor has given me a replacement value certificate for £100 for Insurance. Have replaced nothing else. The other items I consider lost to me.

TUESDAY, 7 MARCH

Edward Stebbing
My landlady said she did not think that Churchill was a man for the common people. 'I don't think he'll reign long after this war,' she said. This has long been my view. Only today I was thinking that really Churchill resembles Hitler in several ways – in his

pugnaciousness, his flair for leadership, his nationalism, his cunning in maintaining the domination of his own political party, but he is more subtle than Hitler, less extreme, less brutal. I would not call him a Fascist in temperament, but then British Fascism would not be the same as German Fascism.

THURSDAY, 9 MARCH

Pam Ashford
I had a chat with a captain just back from Malta. He says everything is in ruins. Sometimes the shells of the buildings are there, but mostly it is rubble. The only thing not damaged is the dry dock. He said there were only 1800 deaths, this small figure due to the catacombs. The catacombs of Malta still house hundreds of small homeless children who have been through all the 2000 raids. There is no livestock on the Island; everything was eaten. On one occasion there was only two days' food left.

Edward Stebbing
Nothing seems to satisfy the coal-miners. I don't know much about their working conditions, though I feel certain that they could be much improved and the miners doubtless have a legitimate grievance, but all the same they must be lacking in a sense of responsibility to be continually going on strike.

FRIDAY, 10 MARCH

Pam Ashford
Americans are peculiar. Capt R kissed me goodbye – no secrecy about it either. I could only say to Helen afterwards, 'When you were at Mr Wallace's did you kiss the customers?' She did not. Neither did I anywhere else. In point of fact Capt R is the fourth on my list. I gather it is a token of friendship. Nevertheless Helen's presence (17 and pretty) has had an upsetting effect. She is the subject of never-ending pursuit by a list the length of one's arm. It is amusing – if it stays amusing.

I am glad to be writing the diary again. The nation is on the tiptoe of excitement as the date of the invasion comes nearer. All through the months when the diary has been silent, there has gnawed at my heart the fear that I might not have restarted in time to get the Second Front. All the same, I would have – Course of Journalism or no course of journalism.

415

MONDAY, 13 MARCH

Edward Stebbing
My landlady has got hold of some story that buses will be taken off the roads. Her daughter and I both pointed out that life must go on even when the invasion starts, though it is conceivable that in some areas buses will be taken off temporarily. She was also rather perturbed about the rocket-guns, which the Germans are supposed to have. 'They reckon they'll reach to the East side of London at least,' she said. I said that it was no good looking for trouble before it comes.

Pam Ashford
The Soroptomist Club had a business meeting today. One of the Clubs in California sent us a parcel of good things. We raffled them at 6d a ticket – eight boxes of biscuits, six small cakes of chocolate, a large piece of chocolate, and a box of tea. I got a box of vanilla wafers. Lucky me!

TUESDAY, 14 MARCH

Edward Stebbing
Had the afternoon off. In St Albans I bought some vitamin A&D capsules and an anthology of poetry, compiled by Lord Wavell, called *Other Men's Flowers*. Afterwards I went to the pictures and saw *The Lodger*, an excellent thriller about Jack the Ripper.

WEDNESDAY, 15 MARCH

Maggie Joy Blunt
Last night another big raid on London. Guns here were active and I got all my Red Cross uniform ready. We are not being called but have to use our own discretion about going to the Point. Can hear our bombers going out now. A continual hum, like the dynamo of some fearful machine.

I am sick of this war. Sick of everything. Of the waiting, and the sound of bombers, of my work and my clothes and the general dullness of my complicated and unfruitful existence. Having caught up on the routine work which had collected while I was ill, am left now with nothing to do and very little in view.

THURSDAY, 16 MARCH

Edward Stebbing
Quite a heated discussion at work about the Jews. Our secretary, Miss B, and I were pro-Jewish, another man anti-Jewish, and the third man did not make his position clear, but seemed to be more or less neutral. Miss B and I had the better of the argument. We pointed out several inconsistencies in the anti-Semitic attitude: that objectors to the Jews' presence in this country failed to pursue this view by turning them out or by putting them in concentration camps; they condemned Hitler for persecuting the Jews and then refused the Jews the right to a decent life anywhere else (Hitler was at least consistent in his policy towards the Jews); they expressed dislike for the Jews' way of living – forced on them by centuries of having to fend for themselves in hostile communities – but put in the same position they would do exactly the same things themselves. We suggested that Palestine should be opened to the Jews. The answer was that if we did they wouldn't want to go, but this was met by saying that thousands of Jews had already been refused entry, in favour of the Arabs, a much less civilised race. But the main force of our argument was that those who hated the Jews failed to deal with the problem either way, but just allowed things to drift. I thought the best solution of the problem would be to ignore the Jews as such and admit them to the full rights and privileges of the country in which they happen to be living; eventually they would be absorbed and forgotten.

SATURDAY, 18 MARCH

Edward Stebbing
A man in the barber's shop said that his brother, who had been a prisoner-of-war for two years, had just been sent his calling-up papers! Somebody said he hoped our organisation would be better when the Second Front started.

MONDAY, 20 MARCH

Edward Stebbing
My landlady mentioned a cartoon in the *Sunday Express* yesterday, picturing some Japanese prisoners, and neither of us could understand why in cartoon Japanese are always represented as ugly little men with protruding teeth, because they are not all like that, and why in books and films Chinese are usually shown as the sort

417

that would stab you in the back. This is the type of disguised dishonesty, which annoys me intensely.

SATURDAY, 25 MARCH

Edward Stebbing
I rose about 7.30. It was Saturday, and I had the whole day off. After I had had breakfast at the hospital (porridge, Spam and chips, bread and marmalade, tea) and had been back to my lodgings I went up to London, hoping to get a seat at the Albert Hall for the concert in celebration of Sir Henry Wood's 75th birthday. I went to the Albert Hall and found that there were no seats left at less than a guinea. I didn't feel like paying a guinea, so turned away, but outside I thought, Why not be extravagant for once? And in any case I almost certainly would not be able to get in at any theatre, so before I could change my mind I went back and bought a seat. Afterwards I was not sorry, as all the proceeds without deductions, about £8,000, are going to a fund for building a new concert-hall in London. After lunch (salad, marmalade roll, coffee) at a snack bar and having a little time to spare before the concert, I strolled in Kensington Gardens. There I saw some soldiers in football kit being marched to their game, and was glad that my leisure was not thus disciplined. Then I went into the hall, where there was a great crowd. There was loud applause when Sir Henry Wood came on to the rostrum. This had died down when there was renewed clapping for somebody in the audience. I could not see whom it was at first and turned to an airman next to me to ask who it was. He said, 'Montgomery, I think,' but then I turned again and saw that it was the Queen with the two Princesses. Then we settled to enjoy the concert, which was excellent, though I thought it might have been more varied. Except for Elgar, all the composers represented were German and the programme was rather on the heavy side. I thought that some Russian music, which Sir Henry had done so much to make known, should have been included. Afterwards I went by bus and tube to Piccadilly and had a snack (two dried-egg sandwiches and a cup of coffee).

SUNDAY, 26 MARCH

Pam Ashford
Helen has a babyish face and the manners of an ingénue, and some of it is, I expect, real enough – she is 17. But she has a beautiful and seductive presence and a month in her company has taught me that there is nothing about sex she does not know. There is ample supporting evidence for that too.

418

The position is that Helen was brought in on 21st February to help with the pressure of work. Now that she has learned the ropes, the Captain discovers that we are overstaffed and I must go. 'It is not fair to the war effort to retain a highly qualified worker when it is possible to manage without.' I am very fond of Capt Macgowan and it makes no difference to that regard, though how I wonder at the blindness of men.

The terms he presented to me were unusual in the extreme. My name will be taken from the payroll on 15th April. The cheques (from American Embassy) for 15th to 31st March, and 1st to 15th April will be sent to me. He does not want me to go to work. 'There is nothing for me to do so I may as well have the full three weeks looking for another post.'

Another episode in my life has closed. To think that my uneasiness about the long time during which the diary was dormant was focused upon the possibility of the invasion bursting on the nations, and yet when I take it up again, it is to go through again the story of finding a job!

MONDAY, 27 MARCH

Pam Ashford
Capt Coleman, who is in Glasgow for a long time (repair job), said last Wednesday he read palms and took our hands. Everyone said he had told them the truth. What he said to me was true too. 'I had had much bad health but had been better for a number of years. I had had hard times but my economic position had been improving over the years; I should always have enough for everything I wanted, but I should never make much. I should not marry.' My comment after he had left was that it was true but general. However, on Friday afternoon he took my hand again and dropped it with a shudder saying ,'You'll have terrible trouble in the next two days. You are to have a new appointment.' I said, 'When?' He said, 'Within a fortnight.' I said, 'Will it be more money?' He said, 'It is a better appointment with more money.'

WEDNESDAY, 29 MARCH

Maggie Joy Blunt
People are seething. Nearly everyone I have spoken to about it was disappointed in Churchill's speech. (The one he broadcast last Sunday.) Many want to know why he spoke at all – they resented his cracks at his critics when no one could answer him back, and felt he

419

was trying to win the country's sympathy for a possible coming election. We are restless and anxious about the Second Front – some people think it will start in the Balkans, some favour Norway and few think we shall try through France. And we stick in Southern Italy, while Russia moves from strength to strength . . .

Photographs are needed, for advertising purposes, of certain aircraft components. This means – 1) getting the Part Numbers from the Sales dept., 2) obtaining permission from the head of Central Planning to have the parts released from their despatch batches, 3) contacting Inspection from where they will have to be collected and delivered to the Photographic Dept, 4) getting the Librarian to look them over and decide which are most suitable for our purpose. By the time all this is done the war will be over.

THURSDAY, 30 MARCH

Pam Ashford
Mother's 77th birthday. In the afternoon we went to the Regal to see *The Prisoner of Zenda* with Ronald Coleman.

FRIDAY, 31 MARCH

Pam Ashford
The Citizen's Theatre had a matinee today instead of Saturday. Mother and I went. The Citizen's Theatre opened last autumn. This permanent repertory theatre (in the Athenaeum) is meant to pave the way towards a municipal theatre. The piece was 'Bull Market' by Priestly. For 2/6 we had seats that were good for seeing and hearing, and also comfortable.

My theatre-going days ended 20 years ago with a long period of total incapacitation. There have been Saturday afternoons when I have longed for a reliable friend who would take me by the hand back to the exhilarating atmosphere. Alone I have feared to plunge. Entering half tired from a morning's work I have been afraid of fainting from fatigue in the third act. I came home feeling happy. Under this week at home I am beginning to feel a human being again. I have had my usual evening walk each evening, striding along briskly. For how many years my walk has been like a draught of medicine, something I have taken for the good of my health. How much better is the fading day to the body that is not weary from toil. My feelings are a mix-up – pleasure in my freedom, anxiety (not deep yet) as to what will happen when April 5th comes. The first of the three weeks is nearly through.

SATURDAY, 1 APRIL

Ernest van Someren
No April fooling in this household at all. I went out and did a little shopping and got some cash from the bank in the morning, Kay stayed in bed till noon as usual. I had fetched our meat ration on Friday afternoon, when it was fine.

The doctor came at lunchtime and inspected us all, and advised a little more bed for the children. I taught Laurie to play Casino, which he took to better than Nap. I have played it since I was a small boy myself.

TUESDAY, 4 APRIL

Maggie Joy Blunt
Last week Manny Shinwell MP came down and spoke to our discussion group. His subject was Post War Britain, and more than 300 people came to hear him. He said that he thought world economic and political unity an excellent ideal but we must be realists. He could not see how we could achieve this perfection while such differing ideologies as that of Soviet Russia and that of individualist, capitalist USA existed together in the world. We must realise the competition that would face us from these enormous empires after the war – and possibly China and India – and that we must organise our industrial resources to the very fullest extent if we did not want to fade to a 4th or 5th rate power. It could be done if we willed it. We had the resources and the skill. All the more mature industries and the public services he thought should operate under state direction – but not Civil Service direction, as we know it today, but by personnel drawn from the workers and technicians in industry who thoroughly understand it. It was a stimulating speech, given impromptu without notes, and was received with tremendous enthusiasm.

SATURDAY, 8 APRIL

Edward Stebbing
In the evening I visited my aunt and uncle and, during some talk about the invasion, mentioned that I thought it likely that the Germans would drop paratroops to interfere with our communications etc. My uncle disagreed, but I thought he was being over-optimistic, because he did not like to face up to the unpleasant possibility. I have no doubt that the enemy will do everything he can to upset our organisation.

Ernest van Someren

K took L to the doctor and had to wait over an hour in the surgery queue, which annoyed her very much. She said no one else spoke a word the whole time. Laurie stood it well. In the afternoon went to the library, alone, and took L to practise on his toy bicycle, which he has been learning to ride with me holding the saddle. Today I let go for the first time and he rode about 50 yards.

MONDAY, 10 APRIL

Ernest van Someren

Laurie cycled alone again and fell off rather hard.

THURSDAY, 13 APRIL

Maggie Joy Blunt

On Sunday we opened a wonderful tin of American tongue which N had brought and had with it potatoes and greens, then rhubarb pie.

We discovered a camp of Italian prisoners on the other side of the Common. They were not wired in and were moving about freely – in fact two passed us on bicycles before we came to the camp. They were talking to the villagers who thronged among them. They were in chocolate brown uniform with coloured square patches on the back of the coat and circles on the trouser leg.

Clothes: my underclothes and night attire are the garments which suffer most. Coupons nearly all go on top clothes. I had a fairly good stock of clothes to start with which has been pressed and cleaned and turned and renovated to give variety and interest. Stockings of course are a big item and I have spent several odd coupons on scarves. Have also been able to buy various second hand oddments which I have turned to good account. Hats I rarely wear and therefore seldom buy. As for evening clothes I have forgotten what a long skirt feels like. If I detailed my wardrobe it would look on paper extravagant, but actually most of it is now nearly 5 years old and beginning to look very shabby. I keep a few items to wear on special occasions only, the rest does duty every day – and very hard duty. At home I always wear slacks. And the garments I wear now at night are just fantastic. I only hope I am never bombed out when wearing them.

FRIDAY, 14 APRIL

Ernest van Someren
Stopped at the doctor's on the way to work, as my throat is swollen and rather sore, has been since yesterday morning. He recommended painting it, and inhalations.

SATURDAY, 15 APRIL

Ernest van Someren
To the theatre to see *There Shall Be No Night*, we left our cycles chained by the Stage Door. It was a very moving and well-acted play, Kay saw in it the influence of Priestley and I of Shaw. After that we had sandwiches and a drink at the Waldorf, because it was at hand, and were duly shocked at paying 3/- for cheese sandwiches made from four thin slices of white bread.

SUNDAY, 16 APRIL

Ernest van Someren
Stayed home all day, pottering about garden jobs, such as improving the new hen-run, for which I cast two small cement props. It rained slightly, and I used sheets of asbestos to make a lean-to where I was working. This delighted Laurie and Julia as a 'Workman's Hut' and they have been playing with it a lot since then.

TUESDAY, 18 APRIL

Edward Stebbing
We were talking about holidays at work. The chief said when the invasion started there would not be any holidays, so we had better squeeze a week in quickly. I have an invitation to spend a weekend with some friends, so decided to write and find out if I could get it extended to a week.

The word 'invasion' is on everybody's lips now. It crops up in every conversation.

THURSDAY, 20 APRIL

Ernest van Someren
The night proved eventful, as there was a raid with flares and HE [high explosives] from Rye House to Edmonton. We woke, and had the children in our bed, and listened to the noise with some alarm, as

there were several fires from a shower of incendiaries at Nazeing, in plain sight from our window, and afterwards a few bombs in Hoddesdon and Broxbourne. One fine house had a direct hit and was wiped out, with two killed.

WEDNESDAY, 3 MAY

Maggie Joy Blunt
The long evenings are here again. Weather brilliant, blossom everywhere profuse, spring in all its perfection. Last night about 11.15 a plane dived with a terrific roar over the trees and houses here. I saw a brilliant burst of flame as it crashed and exploded out of sight. The sky in the west glowed for a long time and one could hear crackling and sharp reports. Was told this evening that it was a Mosquito, landed on a common about 3 miles away, set fire to hay ricks but did no other damage. The crew of 2 was killed.

'Salute the Soldier Week' in Slough this week. Again our firm aims at £15,000. Shinwell addressed us in the Canteen at lunch time today.

My tailor from whom I recently ordered a new coat and skirt died very suddenly about 3 weeks ago.

THURSDAY, 4 MAY

Edward Stebbing
I see that Aneurin Bevan may be expelled from the Labour Party for attacking the trade unions over the new strike order. I agree with Bevan; the trade unions can hardly be said to represent their members now; they just tag along behind the Government, under the thumb of Ernest Bevin. Active and virile minds like Aneurin Bevan's are too dangerous for the tame and mediocre leaders of the Labour Party (with one or two exceptions), but by expelling their most able members that party is committing suicide. I was talking to a man who said it was ridiculous that a man, elected by the people, could not stand up in Parliament and express his sincere opinion. Indeed it is the sort of thing that might happen in Germany. It makes a mockery of our Parliamentary system. Men like Aneurin Bevan, alive to the dangers of Fascism in our own country, are the sort of men we want.

Ernest van Someren
After work went round to see the HM of our local C of E village school about the prospect of sending Laurie there next year. He says

that the children between 5 and 10 are a good mixture, but there are only 4 teachers for about 190 children, in three classes and a nursery or kindergarten class. It seems a bit tough to move Laurie from a class of 8 to one of 48.

TUESDAY, 9 MAY

Ernest van Someren
In the evening went to a film show, arranged by the County Youth Organiser for clubs, of *When We Build Again, Fish Face*, and a Mickey comic on building and a film about the Gold Coast. The main item was a film on housing by the Bourneville Village Trust, quite a good piece of work with excellent shots of bad Birmingham.

WEDNESDAY, 10 MAY

Ernest van Someren
In the evening went to the movies with K, saw *San Demetrio, London* and was much impressed by it. One party who went in a car to the cinema caused a few caustic remarks afterwards.

THURSDAY, 11 MAY

Edward Stebbing
Today has been dominated by my having one of my front teeth out. It started to ache yesterday, got worse during the night, so this morning I went and had it out. I had hoped to go to work in the afternoon, but felt so queer that I had to lie down. Now as I write this the pain has worn off and I feel myself again, but the gap in my teeth looks very unsightly and it will be over a fortnight before I can have a denture.

In the evening I had a visitor who said she had heard a rumour that holidays had been cancelled.

TUESDAY, 16 MAY

Ernest van Someren
Very cold again. After supper went to the Stranges and did sword-dancing practice, four men and Helen Strange as our fifth man failed to turn out.

TUESDAY, 23 MAY

Ernest van Someren
In the evening to a meeting of Fire Guard street leaders, at the Sector Captain's house, a long talkative meeting at which we learnt something and decided very little. We decided, quite illegally, to make copies of the Sector Map for each of us. Such copies are officially banned, and our sector contains no important buildings. We intend to get hydrants marked on the map.

WEDNESDAY, 24 MAY

Edward Stebbing
Went to a dance at which some American soldiers, as well as some British soldiers and naval officers, were present. I asked three of my partners what they thought of the 'Yanks'. One said, 'As a whole they're not too bad, but individually they're awful.' The second said, 'The ones I've met have been very nice.' The third said, 'I danced with one; he was a very nice lad. But I've no time for them really.' A man I spoke to was rather more emphatic, 'I don't like 'em. They think they're It. This is our country and I'm an Englishman etc. . . .' There seems to be a good deal of prejudice against the Americans; it is more or less fashionable to make rude remarks about them. I must admit that they do not make a very good impression on me: they have a natural assertiveness and conceit which is rather unpleasant (they probably can't help it, but this does not alter the fact), but I refuse to share in a vague generalisation which makes all Americans (or all Germans) uniformly contemptible. At the dance tonight they were quite as well behaved as our own troops, if not better.

Ernest van Someren
Another hot day, went with Laurie at about 11 with Joe to see a man called Fennell who lives at Nazeing, he showed us a most remarkably good wireless reproducer and gramophone pick-up, and also an oscillograph. Laurie was most impressed. We came home to lunch, leaving Joe there. In the afternoon we went with both children through Wormley, looking for a brook where they could paddle, but both brooks we tried were about dry. We had a picnic tea, and amused the children with a tiny 'camp fire'.

TUESDAY, 30 MAY

Ernest van Someren
Really hot again, so I didn't get much done at work, my room is about the coolest in the building. People are saying that if the Second Front was only waiting for fine weather it would start now, and it looks as if we had missed our date, or something. One man came back from a week at Minehead very sunburnt.

WEDNESDAY, 31 MAY

Ernest van Someren
Draft Memorandum in reply to Questions issued by the County Youth Advisory Committee.

1) There has been some increase in the use of public houses by people under 24 in the last five years.

2) It would assist if British restaurants and cafes were more generally open in the evenings. Food and drink should be available. There should be no public suggestion of age discrimination in this matter.
   The British restaurant in Hoddesdon might well be opening in the evenings, from 6 to 10.30pm. It is important that it should be available after the cinema is closed.

3) The increased use of public houses by young people has not led to a great increase in intemperance, since it has been caused as much by the need for a social centre as by the need for refreshments. The high cost of spirits and the weakness of beer is a further temporary factor in preventing intemperance.

THURSDAY, 1 JUNE

Ernest van Someren
Laurie went to hospital to have his tonsils out, but as K was having a day in town and the hospital gave us only one day's notice she didn't take him till evening. I put Julia to bed and had supper, then the daughter of a WEA member, Joan Bugg, came to see me and talked about the need for British restaurants or cafes to open in the evening.

FRIDAY, 2 JUNE

Ernest van Someren
At work spent some time making a glass tubing toy for Laurie.

SUNDAY, 4 JUNE

Edward Stebbing
The Italian campaign takes an added interest now that Rome is almost in our grasp. Previously, because of the hard going and relative insignificance of the territory involved, the campaign has seemed rather dull. Now we see that it has been a very skilfully conducted battle since we began our last offensive and that, over difficult ground and against strong opposition, the advance has been surprisingly rapid.

MONDAY, 5 JUNE

Edward Stebbing
The capture of Rome has come even sooner than I expected. It is perhaps the biggest triumph our troops have had, at least it seems so, because Rome is the largest and most famous city they have yet captured. Even it if had not been, the enemy's resistance has probably been the strongest they have had to face, so in any event it is a splendid victory.

TUESDAY, 6 JUNE

Maggie Joy Blunt
INVASION DAY. It really is rather thrilling to hear that the long awaited action of our armies is at last taking place. The BBC announcement was being relayed over the work broadcast at noon today. We crept to our places in the Canteen in a cathedral-like hush. 'There'll be many worried homes today,' said LS. Work went on as usual in the afternoon with a sort of subdued excitement prevailing. Several people suggested that we have been waiting, not for any particular day, but for the fall of Rome. Many claim that they had 'feelings' last night of pending events.

Went to see Meg and Roger on Sunday and their son and heir, born on Easter Saturday. Meg is trying to cope with baby and belongings in two rooms in someone else's house – sharing kitchen and bathroom. Roger when he comes home at night washes the nappies. I have never heard of a father doing this before but Meg mentioned several others who do the same now. What a war will do to the middle classes.

Bought a new coat and skirt at Peter Jones. 'The Govt. want us to go about badly dressed – that's what it amounts to,' said the assistant. She told me of other difficulties too – like having the Gestapo at your elbow all the time, she said. But in spite of this the saleswomen, in the two-piece dept. at least, are courteous and anxious to please and the tailor an artist, taking great pride in his work.

9.30pm. HM the King has addressed his people, on a very strong religious note, with the stammer in his speech more marked than I have noticed for a long time. This was followed by long and detailed news and accounts of the Allied landings and speeches of the commanders which is still going on. How comic to think of all the speculation and scepticism there has been about invasions – that we should strike from Norway, from the Balkans, that we had struck and been defeated in Italy and so on, and then we do the obvious thing which most people anxious to be clever had discarded as a possibility and cross the Channel!

Edward Stebbing
During a somewhat busy day at work I have done my best to keep a record of people's reactions to today's great news of the invasion of France.

Even before I got up this morning I thought something big was happening because of the number of aircraft going over, many more than usual. Going to work there seemed to be fewer people about and there was only one other person on the bus, which heightened my presentiment of a great event.

But it was not until after I arrived at the hospital that I heard the news, from a patient who has been coming to do a few jobs for us. I was not very surprised, for the above reasons and because for some time past I have been prepared to wake up and find that the invasion has started. One of the first things my boss said was, 'We can expect a few air-raids now.'

What struck me particularly was that the invasion has come immediately after the fall of Rome. Were they waiting for this to increase the element of surprise and to take advantage of a time when the enemy had suffered a bad blow to prestige and morale?

My boss and Mr W continued to talk of what Churchill had said about the organisation required for such a vast operation. My boss said, regarding Churchill's post-war position, 'He seems to be a man of action. I think he'll get things done.' Mr W: 'All I hope about the present Government is that they're in office long enough to see their

429

post-war plans materialised.' His tone of voice seemed to indicate that he thought this might not happen.

A nurse came in and said, 'I wish it didn't have to happen. Still, it will soon be over now it's started – in a couple of weeks, do you think?' I said, 'Probably six months or more.'

Listening to the news afterwards, I was impressed by the overwhelming strength of our attack and by the elaborate arrangements which the BBC had made to give the news at first-hand to the public. The weakness of the enemy resistance was also surprising, but no doubt the Germans have something up their sleeve. 'It seems too good to be true,' commented my landlady.

Ernest van Someren
Interesting news at eight, and before lunch the rumour got round at work that it was really the invasion. At one about 100 people gathered in the canteen to hear the news bulletin, and seem impressed but hardly said anything. There was a local directors meeting and people were busy.

WEDNESDAY, 7 JUNE

Edward Stebbing
A quiet night last night. A quiet day, too, for me. I did not come into contact with many people, but the main point arising in conversation was the expectation of a German counter-attack. One man brought a portable radio to work in order to hear the news.

I cannot help feeling a sense of wonderment that life goes on just the same here, while not so very far away one of the most momentous events in history is taking place.

THURSDAY, 8 JUNE

Ernest van Someren
Had a phone talk with my Mother, I agree with her that our news service about this invasion is marvellously good, especially the BBC War Reports. People don't talk about it much, but seem a trifle more cheerful in a rather subdued way, I suppose we are glad to know it has begun.

FRIDAY, 9 JUNE

Ernest van Someren
Kay fetched Laurie home from hospital yesterday, after a week, he was fairly fit and at once said, 'What are we going to have for dinner

today.' He had not been told about the invasion and was very interested. Today he stays in bed except for a short period, and has the kitchen loudspeaker in his room so that he can listen to the school broadcasts.

In the evening went to a WEA meeting for a discussion on private and public schools in education, opened by the head of Laurie's school, who is an amusing speaker but not profound. Adjourned with a few to the Golden Lion afterwards, as we were very thirsty. I had resolved not to drink beer just as a friendly gesture, and therefore to stop when I am no longer thirsty, even if people think it odd. The irrational idea that drinking should continue in symmetrical 'rounds' is stupid enough to be disputed.

FRIDAY, 16 JUNE

Edward Stebbing

The air-raid warning went at about a quarter-to-twelve last night, and after a little while there was a big explosion, followed by some gunfire. After an interval there was some more gunfire, nearer this time, so I got up and came downstairs. By the time I had done this everything was quiet again and after about three-quarters of an hour in which nothing happened I went back to bed, although the 'All clear' had not gone. When I got up this morning the 'All clear' still had not gone. My landlady's husband came home from night duty and said he had heard a rumour that the Germans had made a landing at Dover. I was inclined to give some credence to this, because I thought something queer must have happened for the warning to be so prolonged and because I thought it likely that the Germans would try some form of 'attack as the best form of defence'. My landlady said she had a premonition that something like this was happening.

Soon after I got to work the 'All clear' went. One man said he thought perhaps the Germans had been firing rocket-guns. Another man, who had been fire-watching all night, mentioned radio-controlled bombs; somebody else spoke of radio-controlled planes. I had taken my portable radio to work, and at twelve o'clock we heard the news of the pilotless planes. Mr U said the Germans must be daft to use them. I was glad there was no truth in the rumour about a German landing.

At lunchtime there was much talk about the new weapon. One man remarked that people seemed to be pleased rather than depressed about the news, their attitude being, 'Hurrah! The Germans have got pilotless planes.' I suggested that it was because

431

they had expected something much worse. I said I thought it would be fairly easy to find an answer to them. Opinion was more or less unanimous that the Germans would not be able to do much with them, because of the apparent impossibility of using them with any precision. 'Just a clever gadget,' was one remark.

Ernest van Someren

Was fire-watching last night, stayed up till one and then went to bed in spite of no all-clear, rather puzzled by being woken later by loud bangs at long intervals. Guessed it was pilotless aircraft, and went to town after breakfast. Found everyone talking about them, especially my barber. A total stranger interrupted my reading in the bus to say that he thought that perhaps the gliders were towed over here and then released as bombs.

SUNDAY, 18 JUNE

Edward Stebbing

Interest in the P-planes outweighs all other news, even the fighting in Normandy.

MONDAY, 19 JUNE

Edward Stebbing

Talk about the pilotless planes is almost endless, and I simply cannot remember nor have I had time to make notes of everything that people have said about them today. Already I have heard of many places where they have fallen and listened to a detailed description of them from a person who has seen one. It seems that they travel at a great speed and at a low height – too low both for radiolocation and for the anti-aircraft guns. One man said, 'They must have a terrific store of them,' and said someone had told him that they were sent over at a rate of one every three minutes. Another person, a woman, said they came over 50 at a time and the trouble was 'they can't do anything to deal with them'. I can't see that they're any worse than an ordinary air raid. The question uppermost in people's minds is probably: will we be able to find an answer to the P-plane (or Bumble-bomb as one man called it)? I think we shall, but it seems more difficult than I at first thought, because they are not apparently radio-controlled, as I had imagined. Yet I must admit that these things have put my nerves on edge more than ordinary raids. I suppose the novelty of them, the devilish ingenuity, has something to do with it. It is with a mixture of fear and curiosity that we look up at almost every plane that goes over, half-expecting it to be a pilotless one. Everybody seems to want to be able to say they've seen one.

TUESDAY, 20 JUNE

Ernest van Someren
Did some experimental filming with a cine camera on a difficult subject at work. The Dixons came to visit the Stranges for a night, and will then occupy our house while we are away. Stella D has a baby of 2 months and a girl of 19 months in hospital in SE London, her husband Cecil has recently had flu and they have been very worried by P-planes. They are not really married.

WEDNESDAY, 21 JUNE

Ernest van Someren
Caught the Cornish Express at 10.30 and got seats with a little difficulty, it was reasonably full. We had lunch in the train from one rucksack, and got out at Taunton, the first stop. After a long wait there, during which I cycled down to the town for a little shopping, we caught a local slow train to Minehead, which was quite full. Got there at 3.40, punctually, and went on by bus to Porlock, leaving the cycles to be delivered by the railway van next day. At Porlock our landlady Mrs Ridiler gave us a good tea and we put the children to bed. Later we had our supper, and went for a little stroll at about 9.30. The Hurtstone Point, a moorland fill used as a Tank Range by the US Army, was on fire, giving a most picturesque smoke cloud across the bay.

THURSDAY, 22 JUNE

Edward Stebbing
Received a letter from my sister. Regarding the pilotless planes she says, 'I think they are uncanny, as there is no human element.'
   I went to have a look at the destruction caused by a P-plane which fell in Tottenham Court Road three days ago. I was surprised by the small extent of the main damage. I could not get a close view as the area was roped off, but the really bad damage seemed to be confined to quite a small area, with damage due to blast (windows out, smashed woodwork, etc.) extending for a good way around. Another man who was looking at it said to me, 'If it wasn't for the loss of life, we could thank 'em for that,' and, looking at the squalid buildings which had been ruined, I agreed.

When I got home I found my landlady feeling disappointed because she had missed the opportunity of buying an enamel saucepan this afternoon, not having heard about them until they had all gone.

Ernest van Someren
We went down and looked at the beach, a mile away, which is stony and steep and lined with barbed wire, with convenient gaps for access. The tide was in, but it wasn't warm enough for bathing, though fine. We then explored the marshes between the beach and village. We had to wade across one brook and Julia fell in before we were ready to carry her, fortunately we had a bathing suit to put on her while her things dried in the sun.

After lunch we went on our cycles with the children to the hamlet of Horner, left the cycles and went up a millstream which we explored and paddled in, and then had tea near it. Julia was frightened of a horse in a field there.

SUNDAY, 25 JUNE

Maggie Joy Blunt
The Germans' new weapon, the robot-plane or pilotless aircraft, or as they are being called about here, those 'flitter-bombs', have been causing interest and excitement this past week. The first day they came over we were sent to the shelters. I took one look at them and fled and a great many other people did the same. We have not been sent since although we have had many alerts. One or two of the bombs have fallen quite near. I never hear the alert but am awakened by the vibration of the bomb as it lands. The blast is terrific, everything shakes. N writes that their effect in London is demoralising, to hear them coming and not knowing where they will fall. There is no defensive gunfire. She says she prefers the ordinary blitz and has I gather had very little sleep recently. She has even sent me a copy of her will to keep in a safe place. Have been told that these bombs are designed to damage by blast rather than explosion, and also that there are only enough to last another fortnight when they will be replaced by some other Secret Weapon.

The feeling that the war is nearing its end at last is not viewed by all of us with unalloyed jubilation. In fact I have seen no evidence of jubilation anywhere at the thought. The question that is in everyone's mind is – what will post-war conditions be like? Shall I be able to keep my job or get another of the kind I really want? We feel too that preference will be given to people coming out of the Services – who

434

have of course lost contact as much as any of us. It will be largely a matter of luck and of knowing the right people. It will be a ghastly scramble for work.

What our firm will do or intends to do no one seems to know or will say. We have just launched a New Company 'to co-operate with designers and manufacturers in all industries on the use of light alloys for post-war purposes'. We have put out some splashy advertising.

Ernest van Someren
We took the children to church, at their request, a Methodist church, and out before the sermon. They were only fairly good. Then we walked down to the beach and back. The fire on the hill was beaten out yesterday by soldiers and civilians.

MONDAY, 26 JUNE

Edward Stebbing
Saying that he had heard that an anti-aircraft battery on the South coast had shot down 1400 flying bombs, a man estimated that so far the Germans must have sent over 5–6000 of them.

My landlady said that the baker told her he had not got enough bread to finish his round, as those who worked in the bakery had to stop work continually for the flying bombs.

TUESDAY, 27 JUNE

Edward Stebbing
I heard one of the flying bombs for the first time last night – and I hope it is the last. It seemed to come low over the houses and the noise made the house vibrate, then abruptly the engine stopped and I thought our last hour had come. I put my head under the bedclothes and waited, but nothing happened for about a minute and a half, when there was a faint thud in the distance, miles away. I had expected a deafening roar. I lay awake for some time afterwards, listening to others exploding some way off. When I came down in the morning my landlady said she had still not recovered from the shock.

At work, a girl who lives nearer London said it had been London's worst night.

Ernest van Someren
Rain in the night, and showers in the day, we went out shopping and bought Julia a mac cape, and had 11s at a café. After lunch by bus to Porlock Weir with my chief and family, it was damp at times but we

435

had a short walk in the woods and a good tea at the Ship Inn there. It's a casual place and chickens came to collect the crumbs under the tables.

WEDNESDAY, 28 JUNE

Ernest van Someren
Rainy, to Minehead by bus and met my chief, who is leaving today as there is a child apparently with whooping cough come to their hotel, and they don't like the weather anyway. We had a poorly cooked lunch at the British Rest., and went for coffee afterwards to a café, a good one. Then to a cinema, as it was raining again. Saw a silly film called *Moonlight and Cactus*, then part of a Technicolor thriller called *The Phantom of the Opera* but we left before the end as the children were bored and we had to catch a bus back. Julia refused to go to sleep in the cinema, to our regret.

THURSDAY, 29 JUNE

Pam Ashford
The Proms have been coming through this week. Last night at 8 just after the Coronation Anthem, Zadok the Priest, had started, the BBC suddenly switched over to records. My interpretation is that when the M. of Air tells them pilotless planes are about they go on to records. Miss Ripon had a 'phone conversation with a sister in London last night. She said that yesterday was the worst so far. The laconic terms in which the wireless gives the news, 'There were pilotless planes over last night,' or some such words, is considered to prove how very bad the damage is. 'They are not saying anything' is the grim comment.

Edward Stebbing
When I arrived at the hospital I was surprised to learn that a flying bomb had fallen just at the back of it, for I had not heard it explode, though my landlady said she heard a terrific bang in the night. It had fallen in a field about 20 yards from the nearest building and the blast had done a considerable amount of damage, but fortunately only one person was slightly injured.

One man, who was sleeping in the wooden hut nearest the site of the explosion, had a miraculous escape from injury, went back into the wreckage after a half-bottle of whisky, which he found upside down, but intact, and which he and another promptly consumed.

SATURDAY, 1 JULY

Edward Stebbing
There are two main attitudes to the flying bombs, from the point of view of personal safety – those who think it safer to sleep downstairs or in a shelter and those who think the chances of being killed or injured are the same either way and prefer not to sacrifice comfort for the doubtful advantage of sleeping downstairs. I am one of the more fatalistic ones; if a bomb is going to get me, it will get me, it is no good trying to dodge them. It is better to lose as little sleep as possible than wear oneself out in the effort, perhaps futile, to avoid extinction. I admit that those who shelter in the Underground are fairly sure of survival (though there is the risk of death from pneumonia or some other illness), but we have no shelter near us, so I continue to sleep upstairs.

SUNDAY, 2 JULY

Edward Stebbing
Returning to my lodgings tonight, found the train so crowded that I had to get in the guard's van. In the tube stations the shelterers had returned in force.

TUESDAY, 4 JULY

Pam Ashford
Mother, back from an English Society Whist Drive, tells me, both with confidence and in confidence, that the pilotless planes, or flying bombs as they are becoming more generally known, are being manufactured in Spain and Franco is sending them forward in a steady stream. I queried this. However, it was supposed to be authentic as 'the BBC had said so'. I said to Mother, 'You listen to the BBC four times a day, have you heard them say that?' She had not. Nevertheless this colourful rumour is spreading out from the English Society (who no doubt got it from somewhere else).

Moores Caron & Watson [new employers] act as secretaries to quite a lot of associations and Mr Houstoun has two, viz. the Scottish Pitwood Importers Federation (with the Pitwood Association of Scotland – the same people are members of both) and the Scottish Fireclay Pipe Association.

FRIDAY, 7 JULY

Pam Ashford
From Mr Churchill's speech the position in London appears worse than I myself believed. It might be that is an exceptional point of view, or it might be that it is only the people who like to look at the black side who talk. Mother met Mrs Wallace, who told us that an Army doctor friend of a friend of theirs was prevented from attending a Church parade. A flying bomb struck the Church. Every soul was killed, except the minister. I said to Mother, 'I read of a Church that was struck but the minister (in the building) was not hurt. I also heard of a Church service at which 70/80 soldiers were killed.'

Edward Stebbing
Churchill's statement on the flying bombs must have modified the ideas of both those who were inclined to exaggerate and of those who were inclined to belittle their importance. For a while I thought that more bombs had been sent over (a few days ago I mentioned the figure 5000 – nearly twice as many as have actually been launched), the casualty figures (one killed and about four injured per bomb) were higher than I expected. At first I did not think the flying bombs would be much more than a nuisance, but now I think they have had a considerable effect: doing quite a lot of damage, causing many casualties, and fraying people's nerves tremendously.

SATURDAY, 8 JULY

Edward Stebbing
I had a ticket for the Promenade Concert this evening, but as these have been cancelled I went and got my money back and went to a play instead. There were plenty of people about London still, but the fact that I was able to get a theatre ticket late in the afternoon proves that the flying bombs were keeping many away from the theatres. Several theatres are closing down. The play I saw was *Uncle Harry*, a finely acted drama of the psychological thriller type, but I thought the acting was rather wasted on a not very elevating theme.

TUESDAY, 11 JULY

Pam Ashford
All the clerks have given me piles of work. Now that we are past the peak of the season, we are working on taxation computations.

MC&W are 209 West George Street.

Miss Sinclair continues to keep us wise about the flying bombs. The Marble Arch has been hit. The Gillette razor blade factory has been hit. Yesterday was the worst day so far. This morning London children evacuees arrived in Glasgow and were taken by bus to Lenzie. They had their names on cards around their necks. The bus conductress did not understand a word they said – Cockney. Miss Sinclair says that Singers are turning from war work to sewing machines at the end of the month.

THURSDAY, 13 JULY

Edward Stebbing
Went to see a new British film, *The Way Ahead*, depicting Army life from the arrival of some new recruits at a training depot to the time when they go into battle. This film, in my opinion, is a masterpiece. Perhaps because I have been in the Army I appreciated it more, but it was so vividly real that I felt that I was living the same life as the soldiers in the film. The last scenes were as thrilling as anything I have seen on the screen. British films have undoubtedly reached a very high level since the war. Films like *Desert Victory*, *San Demetrio, London*, *In Which We Serve*, *The Way Ahead*, and others, make Hollywood attempts at depicting war seem pitifully unreal and childish. These British films have original treatment, inspiring themes, acting of the highest quality, gripping realism, superb technical skill in the making of them. I only hope the good work continues after the war.

FRIDAY, 14 JULY

Pam Ashford
In September 1939 I referred to an afternoon with Anna Fraser. Today I contacted her. I told her I was a shorthand typist at MC&W. She said, 'You are wasting your qualifications. Cannot you get somewhere else?' I said, 'They pay me very well and I doubt if I should get as much in a job where I could use my qualifications better.' She said, emphatically, 'You would not.' There are very few jobs as high as £5 a week. That is what I have too. The Ministry of Labour in London circularises the Appointments Department with all posts for women graduates. Often I have seen vacancies for London MAs, fluent French and German essential, at £3 to £4 a week to work in London itself. Wages never went above £5.

SATURDAY, 15 JULY

Pam Ashford
THE GLASGOW FAIR – Holidays for Stay-at-Homes.

All this week *Snow White and the Seven Dwarfs* has been drawing large audiences at the Picture House. Today's queue at 10.05 was 20 yards long. Doors opened at 10.15, show began 10.40. House then three-fourths full. Remembering my dislike for the two long Walt Disneys I have seen (*Pinocchio* and *Fantasia*) I wondered how Snow White would stand the test. It is very pretty – in its conception, drawing, colour and music. I enjoyed it. Another quarter of an hour and my attention would have flagged – as it did with *Pinocchio*.

Edward Stebbing
Started my holiday by standing up all the way home in a packed train. Travelling is no fun these days.

SUNDAY, 16 JULY

Edward Stebbing
One of the sunniest days we have had since March. Spent most of the day at my sister's, playing with my nephew (now about 16 months old), reading Proust, and gathering mushrooms in a nearby field.

Pam Ashford
In conjunction with a number of societies the Corporation has put on at the Winter Gardens of the People's Palace (Glasgow Green) a prize competition for 'fur, feather and fish' – rabbits, budgies, pigeons and fish (small tank aquaria). There are also shown butterflies in cases and goods made from rabbit pelts. The Zoo has given a big glass case with stuffed pheasants, and there is a café among the palm trees. The budgies, in three tiers, occupy the wall dividing the museum from the Winter Gardens. The fish in tanks run from that wall to the East exit. The pigeons (two tiers) from the East to the South exit. The rabbits (one tier) from the South exit (past the West exit) and up to the wall, meeting the budgies there. The place was crowded and rather warm, particularly near the fish.

THURSDAY, 20 JULY

Pam Ashford
I worked like a slave on Thursday and Friday last week. Oh how hard I have to work. Often I think of avenues of escape from

MC&W. But then there are powerful motives for sticking it out. My big pay envelope for one. The nice environment of a professional office. The good peacetime conditions which one supposes will return after the armistice and which I might inherit. I don't want to be high and dry when the armistice comes. What a rotten economic system we do have. There is no separating the mass mind from the belief that the armistice will herald mass unemployment. I do not think it will. With me I know I am at an age when before the war a woman had little chance of employment outside the housekeeping category. That is over for the war, but . . .

I got home early (Mr Houston's holiday) in time for the six o'clock news. How I 'registered' the news that a bomb had been thrown at Hitler!!! But could I get Mother to appreciate the point? She said the news was that General Wavell had been wounded. That is what comes of having a deaf parent. The BBC did not repeat the news headings at the end. So here I am at 7.45 writing what ought to be a thrilling diary entry . . . and all I can say is, 'We will wait till 9 o'clock.'

FRIDAY, 21 JULY

Pam Ashford
On the tram at lunchtime I met Dorothy Wallace, who had not listened to the wireless last night and was quite unprepared for the turn of events this morning. When John brought in the evening papers at 5 feeling ran high. 'German Army in revolt' was what the newspapers were reporting. I hurried home, getting in about 6.10, but the BBC again did not repeat the headlines. Mother said that 'Germany was a closed country. All telephone wires to the outer world were cut, so that nobody did know what was going on inside.' I am longing for the 9 o'clock news when I can hear the news with my own ears.

SATURDAY, 22 JULY

Pam Ashford
Miss Sinclair said she felt energetic last night. For months she has done the housework with weariness. Last night she felt different and then went out and cut the grass. She said, 'Year after year the war has gone on, without a sign of change. Now we can believe it will end. What *will* we do on the day the war ends?' Mother said, 'I shall go into hysterics.' That is how I feel myself. (This note is being written on Sunday evening and frankly I feel shaken right through by the

441

unmistakable sign of what I always knew would be – one day. The crack-up of Nazidom.)

In the afternoon I went to the Girls Training Corps Exhibition at the Art Galleries. It was very enjoyable. I overheard someone saying, 'The war is almost over. That will be one duty the less.' I wondered what the duty was.

Chapter Fifteen

THE LIBERATION OF PARIS

It will really happen soon: British troops march through a small English village on the eve of D-Day.

26 July–18 October 1944

31 July Allied troops advance from Normandy into German lines at Avranches.

1 August Polish uprising in Warsaw.

4 August Anne Frank betrayed to the Gestapo after two years in an Amsterdam attic.

15 August Allies open Second Front at Cannes as US forces approach the Seine 40 miles from Paris.

25 August Paris is liberated by Allied troops and the French, and de Gaulle enters the city.

28 August The V1 flying bombs, which have killed more than 5000 people, are proving less effective as most are intercepted by RAF Channel patrols and anti-aircraft guns; but V2 rockets are not far behind.

8 September Brussels liberated.

9 September Soviet troops advance through the Balkans.

11 September US forces begin fighting on German soil and renew offensives in the Pacific Ocean.

20 September British paratroopers ringed in by German forces at Arnhem, and an early end to the war seems doubtful.

22 September US forces launch air-raid on the Philippines.

3 October Polish forces defeated in struggle for Warsaw.

5 October British paratroopers land in Greece.

14 October Athens liberated by Allied troops and Greek partisans.

WEDNESDAY, 26 JULY

Edward Stebbing

Mrs S asked me this morning if I had heard that civil war had broken out in Germany. Someone told her that it had been announced on the wireless.

I went to London later in the morning. In the café where I had my lunch two men were talking about the attempted assassination of Hitler. 'Germany has cracked,' said one.

In the afternoon I went to the Zoo, where I had not been since I was a child. Some animals and reptiles have been removed for the duration, but there are still plenty of interesting exhibits. The Giant Panda (which we may never see again in this country) I thought a little disappointing; a smaller and less publicised variety of panda seemed a more attractive animal.

SATURDAY, 29 JULY

Pam Ashford

Being so fresh at 12.30 I felt I must do something outstanding. So I went down to the Forth & Clyde Coal Company Ltd. I long for news of Mr Mitchell. He has never called. Miss Bousie told me what Miss Gibson said on 2nd April that she would not join the Women for Westminster Movement because she believes the secretary is a florist who swindled the F&C over the wreath for Mr Hutchison's father's funeral.

SUNDAY, 30 JULY

Pam Ashford

After lunch I began my holiday preparations. This involved going through my big stack of respectable new lingerie, hoarded since before the war. Everything had to be washed, partly because of house dust, but chiefly because of the mothball smell.

The BBC are giving out that Rommel probably has been killed.

MONDAY, 31 JULY

Edward Stebbing

Flying bombs are still a major topic of conversation. The other day someone said that in certain pubs anyone who mentions them has to stand drinks all round. At lunchtime today there was a good deal of discussion on the effectiveness of the balloon barrage. Nobody seemed to think that it was of much use.

THURSDAY, 3 AUGUST

Edward Stebbing
At last we are making the progress we have been waiting for in France. This, combined with the spectacular Russian successes, makes one feel that the end is drawing near.

Pam Ashford
Mr Churchill says that the war is crashing to its end. The war does not, however, get talked about much. So far as Elaine goes talk is about her boy friends – 16 in number, and all in the Forces. When two are on leave simultaneously she gets tied in knots.

Mrs Wallace said this morning's post brought an envelope headed War Office. It contained a notice of her allowance being increased. She, however, thought it was bad news from France and had to sit down on a chair for several minutes before opening it. I said, 'Bad news is sent by telegram.'

Ernest van Someren
Stopped on the way back from work and called on Mary Lawton, who came swimming with me. Her husband John was in the RAMC in Normandy, last weekend he was reported seriously wounded, and today he was reported dead. She has been married only 3 years, and they are very hard up. She is remarkably courageous about it, and has to put off telling her parents as her father is gravely ill and her mother would be too upset.

SATURDAY, 5 AUGUST

Maggie Joy Blunt
Cornwall. N, no longer able to endure the doodles in London day and night, came to stay with me – travelling to Paddington and back each day. When my holiday began on July 22nd I had made no definite plans for it and she said, 'You must go away.' The ban on Cornwall having been removed I phoned June to find out what she was doing and I travelled with her and T last Monday, and here I am.

We expected the journey to be grim. The weekend before conditions at Paddington had been simply appalling – I heard nothing but the most depressing tales of crowds and jammed corridors. Yet on the Monday we all managed to meet without much difficulty on the platform, and when the train came in we split into three directions to get seats. Settled eventually in corner of non-smoker, two Canadian sailors sat opposite. We gave them some of our sandwiches and just before they embarrassed us enormously by showering quite a dozen packets of chocolate from their kit bags onto our laps.

We were met by Muriel (June's eldest sister) whose husband is stationed with the RAF Transport Command at Newquay. They had just moved into a cottage at St Mawgan and insisted upon my staying with them. All round here is full of RAF and evacuees. Was told of one little boy who had been in bad raids in London who threw himself flat at the sound of the first plane overhead.

Pam Ashford

Discomfort yesterday, increasing during the night, prepared me to find that yet again I have my inside upset. I did not mention it at home till the evening when Mother said that every day this week the milk had been thick in the morning. Of course, I believe the widespread trouble is due to stale milk. In the Sunday paper there was a statement that in the large Scottish cities there was much sub-health, attributable to deficiencies of vitamins A and C, and that rheumatism and stomach ailments were rife.

I went on to the Army exhibition at Queen's Park Recreation Ground. At 1.30 things were quiet and I went through 'War in the Jungle' and 'Mountain Warfare'.

'Jungle Warfare' is a shed fitted up like Jungle with tropical vegetation from which (stuffed) monkeys hung, and with (model) birds (brightly coloured) on the boughs. It was dark, lighted by coloured lights cunningly placed. In the trees were model soldiers and real guns. Overhead a gramophone record was producing the song of tropical birds (raucously).

SUNDAY, 6 AUGUST

Edward Stebbing

A marvellous batch of news today: the whole Brittany peninsula cut off, the Russians fighting in Prussia, Florence captured. If it wasn't for the 'doodlebugs' there would not be much to worry about.

Later. Although all this morning's news was not strictly true – the Russians being not yet in Prussia and Florence not fully in our hands – these events are probably so near as makes no difference. I and two other men were talking about the general situation. One of them said, 'I don't think the end is far off.' He thought the Normandy front was the most important. The other man said, 'Well, I hope old Joe Stalin gets to Berlin first. Our people would be too soft with 'em.'

MONDAY, 7 AUGUST

Edward Stebbing
'What's the betting Hitler won't use gas?' my friend K said to me this morning. I said I doubted whether he would use it over here, but he might use it against our troops. Somebody else remarked on the possibility of gas-containing rockets being sent over.

Ernest van Someren
Bank Holiday. We went on our cycles to Balls Park, Hertford, to a horse show and gymkhana. There should have been paratroops dropped there, but they didn't. There were side-shows, not much fun, and the bar was open all day and extremely crowded.

TUESDAY, 8 AUGUST

Ernest van Someren
After work I went and gave a blood transfusion. Collection is being done in Hoddesdon for the first time today and they called on my wife for the fourth time, me for the first. I was surprised at how simple and undisturbing it was, and felt no after-effects except a stiff elbow for three hours.

SUNDAY, 13 AUGUST

Ernest van Someren
Home, pottered about with garden jobs in the morning after a fairly quiet night. A lazy rest after lunch, then we took our tea out and the pram, to the edge of some cornfields where we gleaned a little. Julia was stung by a wasp, but lightly, and I sucked it vigorously so that the pain soon went off. We played hide and seek with L. While K put them to bed I went and had a swim at Carol Morrison's, alone. She has nine cats now.

TUESDAY, 15 AUGUST

Pam Ashford
As forewarned, I have not written for a week. The new page starts at Eyemouth – the fortnight's holiday, for which sake the other fifty weeks become endurable. The guests at our boarding house, Gunsgreen, come from Scotland and Newcastle chiefly. People are obviously wondering, 'What will they do on the day the war stops?' People mostly want to take the end of the war quietly.

WEDNESDAY, 16 AUGUST

Pam Ashford

Speaking for myself I have found the invasion of South France outstanding news. Mrs Turnbull (Newcastle) at teatime said, 'After this war it will be exactly the same as after the last war. The dole. Why, in Newcastle there are already long queues waiting to draw the dole.'

The fact is, of course, that most people are working longer hours. Wages representing those longer hours are taken by the Government as Income Tax and you are back where you started.

This morning a soldier on leave came and sat beside me and another 1½ hours fled. Personally I preferred his talk, as on a more human, if lower plane. He was a fisherman who went into the army five years ago. He is an AA gunner at Dorset and has come here for three days' leave. The soldier is spending his holiday in fact gutting herrings for his uncle and cousin (with whom he is staying). Herring, herring, herring. Kipper, kipper, kipper. He spoke of lovely greasy ones that you did not need to put fat in the frying pan for. Certainly the people here do not share the general dislike for this fish – but between the bones and its fattiness, the dislike has justification. Mother and I cannot but remark on the large numbers of obese fisherwomen here, and I am sure it is this excessive eating of herring.

THURSDAY, 17 AUGUST

Pam Ashford

This is the fifth full day of our holiday and I have given no account of what we do. The answer is feed and loaf. Loafing and feeding, feeding and loafing! Have I done anything else? Yes. I have read a novel. I brought Hardy's *Return of the Native*. I read it in 1924. It went to my head then. I *had* to read all his important novels and for years you could not mention Hardy to me without my pulse quickening. Many's the time I have said that he was the greatest English novelist. Yet my reaction was different this time. As a picture of rural life I enjoyed it intensely. I liked the rustics and the descriptions of nature best. They both were real. But it seemed to me that the language in which the characters spoke was artificial.

FRIDAY, 18 AUGUST

Edward Stebbing

'Best news we've had. I think this *is* the beginning of the end,' said one man today, regarding the merciless destruction of the German army in Normandy.

This evening I saw my first flying bomb by daylight. I had a good view of it, as it passed almost overhead. Seeing it, I felt almost the same as I imagine a savage must feel on seeing an aeroplane for the first time, a kind of awe and fascination, but no fear, because I could see it was going over (and, in fact, it flew out of hearing). With its cross-shaped body and flames coming out of its tail it seemed like something supernatural and malevolent, a strange fiery symbol, an evil apparition.

Ernest van Someren

Very good news this morning, but we had three local alerts during the day's work. After work I went for a swim at the Morrison garden with Mary Lawton. We had supper in the garden, Mary sat with us, and afterwards I only had the energy to do a little watering.

WEDNESDAY, 23 AUGUST

Edward Stebbing

The liberation of Paris gives one a kind of exaltation. I am rather surprised that the French people managed to get rid of the Germans themselves, but the fact that they did makes it more pleasing still, for the Germans must have been weak to give in to the citizens of Paris. This act is in the greatest French tradition; surely it will rank with the barricading of Paris and the storming of the Bastille. One feels that events are moving swiftly; our armies will race through France and will soon menace Germany itself. We, who have had to bear the ordeal of flying bombs, hope that the territory from which they are launched will soon be overrun.

THURSDAY, 24 AUGUST

Pam Ashford

At 7am I overheard the wireless in the family quarters and thought that Roumania had capitulated. It turns out that the BBC had given this 10.30pm last night and that the din had subsided enough for most of the guests to hear the news, which had caused them excitement.

Mr Turnbull said in Newcastle it is possible to swindle Americans by selling them bottles of whisky that is really cold tea. The Americans there (as in Glasgow) spend money freely on whisky. Mrs Turnbull dislikes the Americans. 'It is them that has led our lads wrong.' Mr Brown is another person who dislikes them. 'Playboys over here for a holiday, while our boys are fighting.' Petrol restrictions was his complaint. They have high-speed cars that drink petrol and they think nothing of taking the car out just to buy a box of cigarettes.

TUESDAY, 29 AUGUST

Pam Ashford

It is difficult to judge the flying bomb stories. I think it is possibly this, that the people who can't stand flying bombs bolt into the provinces and spread these tales, whereas the Londoners who don't mind the bombs much stay behind and their views don't get anything like the same publicity.

Having expressed that view in the office I quite unexpectedly got confirmation from Mrs Blane. Her brother, who used to feel very bad about them, now takes no notice. 'You get used to the idea that in the next minute you may be dead, and having got used to the idea it does not trouble you any longer,' was Mrs Blane's report on her brother's sentiments. He and a fellow sergeant, she said, were in Oxford or Regent Street looking in a shop window. A bomb, which had its engine stopped and had drifted a long way thereafter, fell beside them. They saw it falling and darting for cover (for which there was none), it came about that they were standing each in front of a different plate glass window. Her brother's plate glass window fell inwards, a small splinter entered his hand and, being jammed there, his hand did not bleed. The other plate glass window was loosened in its frame but not broken. It just sagged outwards and the fellow-sergeant held it up with his hands, gently lowering it to the ground. In point of fact he had had a hit from a piece of glass from her brother's window, which had cut his uniform and was stuck in his shoulder. He was so excited about holding up the plate glass that he was alongside of that he never noticed his injured shoulder. So her brother and the sergeant then went up to one another and both said, 'I'm all right, how are you?' 'Oh, I'm fine,' and they walked away, but only for fifty yards, when the fellow-sergeant quite suddenly lost consciousness and without a hint of anything wrong just fell on the pavement at her brother's feet. It was a shock.

FRIDAY, 1 SEPTEMBER

Edward Stebbing

The terrifically swift British advance to Amiens and the promotion of General Montgomery to Field Marshal are the two most exciting items of news today. 'You can't keep pace with it,' a man said of the advance.

Pam Ashford

Listening to the 8pm news I just could not believe my ears. Each item seemed better than the one before, it was the sort of thing that might happen in a dream, but in real life, it seemed as if it could not be true.

Reading her paper at 5pm, Miss Sinclair said, 'This paper will be out of date by the 9 o'clock news. It says here that the war is moving so fast that by the time Head Quarters gets to know the news, the news is already stale.'

Oh yes, we are all feeling very happy, and all of us following the news, and studying the maps.

SUNDAY, 3 SEPTEMBER

Edward Stebbing

The fifth anniversary of the outbreak of war. Looking back, my main feeling is one of awe at the huge panorama of events which we have lived through. What a lot of things have happened, to me personally and to people in general. In the comparative safety of what I feel to be the last weeks of the war, I can say that I would not have missed it for anything. (No doubt, if I had been in the battle-line I would not say that.) During these five years we have run the whole gamut of emotions, have seen human nature at its most naked. We have had to put up with many unpleasant things and now we feel that our patience and fortitude have been rewarded. Today the news is better than ever – Finland out of the war, Allied armies on Germany's doorstep, a new offensive begun in Italy, the Red Army preparing for its final attack. Victory is in the air.

MONDAY, 4 SEPTEMBER

Pam Ashford

The feeling of elation is growing markedly. At 2.30 both Miss Lamberton and Miss Sinclair reported that their respective mothers had heard on the 1 o'clock news that Brussels had fallen. Miss Sinclair stated, 'We shall next be hearing that Antwerp has fallen.'

Sure enough, when John brought up the papers that was the latest.

In opening the new session of Soroptomist Club, Miss Walker, President, contrasted last September with no sign of an early conclusion, and 'This September, when we may think of the war ending in a matter of, shall we say, weeks?' – someone called 'Days'.

Ernest van Someren
After work I went to see the doctor, then to a stranger's house where I bought a second-hand doll's pram, which we had located by 'phone. It cost 35/- and was quite nice. Recently I saw one advertised in the *Times* for £10. Julia is delighted with it, and most grateful. We slept upstairs.

TUESDAY, 5 SEPTEMBER

Edward Stebbing
My landlady said victory must be near because several products are being sold in red, white and blue packets. She had a packet of starch substitute with a Union Jack on it and the admonition 'Buy British Goods', a slogan which has been missing throughout the war, because it has been unnecessary, and now seems premature. The other day my landlady had a large rib of beef from the butcher's, a joint which she had not had since the beginning of the war and which, she said, was a sign that the war was nearly over.

Pam Ashford
Mother was quite excited at 1.15, telling me that the Allies were in Luxembourg. During the afternoon there was a rumour that Germany had capitulated – it was received with utter disbelief in our room. From the talk it is certain that the British Nation – the element here, at least – is determined to defeat Germany inside Germany this time. I could not help thinking of the saying that the British never know when they are defeated – it would seem that the British never know when they are victors, either, but want to go on still. There was talk about the way we shall get to know that the war has ended. 'Over the wireless they will say "Stand by for an important announcement" and keep us all on tiptoes until they think everyone in the country is listening.' (Personally I don't think it will happen that way – I think we shall get the news largely by word of mouth. The press and the radio will begin to announce it, and everyone as he gets to know will run to tell his neighbours.) 'I shan't believe it until it is given over the wireless', 'Oh, I should not trust a newspaper' – such were the comments. I said, 'The Government, I think, envisages

454

everyone taking a couple of days' holiday.' In reply it was said that no one would be fit to come in the next day. There is talk galore about celebrating the victory in wine and whisky – with many references to meringues – I don't know why that particular war cake is favoured over other delicacies. There is unbounded confidence in a very speedy conclusion. Japan does not seem to come into anyone's ideas.

Elaine is having a week's holiday at Skelmorlie at her grandfather's house. She went, bemoaning the impossibility of getting 'clicks' (flirtations) there. The office, however, thinks Elaine will manage to get off somehow. Is it generally felt that she is quite out of hand. 'It is because of the war,' Miss Sinclair explains. 'It will be a good thing when she gets into the army, she lacks discipline. They will cut her hair for a start. Her parents have no control over her. She wants a sergeant major to train her. She thinks of nothing but the boys.'

Elaine during her week wrote that at Skelmorlie, there were nothing but cows and sheep, and sheep and cows, and she was going nuts.

WEDNESDAY, 6 SEPTEMBER

Pam Ashford
I had noticed that Miss Dunn (Hyndland draper) and Copland and Lye (Sauchiehall Street) had red, white and blue ribbons. In the office they are saying that Coplands are advertising their red, white and blue ribbons. They say that when victory comes there will be a shortage – so we should buy now.

If peace is not just round the corner . . . but, of course, it is . . . what a flop! The prospect is bringing life into our oh-so-weary souls, we are growing gay again. Nevertheless, the quietness with which we take these stupendous events is almost uncanny. Everyone knows that we are a nation that takes its pleasures 'sadly', but the horrors we have prepared against – and which have not come to Glasgow at any rate – have sobered us still more.

Edward Stebbing
Heard a woman say, 'The gas-man said it will be over in ten days.'

Ernest van Someren
This afternoon Kay came home with the children and found our French window broken again, a large bottom pane, rumpled rugs in the hall and a dog collar on the floor. Later a woman called to ask if her dog had left a collar somewhere here, she said he was keen on cats, so we supposed he tried to chase ours, through a window. She

has offered to pay for it, but glass is scarce round here and it takes a long time to get it replaced. Listened in to the BBC symphony concert in the evening.

THURSDAY, 7 SEPTEMBER

Edward Stebbing
The lifting of the black-outs is as though the chains of imprisonment have been thrown off. For so long we have been forced to grope about in darkness at night that at first the light seemed strange and unnatural. One man said, half-jokingly, 'For years afterwards we shall have a feeling of fear when we switch out a light, a feeling of being haunted.'

Pam Ashford
Before taking up my pen tonight, I asked Mother her views. 'Oh, what is the use of my view? I am nobody,' I said, '*Your* view's no use! You? A representative housewife?' She said, 'The end of the war will mean a new life. I want to see the end of the queues. I want to be able to go into a shop and buy what I want, without being told "For registered customers only".' I said, 'Like the dates at Lennie's this afternoon.' She said, 'Yes, no more queues and the end of the black-out.' The home feels happier tonight.

Mrs Blane read us an interesting letter from her husband. He has been moving forward through France very rapidly. The French shower them with flowers and apples, but he has had no kisses. The French villages have suffered little damage. He paid high tribute to the Maquis in preparing the way, and hopes that when the war is over full credit will be given them. The Germans are very nervous. They found one German body with upstretched arms, one hand clutching a sheet of white paper. They thought the Maquis had shot him as he was seeking surrender. At any rate, someone had removed the boots from his dead body. In that particular village the Germans had shot a large number of hostages, and the hatred of the villagers was terrible.

The canary, after weeks of sulks, is amiability itself and ready to receive such adulation as you like to give him. Still, with him, it is more likely the end of the moult than the end of the war.

FRIDAY, 8 SEPTEMBER

Pam Ashford

Only rarely have I made a close friendship with a member of the opposite sex. Mr Mitchell is an outstanding example. But one came in pre-diary days, viz. Max Towers. A paragraph in the newspaper early in the war gave me the idea he was engaged in civil defence, and a chance encounter at the Forth and Clyde with a commercial traveller who knew him confirmed that. Last winter I met Max on a bus, dressed in his civil defence uniform. What a happy encounter. He came from Bishopbriggs, so I asked Miss Sinclair, and *of course* she knew Max and his wife Betty. Also about the civil defence job. Today she says with the reduction of the civil defence staff, people like Max Towers will be put into the Forces. I said, 'Max could never fit into the Forces. He dreads blood.' She said, 'Plenty of others do.' I said, 'Max could not take life. He would not mind risking his own to save others.'

Miss Sinclair: 'So the war did not end on the second hour of the such and such day after such and such an occurrence' – some prediction that John the office boy has been predicting as infallible, and which is now past.

Ernest van Someren

In the evening my friend Lucas, one of the men who lunches with me daily, came up to see our Japanese sake cups, and was very interested in the collection. He is an accountant, who shares my interest in statistical methods.

SUNDAY, 10 SEPTEMBER

Edward Stebbing

Went to a concert given by a symphony orchestra formed by employees of a local aircraft factory. It was a very laudable performance, though they attempted some works which are too difficult for a young orchestra and there was a very poor audience which must have been discouraging for the orchestra. Being at the concert, I did not hear the gunfire which other people heard and which, we learned later, was coming from the French side of the Channel.

Pam Ashford

When I got home at 10.30, I found Charlie taking down the black-out curtains. The blinds will do now. Mother was fairly dancing about with joy. Both of them feel much more strongly than I do about the black-out. What are we to do with the curtains now? We never want them up again as curtains. I think they could be cut down for knickers, and we would get enough pairs to last us both for twenty years.

MONDAY, 11 SEPTEMBER

Pam Ashford
Today the Soroptomist Club had a business meeting. A movement to 'Save the Children' of Europe has raised its head, and we are asked to send a representative to an inaugural meeting, which representative will go on the committee. We are letting the appeal lie on the table, wishing our money for this other cause.

Dr Stevenson, when in London, received information that when Children's Allowances are introduced, the Government is going to make them payable to fathers, not the mothers. Each individual Soroptomist is being asked to protest to her MP, so that the thing will not slip through without being noticed.

Mrs Muir repeated what Judge van Someren said about the Channel Islanders being tricked into giving the Nazi raised hand. At a meeting they had been told, 'Everyone who can speak English raise his arm.' All did. A film was shown in Germany of the Channel Islanders giving the Nazi salute.

Mrs Froud said that Wodehouse was in Paris and justifying himself. 'He wanted his friends to know where he was.' No one could remember what it was he had said. I said, 'He said he was staying at a comfortable hotel, well fed and quite happy.' They said, 'What was wrong with saying that?' Well, as I had put it, it did not seem very wrong, though at the time I had known it was. The table said it was because he had been on the Nazi wavelength giving out propaganda.

TUESDAY, 12 SEPTEMBER

Pam Ashford
Miss Sinclair (Girls Training Corps) reported that the janitor at the school is convinced that the war will end on 15th October, going on and laughing, 'We should draw up a list of all the dates we hear.' I myself am banking heavily on 9th October, my birthday. Almost immediately after she said, 'So we are in Germany – before the Russians.' Item after item of the 8am news was repeated by the various members of the room. The air attack on Germany – with figures.

Soon we were off again – this time on demobilisation. Miss

Sinclair: 'The demobilisation plans are not ready yet. It is hoped the war won't end too soon. They are to be out next month. Whatever they are, there will be an outcry.' Mrs Blane: 'First in, first out.' Miss Mackinnon: 'It depends on *where* they are. Married men with families – what about you, Mrs Blane?' Mrs Blane: 'I cannot manage that now. Let the men without families out first so that they can do something about it.' Miss Mackinnon: 'They are crying out about the birth rate, but it is higher now.' Miss Sinclair: 'It is the wrong kind who are having the babies.'

Edward Stebbing
About four days ago there was a big explosion in the evening which shook our house and was heard at several widely scattered places. Since then I have heard various rumours about its cause, the most popular being that a munitions factory or a gasworks blew up. Several agree, however, that it took place at Chiswick. Early this morning there was another explosion, which I didn't hear, but which has set everybody talking. People are beginning to think that these explosions were due to the German V2 weapons, probably rocket-bombs. It seems quite likely, but if so, why have they not been more frequent? They are rockets which travel at 800mph, she said. One left a crater 17 feet deep. Five came over last night. Stories are spreading, all somewhat vague, but one thing is certain: there have been several unexplained explosions, too frequent to be gasworks or munitions dumps blowing up.

Ernest van Someren
Before breakfast, in a Mendelssohn broadcast the announcer mentioned 'The Bees Wedding', and Laurie said, 'I wonder if one of the bees took photographs, like Daddy did at the wedding here?'

WEDNESDAY, 13 SEPTEMBER

Pam Ashford
Miss Sinclair's brother has seen a letter from someone in London saying that the V2 bombs – 10 ton rocket bombs – are already falling there.

Miss Sinclair referred to a man 'when he came back from the last war, he got a good job', as if this was extraordinary. I said, 'The post-war boom lasted into 1921. If Government control remains firm, the post-war boom this time could be spread over a much longer time. In fact, I have great faith in Mr Churchill's 4 year plans.'

THURSDAY, 14 SEPTEMBER

Pam Ashford
A woman was sitting on a tram. The passenger beside her said, 'Will you let me pay your fare?' Looking at him, she found he was a Chinese. She said, 'Why should you pay my fare?' He said, 'Because you have left your handbag at home.' She found that she had done so. She said, 'How do you know that?' He said, 'I have second sight.' She said, 'Then tell me where I have left it.' The Chinaman said, 'It fell on the bedroom floor.' She said, 'Since you have second sight, when will the war end?' He said, '26th October.'

On reaching home, she found the handbag on the floor.

SUNDAY, 17 SEPTEMBER

Edward Stebbing
First night without black-out. The effect was a little disappointing in our neighbourhood, but not so much as to be insignificant. Coming home at about 10.45 I saw only a few scattered lights, but even these gave some relief to the darkness, hinted at better things to come. When I got home I found that my landlady, though dispensing with the boards which used to black-out my bedroom, had put up the thick curtains as well as drawing the thinner ones, because, she said, 'The thin curtains don't come right across.' I found, however, that they could just be made to cover the windows and took the thick curtains down.

MONDAY, 18 SEPTEMBER

Pam Ashford
Thousands of Glaswegians must have gone into the city to see the lights on last night. In fact the word 'illuminations' has been used seriously and without consciousness of exaggeration. At 8 o'clock we had looked out of the window at the standard lamps in Hyndland Road, and Mother with disgust had declared that they were the same as last year. They looked the same – perhaps they were. It has been said that the dim-out is to raise morale. There is no doubt that the black-out was the wartime inconvenience most disliked.

Edward Stebbing
Mr B talking about the dim-out, as it is now, said he saw only one or two bright lights last night. 'I don't think it will make much difference. People haven't got alternative curtains,' he said. Another man said, 'I felt a bit guilty with the light on.'

WEDNESDAY, 20 SEPTEMBER

Edward Stebbing
Spent most of the day exploring the cliffs and beaches at Newquay. Weather excellent, sunny all day.

I have struck lucky with my hotel. The food is splendid, almost more than I can eat and of the best quality. The room is comfortable and well furnished, the people are pleasant, and the house is only about three minutes from the sea. But it is a pity the black-out is not lifted here.

Pam Ashford
The terribleness of the modern girl is a subject of which I am never likely to lose sight, for Elaine – and particularly by Miss Sinclair – is constantly being held up as a horrible example. I am fond of Elaine, though. She brings life and laughter to the place. Mrs Blane said to me, 'She is flighty. She talks about "luv", but does not know what love is.' However, Dorothy Lamberton looks like being passed into the same class of undesirable – being a modern girl of 23. This time it was Mrs Blane who raised the subject, and she is not difficult to please. Dorothy spent a day reading a new book from Mrs Blane's desk and returned it with the corners turned in and a page torn out.

SATURDAY, 23 SEPTEMBER

Edward Stebbing
Some of the other guests were talking about the American troops at breakfast-time, generally deploring their lack of civility, and I was rather surprised to hear one woman say, and the others agree, that the black Americans are much nicer than the white ones.

MONDAY, 25 SEPTEMBER

Pam Ashford
There has been a fair amount of comment on the Beveridge Report, I should say the Government White Paper. A year ago people were commenting on the benefits, now they are looking at the costs. People say that private superannuation schemes as well as life assurance will come to an end. Employers – and employees – won't be able to afford both. A workman said that large engineering firms will reduce their staffs, as they won't be able to pay out such large sums as insurance. Along with these comments are congratulatory remarks, 'Social security is what we need.' 'This will buck up the troops no end.'

Kelvingrove's latest exhibition was opened in mid-August, just about the same day as the Glasgow rates advance, and there were many facetious comments thereupon. There was a large attendance but it was possible to see everything.

Transport: Model (hypothetical) housing scheme with trams (1) using bridges at cross roads, (2) using tunnels in the streets, (3) using a roundabout. Models and tram, bus and airplane of the future. Air transport – maps of Atlantic routes. Model of Prestwick airport.

Gas: (1) Chemical – bottles showing how crude tar is broken up, (2) crude benzole assay, (3) industrial uses of gas – photographs, 5 gas-ovens, 3 dated 1910, 1939, 1944. Refrigerators. (1) built-in, (2) silent. Freezing by gas plant. Gas radiators. Circulators. Ascot water boiler.

Electricity: Electric blanket, iron, clock, lamps, hoover, 4 electric ovens, water heater, small oven for one, laundry equipment, refrigerator.

Police: Exhibit of knives, cleavers, daggers, etc., with which various Glasgow murders have been done, including a piece of flooring with the murderer's footprint in blood. Knuckle dusters and ingenious razor slashers.

Edward Stebbing
At a little village near Newquay I saw a notice calling a public meeting to appoint a committee 'to raise funds for the Welcome Home and the Peace Celebrations', which I thought a little premature.

A strange shortage of sweets about here.

TUESDAY, 26 SEPTEMBER

Ernest van Someren
To the Royal Photographic Society for a quick look round at the annual exhibition, on dried emulsions.

WEDNESDAY, 27 SEPTEMBER

Edward Stebbing
One rather obscure point about the Government's social insurance plan is how it affects medical treatment. If everybody is to be included in the insurance scheme, then everybody will be entitled to free medical treatment. Yet previously the Government stated that doctors can still keep their private practice under a State medical service. The new plan seems to be inserting the thin end of the wedge of State control behind the doctors' backs. I think it is a good thing,

but what will the doctors have to say? No doubt the big insurance companies will put up a lot of opposition, too.

Pam Ashford
This is very bad news from Arnhem. I rather think that the diminution in talk about the war means that people don't want to talk about bad news, and that last week there was an apprehension that the airborne troops would be cut off.

Ernest van Someren
Tom Griffiths dropped in, he has done me another poster for the WEA lectures. He stayed and talked till 10.30 when he politely asked if he ought to go, and was told truthfully that it was our usual bedtime. He and I were starting a general discussion about art and religion and the meaning of life, so of course we hadn't finished it.

THURSDAY, 28 SEPTEMBER

Pam Ashford
The news from Arnhem is unfortunate. It has received little open reference, but clearly stirs up considerable feeling – how could it be otherwise. A leading theme is pity for the suffering and endurance of the 8000. Most people seem to believe that the 3000 or 4000 unaccounted for in the figures given must be killed – not prisoners. People are calling them our best forces. I said comparing our losses with the German losses, our figures did not seem very great. I am told, 'If your man were one, the British losses would seem great.' As a result of the news the almost universal belief that the war in Europe would be over in a few weeks is ended.

SATURDAY, 30 SEPTEMBER

Edward Stebbing
Last day of my holiday, probably the best I have ever spent. This was largely because it is the first visit I have ever made to Cornwall, and Newquay stands in what must be one of the loveliest stretches of coast in Britain. There was an abundance of places to see and marvel at. But also it was because I escaped from the war to a great extent. Here there was plenty of good food (in spite of rationing), no sirens, no doodlebugs, pleasant company, little talk about the war, no fire watching to do. Only the presence of a few English and American troops and wounded soldiers, the newspapers and the black-out reminded me of the war. Of course, there were other signs, as

everywhere, such as fantastic prices in the shops (25/- for sunglasses, for instance), poor travel facilities, stretches of barbed wire, etc, but we are now so used to these relatively minor, or less conspicuous, signs that they no longer seem special to wartime conditions.

Ernest van Someren
We cycled back to the river and down the towpath to Maidenhead, past the lovely woods of Cliveden. Then inland to Burnham Beeches, which we found full of army vehicles.

TUESDAY, 3 OCTOBER

Pam Ashford
Mr McDonald is anxious to apply for a vacancy as assistant to the General Manager of the Glasgow Transport System. He said a fortnight ago a strike was threatened because the bonus for driving through the black-out was to be withdrawn. To avert the strike the Transport Department continues to pay black-out bonus in dim-out.

THURSDAY, 5 OCTOBER

Edward Stebbing
At lunchtime today several anti-Semitic remarks were passed, or rather anti-foreigner remarks. 'What fools we were to have them (refugees),' said one man, who later asked what were Captain Ramsay's activities before he was imprisoned. Another man said he (Ramsay) had a club whose slogan was 'Britain for the British'. 'Well, can't we join?' was the rejoinder. This kind of feeling is undoubtedly growing, as is the desire for harsh treatment of Germany after the war. I, too, am more in favour of stern measures in dealing with Germany than I was, but my chief motto is still 'Live and let live'.

FRIDAY, 6 OCTOBER

Pam Ashford
Elaine is 18 next month. She has hitherto expressed satisfaction with the progress of the war, which looked like ending in time to save her from national service. The outlook of the community has completely changed since the Arnhem setback and Elaine's mind sways between volunteering for something or waiting till she is called and having no choice. One minute she says she wants the Wrens, another the WAAFs. We don't discourage her by mentioning that these two are particular as to whom they take in and that most girls find there is

only the Army. Elaine does not want Industry. Miss Sinclair is recommending her to go into the Exchange and ask what there is that she can volunteer for, but not to sign anything. Elaine has been making enquiries from a girl in nursing and has a depressing view of that. This nurse is at Strathavon. The patients are fed well, but the nurses badly. The nurses have cabbage water instead of soup. The potatoes are boiled in their skins and then mashed, so you swallow the skins. The potatoes are only peeled when someone has been put on that job as punishment. This nurse said no one could imagine what the casualties are like. You need to see them. An ambulance train arrived at Strathavon with 500 men straight from the battlefield, still dirty from the battle. Everyone had a part of his body missing. Mines blow off a man's leg. The men are like children and cry.

SUNDAY, 8 OCTOBER

Pam Ashford
I got up early – 10.30, and put in a walk from 11.15 to 1.15. This was to let me have the afternoon indoors, so as to hear Yehudi Menuhin. I got out the knickers to Bartok's concerto – which I knew would be incomprehensible having heard a previous broadcast. Then I got some diary done in the 45-minute interval. Then Mendelssohn's Violin Concerto – Yehudi Menuhin is wonderful.

Ernest van Someren
Went out to church in Hoddesdon at 9.55, to a small service arranged for conference delegates, taken by the Vicar of Hoddesdon with the Broxbourne vicar giving the address. Then on to the Hostel, where I gave them the morning talk on 'Youth Councils and the Community', a subject which I treated rather widely, leading from the reciprocal influences of the individual and the local community to the conception of the world as potentially one big community.

After tea Faith van Someren rang from London, then came out by train to stay with us for a few days. We had supper and spent the evening talking about her troubles with George Hysketh, her lover, who has been neglecting her lately. He now says that his wife has refused to divorce him, and Faith has been trying to make up her mind to give him up.

MONDAY, 9 OCTOBER

Edward Stebbing

The stiff German resistance on all fronts is tending to disillusion those, like myself, who thought the war would be over this year.

Pam Ashford

My date for V-day, simply because it is my birthday. Somewhere about 26th September I said, 'The Sunday papers have always stressed that if we were not into Germany by the end of September it was doubtful if the war could end this autumn. October is too uncertain a month in regard to weather.' In fact the community is settling down to another winter of war.

Miss Sinclair referred to a statement of John Hilton that only 4 million families out of 12 million in this country possessed between them more than £100 capital. The statement both intrigued and mystified us. Mr McDonald said, 'Going into the Home Guard brought me right up against a type of man I had never met before. These fellows have never had any money till the war. Now they have big pay packets. They save nothing. Night after night they get foul (drunk).' The suggestion was made that some of the former poor were saving now. Mr McDonald said, 'I doubt if any of the poor souls will have anything left 2 years after the war. All their savings will be used up during unemployment.' Complete assent.

WEDNESDAY, 11 OCTOBER

Maggie Joy Blunt

Life at work is all shamefully 'cushy' but I don't know what to do about it. I sit back watching events and personalities, fascinated. Our Production programme has been greatly decreased. Shops are closed and men turned out by the 100 (they say there are over 1000 unemployed in Slough now – Labour Exchange has no work to offer them).

Attended a meeting with Sir George Schuster on 'Can We Afford the Peace?' His speech followed the theme of several of his recently published articles on the same subject – that is, that we can afford the peace if we work for it – we must concentrate on increasing our industrial productivity, make plans for industry at home first so that full use is made of our natural resources and industrialists should come forward to the Government with their own plans.

I read somewhere the view that the change from war to peace would be so gradual we should hardly notice it. It will not be something definite and spectacular like lights up, bananas for all, unlimited fully fashioned real silk stockings at 2/6d a pair and everyone with a job they like and able to afford their own plot and bungalow. Recent relaxation on black-out restrictions has made very little difference in this area at least. One occasionally passes a house with lights showing through the curtains, but there is hardly any street lighting and what there is, motorists tell me, makes driving worse rather than better. In the cottage I am no better off – the kitchen windows never had curtains and I am certainly not spending coupons to get material now or go to all the bother of having them made and fixed, and the same applies to the small window in the sitting room which has always had only net curtains. So the black-out screens go up as usual and the thick curtains, still tacked to the walls at the side, are drawn, but perhaps not quite so carefully. There is not the same urgency, either, to turn out the kitchen light when the back door is opened. Think a great many people feel as I do – they have got so used to their black-out arrangements that to change them at this uncertain stage of the war is more trouble than it is worth.

Spent my day off last week shopping in London – searching for a jumper for my new coral red suit. (At friends that evening all the women were wearing red. A feeling abroad that one must get into something cheerful – one is so tired of greys and neutral useful colours.)

Lunched in D.H. Evans self-service room – rather uninteresting scrambled egg, tomato, potatoes and stringy beans, blancmange and coffee. But it was quick. Saw *Lady in the Dark* (Ginger Rogers).

Pam Ashford
Someone said – and there was general assent – 'that whatever the Germans were, they were good fighters'. Next, 'When this war is over, they will start preparing for the next.' 'We should do the same.' 'It is natural to fight . . . fighting goes right through human nature.' 'Look at the quarrels in the Church.' 'There will never be an end to war.' 'The third war is inevitable.' Mrs Blane: 'Let us finish this war and have a rest in between.' Miss Mackinnon: 'Let us hope that the third war will not start till we are 60.' Miss Sinclair: 'They can keep the Beveridge Plan. We shan't be needing our old age pensions' (i.e. we will be killed in the third war).

THURSDAY, 12 OCTOBER

Ernest van Someren
There was a V2 rocket at Walthamstow during the night, which fell in the garden of one of the secretaries at our works. Their house has

been slightly damaged twice before, and is now quite uninhabitable, with the roof off and some walls down. The girl and her mother sleeping in a Morrison shelter were unhurt, no one was killed but several injured.

SATURDAY, 14 OCTOBER

Edward Stebbing
Went home for the weekend. Between Liverpool Street and Stratford I noticed, from the train, fresh destruction along the grimy houses which line the railway, probably due to flying bombs, possibly to rockets. Always an ugly part of London, it looked even uglier now, but somehow those rooftops, church spires and factory chimneys seem so friendly that I could not help feeling sorry for the humble families who have been deprived of their homes.

In Chelmsford I had a haircut and tried to buy a copy of Somerset Maugham's latest novel, *The Razor's Edge*, which I had already tried to get, without success, in St Albans, but with an equal lack of success. New books go out of print very quickly now. I am now reading *Kilvert's Diary*, which I had bought as an alternative to Maugham's book. This is a delightful diary and I am very pleased to have it.

SUNDAY, 15 OCTOBER

Ernest van Someren
One alert and a P plane at Waltham Cross, near enough to the works to shake down a bit of one ceiling in the lab. Several people were killed, as it fell on a row of small houses.

WEDNESDAY, 18 OCTOBER

Edward Stebbing
Hearing the news that the Germans had begun to wipe out the Poles in their concentration camps, Mrs H said, 'They (the Germans) want exterminating. That's the only way to deal with them: do the same to them as they're doing to others.'

Rabbits (for eating) seem to be fairly plentiful now. I have had three or four meals of rabbit recently. We were having a supper of delicious stewed rabbit, potatoes, turnips and carrots tonight as the radio newsreader was telling us about the starvation in Greece.

Chapter Sixteen

WAS CHURCHILL SOBER THIS TIME?

Social security is what we need: the Beveridge Report gathers momentum during a by-election.

20 October 1944–26 January 1945

20 October General MacArthur returns to the Philippines with 600 ships; partisans and Russians free Belgrade.

24 October Huge naval battle around the Philippines involving 282 warships.

30 October Cologne under heavy attack by RAF bombers.

5 November Zionist Stern Gang terrorists assassinate the British minister Lord Moyne in Cairo.

8 November Roosevelt wins fourth presidential term.

10 November Members of the Red Cross have a guided tour of Auschwitz, but are shielded from the atrocities.

12 November The *Tirpitz* finally sunk in Tromso Fjord by Lancaster bombers.

25 November 160 die and 200 are injured when a V2 bomber hits Woolworth's and other shops in South London.

28 November A government white paper reports that in the last five years Britain produced 102,600 warplanes, 25,000 tanks and 722 warships; one civilian has been killed for every three in the forces, and one in three homes have been damaged.

15 December General MacArthur's troops land on Mindoro in the Philippines as part of the second phase of the invasion, but face resistance from kamikaze pilots.

16 December Germans launch effective counter-attack in the Ardennes, culminating in the Battle of the Bulge; General Patton liberates Bastogne ten days later.

5 January 1945 Construction begins on the first prefabricated homes in Britain.

12 January Red Army begins winter offensive at German positions in Poland and East Prussia.

17 January Warsaw falls to Red Army.

18 January Churchill warns Germany that surrender would save thousands of lives and mass destruction.

FRIDAY, 20 OCTOBER

Edward Stebbing

Riga, Athens, and now Belgrade – one by one the capitals of Europe are returning to their rightful owners. Budapest will probably be the next.

Listened to the Dutch Prime Minister describing the plight of Holland, beset by flood and famine, threatened with epidemics, its people massacred and deported by the Germans. I felt overwhelmed with pity. Why do such things have to be? Poor suffering world, filled with misery and destruction when there is no need for it.

Pam Ashford

The pair of breeks I am making out of the scraps of stuff from a dress made in 1925 are almost finished. Really I am proud of them, for they involved joining nine pieces of stuff together. My summer knickers are in rags. However, the four new cotton pairs I have made during the last two months will be a boon next summer. A Sunday newspaper was commenting on girls putting lipstick kisses on their letters. I have seen Elaine do this. It is said to be common.

Last Monday Dorothy Lamberton reported that she will be getting married at her friend's next leave, in January probably. He is buying her underclothing in Iceland.

Ernest van Someren

A quiet night, to work by train again. In the evening went to a meeting of the Psychology Club to hear the Congregational Minister talk about the psychology of conscience. It was the third of a series of three talks, to an audience of only 7 as he is not a very good speaker.

SATURDAY, 21 OCTOBER

Pam Ashford

I went to the Dolcis shoe shop. They had a pair of shoes that fitted me at 55/6 so I took them. Is not that a dreadful price to pay! They have leather heels and I think they will wear. There were 12 assistants standing about, no other customers and I should think not more than 12 boxes of shoes on the shelves. The downstairs section is closed.

After lunch I went to the Art Galleries to hear Mr Hannah speak on 'Art Appreciation, can it be acquired?'.

TUESDAY, 24 OCTOBER

Ernest van Someren
Another P plane passed over low in the night, so that we got up and supported the children while it burst, which it did near enough to break the glass in our front door. We later heard that it was about a mile away in the woods again. Hastily put some linoleum in the front door after breakfast, then went to work by train.

THURSDAY, 26 OCTOBER

Pam Ashford
The bill to enable British women married to Allied soldiers, etc., to divorce them in our Courts has come at a time when this theme is constantly being discussed. I heard of an instance in which a Pole and British girl wanted a Church of Scotland minister to marry them. The minister thought the Pole did not understand enough English to follow the marriage service and a few days before he had the man round and went through the service word by word with the Pole. In the course of this instruction the Pole revealed that he meant the marriage to last only so long as he was in this country.

Demobilisation is very much a subject to the fore, and Mr Churchill's statement to the House that grim fighting may lie ahead was timely. It is women whose husbands are in the Far and Middle East who are making the fuss, of course. I said that 'these women will be giving the Germans the idea that they can get off with a compromise peace'.

SATURDAY, 28 OCTOBER

Edward Stebbing
Spent an hour or so this afternoon looking round bookshops in Charing Cross Road. As usual, I saw about a dozen books I would have liked to buy, but had to be content with a cheap copy of Evelyn Waugh's novel, *Put Out More Flags*. In the Underground I saw a poster, quoting, in large letters, Nurse Edith Cavell's words 'I must bear no hatred in my heart', and I wondered who, in these days when it is thought rather unpatriotic not to hate the Germans, had caused the poster to be exhibited.

MONDAY, 30 OCTOBER

Edward Stebbing
We were listening to *Monday Night at Eight* when there was a fearful explosion, followed after a few seconds by another a little less loud. We were all pretty scared, but there were no more bangs, so we went outside and had a look. Mr and Mrs H thought it had been an enemy plane dropping bombs, but I thought, from the distinct double bang, that it was a rocket. A young man who lives next door said it was a rocket. He said that the two explosions were due to the fact that the rocket first exploded in the air and this explosion threw a warhead to the ground, which caused the second explosion.

WEDNESDAY, 1 NOVEMBER

Pam Ashford
Miss Page has a brother and sister-in-law up from London and they report a jet-propelled rocket, containing terrific explosive powers. They make craters which would bury two buses. Foundations shake for six miles radius. Unlike the doodlebugs – comparatively manageable nuisances – you don't hear the rockets coming. There is this tremendous bang. The shock with which they wake you is such that you cannot sleep again, your nerves are knocked to bits. One night (Saturday or Sunday last perhaps) seven came over London. Fortunately they are not numerous. One's nerves could not stand up to continual jet-propelled rockets. They come from an immense height, and being fired from aircraft from an unpredictable source, they come in unnoticed. I said, 'If Londoners feel like that about seven jet-propelled rockets, what is Cologne going to feel like over our air-raids?'

Edward Stebbing
With a good deal of speculation going on about when the next general election will be, I have been thinking about how I should vote and tentatively decided that the Liberal Party holds the most attraction at the moment. Strictly speaking I would prefer a more Socialist government, but both the Labour and Communist parties seem to me too weak and insincere to deserve support, while the Liberal Party has a vigorous and practical policy. Not long ago the Common Wealth Party appealed to me strongly, but it does not seem as if it will survive as a separate party, whereas the Liberal Party is firmly established and previous Liberal Governments have a good record. I would not dream of voting Conservative. Probably Sir

William Beveridge's entry into Parliament as a Liberal has helped to crystallise my ideas, but only brought to the surface an already strong underlying inclination.

SATURDAY, 4 NOVEMBER

Ernest van Someren
Our Morrison shelter that we ordered in the spring was delivered yesterday. We had to confirm the order a day or two ago and did so after some hesitation, as there are still V2s about, and we thought we could make it comfortable enough for the children to sleep in regularly. I bought paint and a paintbrush and some wood.

SUNDAY, 5 NOVEMBER

Ernest van Someren
Did some wire-brushing and painting on the shelter, which is very rusty, working partly in the greenhouse and partly outdoors until the afternoon, when it rained. The wartime paint is queer stuff, spreads well but dries badly. After tea there was a V2 at Highgate which made us all look up, thinking it was near. Mother rang up later in the evening and it was near her home and broke some of her windows, 13 miles from our house. Played piquet after supper.

MONDAY, 6 NOVEMBER

Pam Ashford
Isabel Sinclair said that the last time she went to London, in the first class carriage was Sir William Mactaggart (the man who builds housing schemes) with an expired return ticket. The ticket was examined four times by ticket collectors and each time there was a verbal fight, which resulted in the ticket collectors taking Sir William's name. He was truculent. 'The Government has told the people to stay out of London. He had done so. The railways were owned by the Government. They must therefore take the ticket of anyone who had stayed away under Government instructions. He was not taking this action for himself. He was taking a stand in the interests of bombed out families.'

Sir William left an unfavourable impression all round. At the station before the start someone took a corner seat and Sir William stamped in from the platform exclaiming, 'That seat is engaged. Get out.' Isabel said, 'Everyone in the carriage knew it was not, but we did not like to say otherwise.' The seat was taken by a South African army officer eventually, whose acquaintance with Sir William was obviously quite meagre. At lunch Sir William did share with him the bottle of champagne in his hamper. 'Champagne!' said Isabel Sinclair. 'What a spokesman for the bombed out families!'

Miss Page (46) spoke of a girl of 18 who joined the Land Army, and has now become engaged to an Italian Prisoner of War. 'Her mother is heartbroken.' The Italian is 20 and entered the army at about 16. He has no prospects of a career when he returns to Italy. Miss Page sees nothing but trouble. Here are some comments. Miss Page: 'It would be pity that would move her.' Miss Sinclair (about 38): 'Oh no, with these young girls it is anything in trousers.' I: 'The Italians are wonderful lovers.' Miss Page: 'That's it. These land girls go down like ninepins before their rolling eyes.' I: 'The foreigners in this country have fairly shown up the ineptitude of our own young men in the art of lovemaking.' Miss Page: 'Some girls of 18 have gathered up as much knowledge about men as you would not have had till you were 30 in the old days.'

WEDNESDAY, 8 NOVEMBER

Edward Stebbing
I was at a dance tonight when the siren sounded, but nobody took much notice. I asked a girl I was dancing with if she came there often. She replied, in a matter-of-fact tone of voice, 'Monday, Wednesday and Saturday, every week,' as though stating her hours of business (which perhaps she was).

Pam Ashford
It began with the office boy telling us that Roosevelt was in, and smiles all round. Dorothy (25) said, 'I like Roosevelt's face, but I don't like Churchill's. Besides, my mother said that Churchill may be all right for the war, but before that he was a turncoat, utterly devoid of patriotism. I liked Neville Chamberlain much better.' I said, 'I liked Chamberlain.' Elaine: 'I liked Mr Neville Chamberlain.'

At the Royal Philosophical Society, Sir Kenneth Clark (director of the National Galleries in London) spoke on 'The Human Face', i.e. portraiture. He is a fluent speaker, witty and agreeable. The talk was illustrated by lantern slides, which ranged from busts of the Roman Empire through the medieval schools to the 16th/17th century. The last phase brought in Flemish Art, but the bulk of the illustrations were Italian. His subject was, however, clearly above the heads of the audience, not that that in any way rendered them unappreciative. In his concluding remarks he spoke (without illustrations) about the modern tendencies, upon which he showered veritable streams of wit. The portrait painter looks in vain for 'good' faces among the present generation. The Renaissance period painters were more fortunate in that respect. Nowadays 'tepid lives give half-baked faces'. However, war service may improve the nation's faces from the portrait painter's point of view.

THURSDAY, 9 NOVEMBER

Edward Stebbing
I am glad that Roosevelt has been elected for a fourth term as US President. This will ensure active American cooperation in post-war measures to preserve peace.

At last the Germans have let out a few comments about the rockets and the papers have been able to print some conjectures on the nature of the weapon. I heard a good deal of talk about them today. One that hit a factory at Luton is said to have killed 180 people. I heard of a woman who has only a kitchen and an air-raid shelter to live in, but refuses to leave.

It is an appreciable pleasure now to wake up in the morning and find oneself still alive. One never knows when a bolt will come out of the blue and put an end to one's earthly activities.

My landlady and I listened to Churchill's speech broadcast from the Mansion House. We both thought he sounded a little tipsy.

WEDNESDAY, 15 NOVEMBER

Ernest van Someren
Laurie had a septic fingertip and was depressed until after breakfast.

One of our directors had his house severely shaken in the night but no glass broken. He reports than an electric switch that was out of order now works perfectly – the first good result from a V2.

SATURDAY, 18 NOVEMBER

Edward Stebbing
Went out this morning with the intention of doing some Christmas shopping. I spent some time in the 'bargain' basement of Selfridges and bought a padded coat hanger, a calendar, and some Christmas cards, all grossly over-charged. That was all the shopping I did. It seems to me that certain people collect all the rubbish they can, such as wood-shavings, old tin cans, bits of paper and string, and make something out of them, and then charge fantastic prices for them. I

saw some tablemats, made by mixing wood-shavings with some sort of glue and pressing them into flat squares, priced at 1/- each. This is just brazen robbery.

In the evening I went to the Adelphi and saw *Anglo–Russian Merry-Go-Round*, a pot-pourri of singing, ballet and comedy representing English and Russian characteristics and designed to promote Anglo–Russian friendship. George Lacy was superbly funny as a female impersonator; Nina Tarakonova's dancing was of an equally high standard. Altogether it was a very pleasing show. Coming out into the Strand, I found that the new street lighting enables one to walk without the aid of a torch.

FRIDAY, 24 NOVEMBER

Pam Ashford
Mr Churchill and Mr Winant spoke in a Thanksgiving Day Celebration (23rd), which was broadcast from the Albert Hall, sponsored by the American and British Commonwealth Association. Mentioning it today I got, 'Was Churchill sober this time?' Everyone knew he had been drunk the last time he spoke: 'His speech was thick', 'He was badly sozzled', 'He should not have been allowed on the air.'

Ernest van Someren
One night alert, and while we were listening to the 8.00 news there was a V2 very loud. I afterwards heard that it burst in the air about 3 miles away. Hence it was only a single bang, normally there is a double bang, with an interval which varies with the distance, first comes the earth-borne sound then the airborne. After work I went to see my Mother, took her some cheese and some chrysanthemums from my garden. Tony was there, my RAF brother, and told me more about his job in a psychiatric hospital.

TUESDAY, 28 NOVEMBER

Pam Ashford
Among many stories of factories being dispersed, now please include the torpedo works at Greenock. A deputation has visited Mr Alexander to try and persuade him to continue to manufacture torpedoes so as to save unemployment hitting the workers.

Edward Stebbing

It is strange that no sooner is a European country liberated than its natives start quarrelling among themselves. The French, the Belgians, the Italians, and even – or rather, especially – the Poles, whose country is not yet freed, are all bickering over who shall rule. The more I read about their squabbles the more I am glad that I am an Englishman. We are so much more sensible about our differences of opinion.

WEDNESDAY, 29 NOVEMBER

Ernest van Someren

After supper Joe D and Doug Lea and a new acquaintance called Captain Rodney Peel came to see us. He is an administrative officer of a district in Eritrea. In ordinary social life he is very shy and meeting strangers makes him sick – we heard afterwards that he met the other two at a pub before coming to see us, and was sick once. He is an ex-rugger player for Cambridge and seems as tough as would be expected of a soldier who has been through an African campaign or two.

FRIDAY, 1 DECEMBER

Pam Ashford

Today (Friday) was the third lecture in the series on Post-War Problems of Economic Reconstruction, and I enjoyed this one better than the others. What does astonish me is to find how much *I* have changed in twenty years. Between 1922 and 1925 I studied Economics at University and was then convinced of the rightness of the laissez-faire. During the period 1935/1942 I saw the coal trade undergo a transition from freedom of enterprise to stringent control. During the war I have approved of tight Government control. Living through these changes, I did not realise how profoundly our economical society was changing, and I with it.

TUESDAY, 5 DECEMBER

Pam Ashford

Mrs Blane said that the Ayr paper had columns of births last weekend. 'It is 9 months since those men came home. They went on to become the Army of Liberation and have not been home since.'

A paragraph about the amount of boot polish used by the Americans has angered Miss Sinclair. 'It is no wonder we have been so short ... I have yet to see a smart looking American ... With their hands in their pockets ... A British soldier would not be allowed to do that ... And American officers chewing gum! None of our men or officers would do that.'

THURSDAY, 7 DECEMBER

Pam Ashford
Mrs Blane had a permanent wave put in. She sat in the hairdresser's chair from 6.30 to 9.30. Dragging on the hair they dragged the skin up too. She had little sleep for no matter which way she lay her head on the pillow, her scalp hurt. But when Dave comes home it will be to a curly pate. One of Dave's relations, astonished at this particular preparation for his homecoming, tactlessly said, 'Dave's not particular.'

FRIDAY, 8 DECEMBER

Pam Ashford
Last Sunday there was an alert lasting five minutes. Of course it must have been a false alarm. Yet Miss Fuller has been telling Mother about it. She and Mr Fuller immediately got into what I used to call the 'Prepare to meet thy God attitude'. They got the buckets of water ready, actually put their gas masks on, got their money secured about their persons, put their attaché cases with essentials at the front door so as to be able to make a quick getaway. I have said, 'I don't know how they got through so much in five minutes.'

SATURDAY, 16 DECEMBER

Edward Stebbing
The Labour Party conference has given me a little more confidence in its general membership, if not in its leaders. On more than one issue the rank-and-file rebuffed the council and many of the speeches struck a bold and challenging note.

Visited some friends, one of whom said that Churchill is going out of favour with the Forces. One of her brothers had written unfavourably of him. I think Churchill has little appeal to the majority of young people.

SUNDAY, 17 DECEMBER

Edward Stebbing
Political affairs are like a leaden weight on the trend of the war. A little while ago everything was going fine for us and we were looking forward to a speedy victory. Now what Germany has been hoping for – political dissention within and amongst the Allies and the liberated countries – has happened, threatening to split the coalition in this country and the unity of the Allies and thus to prolong the war of which everyone must be sick and tired. Although I do not say that we are the only ones to blame – far from it – it does seem that the British Government's policy on the liberated countries and those still to be liberated is still too rigid and high-handed.

TUESDAY, 19 DECEMBER

Pam Ashford
The view has been expressed by Miss Sinclair that Labour will sweep the country at the general election. The Conservatives will press for an election as soon as possible after the fighting stops so that they can get the utmost out of Mr Churchill's reputation, and Labour will want the election delayed so that the country can have a taste of Conservative (mis)management of post-war problems. Miss Sinclair said, 'They have no business to have a party election when the country wants a coalition to settle the post-war problems,' and I have said, 'Mr Churchill wanted a coalition to continue. That might complicate the election issue still more.'

FRIDAY, 22 DECEMBER

Edward Stebbing
Didn't do much work today; most people were celebrating in a restricted fashion. I went to a dance in the evening with P. It was crowded with Yanks and silly little girls and unfaithful married women, jitterbugging for all they were worth and generally mis-behaving. Two Yanks started fighting. The atmosphere was distinctly rowdy and unpleasant, but it was instructive to watch. There was a good band and we did our best to dance, but were continually obstructed by the jitterbugs. When we came out P said, 'I think our men must wonder what we're fighting for, when they come home and see the women prostituting themselves like that.'

SUNDAY, 24 DECEMBER

Edward Stebbing
Went home for the Christmas holiday. The train was very crowded;
I had to stand all the way home.

A rocket had fallen on a factory in the town the previous week,
ruining many people's Christmas. About 40 people were killed and
many more injured.

CHRISTMAS DAY

Edward Stebbing
A very sharp, frosty day, everything covered in white.

We spent a quiet Christmas Day at my sister's. The two downstairs
rooms were decorated with a little holly and one or two paper
chains. For dinner we had chicken, followed by Christmas pudding.
(In spite of the shortage, everybody I know had some kind of poultry.
Many of the birds were very small, however.) In the afternoon some
relatives came round for a short time and small gifts were taken off
the Christmas tree. In the evening we played a card game and had a
glass of port. There were a few nuts and some dates and sweets.
Considering that this is the sixth year of war, I think we did very well
for Christmas fare.

SATURDAY, 30 DECEMBER

Pam Ashford
Here is a good story culled during the 13 days I was not writing.
Scene, the fish shop at Westerton, the garden suburb. High class
neighbourhood. A long queue stretched out past the door and round
the outside of the window, open, with the fish lying on the marble
slab. A Jewess in the queue leant over, picked out the fish she liked
and laid it to the side till it would be her turn. A woman nearer the
door resented this and in the ensuing argument, she seized the fish's
tail and swiped the Jewess's face with it. The uproar was so bad that
the police had to be called in.

SUNDAY, 31 DECEMBER

Edward Stebbing
Well, another year of war has passed. I think everyone is more than a
little tired of war, a little disillusioned about the prospects of the
peace. For, though the coming year should almost certainly see the

end of the European war, the hopes of international co-operation and progress after the war are rapidly fading. From one end of the world to the other one sees nothing but trouble and disorder. The peace, as I see it, will be a turmoil of quarrelling.

NEW YEAR'S DAY, 1945

Pam Ashford
There are 13 unrecorded days from 17th December to 30th December. I have jottings but doubt if they will ever be expanded. Over that period I had to devote my evenings to Christmas and New Year letters. Through Mother being ill 12 months ago I wrote no letters so that I cannot omit anyone at all this time. Even if I had felt disposed, it was impossible to send Christmas cards this year as the shops ran out.

In regard to the Christmas holidays:

23/12/44 Citizens Theatre, and Russian book Exhibition
24/12/44 Film Society (with Alice) to see a film about Naples
25/12/44 Church in morning. 'Journey Home' and King's Speech while washing up.

TUESDAY, 2 JANUARY

Ernest van Someren
Soon after nine we had our nearest rocket to the works, which fell on a small factory nearly half a mile away and only broke one or two of our many windows. Nine people were killed and over a hundred injured. I rang up Kay soon afterwards, as she would hear where it fell and might be anxious. She went to the dentist's so she would be in a position to get rumours.

WEDNESDAY, 3 JANUARY

Pam Ashford
Do you ever wonder why I refer so seldom to Mr Houstoun? Shyness and bashfulness (with a stutter) prevent him from talking to women, and he has also this impersonal manner. I am no different from a Dictaphone into which he might talk if he had one. One knows he is the same with everyone. My own belief is that if only one could get to know him one would find him quite nice. For long I treasure the one gem of conversation to which he had treated me in eight months, viz. in June he pulled down the blind and said, 'That will make the room

483

cooler,' and I said, 'It *will* make the room cooler.' But we have made astonishing progress in three weeks. On 15th December when booking the lunch for the Pitwood members meeting in Edinburgh on 22nd ult., he said to me, 'I hope they give us seasonable fare,' and I said, 'Perhaps you will have turkey,' and he said, 'I hope so.' Then about three or four days after that the siren went when he was dictating and taken aback I looked straight into the man's eyes, and he said, 'It is only a false alarm.'

FRIDAY, 5 JANUARY

Pam Ashford

There was talk about demobilisation, really a comparison between last time (to most of them hazy) and next time (whatever it will be). I said, 'It was 1921 before everyone was out.' Mrs Blane: 'If Dave is kept for two years after hostilities I shall go crazy.' Miss McKinnon: 'They will have things worked out before.' I said, 'They will be demobilised more slowly at the outset. I cannot imagine what the tempo will be like after two years.' Mrs Blane went out of the room then.

This morning Miss Sinclair referred to an article in yesterday's *Express* by Hilda Coe assuring men in the forces that their women folk were faithful to them. Everyone agreed that for one unfaithful woman there were 'ten thousand' longing for their men to come home.

During the week preceding Christmas I made various purchases and found the shops practically empty of customers. Overhead – 'There is something wrong with Christmas.'

Adults showed a greater interest than ever before in children's toys. By this stage of the war parents find that all their children's pre-war toys are gone – the children may even have been too young to have had pre-war toys. If they don't buy them toys now, the children will never have one of the main joys of childhood. I seem to have kept on hearing about second-hand Hornby engines. Mrs Blane had a friend who gave her little boy a Hornby engine on Christmas morning. She went to wind it up and the spring snapped as she turned the key. The engine was broken before it had even been run once (it was second hand). This mother spent all Christmas Day crying. Every time she looked at or thought of the engine she burst into tears.

Ernest van Someren

Today Laurie went shopping for K and when he came back said, 'I've got a present for you, would you like it now or shall I keep it for your birthday?' As Kay's birthday is in July she asked for it now, and got a packet of cigarettes bought with some of his own Christmas present money. She was very pleased.

MONDAY, 8 JANUARY

Edward Stebbing

Conversation at lunchtime was largely about rockets. One man said, 'These things are getting me down more than the doodlebugs . . . Whatever will the next war be like?' 'It doesn't bear thinking about,' said another.

TUESDAY, 9 JANUARY

Edward Stebbing

Snow on the ground. Mr B, one of the men mentioned yesterday, said today, 'I prayed last night, as I've never prayed before, for the people who were bombed-out yesterday.' He said that 21 rockets fell on London the day before yesterday. 'Still, when we're pouring phosphorus on German towns what can you expect?' he asked. In this wintry weather it is certainly dreadful for those who are bombed out of their homes.

Ernest van Someren

Snow, and a notice was put up at work about snowballing, requesting work people to confine this to the playing field and not get too much snow into the canteen or works. There are a lot of adolescents, mostly girls, to whom snowballing is inevitable though insufficient in most cases. No rockets.

THURSDAY, 11 JANUARY

Edward Stebbing

The bread we are getting now is markedly different from the brownish-coloured bread we used to get in the early days of wholemeal bread. Now, while not officially white, it looks white and tastes as nice as pre-war bread.

FRIDAY, 12 JANUARY

Pam Ashford

Miss McKinnon: 'Social security or no social security, the end of hostilities will mean that thousands of us will be starving.'

Elaine: 'Well, I'm not going to starve. I reckon I am good-enough looking to get a rich man. I don't care if all my hair does fall out after I've got him in.' (A reference to frequent corrections given her by Miss Sinclair and Miss McKinnon on the way she is converting her brown hair into golden by means of peroxide.)

SUNDAY, 14 JANUARY

Edward Stebbing

Two heavy explosions shook our house this morning. Rockets are coming over much more frequently now. Will this bombardment never end?

Ernest van Someren

There were two rockets, one in the woods 2 miles away and one at Cheshunt near the cemetery. This killed several people, among them the parents of a girl killed 10 days ago, who were on their way to visit her grave.

MONDAY, 15 JANUARY

Pam Ashford

Jack Smith, an office boy who was called up some months ago, has been visiting the firm. His intentions are to become a paratrooper. That is the best service because 'You have four or five days and then you are out of it, if you are not killed. The infantry are in for months.'

In the office someone asked how long the war had been on. 5½ years. In memory the year before the war seems just like the first year of war. We have a job to remember what peace was like.

Miss Sinclair says there is a lot of consumption among the girls at Rolls Royce, two having died recently. Another girl is living in an iron lung. The cause has been overwork, 12 hour shifts and working on Sundays.

TUESDAY, 16 JANUARY

Ernest van Someren
Laurie's birthday, seven today. Kay knitted him a scarf, Mother sent him a model farm with some animals, in cardboard. Alice Coats sent him a book on Architecture, 'Balbus' and a savings certificate gift token. The Dolby grandparents sent him 10/- and my sister Esmee sent him a pair of leather gloves. In the afternoon he had three friends and two parents to tea, for a small fairly quiet party, which they ate by candlelight off the top of the Morrison shelter.

WEDNESDAY, 17 JANUARY

Edward Stebbing
How exhilarating is the news of the sweeping Russian offensive. The swift capture of Warsaw was a marvellous surprise. At our lunch table today we were making guesses on how long it would take the Red Army to reach Berlin. One man said two months, another three months, I said six months.

Pam Ashford
There is a coal shortage. Dorothy Wallace said that the M. of Supply had no coal at all. One radiator in a private room was all the heat for 50 persons.

When I got home Mother was excited about the capture of Warsaw. I said, 'The war has almost come round full circle now. What will the Poles say of the Russians.' Mother spoke of the enthusiasm of the Poles. My own feelings are less certain. This morning the Russian advance was being commented on favourably in the office.

Ernest van Someren
I X-rayed our electric bed warmer and found the fault in it, and repaired it by soldering in the afternoon, and brought it home to be sewn up and put back into use. It is much better than a bottle but is old and this is its fourth repair in three years. In the evening listened to the Tippett oratorio.

THURSDAY, 18 JANUARY

Pam Ashford
There was a discussion as to how far from the German frontier the Russians were. I said 17 miles. Mrs Blane had learned from a newspaper 14 miles.

SATURDAY, 20 JANUARY

Edward Stebbing
About 11 this morning, while I was at work, we heard a rocket go down, which sounded a good distance away, but the cloud of smoke which went up seemed quite near. Later I discovered it had fallen about a mile and a half from my landlady's house. It had fallen near the main road and buses were being diverted round the scene. Smoke was still rising when I went by about three hours after it had fallen.

I went home for the weekend, snow falling thickly when I arrived. Talking about the rocket to my father, he said that the nearer you are to them the less you hear of them. Some people living near a factory in the town which was hit by a rocket recently heard nothing until the ceilings started falling in.

Ernest van Someren
In the afternoon Laurie had his Boys party. Julia went out to the Perhams and six boys came to see L. They had a little game in the snow first, it was sunny and cold with nearly 3 inches of loose snow. Then they had games indoors, and a large tea, eaten off the Morrison shelter by the light of nine candles, mostly stuck in the necks of bottles, looking very gay. Kay made button biscuits ½ inch in diameter with two holes in each, about a gross of them, which were very popular. Also imitation ice cream of cold custard between iced wafers, and there was an iced cake too.

More games after tea, and at about six I showed them some films, holiday films and some of swimming. By this time one of the fathers had come to take a boy home. The visitors were all 7–9 year olds, and only one was hurt enough to bleed.

TUESDAY, 23 JANUARY

Edward Stebbing
I now hear that 28 people were killed by the rocket. Considerable damage was done, too.

WEDNESDAY, 24 JANUARY

Maggie Joy Blunt
Am trying out a new method for this Diary in the hope that it will help me to keep it more regularly. The cottage getting shabbier and shabbier, but have so far managed to keep it warm enough to save pipes from freezing. Have not yet run out of fuel.

THURSDAY, 25 JANUARY

Ernest van Someren
Started a new job at the factory, part time of course, testing a new drying oven about 50 yards long. It's delightful in this weather to spend one's time moving up and down a long oven with an air temperature of 80 degrees, checking red heats and adjusting thermo-regulators.

FRIDAY, 26 JANUARY

Maggie Joy Blunt
After Sir George Schuster had addressed our Discussion Group in October he put forward the suggestion that we might use his theme as a programme for the winter session and produce a book from it. And this is what we are doing – or trying to do. His theme – that in order to meet our Post-War commitments we must increase our industrial efficiency – has been divided into 3 parts – i) the jobs to be done, ii) organisation – i.e. the relations between government and industry and iii) the human aspect. Schuster came down again with Ellis Smith to restate the case and Ellis Smith to give his views. Mr Q has managed to get hold of Sir William Beveridge for our next big meeting on Feb 7th.

Pam Ashford
25th January was 'the coldest day yet' – I have heard that phrase over and over again. I wonder in my mind whether it *is* the 'coldest day of my whole life' (an almost unanimous opinion) or whether the rations have lowered our resistance. My own health has kept good from that angle. I eat quantities of cabbage, sprouts, endive, lettuce, etc. My great battle against obesity forces me to go meagrely with the fats ration.

The announcements given out with each BBC news bulletin that the Ministry of Fuel wants us to cut down our electricity is received in all quarters with ironical laughter. One of the girls at the table was saying that shop assistants are being allowed to wear their gloves.

I read three boards with 'Russians enter Berlin suburb'. What would you make of that?

Chapter Seventeen

BERLIN WITHIN 39 MILES

STRETCHING YOUR RATIONS

★ Here's one week planned for you! ★

SUNDAY	Steak and Potato Pie—Mashed Potatoes—Spring Greens—Sago Pudding—Stewed Fruit
MONDAY	Curried Vegetables—Steamed Potatoes—Baked Carrots—Brown Betty
TUESDAY	Belgian Soup—Stuffed Baked Potatoes—Steamed Batter Pudding and Jam
WEDNESDAY	Vegetable Casserole—Baked Potatoes—Honey Apples
THURSDAY	Sausages—Mashed Potatoes—Salad—Steamed Apple Pudding
FRIDAY	Fish Pudding—Cauliflower—Chocolate Pudding
SATURDAY	Oatmeal Toad-in-the-Hole—Bubble and Squeak—Baked Jam Pudding

★ SEND A POSTCARD to the Stork Margarine Cookery Service, Unilever House, London, E.C.4, for Stork Margarine Cookery Service Leaflet No. 11

"MAKING YOUR RATIONS GO FURTHER"

—two weeks' dinners for families of 2, 3 and 6 people, complete with recipes.

THE STORK MARGARINE COOKERY SERVICE is sponsored by the makers of Stork Margarine in the confident belief that when Victory has been finally achieved Stork Margarine will once again be available to the discerning housewife.

JSC 27-22

People not knowing how to use their coupons: Stork Margarine helps the rations go further.

27 January–28 March 1945

27 January The Russians liberate Auschwitz.

31 January Red Army is in Germany and captures Driesen, 95 miles from Berlin.

6 February General MacArthur leads US troops into Manila.

9 February British and Canadian troops penetrate the Siegfried Line.

11 February Churchill, Roosevelt and Stalin announce the future shape of Europe at their conference in Yalta, dividing Germany into four zones of control and announcing plans for the United Nations.

13 February Budapest falls to the Russians.

14 February Allied bombers devastate Dresden, with 50,000 feared dead.

23 February US marines conquer Iwo Jima.

26 February More than 1000 bombers attack Berlin.

7 March The US army crosses the Rhine.

10 March US bombers attack industrial areas of Tokyo, with an estimated 100,000 fatalities.

12 March Anne Frank dies of typhus in Belsen.

17 March The Germans intensify V2 rocket attacks on Britain from the Netherlands.

20 March Mandalay falls to the British; Churchill says: 'Thank God we have got a place whose name we can pronounce.'

SATURDAY, 27 JANUARY

Pam Ashford
The cold was the immediate subject of conversation as each one arrived this morning, many people being very late indeed. There is an increasing percentage off ill. Miss Sinclair had to walk to the Bishopbriggs car terminus as the bus service serving their outlying housing scheme had gone on strike. She said a man on the tram had an icicle on the tip of his nose. In order to keep her ears warm she is sleeping with a scarf tied around her head.

Charlie travelled from London to Glasgow on Thursday evening and reached Glasgow at 3pm instead of 7am. He says that Glasgow is the warmest place in the Kingdom. London is much colder, and the snow in England very deep.

MONDAY, 29 JANUARY

Maggie Joy Blunt
S thinks the war will be over in 6 months, TH thinks it's a matter of weeks but that surrender will be not total. I don't know, but think it may be longer that than – longer than 6 months. The Germans, as S says, have their 'backs to the wall' and are in the mood to die fighting to the end. Valhalla and Wagner, 'A splendid chapter in German history' and so on.

Ernest van Someren
Min temp of about 10°F last night, and rockets this morning at Waltham Cross and Amwell, near friends of ours. No one killed or even hurt by either incident. One of my colleagues, a girl of 17, had her house damaged for the fourth time by enemy action. Her mother is getting rather upset, father on service. She didn't come to work, except for an hour in the afternoon. Said that people were indecently curious, sightseers came round and stared at them through the broken window. No one offered to help.

TUESDAY, 30 JANUARY

Maggie Joy Blunt
What I complain of in this war is that for civilians like myself there is never time to relax and do nothing with a free conscience. I sit now in the sitting room still untidy and unswept from the weekend – ashes of Sunday's fire in the grate, Sunday's crumbs on the carpet, Sunday's dust on the sideboard. In my writing case half a dozen or more letters

to be answered (some of them from Xmas) and a pile of Income Tax demands which perplex and frighten me. I must tackle them tonight and leave the sitting room until tomorrow evening. What I *want* to do is to go to bed with a nice book.

Snow this morning quite 12ins thick fallen in the night. Came right over the top of bootees as I ploughed my way to the bus. Stockings soaked. Buses late but running. Our conductor very cheerful.

Frantic day at office with Beveridge meeting arrangements. Our chairman is away with flu just to make things more difficult. Mr Q yesterday on Beveridge: 'This little man, quite determined that his plan for Social Security is possible. Nothing daunts him. He is a big draw. Prepare for an overflow. You know, when his report was first published the BBC and press were told to pipe down on it. But they couldn't. Public demand was too strong for them.'

Health this winter has so far (touch wood) been good. Not even a cold but mustn't boast too soon. Definitely the colder weather suits me. I dislike its discomfort but I have much more energy. But from time to time get very despondent. No interest in my work, tired of trying to keep pace with housekeeping. Have no post-war plans or ambitions. Don't know what I shall do and may in that mood let myself be 'directed' if the Government goes on directing us after the war. One's life isn't one's own and won't be as far as I can see for several years yet if ever.

Must now try to sort these Income Tax papers. Obviously shall have no 'unearned income' after the war and capital will all be used to pay taxes so shall have to earn my living somehow. No doubt very good for my character. Indeed we must not complain. What fate was it decreed that I should be born British?

WEDNESDAY, 31 JANUARY

Maggie Joy Blunt
A busy day at the office. A film on Castings (on the lines of our one on 'Forgings') is just completed and the firm is giving a premiere to the Aircraft Industry on Feb 16th and invitations are now being dealt with by our department. Arrangements for the Beveridge meeting have to go on too. But now I am going to sleep. Should have written a letter but have owed it now so long one more day won't make much difference.

Edward Stebbing
Hitler's speech last night was defiant, but it was the defiance of defeat. Why don't the Germans admit defeat and save much needless bloodshed?

Pam Ashford

On Wednesday evening the Royal Philosophical Society had a substitute lecturer, Dr Balls, on the Vegetation of Ceylon. His talk was illustrated by hand-coloured photographs which he had taken out there, and they really were worth looking at.

On arriving this morning Miss S took the stand that we shall hear of the fall of Berlin on the 9 o'clock news on Sunday. Mrs Blane: 'You cannot imagine it now. It seems unreal. For so long we talked about when we got into Germany, and now it has happened, we cannot believe it' (a true reflection). Twice this week discussion has turned on the future of Hitler. I myself believe him a raving madman by now. I don't think he will ever be tried (not on the grounds of non compos mentis) but because unless he commits suicide (which I think the unlikelier course), the Gestapo will murder him in order to keep the Hitler myth alive. This line of thought does not receive much support. Mrs Blane: 'I want him to be tortured to death.' Mr Barlow: 'He will retire, write his memoirs, and live comfortably on the royalties for the rest of his life' (sarcasm no doubt).

At 5 o'clock the newspapers had Berlin within 39 miles.

Ernest van Someren

Slushy weather, Kay gave a blood transfusion in the afternoon. I should have done so too, but unexpectedly went to town for a meeting with the Institute of Welding on elders training and higher education.

SATURDAY, 3 FEBRUARY

Maggie Joy Blunt

Snow and frost all gone. Not a sign of it remains and it was hard to believe this morning that only a few days ago the whole world was white. Last night the stars were brilliant. As I waited for the last bus home, operation bound bombers trailed a curtain of sound over our heads. They seemed at first invisible but watching carefully you saw that some of the stars were moving. A procession of stars moving steadily south-eastwards just a little ahead of that insistent, deadly drone.

There is a great and unaccountable shortage of shillings and a superfluity of halfpennies. Fortunately I don't depend on a meter, but people who do are having great difficulty. Woman in chemist's shop yesterday asked if anyone there (4 other customers) had one. No one could oblige. She said that even the bank had none and went out looking really worried. Someone else then said she had heard a shopkeeper say the day before 'Shillings? If I had any they'd be going into my own pocket.'

Washed my hair tonight. Don't remember doing this for at least 2 years and maybe 3 – (I don't mean that my hair hasn't been washed for 3 years!) Found a 'Camilatone' shampoo and Golden Rose stored away with astonishing and heart-lifting assortment of fine hairpins, Kirby-grips, setting combs and curlers and setting lotion. Also turned out my soap and toilet roll store (toilet rolls and sanitary towels now very difficult to buy I am told – I always keep a store of both but will have to see about replenishing).

The cats very sulky that I am taking up all hearth space and *their* chair for writing this on. Dinah has now come and sat herself across the page.

SUNDAY, 4 FEBRUARY

Maggie Joy Blunt
A pleasant weekend, all to myself. Such a change. Sunshine gave me a turning out urge and have pottered indoors and out (gardening) all day. I yearn and yearn for whole uninterrupted weeks of this. So much I want to do in the cottage and garden. So much I want to do for myself. To be my own mistress again. No office to go to. No Income Tax to grapple with. No queuing at night for buses. No returning tired out to ice-cold empty house.

A phone call from Ella at lunch time. She and Aunt Aggie have been away from their home (Sudbury, near Harrow) for 8 months now on account of the V bombs which have been falling in their area though have not as yet affected their house. But they have this week been brought rushing back on account of burst pipes. Carpets, lino, grates – everything in a terrible state. Books damp.

Must feed myself now and prepare for another trying week at the office.

WEDNESDAY, 7 FEBRUARY

Ernest van Someren
At teatime a rocket fell about a mile away from our works, in the Royal Gunpowder Factory, doing some damage but causing no casualties.

497

THURSDAY, 8 FEBRUARY

Pam Ashford
People are following the news closely. The speed at which the Russians came through Poland and the Eastern part of Germany was stimulating.

One of Miss Sinclair's friends is in an office where they have opened a fund to have a night out on V Day. I said that, 'That idea does not commend itself to me. I would much rather live in the streets. I did not think I could bear to be confined. I would want to move about and get the excitement worked out of my system. That was what it was like in 1918. What a lovely day it was and how the crowds roamed up and down' . . . and I was actually disbelieved. The others thought that the right way of spending the Armistice Day to come would be at the pictures and they were prepared to stand in queues for hours and hours, since everyone would have the same idea.

FRIDAY, 9 FEBRUARY

Edward Stebbing
At last our own offensive has begun. If only we did not need to have to keep slogging at the Siegfried Line and over flooded country we could, no doubt, advance as swiftly as the Russians. However, this advance is probably only the beginning of a general offensive all along the line. I don't think it can be long before the German front cracks somewhere.

SUNDAY, 11 FEBRUARY

Edward Stebbing
My landlady's grand-daughter, aged two or three, was busy this afternoon building a house out of dominoes and draughts on the table, knocking it down and saying – as well as she could in her unformed speech – 'Bombed-out'.

Pam Ashford
Mrs Stewart then spoke of an establishment known to her. The wife of a man in the Services repeatedly said to her mother and sister (married) that she wanted to bring home a man to sleep with – it did not matter what man, so long as it was a man, and if her husband were killed, she meant to do so immediately. The mother and sister went to see the family doctor. He said he had case upon case of the

same thing. He could prescribe glandular treatment. The doctor said that cases among single women were as numerous as among married women. People with strong willpower and active glands could and did adjust themselves. These patients were all people with weak willpower. It was not so much a craving for sexual experiences as a craving for affection.

MONDAY, 12 FEBRUARY

Maggie Joy Blunt
Our first rocket fell on Sunday about 5am. Landing on Stoke Common – roughly a mile from my cottage – it shook me from a deep sleep and I heard the whistling sound of its descent after the explosion quite clearly. Am told one person killed, 2 old people taken to hospital with shock, many houses in adjoining village damaged, and ceilings in house of one of our directors down.

TUESDAY, 13 FEBRUARY

Edward Stebbing
I could not help laughing at the picture of Churchill, Roosevelt and Stalin taken while they were conferring together in the Crimea. Churchill, especially, with his Russian fur hat and cigar, cuts a comic figure. I said to my landlady, 'They look like three music-hall comedians.' She replied, 'That's a fact. There's nothing inspiring about them.' However, the declaration which 'The Big Three' have signed sounds very promising.

FRIDAY, 16 FEBRUARY

Maggie Joy Blunt
Letter from S on Wednesday. The first news of him since he left England a fortnight ago. He began to write as he crossed the North Sea. 'Have faint impressions of telegrams and a hasty letter, a rushing to War Office and a flush of staff captains, a night on an Essex marsh in a purgatorial transit camp. Tents rainswept and damp blankets on evil straw. Refusal to sleep and a 2 mile tramp with a Polish officer to the nearest village. Time for a drink – and an offer of a bed in a private home. Delightful room and hot bath. Two boiled eggs – true – for breakfast and a happier mood for the march back. Much hoisting of packs on unaccustomed shoulders – long trip in open truck with sad-faced soldiers going back from leave. Tramping aboard and, feeling blasé in contrast to young subalterns, rolling my overcoat for

a pillow. Wake an hour later at sea. Feel I should have some emotion but feel nought. Nothing new maybe and no invasion nerves. Touch wood and whistle.

'. . . And here I am off to war again. The final round I think. Not happy, not unhappy. The old desire for nothing-round-the-corner. What is there? Fear, a sharp twinge for the post-war future. No other. I shall welcome your letters . . .'

Then on 12 Feb he continued: 'Rain, sleet and a bumpy truck to Brussels where I fell among friendly thieves, lost my hat, got stupidly drunk and woke with super hangover. My mind barely working. Yesterday feverishly tried to discover where I was being sent. Met a mad Canadian Major I dug out from the ruins of Caen last July. We celebrated gingerly for fear of pink rats scurrying over the unswept floor of my brain.

'And so today en route again to a town I know well, though my old flat has been V-bombed to ruins and the lovely Claire dead and buried beneath them. By some strange irony it seems that the bomb which killed her was the direct cause of my return here for it killed an officer for whom I may be the replacement. Tonight I shall sleep early and long and tomorrow commence duty with sober mind.'

SATURDAY, 17 FEBRUARY

Maggie Joy Blunt
Have been reading through 1944 entries, and forgot all about pork chops cooking and they are now leather.

Work: Redundancy 'purges' have been carried out periodically among the staff since the autumn and now the Central Production department – already reduced to about 13, has been told that it will cease to function by the end of March and they can all look for other work. The stamp shops will be closed down entirely by then – most of the plant I understand is being transferred to our Birmingham factory – and over 200 staff are to go. Already familiar faces are missing, like candles on a Xmas tree being blown out one by one.

Now I am not one of your hard boiled, pushing, careerist women or I'd have stormed about my situation long ago and probably left for a much better job. But for the sake of my pride I must stamp a little and soon. What *do* they intend to do with Publicity and me in particular? I know more about its present work and past history now than anyone in the firm – surely that has some value – and given the right kind of, progressive minded boss – with experience – I would make a good assistant. But, as S says, I don't want to devote my life to the Higher Metal. (Unfortunately I don't know what I want to devote it to and never have. For 5 years I have clung with utmost selfishness and determination to my cottage which has given me and a vast number of other people infinite pleasure).

To whom can I appeal for advice? No one. Because whatever I say and to whomever I say it I have to complain about my present boss. I have to say that he obviously has not the slightest idea of how a publicity department should be run or any inclination to find out, and that it is a reflection on the management to have allowed such a man to take the job in the first place. I am afraid I have not much opinion of any of the gentlemen who direct this firm.

This looks very like a 'sour-grapes' attitude but it is shared by a great many other underlings. The firm one feels has potentialities, it has done good work during the war, but it is badly managed.

Why in spite of all this argument do I still want to stay?

The answer to that would take too long. It is partly personal, partly convenience and fairly good money. And partly fascination. I have watched events and personalities there so long I want to see what happens next, what the next act is to be.

My story is but one. There are hundreds of others far worse. The Labour Exchange has no work for the men turned down. At our Wycombe works there has been a strike because 20 men were sacked and 20 Italians taken in place of them (lower rates).

SUNDAY, 18 FEBRUARY

Maggie Joy Blunt
A marvellously lovely afternoon, reminding me of all the forgotten summers. I stayed in bed until 2 o'clock but by then the sun was shining in at my window, the day was too good to waste in further idleness. I broke wood to dry under the stove, did out the kitchen, made my bed, swept the stairs, and then turned my attention to the garden. About 4.30 Lys called with her friend C who is just recovering from a sad miscarriage. C is staying with her parents nearby and was out this afternoon for the first time since her return from the nursing home.

Snowdrops are out, crocuses and aconite – a few primroses have been in flower since October. Bees and flies were in evidence. A fortnight ago I saw a Red Admiral butterfly. Moths have been flying into the kitchen at night. This afternoon there was a great flock of wild grey blue pigeons in the woods. They whirred about the trees here for some time, the sound of their wings was like a heavy shower or sleet, and then vanished. Have never seen such a quantity before.

In Windsor yesterday afternoon – after a hair appointment –

bought some scrubbed carrots. When I remarked on their cleanliness the woman said that it was still a penalty to scrub root vegetables.

MONDAY, 19 FEBRUARY

Pam Ashford
On Monday evening I went to the Town & Country Planning Association where they had a discussion between Bailie Gray and Mr Tupling (Factory Inspector) on 'Flats or Houses'. Dr Dunlop: 'The speakers have guaranteed not to speak for more than 30 minutes. (Digging Mr Tupling in the ribs, he pointed to the clock which has stood at 3.15 since last September.) The clock is stopped. So has my watch. (He placed it on the table.) I might have brought my electric clock but I had to mend it a fortnight ago and now it goes backwards. Perhaps it is as well I did not bring it or the speakers would have had more than their 30 minutes. Could anyone lend me a watch for the meeting?' Bailie Gray obliged. Mr Tupling was obviously watch-less. Ah, yes, at least half the clocks that adorn walls no longer work, and the number of people carrying watches has dwindled to – dare I say 12½% – certainly far more people have broken watches than sound ones. When the watch repairers come back from the war, they will be in full employment for years to come.

Maggie Joy Blunt
A letter from S: 'This office is a military almshouse for the lost and lame – I fear contracting the palsy. The Demon Rum is a great evening temptation and I sit with another Desert Rat beside a wood stove in a café and reminisce garrulously. Verily we have become Desert Mice. Have not reconnoitred the local blonde market yet but preliminary observation not encouraging. Their teeth are bad after four years of Boche occupation. Anyway, only Yank privates and British quartermasters can afford them. I hear there is a war off somewhere near here but can scarce credit it. Slough is more embattled.

'There are good officers here, eating their hearts out with restlessness. The work is important and useful – for those who see it as such in its entirety – but even if one knows the importance of being earnest it does not stop one's wish to wave Lady Windermere's fan! I pray for your letters.'

TUESDAY, 20 FEBRUARY

Maggie Joy Blunt

A telegram from S yesterday to say he was coming to England on duty and would phone me tonight. Another telegram this evening to say he was in hospital with a broken wrist.

FRIDAY, 23 FEBRUARY

Pam Ashford

Mrs Blane in her parcels to Dave is very particular to declare the full contents and to exclude food. Dave writes that practically everyone is receiving parcels of food. Mrs Blane said, 'Then Dave is not going to be left out. I thought it was right to comply with the regulations but I shall do so no longer.' She is listing the food she can send him. Her rations in sweets, jam and sugar, coffee, tea, biscuits, tins of meat, beans, the pots of lemon curd she has made, chocolate spread.

Ernest van Someren

Busy at work on odd jobs, and interviewed two applicants for work in the morning, sensible chaps studying for an engineering course, but not clever.

One of our office staff asks any young applicant for an office job, 'What is five percent of a hundred pounds?' and so far only three of several dozen have given the correct answer.

On the way home from work stopped to see the Marx Brothers film *A Night at the Opera*, which I had seen some years ago and enjoyed it immensely.

SATURDAY, 24 FEBRUARY

Maggie Joy Blunt

In a vile mood all yesterday. East wind, grey sky, indigestion. Nothing to do at office and rain as we went home. At home another letter from S asking me to find an unfurnished house or flat in this area for some special friends of his. He might as well ask for the moon. Felt thoroughly angry.

Men in the Services who have spent most of their time abroad during this war don't seem to have any idea how difficult things have become for the civilian and imply that we make an unnecessary moan about conditions. A good story could be written round this – husband returning after 3–4 years in Middle East, wife doing full time war job trying to keep house together, or looking after children on her own, nerves jaded, finds husband utterly unreasonable – thinking that he has had all the hardships and so on.

Tomorrow I hope to spend with Meg and Roger. And if I know of any vacant flats or house they are the first people I'd inform.

Pam Ashford
Now so far as my ordinary contacts go, Lord Haw Haw is as dead as mutton. To Capt. Macgowan he is a new discovery and he listens every night at 10.30. I had great difficulty in getting him to believe that I know who he meant (I had even to supply the name of William Joyce, with such biographical details as I could recall), and further that in 1939 a large part of the British public used to listen as a joke (Helen then 12½ years old did not know this). Capt. Macgowan likes Lord Haw Haw 'for speaking the truth'. Capt. Macgowan said in Crimea Roosevelt, Churchill and Stalin had been spending their time boozing. I said 'Can't you see for yourself that that one is a lie,' but he could not.

Edward Stebbing
Went home for the weekend. In the train a soldier was bemoaning the fact that his wife had left him for another man and wondering what he could do about it. A good many problems like this are arising now, and it is no good turning round and saying that the woman or the man is to blame for being unfaithful. It goes deeper than that. Prolonged separation is bound to have a disturbing psychological effect, and even when neither party has been unfaithful it will often be difficult, especially for young couples, to regain their old relationship.

SUNDAY, 25 FEBRUARY

Edward Stebbing
Returned to my digs and Mrs H asked me how my nephew was. I told her that he was extremely active and self-willed, though very intelligent. We began to discuss why so many children are restless and uncontrollable. We put it down to the times we live in. I thought much of it was because parents were neurotic due to the war and this was bound to affect their children's behaviour. For the same reason parents could not stand the further strain of controlling their children and were inclined to let them drift.

Maggie Joy Blunt
Reading my diary from September 1939.

On 12 Sept: 'Lethargy envelopes me. It is a warm, brilliant day. What is Hitler saying in Nuremburg? Shall we this time tomorrow be involved in war?'

20 Sept: 'I have planted some bulbs, I have typed an article, I have been with June and Stella to see Snow White and have eaten supper at a café near Hampstead station. And somewhere during this . . . horror and despair threaten to return.'

27 Sept: 'War, war and yet more rumours. Why must everything threaten to crash just as I am beginning to get a grip on living? God, please let there be no war.'

28 Sept: 'What, said G at lunch, are Hitler's thoughts and feelings at this moment? Triumph, exaltation, "I am God" – and the people who will suffer most will be the poor people. Chamberlain fighting for peace and the privileged classes, and although I don't agree in theory with having any sort of privileged class, I admire Chamberlain. He seems to me a very fine man. Midnight. And now the four powers are to meet tomorrow at Munich. Perhaps Hitler will in the end be the means of creating a real world's peace and a real League of Nations.'

29 Sept: 'I return to a London plunged in a kind of fatalistic gloom. Stella was preparing to take all her belongings and Geoff to Clare (Suffolk). This panic to get out of London leaves me in a cold fury. Why run away? But then I have nowhere to run, and we have been told that anyone who can get out of London should. Tomorrow I have to be fitted for a gas mask. And yet underneath I cannot believe there will be a war.'

And now we have had nearly six years of war and here am I still with an unfulfilled passion for writing. I have returned now to the cottage on Monday evening, February 26th 1945. I don't think my own life has altered very greatly – not the essential pattern of it. Am driven still by the same desires, suffer the same fears and frustrations. Like knowing lots of people doing all manner of trivial things, possessing lots of books which I never have time to read, I value my independence above all else. Guided always by what I most want to do, never by what I think I ought to do. And never do quite what I want to do.

Cycled to see Meg and Roger today. A windy day but not unpleasant. They are still in two rooms and hating it. The baby is a darling and has grown out of all recognition since the summer. He's eating fish, and cheese and eggs now – and white meat if Meg can get it which she never can.

THURSDAY, 1 MARCH

Maggie Joy Blunt
At 6.15 tonight 4 short films were shown in the canteen: *Pipeline* and *Tennessee Valley* loaned by the American Embassy and 2 English Technicolors, one about pottery manufacture, and *Steel Teeth*. All excellent. Gives one faith and pride in this age – and hope for the future.

RW telling me this afternoon domestic details of the Royal family. She and her parents have lived in Windsor all their lives. Her father owns a pub. They know several of the Castle staff and hear a good deal of gossip. The Queen, they say, is very lazy. Does not get up until 11am then has a bath and goes to bed again. She does as little for herself as possible – if she wants a book, for instance, she rings for someone to fetch it for her although she may be sitting in the room near the book required. She goes round the servants' quarters, pulling their work to pieces, she is said to have a very bad temper. Sounds to me an unhappy woman with not enough to do – energy going to waste. Delicious food of course all the year round – peaches and so on from their own hot houses.

Of the two Princesses, Margaret Rose is the most popular – she chatters to the servants and takes a lively interest in their activities. Elizabeth acknowledges them but remains aloof. One or other of them often accompany their mother when she goes on her tours of inspection. There is an air-raid shelter 12 feet below the castle – made as a flat with every convenience – and stock for a six month sojourn.

Soup for supper and an orange. Did not feel very hungry.

FRIDAY, 2 MARCH

Edward Stebbing
Food shortages have been more of a problem than ever recently. Meat has been in short supply this week. My landlady said this morning, 'If I can't get any fish, I don't know what I shall give you to eat tonight.' However, she managed to get some fish.

Pam Ashford
I am told that the wireless announced recently that there is to be more elastic available for underwear. Knickers in brief. No one has any shyness on the subject in this sixth year of war.

SUNDAY, 4 MARCH

Edward Stebbing
The Germans apparently are going to have a final fling at us before they yield. Piloted planes were over last night and dropped a few bombs. I do not think it can last long. With the defeat of the German armies west of the Rhine, news of which is exciting us today, the end cannot be far off. I wonder why the British Second Army is not mentioned in the news about the Rhine battle. It is a little disappointing to think that the Canadians and the Americans are getting all the honours.

MONDAY, 5 MARCH

Ernest van Someren
In the evening went to a meeting on European Famine Relief arranged by the Peace Group. There were about 30 people, a good speaker (Roy Walker) and a lively discussion, during which we decided to set up a small local committee to get second-hand clothing collected for European relief, as food cannot be sent now.

FRIDAY, 9 MARCH

Edward Stebbing
The exciting news (the crossing of the Rhine) has come more quickly than I expected. Almost everyone expects the war to be over soon; one or two are still cautious. I cannot think that it will last more than a few weeks longer.

I was struck by the pictures of Cologne in today's papers. Our bombing has left it a desolate shambles.

Yesterday I was discussing with two other men how the war would end. We more or less agreed that there would be no formal peace making, for there was nobody we could make peace with. We would just go on until we had beaten the German armies, then set up a military government until we could form a suitable civil government.

SATURDAY, 10 MARCH

Maggie Joy Blunt
Drinking lemon tea and listening to Tauber on the radio. His voice is sticky and distracting. But I don't want to turn off – I want to listen to Drinkwater's 'Bird in Hand' at 9.30 while I wash my 'smalls' and if I turn it off now I shall forget the time.

On Tuesday the Management gives a Premiere showing of our new film on Castings to the Aircraft Industry and we have been fairly busy with replies from the invitations distributed (over 100) and the sending out of tickets (with Hay and his class now performing). A message from W's secretary that one of the men invited is dead.

S thinks the war will be over in 6 weeks. He is in England again. Was sent on special mission to track down a deserter, fell downstairs and fractured his right wrist (a fantastic story but quite true). He is to sail for the Middle East in 10 days' time.

SUNDAY, 11 MARCH

Maggie Joy Blunt
War news is excellent. Everyone saying, 'It won't be long now.' Supposing this time it isn't – although I am not myself convinced – the Russians seem to be as far down from Berlin as they were some weeks ago, the Germans are still in Holland, Dunkirk, Northern Italy, the Channel Islands.

Ernest van Someren
Cold rather dull weather. Borrowed the long ladder from the Stranges and did some repair work on the greenhouse, which has needed more glass since some of Laurie's friends poked sticks through several panes.

TUESDAY, 13 MARCH

Ernest van Someren
Another noisy night, to work by train as it was frosty. In the morning tried to determine the sex of the author of a letter by swinging a pendulum over it. Got four people to do this and they all said it was male – the letter was from a parent of a prospective employee. We answered as to the boy's father, quite confidently.

THURSDAY, 15 MARCH

Edward Stebbing
I think most people accept the fact that the people of Europe are, on the whole, much worse off than we are and need food more than we do. At the same time, of course, everybody thinks we have had more than enough of rationing. They are also beginning to realise that though this will be the year of victory, it will probably be the worst year for rationing.

Pam Ashford

Dorothy Lamberton is ill with a chill caused it is said by wearing no vest. Comment on Dorothy has been galore. To my surprise I learned that this last winter many people have been wearing two pairs of knickers and two vests as the only way of counteracting the thinness of underclothing now being sold . . . Oh, these French knickers (which everyone calls pants nowadays), they should engrave a pair on Hugh Dalton's tombstone, or rather on the tombstones of all the people who blame Hugh Dalton for illness cause by draughts up their legs. The manufacturers just won't put elastic around the knees.

TUESDAY, 20 MARCH

Ernest van Someren

Kay bought grapefruit, and we had some for supper, the first in several years, and enjoyed it specially.

WEDNESDAY, 21 MARCH

Edward Stebbing

The Germans are being battered everywhere, suffering great losses, but they stupidly prolong the struggle. Mrs H said, 'I can't understand why they don't give in.' At least by the time it is finished the Germans will have had the meaning of war brought home to them with a vengeance, as it was not in the last war.

SATURDAY, 24 MARCH

Edward Stebbing

Bought an evening paper, something I very rarely do, for I had seen the headline 'Monty Over' and wanted to read the good news. It gave me a feeling as awesome as did the news on D-Day.

Pam Ashford

I was spellbound by the 9 o'clock news and war commentaries of the Rhine crossings. Marvellous.

MONDAY, 26 MARCH

Pam Ashford

Mrs Blane opened up with 'What do you think of the news?' and everyone beamed back 'Fine'. But otherwise things were as they have been. Just scraps read out of newspapers and talk not centring about the war. Satisfaction was several times expressed at the Scottish troops being the first in. This use of the word 'Scottish' was not, however, directed against the English but against the Americans.

WEDNESDAY, 28 MARCH

Maggie Joy Blunt
Allied cruisers are swarming across the Rhine – Churchill says the end is in sight, Eisenhower that the Germans are whipped. Two women in the Doctor's surgery this morning said, 'Why don't they give in now? If they would only give in so much more bloodshed would be saved.'

Developed a septic finger last week, I think from handling some old and dirty forgings – probably metal dust got into the quick. Dr B says I must dress it three times a day with special lotion after soaking in hot salt water and keep my hand in a sling. Says I am run down, must take time off. As it is my right hand it is infuriating. I can't do a thing and shouldn't really be writing this. Had planned to spend Easter spring cleaning, but it looks as though my plans will be thwarted. Maddening. I wanted to do such a lot. Real, hard, muscular work too.

Edward Stebbing
Discussed when the war would end with Mr and Mrs H. The latter said she was speaking to another woman who said, 'If it doesn't end soon we shall all collapse. We're all keyed up to expect the end.' We all wrote down on a piece of paper the date we thought the war would end. Mr H put June 10th, Mrs H put April 25th, and I put April 9th.

Chapter Eighteen

SUCH THINGS COULD HAPPEN IN A CIVILISED WORLD

An unmistakable air of gaiety; VE Day at last at Piccadilly Circus.

30 March–8 May 1945

30 March The Red Army crosses the Austrian border.

6 April US forces land at the island of Okinawa, a springboard for the invasion of Japan; more than 100,000 Germans surrender in the Ruhr.

7 April Ernest Bevin, the Minister of Labour, signals the end of the coalition government.

12 April Roosevelt dies at the age of 63 and is succeeded by Harry Truman; Buchenwald concentration camp freed by US troops.

13 April Vienna, the first foreign capital occupied by Hitler, is liberated.

16 April Red Army troops move to the outskirts of Berlin.

21 April Allied troops move into Bologna; the battle for the Ruhr ends with 325,000 prisoners in Allied hands.

27 April US and Soviet troops link up at the river Elbe.

28 April Mussolini shot by partisans.

29 April German forces surrender in Italy; American soldiers execute more than 100 SS guards at Dachau.

30 April The Reichstag falls to the Red Army; Hitler and Eva Braun commit suicide in Berlin bunker.

3 May The Allies capture Rangoon, the capital of Burma, without a fight.

7 May Germans sign unconditional surrender.

8 May VE Day celebrations.

Japan surrenders on **15 August**.

FRIDAY, 30 MARCH

Pam Ashford

Good Friday, but not of course a holiday in Scotland.

Today is Mother's 78th birthday. Each year Mother's birthday grows more important to us. She is so wonderfully active and well. From Charlie she got two overalls and from me a set of tablemats. Mrs Craigie gave her a beautiful Swiss roll from Fuller's.

Today being the last Friday of the month I went along to the Grosvenor Tea Rooms to lunch with Mrs Petrie and her circle.

Their great desire is always to get 'trifles' which the waitress, Nancy, a pal of theirs snaffles up for them. I was a little late today, and along with one of the other girls, Miss Nelson, was too late for a trifle. Nancy said, 'The tarts are fine today, real gooseberries, I'll grab two for you.' Oh my Lord! I never tasted anything so foul as those gooseberries in my life. They tasted of mildew, and they tasted of chemicals, and they tasted as if they were unfit for human consumption. They gave me what everyone calls 'enteritis' nowadays.

People in the office pore over their papers on arriving in the morning and again at 5 over the papers which the office boy has brought in. On the trams too one can see more papers being read and with a greater degree of intensity. It is obvious too that the wireless is being missed by no one who is able to listen.

The lack of comment is I think in part due to the fact that if you spoke to someone he would not appreciate your action in deflecting his attention from the particular column in which he was engrossed. And it is partly due to the immensity of the subject.

Ernest van Someren

Pottered round at home and did some work in the garden, moving round clothes and bean posts. Put up a new gadget for Laurie, but it doesn't work yet.

SATURDAY, 31 MARCH

Edward Stebbing

Too cold and windy to go walking far, but I went to look at the place where the rocket fell last December. It was a desolate scene: a few jagged walls standing amid heaps of rubble where several houses had been, on either side the battered hulks of several others, and behind them the gutted roofs of a factory. There were one or two rusty Morrison table-shelters standing by the side of the road, and one had been partly buried in the ruins with its top caved in, and another was upside down on a pile of debris. And here and there amongst the ruins were still to be seen an occasional household article and even a china ornament; on the pavement was a trampled book called *Dulcie King*, a school prize for 1904. These objects had a terrible poignancy. This was the scene three months after the rocket had fallen, and I wondered how many years would pass before all signs of war have been obliterated from England. These areas of destruction will serve as reminders for many years to come.

Maggie Joy Blunt

I wait in desolation for my meal to cook. It has been on the kitchen stove for nearly an hour and a half. Stewed mutton and Spanish onions. My finger is no better, no worse. The Doctor saw it this morning and said, 'It's in the balance now. You *must* keep your hand in a sling or I won't answer for the consequences. That woman who has just gone out – she had the same trouble and now she has lost her nail.'

I went into Slough after seeing the Doctor, to the Bank, to the Post Office, to the library, bought meat pies, fish paste and cigarettes. Reading Georgette Heyer's *Why Shoot a Butler?* An exciting story – the only kind that will keep me still for any length of time! But now they are all living happily ever after and paying, I imagine, supertax.

Everyone I have met recently or heard from is expectant, even exultant. There is much hope in the atmosphere. I offered to take Ella to the theatre for her birthday in February but she did not like the idea of running the gauntlet of V bombs. Now she writes, 'Is not the news thrilling? One wonders just how soon one may expect Victory news. Yes, then you may take me to the theatre. Do! What a treat!'

Ernest van Someren

More good news, but cold weather. One of Laurie's school friends, Paul Veugan, came over for the day and they played in the garden in the morning. After lunch we went for a walk, with Jeremy Pigeon as well (not my Mother), and went to a gravel pit where they all scrambled about and got muddy.

SUNDAY, 1 APRIL

Edward Stebbing

We had grapefruit for breakfast, the first of the war for me, as far as I remember.

515

TUESDAY, 3 APRIL

Maggie Joy Blunt
Have tried to obey Doctor's orders – finger looks about the same. To see a Red Cross film show: *Blood Transfusion, A.B.C.D of Health, Green Food for Health, First Aid on the Spot, Conquest of a Germ.*

This evening my friend Cy brought a wireless to replace mine. Mine apparently in a rather bad condition, and Cy owns a wireless and sports shop in Slough and is having this done for me all out of the kindness of his heart.

He has just had a raw deal, he told me, and feels by doing someone a good turn that he gets himself readjusted to living. He has been helping to run a Club but has a very poor view of its members – the petit bourgeoisie of Slough. All out for their own interests, he said, 'And you feed them today knowing that if they saw you in the gutter tomorrow they'd tread on you.' Makes me feel gloomier than ever about the future. When the war is over the fight will continue. We shan't get our Brave New World until people are different – and will people ever be different?

Pam Ashford
Perhaps last week's disinclination to talk about the Allied progress arose from a caution against believing that the end really could be here at last. When our troops raced through France last August we expected too much; and when in January the Russians, in particular Gen. Zhukof (I know my spelling is wrong), raced through mile upon mile to the Oder, again we thought this was the end. But yes, this is the end this time, however that end may come.

WEDNESDAY, 4 APRIL

Edward Stebbing
I and two other men were talking about German propaganda. Even in their defeat the Germans make brilliantly clever propaganda out of it. C was listening to Haw-Haw last night. His line of talk was to the effect that though things were serious for the Germans, they would be much worse for us; the Russians would not stop when they met our armies, they would come on and occupy all Europe, eventually including Britain; in fact, the Germans were doing their best to let us in and hold the Russians back; they weren't really fighting us. Together with this were some more threats about V-weapons. This sort of thing makes you stop and think, for, as C said, 'There's a grain of truth in it.' No doubt the Germans would prefer us to occupy Germany rather than the Russians.

Pam Ashford

Only 2 war commentaries today and both relate to the announcement that persons on Govt. work will celebrate the victory with 3 days leave with pay. Meeting Dorothy Wallace I said, 'You at any rate know what you are to get.' She said that it had been circulated in confidence months ago. She disapproved of the whole thing as being likely to encourage a slackening off in the war effort against Japan.

FRIDAY, 6 APRIL

Pam Ashford

Miss Sinclair: 'I was talking to an airman who has been bombing Germany. One night they gave them leaflets to drop. They read them. The crew was fairly disgusted. These leaflets purported to be extracts from German prisoners-of-wars' letters stating that they were well-fed here. They have accounts of the German prisoners eating turkey on Christmas Day. Turkey! 'Tis many a long day since the like of us had turkey. Who's going to give turkeys to Germans on Christmas Day?'

SATURDAY, 7 APRIL

Pam Ashford

Every day this week Mrs Blane has come to work in an ever-increasing state of excitement. Dave is due on the 9th. Mrs Blane is, of course, deeply in love, and love is a very beautiful thing but really it is not normal to be in this infatuated state after five years of marriage. I *would* indeed like to know what this Dave *is* like, and how far her prostrating herself in front of him like a doormat is her own idea, and how much is his. And the preparations! I don't follow the hair-dressing story in its entirety. Apparently a certain interval of time has to elapse after a perm before you can have another one, 'the hair has to grow in', and the perm inserted last Monday with a view to its having its extreme furrow-field appearance by the 9th did not come up to scratch. This has been a week of nightly hair-washing to get it soft, and tomorrow (Sunday) Elaine is to spend the day at Mrs Blane's at Rosslyn Terrace, when with the hair of the head wet they will first pull it straight and then Elaine (who has a flair for hair-dressing) will reset the whole thing with grips, rubber bands, kirbies and hairpins. Well I can't see that any man on earth is worth all that much suffering, can you?

MONDAY, 9 APRIL

Edward Stebbing
I wish the Government would do something to stop the rampant profiteering in the sale of houses. Fantastic prices are being asked for the poorest class of dwelling. The people who make excessive profits out of the homeless do not deserve to have the war won for them.

TUESDAY, 10 APRIL

Pam Ashford
Mrs Blane was not at the office when we assembled this morning. We wondered if . . .? Yes, at 9.45 she burst into the room (wearing a new hat and summer coat just cleaned). Dave arrived at 8.30am. She had had a telegram last night to say he was on the way. She had already been in to see Mr David Carson who said 'that means you will be off for a month' (his way of speaking). To what a pitch of emotion she had got herself. So she went off.

Miss Smith spent Sunday afternoon at Mearnskirk hospital. One room is called 'the chamber of horrors'. The patients there cannot be seen they are so disfigured or mutilated.

She spoke of two brothers she knew at Dunkirk. A shell fell beside them and one was blown to pieces – nothing left – the other was terribly injured. His parents were sent for when he was got to a hospital here, they just saw a boy completely swathed in bandages and were told that was their son. The hospital thought he could not survive, but he has, and seems to have been able to get back to a useful life (I don't know what as).

FRIDAY, 13 APRIL

Pam Ashford
Elaine has a new centre of attraction. Vic (the engineer on the *Q. Elizabeth*) has failed to communicate with her. So did Leo two or three months ago (the Canadian in Italy). Now Elaine is in love (what she calls love) with a Canadian on leave. It is obvious that this is a person with a vulgar mind (sexy – filthy in fact) and to judge from his dialect (which Elaine has been imitating) a slum dweller – or equivalent.

Edward Stebbing
The death of President Roosevelt is a sad loss, both to America and to the world. I was talking to two men about it today. One said it was

a pity he did not live to enjoy the final fruits of his efforts. The other said that perhaps his name would be more highly honoured because he had died during the war and not after it. He even suggested that it might have been better for Churchill's fame had he been killed when he visited the Rhine recently. If he had died then he would have been a national hero; after the war he might not be so well thought of.

Now for the big news item of today. I heard of Pres. Roosevelt's death while I was dressing in the bedroom. Mother in the dining room was sitting there as she always does, listening. I heard her exclaim out loud, so great was her surprise . . . and, of course, the unexpectedness of it was one of the first impressions with us all. What a shock. The other first-thought was – so far as I can judge everyone had the same one – 'What a pity just as we were within sight of victory.'

Ernest van Someren
Horrified at the news of Roosevelt's death. People I met at work mentioned it, only three of them in the course of the day, but that is more than the usual number of people (0) who talk to me about current news.

To the Army & Navy Stores and bought myself a tweed jacket.

SATURDAY, 14 APRIL

Pam Ashford
Do you realise that I have now completed twelve months with MC & W. My life with Capt. Macgowan and with Mr Mitchell was so much more interesting than accountancy. If I have to stay at MC & W I shall indeed feel that my life is wasted, for it will mean I shall never do anything but typing and shorthand. I never as much as see a customer, let alone speak to one over the 'phone or in person, or write a letter of my own.

I follow the *Herald* advertisements every Tuesday, and answer the good ones, but the fruit market one is the only one that has been answered. 42, educated, and in the £5 a week category – any one by itself is enough to frighten an advertiser away, all three combined is fatal.

Ernest van Someren
In the evening looked up a new resident in the district, an artist named Suwter, a woman with two children. Her husband is the new Education Officer at Hertford, she is a startlingly attractive looking person, to whom I talked about the Music Club.

519

SUNDAY, 15 APRIL

Edward Stebbing
Further confirmation of Nazi bestiality was given tonight by an American commentator's first-hand account of what he saw at the concentration camp of Buchenwald. How degraded men must be to do the things which were done to the prisoners at this and other camps!

Ernest van Someren
We have stopped using the Morrison shelter for the children now, and this weekend restored them to their two separate rooms upstairs.

TUESDAY, 17 APRIL

Pam Ashford
The memorial service for President Roosevelt must have been impressive, judging by Mother's conversation at lunchtime. 'There has never been such a service in this country before.' 'What a lot of Kings and Queens . . . and the Lord Mayor bearing a sword with a pearl handle, etc.' The wireless reports in the evening were, however, not very informative on this subject.

From two quarters I have heard of a film that is being shown in which one sees Roosevelt as he was when he took over 12 years ago and the last picture taken of him, viz. Yalta. Ever so many of Churchill, Stalin and Roosevelt (wearing a cape) at Yalta. We sympathise with Mr Churchill too, whom we are sure must feel the President's passing.

General Eisenhower is properly putting down the rumour (flamed by the Sunday papers) that Mr Churchill would end the war by proclamation on Thursday.

WEDNESDAY, 18 APRIL

Edward Stebbing
Bertrand Russell, writing in *Picture Post* today, points out the futility of the proposals for the new world security organisation to be discussed at San Francisco. The means of preventing aggression will be applicable only to those countries which are too weak to be likely to make war; the big powers will be free to aggress as much as they like. This would prevent small wars, but not another world war. I think it is really useless to talk of a world organisation in the present worldwide mood of cynicism and disillusionment.

Ernest van Someren
Our ninth wedding anniversary. In the evening we got a neighbour to watch the kids while we went out. We went up to the river a mile away and hired a boat for a short row, then had a glass of beer at the pub called 'Fish and Eels'.

THURSDAY, 19 APRIL

Pam Ashford
Mrs Blane came back this afternoon, Thursday, 19th April, Dave set out on the journey back this morning. 'The Germans are receiving our troops very well. It is difficult not to fraternise with people who press friendship upon you. But the information about Buchenwald is enough to put our men wise.' Dave has come all the way from Osnabruck. He crossed the Rhine 2 days after the Rhine crossing by a bridge put up by the engineers. The German towns have been knocked about. One is not rubble, it is just dust.

It is marvellous how well the leave has been organised. There are 4 ships passing between France and Dover with men on leave, and it is when the sailing of a ship is delayed that one hears these wireless announcements telling certain leave parties to report a day late. Dave got an extra day that way.

Conditions for our men in Germany are tolerably comfortable. Plenty of food and good quarters, but it is tiring work. He went back this morning feeing better than when he arrived. Mrs Blane said in regard to food here, 'I did not spare anything,' but he had an emergency food card giving him double rations.

Ernest van Someren
After work went down to Enfield for a meeting of our works discussion group. I gave a talk on 'The Christian Vocation, the Meaning of the Incarnation', which was a rather difficult subject.

FRIDAY, 20 APRIL

Edward Stebbing
Now we can really imagine what the German concentration camps were like. The sickening pictures which have now been published prove that they were veritable slaughterhouses. Two men I was speaking to about it were agreed that the only way to prevent such things happening again would be to exterminate the Germans. 'They're certainly not fit to live,' said one.

Pam Ashford

Last August the report of the Lublin Gas Chambers, etc., human fertilisers in particular, distressed me so much that I have avoided that topic of subject ever since. BBC and newspaper headings and photographs (and some grave (burial) scenes at the Cosmo recently were most distasteful) have been enough to give me an idea. So with Buchenwald and Weimar – I did not read them.

MONDAY, 23 APRIL

Pam Ashford

Miss Murray, Miss Smith and I spoke in a general way about the Belsen horror camp. People fight shy of the details. I said, what I have thought often over the weekend, 'Last August when the reports of Lublin were issued there was no public stir. Why should there be this stir over Buchenwald, which to me is less horrible?' (My own judgement is that last August people did not believe that Lublin was true, they thought it was propaganda, whereas this time they accept the reports. Probably that is because it is our forces which are up against these present horrors.) But Miss Murray and Miss Smith, whom I had to remind of the details of Lublin, said that they thought that was less horrible. If people are gassed they don't suffer. Some of the people at Buchenwald have been there 12 years. And they are Germans too, their own folk.

Miss Sinclair was saying (apparently from a report in the evening paper) that the commandant of the camp had been hung and there was a cry all round the room that that was too good. He ought to be kept alive for years and tortured regularly.

No black-out tonight!!

TUESDAY, 24 APRIL

Edward Stebbing

Had a letter from my sister. About the Belsen concentration camp she wrote, 'What a dreadful place that must have been at Belsen. I just can't forget it. It doesn't seem possible that such things could happen in a civilised world.'

Pam Ashford

Both Elaine and Miss McKinnon arriving at work, spontaneously and without knowledge of the other's views, spoke of the news films last night. Elaine said she could not get the scenes of 'that camp' out of her mind. Miss Sinclair told her that that was why the film had been put on, so as to educate her. Miss McKinnon said that she had seen some dead bodies. I said I intended to reach the Cosmo on Saturday immediately after the news and leave before it was shown again. I did not want to see the films. Miss McKinnon said that the films were not so horrible as all that. I said I had read that there had been protests in London but that the Glasgow cinema proprietors said that the films now showing were not the ghastly ones in London. They were still to arrive – presumably next week.

WEDNESDAY, 25 APRIL

Maggie Joy Blunt

Weather has been amazing. Last week 70 in the shade, everyone in summer frocks and without stockings, trees in leaf everywhere almost overnight – the oak before the ash – and all the May month flowers in bloom – lilac, laburnum, red and white may, irises, tulips, chestnut, with fading forget-me-not, primrose and apple blossom. I saw roses out on a sunny wall in the village. It has been wonderful, beyond describing.

'God is pleased,' said N, 'that we are freeing the concentration camps in Germany.' The horrors that have been revealed by the Allies are past belief. All the people I know cannot understand how any human being in a so-called civilised nation could treat other human beings like that. We just cannot understand it. The authorities who ordered such torture, and the men and women who had to supervise and control the camps, must be mad, terribly mad. One suspected the Nazis of a certain amount of brutality and sadism, but not on this scale, involving the death by starvation and deliberate degradation of 1000s and 1000s of men, women and children – the children the worst of all. All civilised, balanced people must be shocked to the soul at the reports that have come out – German people among them – and it is said that some have claimed and do claim that they knew nothing of what was going on.

It is indeed a terrible lesson to the whole world. Did the Nazis think they would never be discovered? They must have done. As to the whole German race bearing the blame – maybe they should and must, but as M said, when your loved ones are threatened what can you do? Would you be brave if your husband, mother, child might be whisked away from you if you didn't submit to the authorities? I suppose the fault is in being so ignorant and disinterested in 'politics' as to let the State grow to such power. This seems to me the moral – the lesson we have to learn from the story of the German concentration camps – and it should be broadcast and brought home to everyone.

I thought that I should revel in not having to draw curtains any more at night. But as soon as it gets dark an unprotected window makes me feel guilty and uncomfortable. I draw my curtains. Except when I intend to read in bed. Then I can open the window and draw back the curtains before I get into bed and can read as long as I wish, turning out the light when sleepy without having to disturb the sleepiness to attend to the window. That is a pleasure. Five and a half years had passed since I had last done that. Five and a half years seemed to me at once a vast age, a century . . .

I still don't know what I should do. Perhaps I should hang on as long as one can or until something better turns up. At a Mona Rolf London School of Psychology service last Sunday a medium picked on me and said amongst other things that I should remove myself from my place of work if I could as there were influences there not good for me. But she didn't say if I should make the opportunity or wait for it, so am really no better off.

Pam Ashford

Today has been the hardest day so far. Now in the evening I am very tired. Mother urges the suspension of the diary till the busy spell is over, but I reply that suspension is out of the question when Berlin is on the point of falling. Nevertheless I have heard comment in the office only once today, viz. about the presence of Hitler in Berlin. My own view is that Himmler now is master of Germany and is dropping Hitler, who will be bumped off by the Nazis (if he does not get hit by a bomb) in such a way that the story of Hitler giving up his life in defence of Germany can become a legend. Most of the Nazi leaders are of course out of Berlin by now. Most people in the room (led by Miss Sinclair) *don't* believe Hitler is in Berlin. Hitler will disappear. He may be having his face remodelled by a surgeon.

Ernest van Someren

In the evening Mrs Suwter and Tom Griffiths visited us, and we had coffee and lively talk until 11.15. They are both artists, which helped the talk. Later we began discussing vegetarianism. She is a keen one and has a girl of 13 months who has never had any milk, butter, cheese or eggs, and neither did her mother before or after her birth. In spite of the doctor's warnings she is quite healthy.

THURSDAY, 26 APRIL

Maggie Joy Blunt

Several letters from S who is now in Italy. While at sea he wrote: 'I am glad to be overseas again now the war wanes in Europe. But it would be exhilarating to be part of the pursuit in Germany. There will be no glorious finale to this war but a certain anti-climax.

'As for me I am empty and void. What will happen in the days to come? I do not know. But I feel I am following a star, ill fated possibly, but a star.

'The plaster is off my hand but writing is still tres difficile. Blue tranquil seas and idle sunbathing hours. Of the Eusa women only 2 are outstanding – a 19 year old starlet, blonde, self-assured, diamond-hard, and diamond seeking. A 30 year old femme fatale of more generous proportions and temperament who prefers emeralds.

'17 April: Am still in this dirty little Italian town reading endless files to "get the picture" and trying to still the still small voice that urges me to seek action again. Maybe it is the movement of action more than the battle which I desire. Boredom is always close to my shoulder. This last act of the war drags slowly and like many men I cannot see the end as a reality, though I know the curtain is about to fall. "Cease fire" seems in fact as remote now as in 1941. It is this false perspective in my mind's eye that makes post-war planning so futile, a mere juggling with conjecture.

'My only entertainments are an occasional film, reading American magazines, drinking foul Italian gin in the mess and trying to write limericks in dog-Italian. Until the Boche is wiped out in the Po valley, any more seems unlikely. Food is admirable. I feel now that it will be impossible for me to settle down to a desk job after the war – unless my dream of 6 months' peace on an Aegean island changes my philosophy. Any *New Statesmen* you have to spare or *Tribunes* will be welcome. I have not seen an English journal here (except *Picture Post*), though *Time* and *Life* etc. are plentiful.'

In Burnham Beeches the weather has broken. A fine rain began about midday and this evening when I came home the thirsty garden was rejoicing, things growing visibly, I swear it.

Pam Ashford

Mother has refrained from going to the Cosmo this week as she has not wanted to see the news films. I have found out the timing of the programme next Saturday. The news immediately precedes the feature film. I am going to take her in at the precise moment the big film should be coming on. I hope the plan works all right. Mother is,

525

however, saying, 'I must get used to it. They will be showing these horror films all the summer. It may be that the showing of these films in Germany will turn the Germans against war. These films will teach the world what Germany is like. They may mean the end of war.'

FRIDAY, 27 APRIL

Maggie Joy Blunt
The Russians and Americans have met in Germany, in Italy the German Army is crumbling fast. Mussolini, it is reported, has been captured. Dramatic news. Much speculation is as to what is happening now to the Nazi chiefs – evening papers say Goering has left the country with wife, daughter and £5,000,000. I wondered aloud coming home with Mr Ch. in what currency he could have taken it – not German marks. Gold would be too heavy. British notes? Ironical. Or dollars.

At lunch today B from the Lab came and sat with me. He has been with the firm since 1936 and was surprised to hear that my length of service dated back only to 1942. 'One has come to think of Miss B and publicity as synonymous,' he said. 'One can't imagine a time when there was a Publicity without Miss B.' I must be getting a very hoary look. Time I was pensioned. He suffers from the same sense of uncertainty – thinks as we all do that no one, not even the Directors, know what is going to happen.

I think Hitler will commit suicide, and only Hitler. Many doubted it – 'it takes a lot of courage'. But thinking this over, yes it takes courage for the 'normal' person, but suicides are never 'normal', and Hitler is not normal.

SATURDAY, 28 APRIL

Ernest van Someren
Went to Leicester by train, and was met at Narborough by my brother Tony with Gilbert and John, his boys aged 5 and 3, whom I have never seen before.

Tony's psychiatric hospital has moved from Matlock to Littleport a few weeks ago, and he is on leave. In the evening his successor, who lives in a wing of the county mental hospital there, came in for a chat. He is a Rhineland German with a charming sense of humour.

MONDAY, 30 APRIL

Pam Ashford

The news yesterday was, of course, very good, and at 8am I was pricking up my ears more keenly than I had ever pricked them up before.

Other people are the same. Miss Sinclair on arriving opened up with, 'What an exciting weekend,' and there was a buzz of comment, Mussolini coming first. 'What an excitable race the Italians are. Such things could not happen here.'

There is, of course, a lot of bitter comment nowadays about the German POW getting twice as big rations of food as our own civilian population, the POW getting the same rations as British Troops.

Mrs Blane anticipates that Dave will be in the big push. Everyone agrees that the Germans cannot continue for long. 'Once we get Hamburg and Berlin it will all be over.'

Edward Stebbing

Was home for the weekend yesterday and the day before. On Saturday we were excited by the news of Himmler's peace offer to Britain and America; but we knew such an offer would not be accepted unless also made to Russia. But now that a definite desire for peace has been shown, everyone is naturally thinking that it cannot be many days before an acceptable offer is made. The American–Russian link-up, the gradual reduction of Berlin, the final stages in Italy, all point to an end very soon. Yet people are relatively calm about it, because the end has been expected for some time. The war has gone full cycle to a logical and fitting conclusion. What excites interest as much as anything is the fate of Hitler. Is he in Berlin? Is he dead? Yesterday's papers were only guessing. The capture and swift execution of Mussolini by Italian patriots was a well-deserved reward. Events in Europe are coming thick and fast, obscuring news of the San Francisco Conference, where the Polish question threatens to split Britain and America on one hand and Russia on the other.

TUESDAY, 1 MAY

Maggie Joy Blunt

Important hours, important as those days at the end of August in 1939 preceding the declaration of war. This is a tension of a different kind, expectancy, preparations being made for a change in our way of living. But the tempo is slower. We wait, without anxiety, for the official announcement by Mr Churchill that is to herald two full days' holiday and the beginning of another period of peace in Europe. We wait wondering if Hitler is dying or dead or will commit suicide or be captured and tried and shot, and what his henchmen are doing and feeling.

We had ice cream in canteen for lunch today – the first for two or is it three years?

Edward Stebbing

When I came home Mrs H said there was no fresh news. She thought perhaps we were waiting for Hitler to die before declaring peace. I said I didn't think it likely and I thought it quite possible that Hitler's death might be announced as a subterfuge to give him a chance to escape. Shortly afterwards Mr H came home and told us that Hitler had been reported dead, so I stayed up to hear the midnight news, which repeated the German announcement. I was surprised that Admiral Doenitz had been appointed as Hitler's successor and that the Germans were determined to fight on.

Pam Ashford

Dave writes that it was to his Unit that Gen. Dietmar surrendered. At 9.15 there was an unusual amount of fluency on current events. Last night several people saw some ghastly films of the horror camps and related details. Miss Sinclair: 'That shows you what things would have been like here if we had had a dictatorship.'

At 5 people were gasping for their newspapers. Mr Churchill scored a good joke by saying that the position was easier than 5 years ago. At 6 Mother and I listened with bated breath to the report of Mr Churchill's remarks to the House of Commons. The end is near. The end is near. The end is near. We have waited so long. As the years have passed it has seemed as if there would never be an end. I am beginning to feel excited.

WEDNESDAY, 2 MAY

Pam Ashford

On reaching work I learnt that the news had been interrupted last night after 10 for the announcement of Hitler's death. Mrs Blane described herself as struck motionless with a wet dish poised in her two outstretched hands. For myself the element of surprise was slight, and throughout the day I have not heard a single soul accept the story as true. I have always expected that the Nazis would murder Hitler in such a way that they could build up a Hitler legend. I do not exclude the cerebral haemorrhage possibility.

But excitement is growing. Every dog has his day, and V-Day is going to be quite a day. Every flag for sale is being snapped up at once.

THURSDAY, 3 MAY

Edward Stebbing
The surrender in Italy seems to have led people to expect a general surrender within the next day or two. I took my portable radio to work so that we should not miss the announcement if it came. Mr L said that peace would probably be declared tomorrow morning, as some of the local police had received orders to report to London by 10.30 tomorrow morning.

I went to the pictures straight from work. The newsreel of the German concentration camps was being shown. It was horribly gruesome; our feelings were not spared. Still, I think everybody should see it, fully to appreciate the sickening and shameful reality. I find it more difficult than ever to understand, however, how such human degradation could come about.

When I came out of the cinema it was snowing and raining, and by the time I reached home it was snowing hard. This weather is unbelievable.

When I got home I noticed that my landlady had put up four small Union Jacks on the wall. She said she had heard two women talking about Hitler. One of them had said he might have had his face altered by plastic surgery so that he wouldn't be recognised. The other said no, he would escape in a coffin. I said they must have been reading thrillers. I said that if Hitler was in Berlin surely the Russians would have found him, unless, perhaps, he had been cremated.

I asked Mrs H what she would do when peace was declared. She answered, 'I shan't do anything. Some will go mad; others will just heave a sigh of relief, like myself. I don't think there is much sense in celebrating while we're still at war in Japan. There has been too much tragedy in this war, for civilians as well; there's not much to celebrate . . . I might have a drink.'

Pam Ashford
After having Hitler die of a cerebral haemorrhage, now we have him committing suicide. It makes us laugh.

The sale of flags is brisk. I went along to a hawker at Pettigrew's and she said they cost 8s 6d. I said that was too much. She said, 'It is a Government-controlled price. Given out today over the wireless. It should be 10s, but I am selling at 8s 6d because of patriotism.' I said,

'It is still too much,' and she retorted, 'You are not patriotic.' I went to a hawker at Copland's and got a Union Jack (same size) for 5s. Dick, our canary, after complete silence all day, burst into song when shown the Union Jack.

Ernest van Someren
Thought V-Day would be announced at noon, but was disappointed. The news is most encouraging. Stayed on after work to go to a singularly dull meeting of the discussion group at the works, and got home at about 8 very cold and wet. We are thinking of having a sort of party on VE+1 evening if the day of the week is suitable, but I've got a lot of evening engagements just now.

FRIDAY, 4 MAY

Ernest van Someren
The news of the surrender broke today and was very welcome. The continued dropping of food on Holland by the RAF is also one of the best pieces of news this week.

Pam Ashford
The pulse of the nation is throbbing faster and ever faster. There never was anything like it in all our lifetimes.

Maggie Joy Blunt
I asked RW what she intended to do on VE Day and she said that she didn't know. Her people keep a pub in Windsor and they have not decided whether they will keep open or not. If they do (and the brewers want them to) they will not have more than their normal rationed supply and will be sold out by 9.30pm. Her father thinks he will invite in all his pals and keep the pub closed to the public.

Listening now to the repeat broadcast of General Montgomery from Germany this afternoon. My emotions at this moment are indescribable: enormous pride in the fact that I am British, wonder and excitement. 'Tomorrow morning at 8am the war in Europe will be over . . .' The war in Europe is over . . . This is a tremendous moment.

The war is over. I cry a little. I think of my dearest friends, my stepmother, my brother in Egypt, of those men in the fighting services I have known – and I wish I had taken a more active part; it is too late now. But it is not too late to take part in the fight ahead. I am not moved to rush out tomorrow and wave a Union Jack in the village high street. I think it is a good sign that people are saying universally

'Our troubles are only just beginning,' because it would be idiotic to assume they are over with the end of hostilities.

SATURDAY, 5 MAY

Edward Stebbing
I went up to town in the afternoon. Walking from Charing Cross Road to Leicester Square and Piccadilly Circus and along Regent Street, I saw hardly any signs of preparations for celebrations. The shelter at the entrance to Piccadilly Tube station was being taken down. In Regent Street I joined a long queue for the *Daily Express* exhibition of photographs of the German concentration camps. The pictures were as revolting as I expected. Those naked, writhing (though lifeless) figures make one think of Dante's *Inferno*; this must have been purgatory for those pitiable creatures. I think I have now seen enough of this horrifying evidence.

Ernest van Someren
I spent most of the morning glass-blowing because I had a sudden urge to do some handwork instead of the report-writing which is my main job of work just now. Cycled home at lunchtime, rather thinking that it might turn out to be V-Day at 1pm. It wasn't.

SUNDAY, 6 MAY

Edward Stebbing
I stayed indoors during the morning and the afternoon, reading and writing. At 6 o'clock came the announcement that V-Day would probably be before next Thursday. Mr H remarked that they had not surrendered in Norway yet and that the Russians were still fighting hard.

Later I went to a dance at a dance-club. They were selling delicious ice cream there. One girl I danced with was not sure whether it was V-Day or D-Day we were waiting for!

MONDAY, 7 MAY

Edward Stebbing
We have been in suspense all day, waiting for the official victory proclamation.

On our way home F said to me, 'If it's V-Day tomorrow, shall we go on the spree tomorrow night?' 'Where?' I asked. 'Go and see the floodlighting,' he replied. 'That's an idea,' I said. When we got home our two neighbours were putting up flags outside their houses. One of them called out, 'We're not too optimistic, are we?'

At 9 o'clock it was announced that it would be V-Day tomorrow.

Pam Ashford

The tension, excitement and nerve strain was positively painful in the afternoon. At 6 we gathered around the office wireless set. We heard of the surrender made to General Eisenhower. I came home, and the flags were out in strength. Again and again I recognised a display that had been the same one put up for the Coronation. Union Jacks were favourites, with Scottish Lions a good second. Red ensigns were a long way behind in third place, and here and there a French flag, a Belgian flag and once a Russian flag. But Hyndland was not flag-conscious. Mother had not put my 5s flag out and wanted to wait for the declaration.

Then at 9pm the BBC made known that tomorrow would be VE Day (the 'E' has been added). A tenderness came over Mother and me and we kissed each other fondly. Then I ran to the window to find that Hyndland was putting out its flags. The terrific tension of the last week was gone and in its place we felt happy. We gave ourselves up to the happiness. Then at 9.30 we went to bed. But I had a poor night. My mind was seething with thoughts of the eyes of the starving at Belsen . . .

At midnight the ships in the harbour let off sirens.

Maggie Joy Blunt

I had a £1 note taken from my handbag at work this week. Other people have been missing notes recently and when I reported my loss to the works police I was told that they had their eye on a certain office boy.

From Italy S wrote on 1 May:

'Last night German resistance on the northern Italian front ended. I was at my desk with two very young officers and my OC who was a captain with me in Greece in 1941. He said, "It's been a long road." We opened a bottle of Scotch and had a lot . . .

'The end is near now and a great sense of emptiness. A new desert of emotion to be explored and fought over . . .'

Ernest van Someren

Cycled to work, an air of anticipation about. I did some report work, and towards five heard that it was definitely over and the announcement would be made very soon. When I cycled home a lot of shops were already putting flags up, and at home Laurie had a flag over the door. While I had supper a neighbour tried to string a huge old flag across the road on a wire to the house next door, but finally gave it up and tied it over to my house instead. The children were thrilled.

TUESDAY, 8 MAY – VE DAY

Edward Stebbing
When I awoke the first sound I heard was a cuckoo calling. It was a fine sunny morning, but there had been a heavy thunderstorm in the night. The church bell was ringing – the local church has only one bell with a rather mournful note. All we could get was a *Daily Herald*, which we had to share with our next-door neighbour.

Buses were running a Sunday service, but we were fortunate in getting a lift in Dr S's car, an unprecedented occurrence – usually he goes by without offering us a lift.

After lunch we went along to the local pub and had a drink or two, or, to be exact, three. F played the piano and the rest of us, including three or four nurses, sang songs, among them 'She'll Be Coming Round The Mountain', 'Bless 'em All', 'There'll Always be an England', and a somewhat improper one called 'Roll Me Over in the Clover'.

After this we went back to work to finish off a few jobs that remained. At 3 o'clock I switched on my radio to hear Churchill's formal announcement of the end of the European war. I thought his 'Advance Britannia' a bit melodramatic.

We took a bus to the nearest tube station and then went by tube to Leicester Square. At Leicester Square there was a great throng of people coming out of the station, and the street outside was swarming. In a side street at the back of the Hippodrome was a crowd watching some soldiers and girls dancing to a street-band. A little farther on I met an acquaintance whom I had not seen during the war. Then we walked into the square and up to Piccadilly. There were crowds everywhere, but there was room to move comfortably. Here and there were ice-cream barrows and vendors of flags and other favours. In Piccadilly Circus the people were jammed together more. One man was seated comfortably on top of a lamppost. A sailor was climbing up the side of a tall building next to the London Pavilion, while men on the roofs were throwing fireworks into the crowds and emptying buckets of water over them. After several fireworks, which exploded with terrific noise, had gone off, a soldier leaned out of a window and waved a white handkerchief of surrender. The crowd laughed.

We made our way across Regent Street, down Waterloo Place and the steps to the Mall, and under Admiralty Arch to Trafalgar Square. One crowd was going in one direction and another in the opposite direction, but all were more or less orderly, just walking along calmly and looking around, though there was an unmistakable air of gaiety. Now and again a little group would do 'Knees Up, Mother Brown', some were singing, others blowing whistles or waving rattles. We stopped and watched the people in Trafalgar Square for a while, then went down Northumberland Avenue to the Embankment; it was less crowded here. We turned up Parliament Street and went into the Abbey, which was packed with people for the service. We walked round, then came out and continued up Whitehall. There was a crowd outside the entrance to Downing Street, hoping to see Mr Churchill. We saw some mounted police come out of Scotland Yard and go up towards Trafalgar Square. Outside Whitehall Theatre F said, 'Perhaps Phyllis Dixey will have too much to drink tonight and drop her fan.' We reached Trafalgar Square again and listened to some people singing to a banjo played by a man seated on one of the lions. F suggested that we should go to Hammersmith and come back to the West End later, so we walked up to Leicester Square Tube station again and went to Hammersmith.

We went to the Brook Green Hotel, which possesses an organ. F plays the organ and knew the organist there, who let him play for a little while. Two request numbers were, 'There'll Always Be an England' and 'The White Cliffs of Dover'. There was a merry crowd there. We had two beers and an alleged cocktail each, came out about 9 o'clock and passed some people gathered round a loudspeaker listening to the King's speech, but we didn't stop. We went by tube back to Piccadilly, where fireworks were still going off, including rockets and coloured flares. A little group started a bonfire, but a policeman put a stop to it. We stayed there a little while, jostled here and there, then decided to go down to Trafalgar Square again. In Regent Street some servicemen and women were dancing on top of an air-raid shelter. It was getting dark now and some torches were burning on the balcony of a building in Waterloo Place. A column of people marched by singing, and a WAAF girl brushed me in the face with something fluffy on the end of a stick.

Across Trafalgar Square the National Gallery was floodlit. In the square some brilliant lights were playing on the people crowded round Nelson's Column and two searchlights were trained on Nelson from high buildings on either side. We wended our way up the Strand. On the front of the Tivoli a big red neon sign said 'Gaumont-British Pays Tribute to the Soldiers and Workers of the Allied Nations'. The entrance to the Savoy was lit up with green and white neon lights. There were no streetlights – or if there were, none noticeable – but one little side street had all its lights full on and stood out on its own like a showpiece. It was barricaded off, and the only people in it were an old lady talking to a policeman. It was like a brightly lit shop-window on a dark background, with the stationary figures of the woman and the policeman like dummies. (Looking back, this, strangely enough, is my most vivid impression of the day.) We turned into Aldwych, where Bush House was lit up. Buses were still running along Kingsway; there were few people here. We stopped to look at a little group of people round a bonfire in a bombed area; one was playing a guitar and the others were singing. We decided to walk to King's Cross. Euston Road was dazzlingly lit as far as the eye could see and St Pancras Church was floodlit. We caught the 11.50 train and when it got out of the station we saw many searchlights feathering the sky, sweeping rapidly to and fro in a victory signal. Near the station where we got off the train there was a bonfire outside a pub and some girls were dancing around it.

We walked homewards; my legs and feet were aching. One or two houses had illuminated V-signs in their windows, another had a small floodlight in the front garden lighting up a tree with white blossom, lilac I think – it shone with a simple, yet symbolic, beauty. We arrived home just before 1am. I sat down and read the evening paper, then went to bed. On taking my shoes off I found that I had a blister on each foot.

Ernest van Someren

We all four went to the parish church for a thanksgiving ceremony, which was attended but not crowded (about 300). The service was prolonged while a list of serving men and women was read name by name, followed by eight who had been killed.

A quiet afternoon at home as it was sultry and rain threatened. We listened to Churchill's announcement at three. We put up the tent for the children, and let them have tea in it with some chocolate spread for a treat.

Pam Ashford

I never worked so hard as today (accounts deadlines). At 2.55 we went down to the wireless set, and Mr Goodwin joined us. He said that the flag on the J&P Coats building was upside down, and went away to find an encyclopaedia and he spent the entire time that the broadcast was on reading the way the Union Jack should be hung.

During the day Miss Smith looked out of her window to see two urchins of 8 or 9 climbing the railings of the houses facing ours and tearing down the small flags which the owners had put up, and stuffing them in their pockets.

Subjective feelings? I think I can best sum myself up this way. At 6 I walked from the office to Wellington Street in absolutely deserted streets, and I sang to myself out loud (but not very loud) 'The Devil's awa'. By Devil you will, of course, understand Hitler. It was just as if a foul pestilence had gone, and the free world seemed as fair as the Garden of Eden.

Epilogue

To which one is tempted to reply: if only she knew. The Garden of Eden had already transformed itself into a place of austerity and struggle by the time Pam Ashford wrote her last entry in September 1945, not long after VJ Day. Her entries suggest she had a fairly good idea of what life would be like after the war ended, but she forecast a period of deprivation and adjustment lasting a few months, possibly a year. She did not imagine a five-year stretch or more; she could not predict that Britain would spend so long propping up a starving Europe. She could not imagine that rationing could be stricter, nor that bird seed would be almost as hard to find two years after Glasgow hung out its flags.

Sixty years after her last entry I took a cab to her former home in Hyndland Road, one of many brownstone tenements in that part of Glasgow's West End undergoing refurbishment. It was a two-minute walk to the Western Lawn Tennis and Squash Club, with its six all-weather courts and gym with plasma TVs. I also passed the former home of the Forth & Clyde Shipping Co in Hope Street, since converted into an office supply company. Next door was the Solid Rock Café, a Hard Rock Café clone with loud music and framed memorabilia. It was bringing America to Glasgow, just like in Pam's day. One of her last entries records a friend having her hair done in an American style. She writes with optimism about the possibilities of Clement Attlee's reformist programme, disappointed at Churchill's defeat. She hears that her old workmates Mr Hutchison and Mr Ferguson have been quarrelling. She is looking forward to visiting more art galleries and theatres.

Edward Stebbing continued working at Clare Hall Hospital in Potters Bar until 1948. His next job, at the Shenley Mental Hospital, brought him into contact with the Spanish nurse Isabel Gonzales, and the two married in 1955. He retired in 1980 as head of the Cytology Department at the Hospital for Nervous Diseases in Maida

Vale. The Stebbings had two children, the eldest of whom, Phil Stebbing, offered me tea in the summer of 2006 at his home near Horsham in Sussex. Phil remembers his father as 'a very careful thinker, very well read, always looking to improve his mind'. He explained that before the war his father had always wanted to go to university, but had been forced by circumstance to work in a draper's shop. He later enrolled in the Open University, where he attained a BA (hons).

Phil Stebbing remembers his father as liberal and forward-thinking, although he was less than keen on his son's interest in pop music and punk-era anarchy. He was keen on local history, and published a seasonal journal of Shenley's large pond. When he was young, Phil found a neat copy of the diaries his father had sent to Mass-Observation in his father's wardrobe. Edward Stebbing had kept a carbon copy of his handwritten submissions, and had typed them up with the aim of publication. He found no takers, so in 1998 he published them himself through the Book Guild in Lewes, Sussex. *Diary of a Decade* is the full account of his wartime years with a few passages about his post-war travels through Holland and Germany, and closes with a fitting conclusion to the true value of Mass-Observation: 'I have learned an inescapable lesson of history: the past, whether good or evil, cannot be altered.'

Edward Stebbing died in 2003 at the age of 82. He suffered from respiratory problems and prostate cancer, but remained relatively fit until the last year of his life. His son, who has two daughters, is a television film-maker, making documentaries about Greenpeace and terrorism. He is also engaged in promoting an organic lifestyle – healthy food, yoga, healing, spiritual awakening – through the Internet company he runs with friends: http://www.hunabku.biz.

Maggie Joy Blunt fulfilled her long-held ambition to become a writer. She began writing *Lovely Peggy*, a biography of the eighteenth-century Irish actress Margaret 'Peggy' Woffington, not long after leaving High Duty Alloys in Slough in February 1946. She worked on it for five years at the British Museum Reading Room, and it was published under the pseudonym Janet Camden Lucey by Hurst & Blackett in 1952. She continued to write for Mass-Observation until 1950, with many entries about her work for the Liberal Party and her ceaseless pursuit of cigarettes.

Not long after her diaries appeared in *Our Hidden Lives*, her niece told me about the existence of other journals that she kept throughout her life, and among these was a brief biographical sketch. She wrote that her mother was an accomplished pianist before she married. Her father was an architect, and Maggie Joy had trained to follow in his footsteps but found the work too demanding. She instead became an architectural journalist, and after her biography opened up a bookshop near her cottage in Farnham. She specialised in cat books, and the reputation of her stock assured her of many loyal customers overseas. A few years ago I was asked to address the Farnhams' Society about her writing, and there met a dyslexic man who told me he would always be grateful to Maggie Joy for helping him read.

Her biographical sketch mentioned four lovers, but she did not marry and remained childless. At one time she had 13 cats. She died from lung cancer in August 1986, at the age of 76. Her death was announced in *The Bookdealer*: 'Friends and fellow dealers remember [her] for her consideration, straightforwardness and great kindness. She will be sadly missed.'

Laurie van Someren has had many birthdays since the one in January 1941, his third, at which he was delighted to find that the morning's post was all for him. He now lives in semi-retirement with his wife in Bottisham, on the outskirts of Cambridge. From here he supplies his various stress management aids and biofeedback instruments, and takes pride in being the entrepreneurial role model for the success of his two sons, directors and founders of nCipher plc, a company engaged in business cryptography and data protection.

When I visited him in the summer of 2006, I was pleased to see that a dozen roosters and hens were pecking at the rose petals in the garden beyond his kitchen window, a comforting throwback to the days when he helped his father with their mischievous poultry in their garden at Broxbourne.

Ernest van Someren continued to pursue his career in metallurgy for the rest of his life. His firm was taken over by the British Oxygen Company, and in the late 1950s he began at the Welding Institute at Abington, Cambridge. He moved his family to nearby Girton in 1960, retiring eight years later. Laurie attended Eton, found that he was good at science, and followed his father into metallurgy. He worked in Boston for a decade on government-sponsored research, before settling back near Cambridge in 1971. His mother Kay died from breast cancer in 1979, and his sister Julia, who remained single and worked as a librarian, died in 1990 at the age of 49, also from cancer. Ernest van Someren developed diabetes and had a stroke, and died in 1984. He devoted much of his last few years to working on the family tree.

Laurie van Someren told me that he remembers his father typing his Mass-Observation diaries on a folding table, and was pleased to discover that they were still intact and cared for at the University of Sussex. He planned to visit them with his wife when he was next in the area.

The Archive was established at the university in 1970, and continues to provide historians and visiting members of the public with a unique insight into civilian life between 1937 and 1950. It remains a living resource: a major autobiographical project is currently under way, in which hundreds of volunteers respond to regular requests to write in both diary form and in reports on themes about themselves, their families, work places and communities. This material has been gathered since 1981 and continues to the present day. The greater part of it is available for research and teaching.

The Archive is a charitable trust and is managed as part of the Library's Special Collections department. It is partly self-supporting and runs a Friends scheme to finance its work. To join the scheme, please see the website, email moa@sussex.ac.uk or write to

The Mass-Observation Archive
Special Collections
University of Sussex Library
Brighton BN1 9QL

Acknowledgements

I wish to thank everyone who has been so unfailingly supportive of this book at Ebury and Random House. I am also grateful to Laurie van Someren for his suggestions, Phil Stebbing, Babs Everett, Jules Churchill, Laura Macaulay, Jessica Alford, Kitty Laing, Pat Kavanagh and Annie Collie. For the chronology I have relied largely on the superb *World War II Day By Day* (Dorling Kindersley, 2004). I am particularly indebted to the Trustees of the Mass-Observation Archive and Dorothy Sheridan, Sandra Koa-Wing and all the staff at Special Collections at the University of Sussex Library who have been enthusiastic and helpful at all times and an absolute pleasure to work with.

www.massobs.org.uk
www.simongarfield.com

Photo Credits

Endpapers: Diagram showing the works of a V2 rocket bomb published in the *Illustrated London News*, Dec 9 1944 © Illustrated London News

Chapter 1: Two soldiers contemplating entry to the Prince of Wales Theatre in London for the non-stop revue circa 1939 © Popperfoto/Alamy

Chapter 2: Man injured by fall of a V-1 rocket in London, circa 1940 © Topfoto

Chapter 3: Members of the public join in a gas warning exercise at Brighton, with a warden with rattle and bell giving the alarm, circa 1940 © Popperfoto/Alamy

Chapter 4: Article with diagram showing two possible routes taken by Hess, published in *The Sphere*, 24 May 1941 © Illustrated London News

Chapter 5: Fool's Holiday: cartoon by David Low, published in the *Evening Standard*, 1 August 1941 © Centre for the Study of Cartoons and Caricature, University of Kent, catalogue record DL1756 © Solo Syndication/Associated Newspapers

Chapter 6: June 1941. People look through the shop window at Selfridges, London, with a dress going on sale as clothes rationing starts © Popperfoto

Chapter 7: Churchill inspecting the House of Commons Home Guard in Spencer's Yard, London, May 1942 © Hulton Archive/Getty Images

Chapter 8a: Clive W. Black, house steward at the Royal Academy of Music. He helped to organise the Academy's ARP provision, and can be seen here acting as a fire watcher on the roof of the Academy, 1944 © Trustees of the Imperial War Museum, London

Chapter 8b: Britain Shall Not Burn: poster issued by the Ministry of Home Security, 1940 © Peter Newark's Military Pictures

Chapter 9: American soldiers based in England being entertained at an outdoor show, 1944 © Popperfoto

Chapter 10: 11th April 1942. Princess Elizabeth helping her father King George VI with a swimming pool stirrup pump, at the Royal Lodge, Windsor, whilst Princess Margaret and Queen Elizabeth look on © Hulton Archive/Getty Images

Chapter 11: Blackpool, 1943. Polish airmen at the Tower Ballroom wait on the stairs with some local girls © Popperfoto

Chapter 12a: Poster: Is Your Journey Really Necessary? produced by the Railway Executive Committee during World War II to remind passengers to avoid making unnecessary rail journeys during wartime. The transportation of servicemen and war supplies and munitions had to take priority over passenger journeys © Science & Society Picture Library/NRM-Pictorial Collection

Chapter 12b: Don't Mind Hitler, Take Your Holiday. A travel company at London's Victoria Station showing a poster which tells people to ignore the threat of war and book their holidays. Circa 1939 © Alamy/Popperfoto

Chapter 13: Words and music for Gracie Fields' song, 'Wish Me Luck', as performed by Gracie in *Shipyard Sally*, 1939 © Topfoto

Chapter 14: Cartoon: On Your Marks! By Philip Zec, showing Churchill at the ready, 1944 © Topfoto

Chapter 15: British Invasion troops waiting for D-Day marching through a village street, 28th May 1944 © Hulton Archive/Getty Images

Chapter 16: A hoarding urging local voters to cast their vote for Labour Candidate Jennie Lee, wife of Aneurin Bevin, in the Bristol by-election 1943 © Hulton Archive/Getty Images

Chapter 17: Wartime advertisement for Stork Margarine, 1940s © Advertising Archives

Chapter 18: Servicemen watching VE Day crowds from the top of a lamp post, Piccadilly Circus, central London, 8 May 1945 © Science & Society Picture Library/NMFPT/Herald Archive

Epilogue: 15th August 1945. People in Battersea, London, celebrate VJ Day, the end of all hostilities in World War Two © Popperfoto

Index

357, 380, 403–4, 466, 486, 514
biscuits 17, 33, 122, 170, 264, 279, 357
Bismarck 111, 119–20, 123, 125
Black Magic chocolates 32–3
black people 235, 335, 365, 461
black treacle 233
black-outs 11, 25, 45, 105, 171, 230, 384, 395, 461
    driving bonuses and 464
    fines and 348
    lifting of 456, 458, 460, 467, 524
    police enforcement of 268, 334, 348
blanket bombing 377
'Bless 'em all' (song) 80
Bletchley Park 111, 295
Blithe Spirit (play) 111
blood donation 449
BMA (British Medical Association) 390
Boer War 390
Bologna 513
bomb craters 349–50
Bomber Command 191
bonuses 67–8, 271, 280, 464
book drives 360–1
book publishing 205
boot polish 479–80
Boult, Adrian 146
'bouncing bombs' 345
Bourneville Village Trust 425
boxing 220
Boyer, Charles 47
Bracken, Brendan 217
Brahms, Johannes 209
'Brains Trust' 198, 207, 240, 285, 339, 341
Braun, Eva 513
Brazil 283
bread 485
    off-white 227, 230, 243
Bright, Bill 314
Bright, Olive 314
Brighton 364
Bristol air raids 9
Bristol Hercules engines 302
Britain, battle of 111
'British, The' 221
British army 18, 52, 61, 413, 453, 493
    blankets 67
    Cinematography 347
    discharge 134, 138
    exhibitions 448
    films on 439
    food 49, 53–4
    in Libya 180
    marching 90
    mock invasions 166
    parades 64–6
    sick-leave 78, 95–6, 121–2
    training 68, 72–3, 265, 268, 271
    uniforms 69
British Association 166
British Broadcasting Corporation (BBC) 2, 9, 13, 14, 26, 52, 55, 80, 82, 89, 91, 123–4, 150, 154, 155, 175, 176, 183, 195,

243, 250, 269, 285, 288, 320, 328, 378, 393, 398, 399, 428, 430, 436, 437, 441, 446, 451, 456, 489, 495, 522, 532
    War Reports 430
British cinema 4
British Expeditionary Force (BEF) 279
British Legion 207, 337
British Medical Association (BMA) 390
British Rheologists Club 20, 127
British Rubber Producers Research Association 127
Britten, Benjamin 371
Broadcasting House 45
Brussels 445, 500
Buchenwald concentration camp 43, 513, 520, 521, 522
Buck, Pearl 265
Buckingham Palace 84, 260
Budapest 472, 493
budget
    1941 97, 98
    1942 238
budgets, household 54–5, 201–3
budgies 35, 247–8
Builder (magazine) 103, 157
Bulge, battle of the 471
Bull Market (play) 420
Buna, Papua New Guinea 319
burglary 332, 401–2, 414
    see also thieves
Burma 213, 413, 513
Burns Club 82, 106
buses 15, 255, 391
Butler, R.A. 345
Byelorussia 413

Caen 413
Caesarean sections 91
Café de Paris, Piccadilly 77
Cairo 280, 471
cakes 122, 129, 176, 264, 289, 299
Campbell's tinned soup 84
Canadian troops 493, 500, 507, 518
    in England 253, 284, 285–6, 368–9, 448
canaries 13, 29, 30, 31, 35, 85, 247, 456, 530
Cannes 445
Canterbury, Archbishop of (1942) 296
Canterbury air raids 295
Cape Matapan 77
capitalism 337
Cardiff air raids 55
carrier pigeons 13
cars 255
Cassino 413
Cat and the Canary (film) 195
cathedrals 243–4
cats 19, 148, 155, 231, 247, 497, 540
Cavell, Nurse Edith 473
Chamberlain, Neville 5, 9, 14–15, 29, 61, 83, 279, 476, 505
Channel Islands 26, 458, 508
Chaplin, Charlie 9, 56

Cherbourg 413
Chevalier, Maurice 32
Chiang Kai-Shek 377
Chichester, Bishop of 377
chickens 21, 24, 46, 78, 100, 133, 149, 151, 159, 160, 161, 196–7, 236, 281, 282, 305, 306, 382, 392
chilblains 205, 220, 396, 397
childbirth 90, 91–2
children's needs 248–9
China/Chinese 216, 235, 283, 287, 417–18, 421
chocolate 28, 78, 126
Chopin, Frédéric 234–5
Christianity 26, 284, 296, 350, 357
Christie's 102
Christmas
    1940 27, 32, 33, 34–7, 44
    1941 182, 185, 194–8
    1942 315–16, 333
    1943 397–9, 400, 401
    1944 477–8, 482, 483, 484
Church 132, 296, 335–6
church bells 345
churches 243–4, 438
Churchill, Randolph 24
Churchill, Sarah 154
Churchill, Winston 3, 9, 21, 29, 43, 51, 61, 66, 88, 98, 117, 134, 139, 142, 170, 178, 220, 230, 262, 274, 283, 287, 298, 299, 321, 345, 459, 473, 476, 478
    alcoholism 212, 477, 478
    and the Allied invasion of France 429
    and the Anglo-Russian treaty 253
    and anti-Semitism 361–2
    and the Atlantic Charter 137
    in Cairo 280
    and the end of the war 393, 447, 471, 493, 499, 504, 510, 528, 533, 535
    and the evacuation of Greece 77
    fading popularity 480, 519
    and George VI 387
    Glasgow visits 80
    hopes for a common US-UK citizenship 377
    old-school nature 268, 390, 414–15
    post-war election defeat 538
    and post-war reconstruction 352
    public criticism of 214
    replacement rumoured 260
    and Roosevelt 150, 151, 319, 345, 377
    Senate address 198
    speeches 35, 62, 72, 104–5, 107–8, 112, 125, 128, 129, 143, 153, 185–6, 192, 208, 295, 303, 311, 338–9, 363, 394, 419–20, 438, 477, 478
    and Stalin 259, 279, 280, 499, 504
    in the USA 263

547

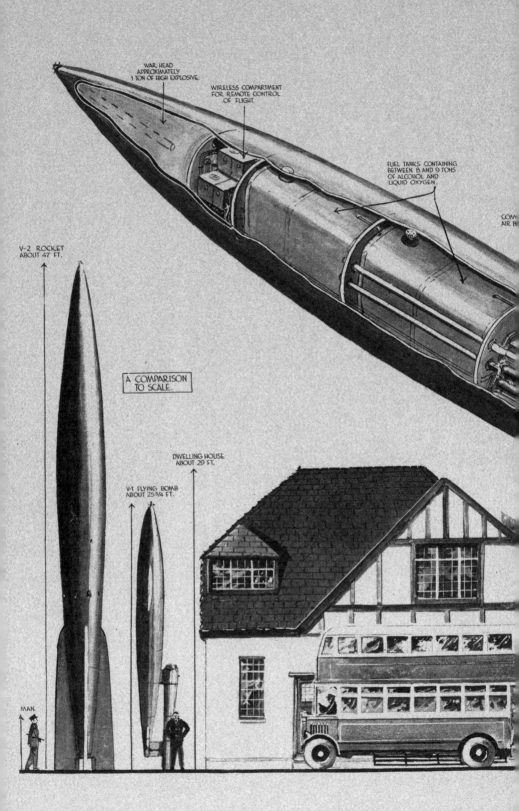

WAR HEAD
APPROXIMATELY
1 TON OF HIGH EXPLOSIVE.

WIRELESS COMPARTMENT
FOR REMOTE CONTROL
OF FLIGHT.

FUEL TANKS CONTAINING
BETWEEN 8 AND 9 TONS
OF ALCOHOL AND
LIQUID OXYGEN.

COM
AIR B

V-2 ROCKET
ABOUT 47 FT.

A COMPARISON
TO SCALE.

DWELLING HOUSE
ABOUT 29 FT.

V-1 FLYING BOMB
ABOUT 25¾ FT.

MAN.